D1300088

INDUSTRIAL ARCHAEOLOGY: TECHNIQUES

Industrial Archaeology: Techniques

Edited by

Emory L. Kemp
Institute for the History of Technology
and Industrial Archaeology
Eberly College of Arts and Sciences
West Virginia University

KRIEGER PUBLISHING COMPANY
MALABAR, FLORIDA
1996

Original Edition 1996

Printed and Published by
KRIEGER PUBLISHING COMPANY
KRIEGER DRIVE
MALABAR, FLORIDA 32950

Library of Congress Cataloging-In-Publication Data

Industrial archaeology : techniques / [edited] by Emory L. Kemp.
    p.   cm.
Includes bibliographical references and index.
ISBN 0-89464-649-4 (acid-free paper)
    1. Industrial archaeology.   2. Industrial archaeology—United States.   I. Kemp, Emory Leland.
    T37.I54   1996
    609—dc20   94-17788
                                                            CIP

10 9 8 7 6 5 4 3 2

FOR JANET

Contents

FOREWORD—Billy Joe Peyton ix

ACKNOWLEDGMENTS xiii

ABOUT THE AUTHORS xv

CHAPTER 1- The Dioscuri: Industrial Archaeology and
           the History of Technology—Emory L. Kemp 1

CHAPTER 2- The Shepherdstown Cement Mill: A Case Study—
           Emory L. Kemp 7

CHAPTER 3- Federal Records/Federal Repositories—Ruth Ann Overbeck 41

CHAPTER 4- Research in State and Local Archives for Preparing Histories
           of Specific Sites—Barbara J. Howe 49

CHAPTER 5- Quadrangular Treasure: The Cartographic Route
           to Industrial Archaeology—Robert M. Vogel 59

CHAPTER 6- The UTM Grid Reference System—Peter H. Stott 89

CHAPTER 7- The Photogrammetric Recording of Historic
           Transportation Sites—Paula A. C. Spero 103

CHAPTER 8- Remote Sensing Technology Applied to Site
           Documentation—Ronald W. Eck 123

CHAPTER 9- Field Work and Measured Drawings—
           Richard K. Anderson, Jr. 133

CHAPTER 10- Large Format Photography—Robert J. Hughes 167

CHAPTER 11-Land Surveying Methods Employed by Industrial
           Archaeologists—Edward H. Winant 179

CHAPTER 12-Integrating Geographic Information Systems and Industrial
           Archaeology: Exploring the Potential and the Limitations—
           Trevor M. Harris and Gregory A. Elmes 191

INDEX 205

Foreword

The first question asked by persons who pick up this book might be: What is industrial archaeology? While the term connotes a number of different impressions, an exact definition remains somewhat amorphic. Perhaps the best definition comes from Dr. Emory Kemp, originator and editor of this work, who refers to "IA" in *Public History: An Introduction* as a new discipline which provides primary information for historians and essential material for sites where preservation is contemplated. Although this new field has not yet gained the professional respectability of either traditional history or archaeology, it does attract a truly interdisciplinary team of loyal and dedicated professionals and amateurs with a myriad of skills and backgrounds.[1] R. A. Buchanan, a leading British historian of technology and industrial archaeologist, says that industrial archaeology "is a field of study concerned with the investigation, surveying, recording and, in some cases, the preservation of industrial monuments. It aims, moreover, at assessing the significance of such monuments in the context of social and technological history. The great bulk of the material dates from the last two hundred years—the period of continuing Industrial Revolution—and some of it may be very modern indeed."[2] Buchanan goes on to say that IA is archaeological insofar as it is related to the examination of the tangible relics of industrialization. But, unlike conventional archaeological studies, it also utilizes documentary evidence in many varieties, and "industrial history" or "industrial architecture" are correct names for at least part of its activities.

So much for the definition of industrial archaeology. The idea for a book on the subject originated long ago in the mind of Emory Kemp, founder and director of the Institute for the History of Technology and Industrial Archaeology and former professor of history and engineering at West Virginia University. As one of this country's leading industrial archaeologists, Kemp taught the techniques of IA and historic site documentation for many years. As a student of his in the mid-1980s, I recall there being a dearth of good source material on the subject. To be sure, there were numerous IA-related journals in publication, including the Society for Industrial Archeology's semiannual *IA Journal* and others of quality, most notably from Great Britain and Italy. However, there were no book-length works published in the United States dealing strictly with techniques of IA. Among the best-known related works were David Weitzman's *Traces of the Past: A Field Guide to Industrial Archaeology*, which still enjoys a wide popularity among IA enthusiasts today, and the impressive work by the National Park Service's Historic American Buildings Survey/Historic American Engineering Record entitled *Made in America: Buildings, Structures and Sites*.

At any rate, lack of an appropriate text on the techniques of IA prompted Dr. Kemp to assemble his own "professor published" work consisting of articles on specific topics relative to the field. Despite the fact that there were precious few instructional pieces from which to choose in those days, this approach served the purpose to teach the rudiments of historic site documentation to small classes at West Virginia University. Within a few short years, the phenomenon of professor published texts passed from the scene, due in part to the desktop publishing revolution and the perpetually puzzling issue of copyright infringement. Alas, as the '80s drew to a close, there remained no standard text from which to teach the techniques of industrial archaeology.

Then, along came the Institute for the History of Technology and Industrial Archaeology in 1989. Building on Kemp's work and West Virginia University's 20-year tradition of academic and professional involvement in the history of technology, industrial archaeology and the history and preservation of engineering works, the Institute is involved in the identification, documentation, study and interpretation of sites, structures and artifacts relative to the areas mentioned above. Part of its mission involves sponsorship of a biannual field school to teach the techniques of industrial archaeology for graduate-level credit. As planning began in 1991 for the pilot six-week session, held at Harpers Ferry National Historical Park the following summer, it became quite clear that a commercially published work focusing on IA techniques was still needed. Enter Krieger Publishing Company, whom we approached with the idea for this book. Needless to say, they liked it.

With a commitment from Krieger, the Institute commissioned a cadre of leading practitioners in the field to submit essays as chapters for the book. After draft essays were received, our staff collated and bound them into notebook form for field-testing by participants of the summer field school. Then, in an attempt to produce the best possible work for educational purposes, we gave each student the opportunity to critique the essays for content and style. Almost without exception the students took their mandate very seriously, resulting in many constructive and relevant suggestions for improvements. Fortunately, the authors graciously accepted these critical reviews and responded with revised essays. In the end, the involvement of students in the preparation of the book helped the authors clarify key points in their essays and proved quite helpful in the quest for a most comprehensive and readable text.

One of the hallmarks of all Institute publications is the copious amount of illustrative material contained within them. Unlike the average scholarly historical monograph with a judicious smattering of maps and a few sketches or photos, this work contains over one hundred maps, charts, photographs and other illustrations—including drawings of the Shepherdstown (West Virginia) Cement Mill as done by the field school participants themselves.

With this book we try to make the point that a wide range of expertise is desirable to actually *do* industrial archaeology, and that skilled engineers, historians, architects, landscape specialists, photographers, surveyors and historical archaeologists are involved. That is not to say that the field is an exclusive haven for persons with impressive professional credentials and advanced degrees. On the contrary, some of the best IA work in the United States and abroad has been accomplished by enthusiastic amateurs and volunteer organizations.

Within these pages is a collection of essays that deal with some of the techniques relating to the practice of IA. There are two major reasons for such a work as this. The first has to do with the fact that no other book deals with the "how-to" side of IA in quite this manner. A second, and perhaps more important, reason for publishing this work is to share the expertise of leading practitioners and convey a true sense of the multidisciplinary nature of the field. If the reader comes away with only one impression, we hope it is the understanding and appreciation of industrial archaeology as a multifaceted field involving certain aspects of the humanities, science and engineering, social sciences, mechanical and graphic arts, as well as environmental and cultural resource management.

For the students, teachers, and IA'ers who will read this book, I simply suggest you enjoy it, use it and learn from it. Let us hope that your copy gets marked-up, torn, tattered and dog-eared, because it means you took it off the shelf and used it in the field where it belongs! Please treat the book as a reference work to spread the IA gospel and help us define for others the meaning of the words "industrial archaeology."

Billy Joe Peyton
Associate Director
West Virginia University
Institute for the History of Technology
& Industrial Archaeology
Morgantown, West Virginia

ENDNOTES

1. Emory Kemp, "A Perspective on our Industrial Past Through Industrial Archeology," in Howe and Kemp, *Public History: An Introduction,* p. 174.
2. Ibid., pp. 175–76

Acknowledgments

The origin of this book stretches back more than 25 years with the documentation of the Wheeling Suspension Bridge for the Historic American Buildings Survey. This project was undertaken before the founding of the Society for Industrial Archeology or the establishment of the Historic American Engineering Record in the National Park Service. Thus, I have grown up with the field and owe a great deal to both of these organizations regarding site recording. Over the years I have worked closely with Eric DeLony and Robert Kapsch of the HABS/HAER program, both of whom have shared my enthusiasm for the documentation of historic industrial sites and particularly historic bridges. I am especially indebted to Robert Vogel and the Smithsonian Institution for support and leadership for more than two decades.

At West Virginia University, graduate students in the history of technology and public history have enrolled in a course on historic site recording and interpretation for many years. It was evident from this experience that no single text was available for either students or professionals in the subject. With the urging of Dr. Barbara Howe, a new course was launched and has been a prime testing ground for teaching materials on industrial archaeology. I am, therefore, most grateful to her and to my former students for supporting this activity over the years.

The possibility for publishing a book on techniques, as opposed to richly illustrated books documenting industrial sites, came after the founding of the Institute for the History of Technology and Industrial Archaeology, at West Virginia University where the idea for such a book was supported by Gerald Lang, a member of the Institute's Advisory Committee and dean of the Eberly College of Arts and Sciences. Thus, in addition to the essayists, without whom this book obviously would not exist, many dedicated staff members at the Institute shared in its preparation and deserve my heartfelt thanks. Heading the list is associate director, Billy Joe Peyton; communications coordinator, Christine Peyton-Jones; delineators, Christina Spyrakos, Paul M. Boxley and John Hriblan; staff associate, Rena Taft; secretary, Carol Lones, and Peggy Walbert, who helped proofread and edit the text. Finally, a special thanks goes out to the staff at Krieger Publishing Company for their unflagging support and enthusiasm for this project.

Emory L. Kemp
Institute for the History of Technology and Industrial Archaeology
Morgantown, West Virginia

About the Authors

Richard K. Anderson, Jr. is a consultant specializing in the documentation of industrial and architectural sites. Anderson earned a B.A. from Princeton University in 1973 and a Master of Architecture degree from the University of Pennsylvania in 1976. He began his IA career in 1978 as staff architect for the Historic American Engineering Record, where he participated in numerous IA recording projects until 1989. He revised and extended HAER's *Field Instructions* manual and wrote HAER's *Guidelines for Recording Historic Ships*. In addition to documenting industrial, architectural and maritime resources across the country, he teaches documentation techniques of the Historic American Buildings Survey as a faculty member of the Historic Preservation Program at the Savannah College of Art and Design, GA.

Ronald W. Eck is a Professor of Civil Engineering at West Virginia University. Eck earned his Ph.D. from Clemson University in 1975. He now serves as director of the West Virginia Transportation Technology Transfer Center at WVU. He is chair of the Transportation Research Board's Committee of Low-Volume Roads and recently completed a term as chair of the Executive Committee of the Aerospace Division of the American Society of Civil Engineers. He is a member of the Institute of Transportation Engineers, the American Society for Photogrammetry and Remote Sensing, and the American Society for Engineering Education. He has published widely in the areas of highway design and maintenance, traffic safety, and engineering education. He is a registered professional engineer.

Gregory A. Elmes is an Associate Professor of Geography at West Virginia University. He received his early geographical training in the United Kingdom, completing a Bachelor of Science degree at the University of Newcastle Upon Tyne in 1972, and in 1979 completed his Ph.D. at Pennsylvania State University. In 1986/7 he spent a sabbatical leave at the University of Edinburgh, completing an M.S. in Geographical Information Systems. On returning to West Virginia University he initiated a GIS curriculum and was awarded funding for projects in the design, development and implementation of GIS and digital mapping for natural resource and forest pest management. His current research projects include landscape study of the dynamics of gypsy moth populations; the development of knowledge-based GIS; a gypsy moth management expert system, funded by USDA Forest Service; and study of the decline of Red Spruce in central Appalachia. A recent article in *Applied Geography*, jointly written with Dr. Harris, discussed the role of GIS on regional planning in North America. Also in 1993 he published (with Dr. K. C. Martis) *The Historical Atlas of State Power in Congress, 1790–1990* a work developed from a GIS database.

Trevor M. Harris is Associate Professor and Geography Program Director in the Department of Geology and Geography at West Virginia University. Harris received his Ph.D. from the University of Hull (UK) in 1982 and rose through the academic ranks to become a Senior Lecturer at the University of Plymouth. He came to the United States in 1990 and, through a series of seminal presentations and publications, has established a reputation as an authority on both sides of the Atlantic on archaeological applications of GIS. Dr. Harris has contributed five chapters to books on archaeological information issues, among them a prospect and review of the adoption of GIS in archaeology in *"Interpreting Space: GIS and Archaeology"* (Allen, Green and Zubrow, eds.). Selected presentations at recent conferences in Denmark and California display his abilities in landscape archaeology, "Danebury revisited: An English Iron Age hillfort in a digital landscape"; in space-time issues of information handling, "4D GIS-whatever next?"; and in environmental impact assessment, "Balancing energy and economic development against environmental coast: A GIS approach." In addition, he has been awarded major grants for environmental assessment of power transmission lines and the development of a state-of-the-art GIS laboratory at West Virginia University.

Barbara J. Howe is an associate professor of history at West Virginia University, where she directs the public history program. Howe received her B.A. in History and B.S. in Education from the University of Cincinnati, her M.A. in History from the University of Wisconsin-Milwaukee, and her Ph.D. in History from Temple University. She was a regional preservation officer for the Ohio Historic Preservation Office from 1976 to 1980. She has been at WVU since 1980, and her responsibilities there include teaching historic preservation and local history research methodology courses, in addition to working with community preservation groups. She co-edited *Public History: An Introduction* with Emory L. Kemp and co-authored *Houses and Homes: Exploring Their History*. Combining her interests in women's history and historic preservation, she wrote the "Women and Architecture" essay for *Reclaiming the Past: Landmarks of Women's History,* edited by Page Putnam Miller.

Robert J. Hughes graduated from Kutztown University with a major in fine arts and photography. His photographs are most often used for "applied" multicultural resource documentation of landscapes, buildings and structures, and industrial archaeology. Projects include a historic Kentucky oil field for the U.S. Army Corps of Engineers, the Lower Bank Bascule Bridge for the New Jersey Department of Transportation, a late nineteenth-century steel and glass building for the U.S. Department of the Treasury, and the mechanical and structural systems of a Harrisburg, Pennsylvania department store and a nineteeth-century canal tide lock in Alexandria, Virginia, for private clients. In addition, Hughes served two terms as the Chairman of the Capitol Hill Historic District Committee which has oversight on more than 8,000 multicultural resource properties in Washington, D.C. His photographs have been published by the U.S. Department of the Interior, in newspapers, and in the book, *Houses and Homes: Exploring Their History*. In addition, many of his photographs have appeared in historic preservation exhibits in the Washington metropolitan area, in Virginia and West Virginia.

Emory L. Kemp worked for leading engineering consulting firms in England before receiving his Ph.D. in Theoretical and Applied Mechanics from the University of Illinois. He came to West Virginia University in 1962 to establish a graduate program in structural engineering. Later, he founded the WVU Program in the History of Science and Technology. Fostering the use of the material culture approach for the study of our industrial past he has researched and preserved historic industrial sites around the country and advocated the interpretation of such sites and monuments for the public. Kemp was a founding member and recent President of the Society for Industrial Archeology, and has been a member of the Historic American Engineering Record advisory board. As a Regents' Fellow at the Smithsonian Institution in 1983–84, he researched the history of suspension bridges for a forthcoming book. In 1991 he received a National Preservation Honor Award presented by the National Trust for Historic Preservation for his contributions to the preservation of this nation's industrial heritage. He specializes in the history of bridges and has been involved in more than three dozen projects, documenting and restoring historic bridges and other industrial structures. He is director of the Institute for the History of Technology and Industrial Archaeology at West Virginia University.

Ruth Ann Overbeck is director and founder of Washington Perspectives, one of the nation's oldest public history firms. She received her BA and MA from the University of Texas. Her backgound in American social history has led to a career that encompasses projects involving land use, demographics, historic preservation, and industrial archaeology. Some of the latter projects include the documentation of a U.S. Navy Civil War coal refueling station, a historic Kentucky oil field, and a World War I U.S. Army Camp that experimented with munitions and poison gas. Overbeck is deeply involved with the computerization of multicultural resource data basses and serves on the Data Base Standards Committee for the Washington D.C. Historic Preservation Office. She is a member of the Washington D.C. Historic Records Advisory Commission and numerous professional organizations. She has designed and led more than 100 tours and seminars for the Smithsonian Institution's Associate's Programs and co-authored the book, *Houses and Homes: Exploring Their History,* which is now in its third printing. Her essays appear in college text books as well as in local and regional publications.

Paula A. C. Spero has been involved in the inventory, survey, evaluation and documentation of historic resources for 20 years. Ms. Spero has a multidisciplinary background, having received an M.S. degree in Engineering from the University of Virginia, a degree in Art and Architectural History from the University of Maryland and graduate training in Architectural Design. Ms. Spero's professional career mirrors her multi-disciplinary training, having served as research engineer for a state D.O.T., architectural historian for a state SHPO, and structural engineer for a major engineering firm. In 1983 she began an integrated career as a private consultant, founding her Baltimore, Maryland, firm, P.A.C. Spero & Company. Her firm, a certified Women Business Enterprise, now employs a number of specialists and has served clients throughout the Eastern United States for nine years through varied cultural resource projects.

Peter H. Stott is an industrial and architectural historian with a 20-year background in historic preservation. After completing Columbia University's Historic Preservation program, he worked for several years with the New York State Historic Sites Bureau, where this article was written for IA. Since 1979, he has worked primarily in the Boston area, initially for the Massachusetts Historical Commission. In addition to work on the UTM coordinate system, his other writings include "A Guide to the Industrial Archeology of Boston Proper," published in 1984 for the 1984 Boston Conference of the SIA; and a guide to the industrial archeology of Columbia County, New York, published in 1993.

Robert M. Vogel is Curator Emeritus of Mechanical and Civil Engineering, National Museum of American History, Smithsonian Institution in Washington D.C. He is a co-founder of the Society for Industrial Archeology and an acknowledged leader in the field with a worldwide reputation. With academic training in architecture, he was an avid collector of archival materials dealing with America's industrial past. His work forms the basis of the Smithsonian collection on civil engineering. He has served the Society of Industrial Archeology tirelessly since its establishment. Most notably, he has served as editor of the SIA newletter, member of the board of directors and president of the society, as well as running the SIA headquarters at the National Museum of American History. His article on the identification of industrial archeology from the USGA quads arose from a growing awareness that this valuable resource was not nearly as well utilized by investigators as it merited.

Edward H. Winant is a doctoral candidate in the History of Science and Technology at West Virginia University and assistant engineer at the Institute for the History of Technology and Industrial Archaeology. Winant received his B.S.C.E. from West

Virginia University in 1989, and his M.S.C.E. in 1991 with a specialty in hydraulics. Research topics worked on include vacuum transport and spillway hydraulics. His master's thesis was on computational methods for the analysis of geometrically complex emergency spillways. He has also written two FORTRAN programs for hydraulics computations. These are SPILLWAY for the West Virginia Department of Natural Resources, and Curve1D for the U.S. Army Corps of Engineers.

CHAPTER 1

The Dioscuri: Industrial Archaeology and the History of Technology[1]

Emory L. Kemp

Historians have long recognized, though in a general way, the dominant influence which technology has played in Western civilization since the eighteenth century. The entire social fabric, with its religious, educational and political institutions, as well as economic system, has been significantly influenced by the technological tide which, like the sea, has sometimes dealt with these human activities in a gentle and benign way, but often with violence. With the advent of steam power, the subsequent development of the factory system and a network of transportation systems, such as railways and canals, the influence of this tide was clearly manifest and the reaction of humanists, artists, architects and men of letters was quickly forthcoming. Such nineteenth-century luminaries as Dickens, Ruskin, Owen, Carlyle, Thoreau, Pugin, Elizabeth Gaskell, Disraeli and of course Engels and Marx, come to mind. With this early evidence of the sensitivity on the part of intellectuals to the industrial revolution, why has the history of technology and its sibling field, industrial archaeology, been so shamefully neglected by academic historians and archaeologists? I believe there are a number of reasons for this.

Compared to the history of science, the history of technology is a recent addition to the broad spectrum of historic subdisciplines represented in academia. In many ways its development is more akin to minority and women's studies, each struggling to find a secure place in the field of history, than it is to the history of science. In the case of the history of technology, it is always tacitly assumed to be part of, albeit a much less significant segment of, the history of science. Unlike the history of science, the history of technology and industrial archaeology does not deal with what was earlier considered to be an "exact subject." I think that in our day we are finding out that science is no longer defined as an

exact intellectual enterprise. The history of engineering or of technology is not related to a field represented in most colleges of liberal arts and science. In fact, it is very rarely assumed to be part of the liberal arts. In Europe, colleges of engineering are often not included in universities at all. This is particularly true in France and Germany and, to a limited extent, even in Britain. It is difficult to relate the history of technology and industrial archaeology to the history and philosophy of ideas. A much easier task, I believe, in the case of the history of science.

From the historians' point of view, industrial archaeology and the history of technology require different research methodologies with an emphasis on nontraditional sources of information, such as engineering drawings and specifications, articles in technical journals, company records and the documentation of historic manufacturing processes. Perhaps the most marked departure from traditional research methods used by historians is the key role the artifact plays as a source of historical evidence. Gleaning evidence from the artifact is the *raison d'etre* of the new field of industrial archaeology. Techniques used include remote sensing, surveying, architectural photogrammetry and hands-on field work to produce measured drawings and large format photography as well as, nondestructive and traditional testing methods for determining the physical and chemical properties of historic materials.

There is suspicion on the part of many historians that the history of technology and industrial archaeology is somewhat folkloric, with little intellectual content, and that it really deals with craft or folk skills in some ways or, at its best, is simply applied science. I think there is a failure to recognize what Victorians always knew when they talked about the art and romance of engineering. That, in fact, like architecture it is a creative art form. Ironically the very people who created this technology have failed to produce the kinds of archival material that historians are so fond of dealing with. It reminds one of the Irish poet, W. B. Yeats, who said "The intellect of man is forced to choose perfection of the life, or of the work."[2] I think in the case of the history of engineering, it has always been the perfection of the work on the part of engineers which has left, in most cases, very little in the way of a "paper trail" to provide insights into the creative design process and problems connected with construction and manufacturing processes. Thus, the artifact becomes, in many cases, an essential part of the investigation and evaluation of historic industrial and transportation works.

Since the field is a fairly latecomer, it was early dominated by internalists who were in the main not trained historians. The internalist perspective places great emphasis on the history of invention as the key to the understanding of the history of technology without the context of social and political history, which, I think, is so important. It has spawned a biographical tradition which remains at the heart of the history of technology, being established by Sir Samuel Smiles early in the nineteenth century.[3] In its most extreme form, this has led to writing the history of technology on a heroic basis dealing with what Sir Kenneth Clark calls "the great field marshals of the industrial revolution."[4] Little regard was given to the industry and society which made these great engineering accomplishments possible beginning in the eighteenth century.

In 1958 the multivolume *History of Technology* by Singer et al. was published in Britain and has become a landmark in the field.[5] Its focus was almost entirely upon internalist issues as the key to understanding this new discipline. It was largely devoid of a contextual background in social and political history. This led Melvin Kranzberg and colleagues not only to propose an alternate view of the subject, but to carry their convictions beyond mere criticism and to found the Society for the History of Technology. This fledgling society was dedicated to an integrated approach combining technological perspectives with contextual history.

Equally significant is the fact that the very men who have literally changed the world through science and technology and could be called the present-day revolutionaries have often been unaware of the role they have played. Fortunately, in the last several decades there has been a growing awareness of the inter-relationship of technology and society. This awareness has resulted in significant investigations in the field of the history of technology and industrial archaeology. It has also given rise to the new field of industrial archaeology which, through detailed investigations of industrial remains, seeks to provide building blocks for the professional historian and essential information for the preservation of historic engineering works. Although this new interest in technology has not yet achieved the respectability of the more classical studies in history and archaeology, it has attracted a truly interdisciplinary group of scholars and inter-

ested amateurs, representing both the humanities and technology. This fact, in itself, is significant. It provides a meaningful bridge between the two cultures. (This term was first used by C. P. Snow in the famous 1959 Rede Lecture at Cambridge University.)[6]

Modern archaeology employs scientific techniques for the study of the relics of man dating from the beginning of human life to the present age. As Childe indicates in his excellent *Introduction to Archaeology,* archaeologists are preeminent in the study of prehistoric man.[7] In fact, what we know about the ancient Middle East is largely based on archaeological evidence. With this emphasis, many in the field have insisted that for archaeology to exist, artifacts and monuments must be excavated. To many in the field of industrial archaeology, this appears to be an undue restriction to a vital field of knowledge. Thus, there has been resistance to apply the term to studies of human relics and monuments associated with the rise of industry during the past two centuries. As illustration of this controversy, there was an exchange of articles shortly before the founding of the Society for Industrial Archeology in America between Robert Vogel[8] of the Smithsonian Institution and V. P. Foley.[9] With most archaeology programs firmly lodged in departments of sociology and anthropology, industrial archaeology has found it difficult to be accepted in academia. As a result, there are few academic programs in industrial archaeology.

However, to accept a broader view of the field one must recognize monuments in terms of existing and often occupied buildings housing industrial processes, and other structures and relics, company records and machinery, for instance. In this connection, one of the early British leaders, Kenneth Hudson, reported that even the Council of British Archaeology, not a markedly revolutionary body, has itself been using the terms without even a hint of inverted commas (i.e., quotation marks) since 1969.[10]

Perhaps the best way to establish industrial archaeology as a subject is to quote Pannell, another leader in British industrial archaeology:

> O. G. S. Crawford, that great field archaeologist, appreciated that as a branch of anthropology, the subject of archaeology could not be confined within dates or periods, but represented the study of man through the physical remains of his past activities.
>
> If we accept this view, then industrial archaeology becomes a subject rather than a chronological subdivision of the main study—archaeology—and should include archaeology of industry in all periods of the past. As, however, archaeologists of prehistoric classical, medieval, and other periods have included the industries of those times in their studies, it has been accepted that industrial archaeology starts where the already established periods end or, in other words, at the beginning of the industrial revolution.[11]

Following World War II with the loss empire and the need to play a new role in Europe, many in Britain sought to celebrate the nation's leading role in the industrial revolution by investigating and, in selective cases, preserving the physical remains of Britain's early industry and transportation systems. In the best British tradition, industrial archaeology sprang from groups of amateurs interested in specific local industries and, particularly, in canals, railways and steam engines. The work of these local groups includes published histories and increasingly the preservation and restoration of industrial monuments. Amongst these preservation activities are notable works in reopening abandoned railway lines, restoring rolling stock, especially steam locomotives and the restoration to operating condition of a variety of steam engines used in pumping, milling and factories. In addition, water powered sources used at textile and grist mills and other industries received the attention of industrial archaeologists. Perhaps the most impressive work has been the canal system, which by the end of this century, will be reopened almost in its entirety for recreational use. The British case, then, was an amateur local development trying to preserve and understand the great industrial revolution in Britain on a local or thematic basis. In the beginning, it found difficulty in establishing a national organization in industrial archaeology, let alone a vigorous discipline in academia. There are certain notable exceptions to this such as the Iron Bridge Gorge Museum and its relationship with the University of Birmingham and the Association of Industrial Archeology in the national group in Britain.

Industrial archaeology in America, on the other hand, is very much a professional activity. It was founded by a group of interested professionals on a rainy Saturday morning at the Smithsonian Institution in Washington in 1969.[12] Very few academics were represented in this group, but rather a spectrum of professionals working in museums and other government and private agencies. This group then was not a grass roots movement, and still it is more national in its outlook and activities than its British cousin. It has failed though in the same way to become a vigorous part of academia. In contrast, one only has to think of the great amateur archaeologists of the nineteenth century, Heinrich Schliemann, Arthur Evans and others, and how these amateurs managed to introduce their interest into academia. I do not think anyone today debates that archaeology is not a central part of the great liberal arts tradition. Industrial archaeology has only tenuous links with this earlier tradition, and has not yet gained the respectability of historical archaeology.

The 1976 Exxon Education Foundation report stated:

> The real riddle of the undergraduate curriculum is what to do about liberal arts. The sense of genuine mission has been eroded from it. As a result, the liberal arts became viewed as a museum of past riches and its faculty members viewed themselves as curators.

One need not restrict these remarks to the undergraduate curriculum but extend them to the entire realm of the liberal arts, or the humanities, to use another term. Thus, it appears that the history of science, engineering and industrial archaeology provide the opportunity of an expanded and exciting new vision of the liberal arts. In fact, one could entitle this as the "New Humanities."

Outside the academy, the nation's rich industrial heritage has been receiving increasing attention during the past two decades as a result of the National Historic Preservation Act of 1966, the adaptive reuse of historic industrial buildings and more recently the establishment of industrial parks at both the state and federal levels. The role of historians of technology and industrial archaeologists have come to include documentation of historic sites, the preparation of mitigation and preservation plans, National Register and National Historic Landmark nominations, together with inventory and evaluation work and more recently, thematic studies of various industries as part of the discipline. The establishment of historic industrial sites under the aegis of the U.S. Congress have involved the National Park Service in the history of technology and industrial archaeology on a very large scale indeed, but not always with enthusiasm, since many in the Park Service have spent their careers in what is now called the environmental field. For example, the National Park Service's involvement in America's Industrial Heritage Project in southwestern Pennsylvania and several other industrial corridors represents the establishment of the history of technology and industrial archaeology as essential related disciplines for the preservation of the nation's rich industrial heritage. Similar activities have been undertaken at the state and local levels on both a public and private basis.

One of the hallmarks of these various initiatives is the interdisciplinary nature of the professionals involved and the emphasis on the artifact as evidence. Perhaps the best way of gaining insight into industrial archaeology is to describe some of the techniques employed.[13] The activities can be grouped from initial inventory and survey work through a series of steps resulting in full restoration of a historic site according to the highest national and international standards for historic preservation.

Inventories are an attempt to obtain basic information on potential sites for a particular geographic region or for a particular industry. They also provide the raw material for establishing a data base and providing background information to produce contextual histories. This then establishes basic information on the distribution and size of a given industry, which would be of interest not only to historians of technology and industrial archaeologists but also to economic and social historians. Such work can also act as an emergency alert system so that interested organizations and individuals can document structures, machinery and other relics in danger of destruction. There is an urgent need to develop a nationwide data base of industrial structures as a practical matter in deciding which sites and structures should be preserved through documentation and which, in selected cases, should receive full restoration or adaptive reuse. Contextual histories based on such inventory work are now in preparation for the iron and steel industry and the coal industry in the eastern United States.

Unlike prehistoric archaeology, the industrial archaeologist usually has access to written records. These may constitute company records and accounts, public records, newspaper, magazine and professional journal articles, records in the Patent Office, local histories, diaries, journals and other written records. Contracts, specifications and catalogues also provide an important source of information. No site should be investigated without a search for written records. Unlike other amateurs in the field, the engineer by virtue of his special knowledge can give valuable insights into industrial processes and in identifying unique features of designs which are important in understanding the evolution of engineering and technology.

With a portable tape recorder, oral records of persons involved in the development of industry should be made by industrial archaeologists whenever possible. Oral histories are often invaluable in documenting obsolete manufacturing processes, and a tape repository of such material is often available in state and university libraries, as well as at the National Archives and other federal institutions.

The importance of actual on-site recording cannot be over emphasized. In the context of archaeology, in general, it is appropriate to quote Childe again:

> The public, I suspect, still thinks of monuments as ivyclad ruins, isolated blocks of stone carved or inscribed. To many, relics are single coins or flint implements turned up in ploughing or ditching if not personal mementoes—a button from Prince Charlie's vest, the joint of a martyr's toe, a tooth of Buddha. None of these, least of all the last group, are likely to be significant archaeological data. To have a meaning that an archaeologist can hope to decipher, an object must be found in context.[14]

It is well then for the industrial archaeologist to note that this means site documentation. This involves preparing site maps and producing measured drawings of extant structures and machinery. Traditional hand methods used in cartography and in architectural engineering practice have emerged as the traditional approach to IA documentation. However, one should be alerted to new techniques which are available, including remote sensing, aerial photography and mapping, architectural photogrammetry, the use of nondestructive testing instruments to determine physical properties of historic materials and the recent, rapidly expanding field of geographical information systems. Thus, recording a particular site usually involves an multidisciplinary team which may include engineers, architects, cartographers, archivists, as well as historians and traditional archaeologists.

When considering the documentation of historic sites in America, and especially the preparation of measured drawings based upon hand measured field notes, one naturally thinks of the Historic American Building Survey and the Historic American Engineering Record. HABS was established in 1933 during the depth of the Depression as part of the Roosevelt New Deal. To mark the fiftieth anniversary of the founding of the survey, two books were published. The first, *Fifty Years of the Historic American Building Survey*

provides a detailed history of HABS, while the second, *Historic America: Buildings, Structures and Sites* presents the work of both HABS and HAER, including 16 essays by experts in the field together with a checklist of sites documented in the HABS/HAER collection.[15] These two surveys have established a national standard for the documentation of historic sites.[16]

If one views site documentation as a secular analogue to canonization, the HABS/HAER standards represent the requirements for sainthood. In terms of international preservation activities, these surveys stand unchallenged in terms of documentation. This documentation consists of ink-on-mylar measured drawings, large format archival photographs and a written history of the site. In all documentary work the measured drawings and photographs should be viewed as complementary ways of obtaining data. In particular, plans and cross sections reveal information which cannot be obtained photographically. On the other hand, photographic techniques can be used to provide essential information in the production of measured drawings. Photogrammetry can be used to produced measured drawings without the necessity of making detailed hand measurements in the field. The recently developed Computer Aided Design (CAD) technology will increasingly be used to produced measured drawings at all levels of documentation.

Harley McKee, one of the early leaders of HABS, indicates that HABS quality drawings and photographs were intended to be illustrative and used in publications or for gallery or museum exhibits. The latest information on the activities and techniques of HABS/HAER can be found in John Burns's *Recording Historic Structures*.[17] If, however, the documentation of a site is to be used for other purposes, such as restoration of a historic structure, then the level of detail including dimensions will be much more comprehensive, with a greater emphasis on producing information to guide the restoration work and less concern for the aesthetics of each drawing.

Even further removed from the HABS/HAER level of documentation are the requirements, also established by the National Park Service, for the preparation of photographs for the National Register of Historic Places and the documentation stipulated by the National Park Service for a wide-range of mitigation studies. Often, when a site is determined to be of archaeological or historical significance, site documentation is required if federal or state funding is to be used.

Thus, with limited time and money it is necessary to consider the level of documentation needed for a given site. This includes determining the number and level of details of the drawings to be prepared integrating the drawings with the anticipated number of photographs. These decisions should be made before any field work is undertaken.

The emphasis of this book is on the essential techniques employed in producing drawings, photographs and written histories. Following the introductory essays, the first topics considered are historical sources to aid in the preparation of contextual site histories.[18] The field work is presented in essays dealing with the preparation of site maps, measured drawings and large format photographs. The final essays deal with an introduction to photogrammetry and geographical information systems that will increasingly be employed by those involved in industrial archaeology.

Much work needs to be done in the field of industrial archaeology to provide the information needed to understand the whole process of industrialization. Little has been said, until recently, about the human side of industrial archaeology, for example, housing, churches, schools and other parts of the built environment associated with industry. The rapidly disappearing craft skills which were so necessary in the early phases of the industrial revolution need to be recorded wherever possible. Such skills are now being replaced by automated machines and by robots. In addition, little attempt was made to understand the conditions to which working people were subjected at home and in the work place in the early phases of the industrial revolution.

Our industrial monuments are rapidly disappearing, thus every effort should be made to organize the field of industrial archaeology as rapidly as possible and to enlist the active participation of a whole host of scholars and amateurs across North America. One of the ways to do that, and the mission of this book is to present the techniques of industrial archaeology to a much broader audience for use in the classroom and in the field.

ENDNOTES

1. Elements of this essay are based upon earlier published and unpublished works by the author: Emory L. Kemp, "Industrial Archaeology- An Avocation for Engineers," *Engineering Issues-Journal of Professional Activities,* ASCE, 99 No. PP4 (October 1973): 481–498; "A Perspective on our Industrial Past Through Industrial Archaeology," *Public History: An Introduction,* (Malabar, Florida: Krieger Publishing Co. 1986), pp. 174–198; and "Public History and the Research in the History of Science and Technology: Has It Made a Difference?", presented at the American Historical Association, (December 1991), unpublished.
2. Yeats W. B. *The Choice,* st. 1, 1933.
3. Smiles Sir Samuel. *Lives of Engineers* (London: John Murray, 1878); *Industrial Biography* (London: John Murray, 1884)
4. Clark Sir Kenneth. *Civilisation.* New York: Harper & Row, 1969, p. 330.
5. Singer C. et al., *A History of Technology,* 1–5. Oxford: Oxford University Press, 1958.
6. C. P. Snow, "The Two Cultures," Rede Lecture at Cambridge University, 1959, publication, C. P. Snow, *The Two Cultures and a Second Look.* Cambridge: Cambridge University Press, 1969.
7. Childe V. Gordon. *A Short Introduction to Archaeology.* New York: Collier Books, 1962.
8. Robert M. Vogel, "On the *Real* Meaning of Industrial Archaeology," *Historical Archaeology* 3 (1969)
9. Foley V. P. "On the Meaning of Industrial Archaeology," *Historical Archaeology* 2 (1968)
10. Hudson Kenneth. *Industrial Archaeology: An Introduction.* London: John Baker, Ltd., 1966.
11. Pannell J. P. M. *Techniques of Industrial Archaeology.* Newton Abbott, Devon: David & Charles, 1969, p.9.
12. Information about the Society for Industrial Archeology can be obtained by contacting the Society's headquarters at the National Museum of American History, Smithsonian Institution, Washington, DC 20560. The Society's newsletter, SIAN, and Journal, IA, are a rich source of information on the subject and current activities of the SIA and its members.
13. The history of the related field of prehistoric and historic arhaeology can be found in:
    Willy Gordon R. and Jeremy Sabloff. *A History of American Archaeology.* London: Thames & Hudson, 1974.
    In a number of cases the techniques of historical archaeolgoy must be employed if excavation is contemplated. A comprehensive treatment of excavation methods is given in:
    Hume Ivor Noel. *Historical Archaeology.* New York: Alfred A. Knopf, 1974.
14. Childe V. Gordon. *A Short Introduction to Archaeology.* New York: Collier Books, 1962.
15. Smith Carol C. *Fifty Years of the Historic American Building Survey, 1933–1983.* Alexandria, VA: HABS Foundation, 1983.
    Stamm Alicia and C. Ford Peatross, eds., *Historic Buildings, Structures and Sites.* Washington, DC: Library of Congress, 1983.
16. Department of the Interior, National Park Service, "Secretary of the Interior's Standards and Guidelines for Architectural and Engineering Documentation", *Federal Register* 48, No. 190 (1983): 44730–44734.
17. McKee Harley J. *Recording Historic Buildings.* Washington, DC: Government Printing Office, 1970.
    Burns John A. Recording Historic Structures. Washington, DC: The American Institute of Architects Press, 1989. This illustrated work by the chief of HABS represents the latest information on site documentation by HABS/HAER.
18. *The Public Historian* (Summer 1991) presents a set of review essays on industrial sites. In his essay Steve Lubar reflects on the Historic American Building Survey/Historic American Engineering Record together with publication from America's Industrial Heritage Project. He urges more attention be paid to contextual history to accompany site histories.
    Lubar Steve. "The Historic American Building Survey/Historic American Engineering Record/America's Industrial Heritage Project: Some Recent Publication," *The Public Historian* 13 No. 3 (Summer 1991).

CHAPTER 2

The Shepherdstown Cement Mill: A Case Study

Emory L. Kemp

INTRODUCTION

During the summer of 1992, the Institute for the History of Technology and Industrial Archaeology at West Virginia University organized a six-week field school in industrial archaeology. The course was based upon draft versions of the essays in this book. In a sense, it was intended to proof test the material in the book, and, in fact, each of the students in the summer short course was required to write an evaluation of each of the chapters of the book. The course was taught by a cadre of professionals drawn from the Institute and faculty from the departments of History, Civil Engineering and Geology and Geography at WVU. It was truly a multidisciplinary teaching team composed of engineers, landscape architects, historians and geographers serving as lecturers.

The course consisted of two parts; namely, a three-week classroom preparation for three weeks of field work. The first part was held at West Virginia University and covered each of the topics presented in this book. Emphasis, however, was on the preparation of measured drawings, the theory and practice of archival photography, land surveying and historical research applied to historic structures and sites. The class was assigned a site on Virginius Island, part of the National Park Service located at the Harpers Ferry National Historical Park, to record some of the early industry on the island. The second site was a natural cement mill on the Potomac River near Shepherdstown, West Virginia, and it is this site which is the subject of the case study. Its location can be seen in Figure 2.1 downstream from Shepherdstown.

Team members were involved in every aspect of the field work. The ruins of the cement mill, the kilns and office were documented and located on a site map. Documentation included the preparation of measured drawings of the extant mill and battery of kilns, as well as producing large format, perspective corrected archival photographs and a series of 35mm and 2-1/4 × 2-1/4 photographs for use in producing the drawings.

Two monographs published by the Institute contain research done on the Shepherdstown Cement Mill, as well as other natural cement mills in the Potomac Valley. This work, undertaken a number of years ago, investigates the entire natural cement industry in the Potomac Valley. Eleven sites were located, the Shepherdstown and Round Top mills being the most important producers of natural cement, as well as having the most significant artifacts left on-site. Because the preliminary historical investigation had been completed, the class was asked not to undertake primary research but to take the data already developed and prepare a National Register of Historic Places nomination for the Shepherdstown Natural Cement Mill. This National Register nomination provides information on the significance of the site, a description of the extant structures and reference materials. The complete nomination can be found in Appendix A.

The field work was organized by establishing a set of three-person teams assigned to the kilns, the cement mill and the office, as well as providing basic surveying data. Before any work could be undertaken, however, the entire team cleared the site of scrub and undergrowth. Once the site was cleared, each of the archaeological features was located on a site map. The work consisted of using a theodolite and level, as well as a 100-foot tape. This is a traditional way of producing a site map. If more time and resources had been available on this study, the field surveying would have been compared with aerial photographs of the area and a contour map of the site prepared using aerial photographs. In a similar way, in the future it would be highly desirable to employ both close range photogrammetric techniques, as well as the traditional hand measuring method of producing field data and subsequently measured drawings. In the case of the Shepherdstown Cement Mill study, traditional hand methods of measurement were employed. All of the archival photography was done

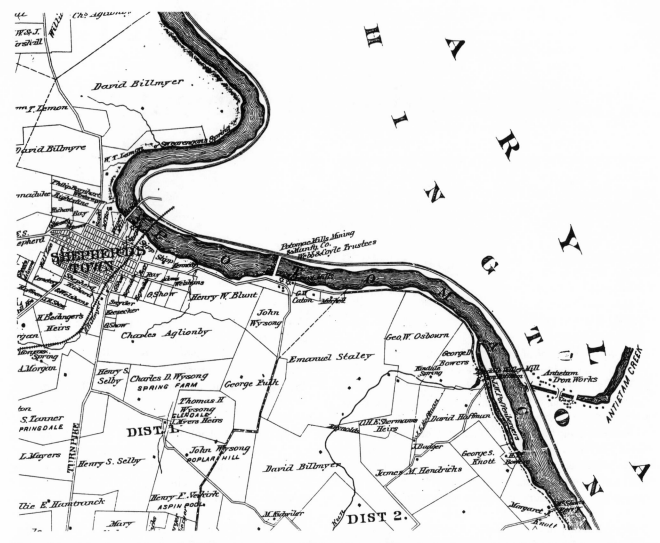

Figure 2.1. A local map showing the Shepherdstown Cement Mill and Potomac River Dam whose pool supplied water to the mill and provided a means of moving canal boats across the river from the Chesepeake and Ohio Canal.(West Virginia Geological Survey, 1916)

with a 4 × 5 inch large format view camera in which it was possible to correct any perspective distortions. The results of this field study are shown in a sequential manner, starting with typical field notes which form the basis of a series of measured drawings. The large format photography is represented by a series of photographs of the prominent features of the site. In addition to large format photography, both 35mm and 2-1/4 × 2-1/4 inch cameras were employed to provide supplementary material to the field notes to assist the students in first preparing pencil drawings on vellum, and finally Mylar tracings of the preliminary drawings. A series of 2-1/4 × 2-1/4 inch photographs of the battery of kilns is presented to illustrate this phase of the documentation. The historical research found a focus in the preparation of the National Register nomination which gives a background history of the site and a description of its prominent features. It should be noted that none of the members of the team had previously served with the Historic American Engineering Record or its equivalent at the state and local level. The results produced here are the due to the skills learned in the first three weeks of the field

school using the essays produced in this book. The results of the work were not only used to evaluate essays in this book but also to provide illustrative material for the chapter of the monograph dealing with the history of the Shepherdstown Cement Mill.

THE SHEPHERDSTOWN CEMENT MILL IN CONTEXT

Before presenting details of the documentation of the Shepherdstown Cement Mill, it seems appropriate to set the stage for the case study by providing a context for the documentation of this particular site.

Natural cement is a finely pulverized product resulting from the calcination (burning or dehydration) of an argillaceous limestone (i.e., of a clay material). In addition to the primary component of calcium ($CaCO_3$) such rock contains significant amounts of clay, slate or other argillaceous materials or sufficient quantities of alumina silicate, which when calcined and mixed with water hydrates again into a solid, making it useful as a building material. Natural cement can be used as a mortar for stone or brickwork or as a binder in concrete. Its peculiar characteristic is that it hardens underwater and is waterproof once it has set. John Smeaton and James Parker of England discovered (more correctly rediscovered) and manufactured natural cement in the eighteenth century. It was John Smeaton who correctly determined that it was the clay component in the limestone that led to the waterproof properties associated with hydraulic cement. Hydraulic, or natural, cement has a long and distinguished history dating back to the Hellenistic Period of the Greeks, and was widely promoted by Roman engineers who had discovered that certain rock deposits produced a waterproof cementitious material. Eighteenth-century engineers used it extensively in Great Britain and later throughout the world. It should be noted that the calcination of limestone devoid of argilleous and/or aluminum components results in the production of quick lime, CaO. Lime was used traditionally for mortar in stone masonry and brickwork.

With the Industrial Revolution came a heavy demand for large public and industrial works. Thus, the hydraulic property of natural cement made it essential for the construction of canals, bridges, aqueducts, dams, breakwaters and causeways throughout most of the nineteenth century. In architectural work, such as buildings and houses, lime mortar continued to be preferred over cement mortar since it produced a softer mortar which could yield if there was any movement in the masonry or brickwork. Lime was, however, not waterproof and could not be exposed to situations where it was in contact with water or used underground. Benjamin Henry Latrobe, the architect of the U.S. Capitol and other well-known structures, was one of the first to apply the hydraulic properties in cement in the construction of the Chesapeake and Delaware Canal in 1804. Latrobe had studied under John Smeaton and the well-known canal engineer William Jessop in England. Loammi Baldwin also used hydraulic cement in the Middlesex Canal in 1796–1797. There may have been other engineers in the United States who also used hydraulic limes or cement in their works, but their deeds are unrecorded. In addition, these cements were of necessity imported from Great Britain and Continental Europe, since natural cement was not produced in North America at the time.

The engineers of the Erie Canal, under construction from 1817 to 1826 in New York State, appear to have been the first to discover natural cement limestone in the United States and to manufacture and use it in extensive quantities. At the beginning of the natural cement-producing period brought about by its use in the Erie Canal, it was particularly sought after for its use in building hydraulic structures on canals and navigable waterways. Its discovery on the Erie Canal, credited to Canvass White, led to the establishment of natural cement mills in New York, particularly the Rosendale Cement, which became well known throughout the period.

Had it not been for the need for natural or hydraulic cement by canal engineers, the natural cement industry would probably not have developed as quickly or as extensively as it did. Conversely, had it not been for the discovery of extensive beds of quality cement limestone in the United States and the subsequent development of the natural cement industry, the growth of the widespread network of canals would probably have been greatly retarded.

After the 1890s, Portland Cement replaced natural/hydraulic cement as a building material because of its more consistent high quality and the fact that the basic ingredients were blended from separate components and thus not dependent upon naturally occurring cement rock in which the necessary components occurred, with only a few exceptions, in only approximately correct proportions. Had it not been for the need of natural cement for canals, the United States might have managed longer with native limes and imported natural cements until the development of the Portland Cement industry. There is a possibility, of course, that the Portland Cement industry might have developed much earlier had it not been for the existence of a thriving natural/hydraulic cement industry. In any event, for a period of about 80 years, natural/hydraulic cement provided one of the necessary ingredients which helped to make possible the industrialization of the United States.

SHEPHERDSTOWN CEMENT MILL

The years of operation of the natural/hydraulic cement plant at Shepherdstown in Virginia (later West Virginia) can be divided into two general periods: pre-Civil War (from 1828–1861); and post-Civil War (from 1867 to the beginning of the twentieth century). The location of this mill with relation to Shepherdstown and the Potomac is shown in Figure 2.2. During its early development, the owners were busy converting part of their grist mill to cement-making operations, erecting cement kilns and opening cement limestone quarries. It is interesting to note that they continued to produce flour as well as natural cement in their grist mill using the same stones! Until about 1837 when the Round Top, Maryland, natural/hydraulic cement plant went "on line," the Shepherdstown plant was the prime producer of cement for the Chesapeake and Ohio Canal. Nevertheless, there were 10 other cement mills producing cement, at one time or another, for the canal and for shipment in barrels on the canal to Washington, Alexandria and other growing urban industrial areas. During the rest of the early period, until destroyed by federal troops in 1861 so that it could not be used by the Confederates, the Shepherdstown plant produced natural/hydraulic cement largely for the Washington, D.C. market.

The Civil War years brought considerable disruption to the trade and industry of Shepherdstown. In fact, one of the battles of the Civil War is called the Battle of the Cement Mill which took place in September 1862. It was not until 1867 that sufficient capital could be secured to erect a new cement plant on the ruins of the original mill. When production began anew it was without the accompanying grain

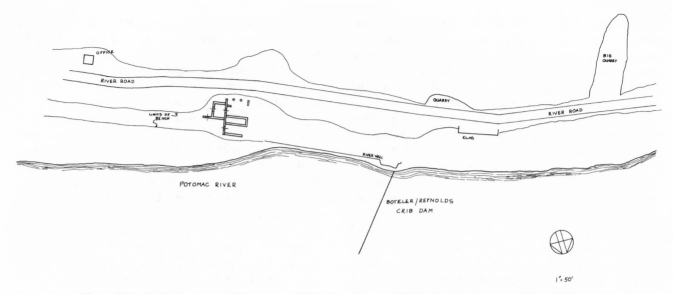

Figure 2.2.   Preliminary map of the cement mill site based upon a field land survey. (map by Edward Winant)

grinding that had taken place in the pre-Civil War years. During the post-Civil War years, attempts were made to modernize the plant, to obtain waterpower from the Potomac River, and to rely on transportation provided by the C & O Canal. Sometimes steam had to be substituted for water power because of insufficient water in the Potomac River, and then local railroads were called upon (instead of the canal) to haul coal to the mill and cement to market. In spite of efforts to modernize the plant and to use the most efficient means of transportation, the plant soon went into gradual decline and ended production with the death of the operator in 1901.

Many years of the operation had been hard ones for the owners and operators. Although the cement plant had never been a resounding financial success, the natural cement produced by the Shepherdstown natural cement plant helped to build the Chesapeake and Ohio Canal, area railroads and many of the public and private buildings in the nation's capitol and surrounding areas.

THE CASE STUDY

The traditional approach to the documentation of industrial and transportation sites has been established by the National Park Service's Historic American Building Survey/Historic American Engineering Record (HABS/HAER) and was used in documenting the Shepherdstown Cement Mill. However, because the history of natural cement of the Potomac Valley is the subject of a separate monograph by the Institute for the History of Technology and Industrial Archaeology, it was decided to have members of the field school prepare a National Register nomination rather than the traditional detailed site history. The usual approach includes using primary source material whenever possible, supplemented with secondary sources which can be used not only to give a more

complete site history but to place the site in context with contemporary social and industrial history. This contextual background is essential in establishing the significance of a given site, and is necessary if the documentation is to serve as a mitigation study mandated by Section 106 of the National Historic Preservation Act of 1966 or as the basis for the development of a National Register nomination.

Because of the length of the National Register nomination, it has been featured in an appendix rather than appearing in the text. All of the work was undertaken by students in the field school, reviewed by the faculty and produced as a single joint effort. It should be noted that this National Register nomination includes a discussion of the historic significance of the site, a description of extant structures as well as, illustrative material and selected references. Also, before any field work was undertaken at the Shepherdstown Cement Mill, the history of the mill was presented to field school participants as well as, reference materials which had been collected for the monograph.

FIELD MEASUREMENTS

In documenting the Shepherdstown cement mill two kinds of measurements were taken. The first was a traditional engineering land survey of the site, done so that a site map could be prepared and all of the important site features located in relation to one another. These included not only the cement mill itself, but the battery of cement kilns on the river front as well as, the original large kiln on the hill side and the office of the company. Figure 2.2 is the copy of the site map.

Following the land surveying, the teams turned their attention to the preparation of field notes which served as primary source material for the preparation of formal measured drawings. These field notes were prepared in the traditional hand measured way, using the format established by

HABS/HAER. A sample of field notes dealing with a cement kiln is shown in Figure 2.3. The students were assembled in groups of three and assigned specific recording tasks on one or more of the structures. Historic photographs showing the mill during its years of operation, Figures 2.4 and 2.5, supplement the student photographs and drawings.

The photography was an essential part of the documentation of the site used in conjunction with the measured drawings to provide information would could not be readily depicted on drawings. In addition, small format photography (2-1/4 × 2-1/4 inch and 35mm cameras) was used to provide a large number of photographs to assist in the interpretation and provide essential information to supplement field notes in the preparation of the measured drawings. A representative set of photographs of the kilns using a 2-1/4 × 2-1/4 inch format is shown in Figures 2.6, 2.7 and 2.8. A view camera with a 4 × 5 inch format was used to produce perspective corrected archival photographs of all of the important features of the site. Representative samples of the archival photos are shown in Figures 2.9 through 2.13. Each of the field school photographs was produced by participants organized in teams of three, so that each member had an opportunity to use the view camera. Although many of the participants had extensive experience with small format photography, none of them had used a view camera before enrolling in the field school.

Following the site work, the teams returned to the drawing office to produce measured drawings. This consisted of a two-stage operation in which preliminary drawings were prepared in pencil-on-vellum. This was later traced in ink-on-Mylar to HAER standards, work that was undertaken by delineators of the Institute. The original drawings produced by various members of the field team are shown in Figures 2.14 through 2.21. It should be noted that the ink-on-Mylar drawings based on this student work formed the basis of the illustrative material for the monograph on natural cement mills in the Potomac Valley. Thus, the members of the field school felt that they were documenting a significant historical site and that information which they obtained made a major contribution to the monograph published by the Institute.

This case study is illustrative of the kind of documentary material that can be developed using a field school as the *modus operandi*. It also shows that a new generation of historians and industrial archaeologists can be trained using these field school techniques. The need for documenting historic industrial and engineering works has increased rapidly with a renewed emphasis on the preservation and interpretation of historic, industrial and transportation sites. It is, therefore, hoped that this and subsequent field schools together with this book can make a contribution to this rapidly expanding national enterprise.

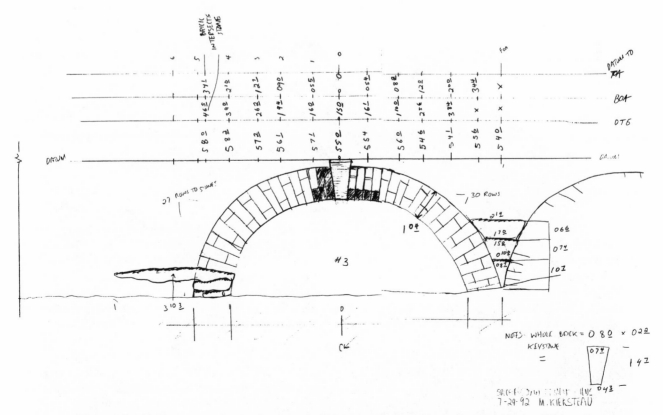

Figure 2.3. Field notes showing details of a typical kiln. (drawing by field school student Matthew Kierstead)

Figure 2.4.   View of the Shepherdstown Cement Mill from the Maryland shore. (Tom Hahn collection)

Figure 2.5.   Close-up of the cement mill in the late 19th century. (Tom Hahn collection)

Figure 2.6. Oblique view of the battery of cement kilns with field school students in the background. (photo by field school student Phil Ross)

Figure 2.9. A view looking north showing the ruins of the main building of the cement mill, with the Potomac River in the background. (IA Field School, 1992)

Figure 2.7. Interior view of the drawpit for kiln #4. (photo by field school student Phil Ross)

Figure 2.10. A riverside view of the addition to the mill on the right and the wall of the main mill ahead, looking upstream (IA Field School, 1992)

Figure 2.8. View of the drawpit of small experimental kiln. (photo by field school student Phil Ross)

Figure 2.11. A view looking NW showing the mill addition. (IA Field School, 1992)

Figure 2.12. A view looking east of the riverside chamber of the main mill building. (IA Field School, 1992)

Figure 2.13. The large kiln located on the hillside above river road was not successful and lead to its abandonment and the six-kiln battery on the river bank. (Emory L. Kemp collection)

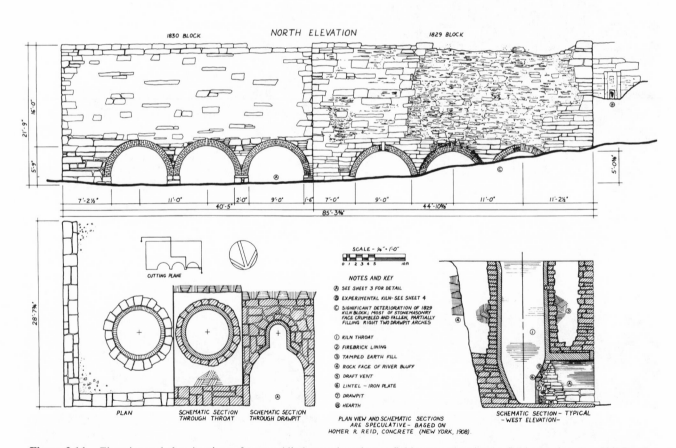

BATTERY OF CONTINUOUS CEMENT KILNS

Figure 2.14. Elevation and plane/sections of cement kiln battery based upon field notes. (drawing by field school student Phil Ross)

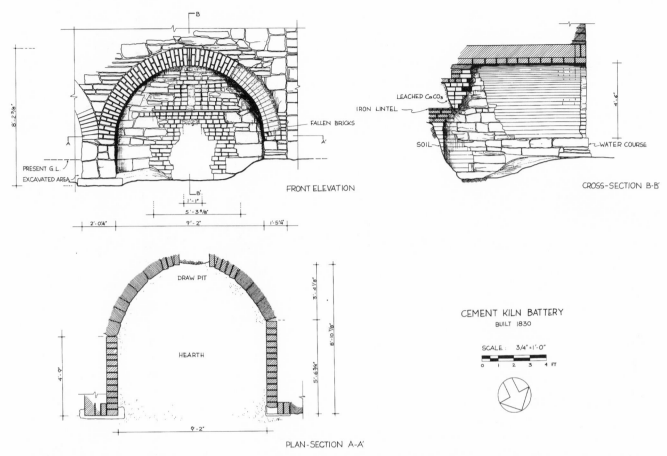

Figure 2.15. Elevation, plan-section and cross-section of one cement kiln. (drawing by field school student Christina Spyrakos)

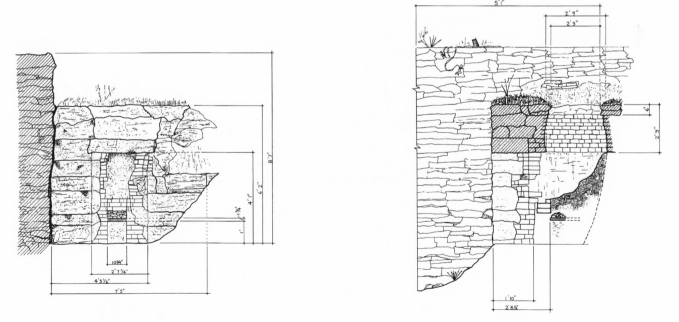

Figure 2.16. Elevation and section of the experimental kiln. (drawing by field school student Brian Coffey)

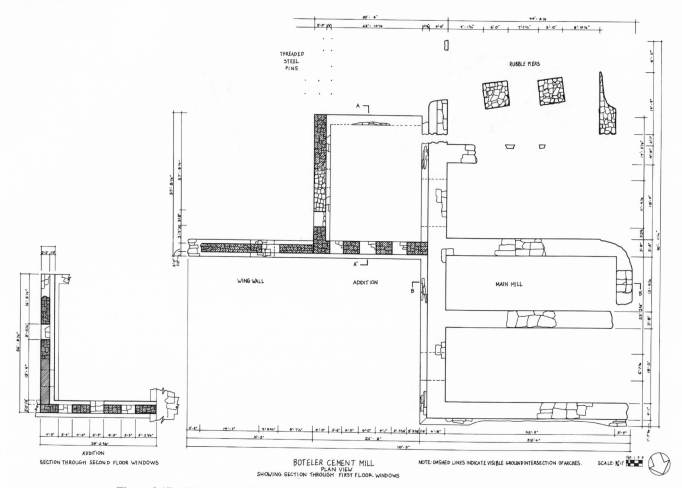

Figure 2.17.   Plan view of the cement mill. (drawing by field school student Matthew Kierstead)

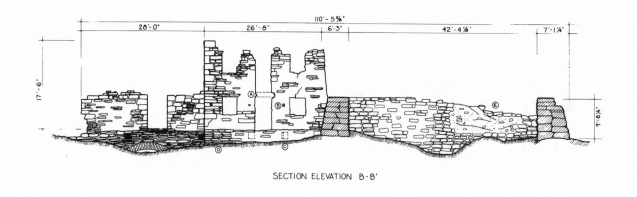

NOTES:
Ⓐ – PROJECTED DOOR LINTEL
ⒷⒸⒹ – VARIOUS BEAM POCKETS
Ⓔ – COLLAPSED WALL

THE CEMENT MILL

Figure 2.18.   Section-elevation of the cement mill. (drawing by field school student D.J.S. Bonenberger)

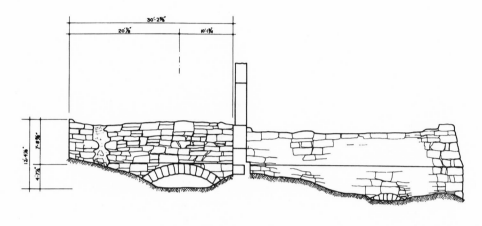

SECTION A-A'

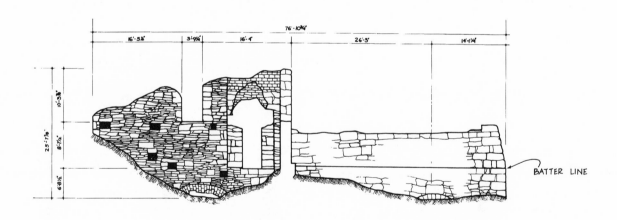

EAST ELEVATION

Figure 2.19. East elevation and section of cement mill addition. (drawing by field school student Bryan Ward)

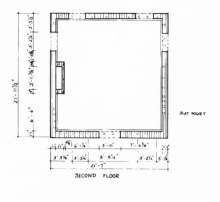

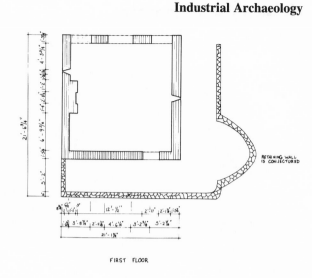

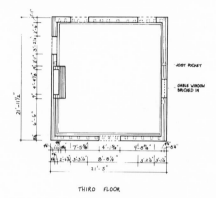

SECOND FLOOR

FIRST FLOOR

OFFICE BUILDING
PLAN VIEW

THIRD FLOOR

Figure 2.20. Floor plans for the cement mill office. (drawing by field school student Shelley Birdsong)

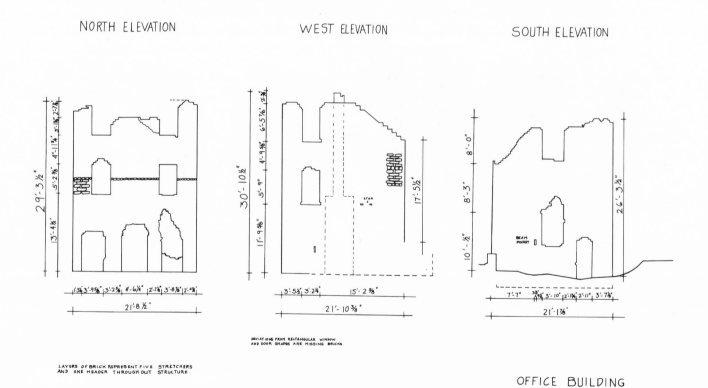

NORTH ELEVATION   WEST ELEVATION   SOUTH ELEVATION

LAYERS OF BRICK REPRESENT FIVE STRETCHERS
AND ONE HEADER THROUGHOUT STRUCTURE.

DEVIATIONS FROM RECTANGULAR WINDOW
AND DOOR SHAPES ARE MISSING BRICKS

OFFICE BUILDING

Figure 2.21. Elevations of the cement mill office. (drawing by field school student Brucella Jordan)

APPENDIX A:

Draft version of National Register of Historic Places Registration Form prepared by field school students.

```
NPS Form 10-900                              OMB No. 1024-0018
(Rev. 10-90)

United States Department of the Interior
National Park Service

NATIONAL REGISTER OF HISTORIC PLACES
REGISTRATION FORM

===============================================================
1. Name of Property
===============================================================
historic name:           Boteler Cement Mill

other names/site number: Potomac Cement Mills
                         Shepherdstown Cement Mill


===============================================================
2. Location
===============================================================
street & number: River Road, 1.3 miles east of Shepherdstown
                                       not for publication ___
city or town: Shepherdstown                       vicinity: x
state: West Virginia         code: WV    county: Jefferson  code: WV037
zip code: 25443
===============================================================
3. State/Federal Agency Certification
===============================================================
As the designated authority under the National Historic Preservation Act of
1986, as amended, I hereby certify that this ____ nomination ____ request for
determination of eligibility meets the documentation standards for
registering properties in the National Register of Historic Places and meets
the procedural and professional requirements set forth in 36 CFR Part 60.  In
my opinion, the property ____ meets ____ does not meet the National Register
Criteria.  I recommend that this  property be considered significant ___
nationally ___ statewide ___ locally.  ( ___ See continuation sheet for
additional comments.)


_____    _____
Signature of certifying official               Date


_____
State or Federal agency and bureau

In my opinion, the property ____ meets ____ does not meet the National
Register criteria. ( ___ See continuation sheet for additional comments.)


_____    _____
Signature of commenting or other official      Date


_____
State or Federal agency and bureau
```

==
4. National Park Service Certification
==

I, hereby certify that this property is:

____ entered in the National Register
    ___ See continuation sheet.   _____ _____
____ determined eligible for the
  National Register   _____ _____
    ___ See continuation sheet.
____ determined not eligible for the
  National Register   _____ _____
____ removed from the National Register _____ _____

____ other (explain): _____

_____ _____ _____
                                   Signature of Keeper   Date
                                                 of Action

==
5. Classification
==

Ownership of Property (Check as many boxes as apply)
          x   private
          ___ public-local
          ___ public-State
          ___ public-Federal

Category of Property (Check only one box)
          ___ building(s)
          ___ district
         x site
          ___ structure
          ___ object

Number of Resources within Property

Contributing	Noncontributing	
2	_____	buildings
_____	_____	sites
2	_____	structures
_____	_____	objects
4	0	Total

Number of contributing resources previously listed in the National
Register: none

Name of related multiple property listing (Enter "N/A" if property is not
part of a multiple property listing.)   N/A

```
==============================================================================
```
6. Function or Use
```
==============================================================================
```

Historic Functions (Enter categories from instructions)
     Cat: industry   Sub: manufacturing facility
            extraction   extractive facility
            processing   processing site
            commerce   business
            transportation   water related

     _____   _____
     _____   _____
     _____   _____

Current Functions (Enter categories from instructions)
     Cat: vacant   Sub: not in use

     _____   _____
     _____   _____
     _____   _____
     _____   _____
     _____   _____
     _____   _____
     _____   _____


```
==============================================================================
```
7. Description
```
==============================================================================
```

Architectural Classification (Enter categories from instructions)
     no style

     _____
     _____

Materials (Enter categories from instructions)
     foundation: limestone
     roof _____
     walls: limestone

     other: arches-brick_____
     _____

Narrative Description (Describe the historic and current condition of the
property on one or more continuation sheets.)

NPS Form No. 10-900-a   OMB No. 1024-0018
(8-86)

United States Department of the Interior
National Park Service

NATIONAL REGISTER OF HISTORIC PLACES
CONTINUATION SHEET

Section 7   Page 1   Boteler Cement Mill
                                                    Jefferson County, WV

The Boteler and Reynolds Mill, constructed in 1828, is located on river
terrace land on the southern bank of the Potomac River, approximately one and
a quarter miles from the center of Shepherdstown, West Virginia. The main
mill site is located between the office building to the east, the 1832 kiln
to the south, and the 6-kiln battery to the west. A high bluff to the south
of the mill complex was extensively quarried to provide raw material for the
production of natural cement. A timber crib dam extending across the Potomac
River provided water power for mill operation and slackwater for navigation
between the mill and the Chesapeake and Ohio Canal on the northern shore.

The function of the cement kilns was to convert the quarried cement rock
to a usable form of cement, a process known as "calcining." This process
converts calcium carbonate ($CaCO_3$) to calcium oxide (CaO, or "quicklime") by
oxidation with moderate, steady heat, driving off carbon dioxide in the
process. Calcining also converts magnesium carbonate ($MgCO_3$) to magnesia
(MgO) and drives off sulphurous impurities as sulphur dioxide (SO_2).

The physical process entailed charging the kiln from the top with
alternating layers of cement rock and fuel (initially charcoal but coal soon
after operations began), at ratio of one ton of coal per 70 barrels of
cement. As the cement was burned, it was drawn from the bottom. Each of the
six kilns operated continuously and had a daily capacity of 50 barrels or 300
barrels a day. Actual production averaged 200 barrels a day. One barrel of
cement is equivalent to three bushels or 200 pounds.

Cement rock was carted from the quarry above the kilns (common practice
in the natural cement industry was to employ a tramway, but no artifactual or
historical evidence confirms this practice at Shepherdstown), and calcined
cement was loaded on scows in the headrace and boated to the mill for
preparation. Thus the headrace served four purposes: water power for the
mill, transporting coal by barge from the C&O Canal to the kilns,
transporting calcined cement by scow to the mill, and transporting prepared
cement from the mill across the river to the C&O Canal. After the disastrous
flood of 1889, Major Blunt built a cable-car tramway from the kilns to the
mill to eliminate reliance on the headrace, which was usable only seasonally
and prone to damage by flooding.

Located on a steep embankment on the southern side of the Potomac River,
approximately one and one quarter miles from Shepherdstown, West Virginia,
the small test kiln of The Boteler and Reynold's cement mill is a
inauspicious but historically important component of the large mill complex.

NPS Form No. 10-900-a   OMB No. 1024-0018
(8-86)

United States Department of the Interior
National Park Service

NATIONAL REGISTER OF HISTORIC PLACES
CONTINUATION SHEET

Section 7   Page 2   Boteler Cement Mill
                                                  Jefferson County, WV

Built in 1829, the small structure was used to test the quality of cement
rock found in a quarry less than a few hundred feet away from its location.
The first kiln built on the mill site was found to have many problems
producing a consistent product, resulting in the decision to try another
design, and a location that would be closer to the mill. While an outcrop of
rock was located in a more advantageous position, its quality had to be
tested before any substantial work on a new kiln or kilns could ensue. This
test may have been the only time the small kiln was fired. After
establishing that the adjacent cement rock was of suitable composition, six
larger kilns were built directly beside it to the east. Both the battery of
six kilns and the test kiln remain intact today.

     The office building is a 2-1/2 story brick structure. It is located
beside the road and fronted by a white picket fence, There is a retaining
wall behind the structure constructed of rough stone. There is also a
fortification type mound faced with rough cut stone on the east side of the
structure. The roof is hip construction. The operation of a factory
requires significant administrative work. It is evident that correspondence
was carried on between the Shepherdstown Mill and the Chesapeake and Ohio
Canal officials as well as with others involved in the mercantilism of
cement. There were certainly letters to write, bills to pay, invoices and
receipts to make, workers to hire and manage, salaries to pay, etc. The
office building was undoubtedly a very necessary part of the cement mill
complex.

     The Shepherdstown Cement Mill is an extant testimony of the tremendous
effort that were made at the beginning of the last century to give birth to
industry, to develop new techniques, and to improve the quality of life,
transportation, and thereof of construction materials. It is part of and is
actually a contributor to the Industrial Revolution and to the process of
industrialization of this country.

Large Mill

     The mill building is comprised of a large main mill building and a
smaller attached addition. The large mill building was rectangular and
judging from present remains the width of the foundation is approximately 55
feet and the existing length of the foundation above the ground is
approximately 75 feet, but photographic and on-site evidence indicate that
the foundation extended further to the south. The building at the time of

NPS Form No. 10-900-a   OMB No. 1024-0018
  (8-86)

United States Department of the Interior
National Park Service

NATIONAL REGISTER OF HISTORIC PLACES
CONTINUATION SHEET

Section 7   Page 3   Boteler Cement Mill
                                                 Jefferson County, WV

operation was three stories high with a shallow hipped roof. Atop the roof
was a short gable-roofed ventilation monitor. The building had numerous
windows on the north and east facades. The addition to the east was three
stories high, but was lower than the large mill. The first floor of the
addition was at the same elevation as the stone foundation wall. The roof of
the addition at the time of operation was a gabled roof with the ridge line
perpendicular to that of the larger adjacent mill. Currently, a single
standing wall project to the east from the addition. This wall has a window
or door opening and interior joist pockets. Other features exist, such as
threaded steel pins and collapsed piers, but their historical uses are
unknown. The mill complex is currently in a ruinous state. Over time the
mill has been subject to various floods and has been affected by road
construction on River Road. The remains include foundations, walls, and some
free standing walls.

    The large mill foundation walls are constructed of a combination uncut
to rough cut, uncoursed to irregularly coursed, dark, hard metamorphosed
limestone or shale of local origin, which is consistent with stone found in
the area. The exterior walls exhibit a batter of one and a half to two feet
which begin approximately three feet from the ground. The large mill
foundation walls are divided into three bays. The center bay measures
thirteen feet by forty-two feet and the outer bays are eighteen feet by
forty-two feet each with a single arch through the east wall. The center bay
was enclosed on all four sides. The flanking bays were open at the west end
to allow water to flow through for milling operations. Remains of a room to
the south consist of two collapsed piers and possible wall remains. The
physical extent of this room is speculative. During production the building
was three stories tall with a shallow hipped roof. The walls were heavy
masonry of unknown composition. The west facade contained two windows on the
first and third floors, which are in vertical alignment and the second floor
had three windows staggered between the first and third floor windows. All
three stories on the east facade were in vertical alignment and of same size.
The roof extends laterally beyond the walls and was supported by exposed
rafters or brackets. Atop the hipped roof of the large mill was a lighting
and/or ventilation monitor. Currently all that remains are the foundation
walls, which have deteriorated most dramatically at the western end.

    The addition to the mill complex rests upon a stone foundation similar
to the large mill. The walls of the addition are composed of rough uncoursed
limestone, which likely was waste rock from the production of natural cement.
The north facade of the addition contained three square window openings on

NPS Form No. 10-900-a   OMB No. 1024-0018
   (8-86)

United States Department of the Interior
National Park Service

NATIONAL REGISTER OF HISTORIC PLACES
CONTINUATION SHEET

Section 7   Page   4   Boteler Cement Mill
                                            Jefferson County, WV

each story. The east facade has a door opening to the first story. The
doorway was filled at some undetermined date with stones at the lower levels
and with bricks at the upper level. On this facade large beam pockets are
evident, suggesting the existence of a floor that supported a heavy load.
The interior of the addition is bounded by three limestone walls and the
battered wall on the east facade of the large mill. The interior walls also
display beam pockets for large support members. The arch through the south
bay enters the addition through the battered wall of the large mill and exits
through the eastern wall of the addition and thence to an arch in the free
standing northern wall. As the walls ascend to the higher stories their
width narrows and at each story a shelf exists, which was likely a rest for
floor joists. On the east side of the addition it appears that at least two
attached one story sheds were built. The sheds were built along the east
wall of the large mill and the south wall of the addition. Lack of
foundations for these sheds suggest that the sheds were temporary.

      Currently a free standing one story wall exists as an eastern
continuation of the north facade of the addition. The wall contains a
rectangular opening and an arch in the stone foundation.

Kilns

      The battery of cement kilns, located about 450 feet upstream of the mill
ruins, consists of two attached rectangular blocks of three continuous-type
kilns, each, built into the side of the river bluff. They are of coursed
limestone rubble construction, approximately 85 feet long and 20 feet high.
Depth varies from 28 feet on the right top side to about 20 feet on the left
top side. The top of the battery is even with the road level.

      The right-side block of kilns was built in 1829 and abuts the small 1828
experimental kiln (see below). This block is symmetrical, with the three
brick-arched drawpits centered in the structure. The left-side battery was
built in 1830 directly onto the earlier block. The drawpit arches are not
centered in this block but are skewed to the right, indicating that the left
wall of the 1829 block was used to support the construction of the newer
block. Otherwise, the two blocks differ little in construction. The 1829
block's brick arches have limestone keystones; the 1830 block has brick
keystones. On the 1830 block, the brickwork of the arch extends back into
the kiln to a point where the walls begin curving towards the drawpit
opening. On the older block, the brickwork only extends inward for several

NPS Form No. 10-900-a
(8-86)

OMB No. 1024-0018

United States Department of the Interior
National Park Service

NATIONAL REGISTER OF HISTORIC PLACES
CONTINUATION SHEET

Section 7   Page 5

Boteler Cement Mill
Jefferson County, WV

courses, where limestone voussoirs support the arch. Additionally, the
arches of the newer block are situated ten inches higher on the structure
than are on the older block. The battery was built by immigrant Welsh and
english stonemasons.

Overall, the battery of six kilns is best-preserved of the remains of
the mill complex, but are moderately deteriorated. The 1829 block is
significantly deteriorated; much of the facing stonework on the right side
has crumbled and fallen, nearly covering the two drawpit arches farthest to
the right. Five of the six brick-lined kiln throats have also collapsed and
filled with decades of organic debris. Depressions across the top of the
kilns indicate that the diameter of each throat was approximately seven to
eight feet, agreeing with historical data. Large trees and brush cover the
top of the battery. Sediment from repeated floods cover at least eighteen
inches of the base of the kilns as well as the fallen stonework.

Limited excavation of the sediment in the right drawpit of the 1830
block (the most intact drawpit) revealed a limestone hearth. Height from the
hearth to the apex of the arch is 6 feet 9-1/2 inches; interior width is 9
feet 2 inches at the widest point; depth is 8 feet 10 inches. The top and
sides of the arch narrow concavely to the drawpit opening itself, which is 3
feet 6 inches high by 2 feet 6 inches wide. An iron plate lintel 1-1/4
inches thick supports the and brick above the drawpit opening; above this
lintel is a vent for the air draft for the kiln. This vent is 5 inches wide,
lined with brick, and rises diagonally into the interior of the kiln. It is
encrusted with calcium oxide leached from the inside of the kiln.

It is difficult to account for the difference in condition between the
two blocks, considering that they were built only a year apart. Some
possibilities are: (1) different grades of limestone were used to construct
the kilns; (2) better workmanship prevailed on the 1839 kilns, as the labor
force then was more skilled than earlier; (3) structural damage incurred
during the Civil War was not fully repaired on the 1829 kilns; (4) the
collapse of the attached shedding of the 1829 kilns may have pulled down the
stone facing.

The historical appearance of the kilns differed in that a sloping shed
roof (visible in historic photographs) covered the front length of the
battery. These sheds functioned more to protect the cement from moisture
than to provide comfort for the laborers, who worked in a very hot
environment.

NPS Form No. 10-900-a
(8-86)

OMB No. 1024-0018

United States Department of the Interior
National Park Service

NATIONAL REGISTER OF HISTORIC PLACES
CONTINUATION SHEET

Section 7   Page 6

Boteler Cement Mill
Jefferson County, WV

Test Kiln

     Dwarfed by the battery of kilns it abuts, the test kiln is a meek
industrial structure. Approximately six feet high by five feet wide, it is
awkwardly located near the top rear of the main battery. Rectangular in
shape and built of a metamorphosed shale common to the region, the test kiln
is void of any architectural style or decorative features; not to assert that
the larger kilns exhibit such style, however, the test kiln's construction is
of a crude and non-permanent nature. Unlike its neighbors, the test kiln has
no arch; rather, a simple post and lintel construction made of large blocks
of roughly cut and suitably sized stones creates an opening on the face of
the kiln approximately two and 1/2 feet wide and four feet tall. This
opening is angled inward on either side and merges with the face of the kilns
draw pit. An iron lintel rests approximately one foot above the hearth and
approximately two feet eight inches deep from the face of the structure.
Extensive erosion has exposed the outside surface of the brick lined interior
and in some areas, has caused much of the bricks to fall away from the kiln.
What is most likely a vent, is located directly above the iron lintel and is
approximately four inches high.

     The top of the kiln is accessible and open, revealing a bottle-shaped
interior not unlike many lime kilns of larger proportions. The cylindrical
interior is two feet, three inches wide at its opening and nearly six inches
wider at its approximate middle. Dirt and rubble have filled much of the
interior of the kiln. The kilns hearth was uncovered after excavation and
was found to be made of a more finely hewn stone than that of its outside
construction.

     It can be assumed that coal was used to cook the cement rock as many
pieces of coal were found both as loose fragments and in component form with
cement rock.

Office

     From oral interviews with neighbors it was derived that the house was
probably inhabited until ca. 1927 and was abandoned ever since. Today, only
the four exterior walls remain in place, in fairly good condition. The site
is seriously overgrown and fallen trees on the walls threaten the stability

NPS Form No. 10-900-a   OMB No. 1024-0018
(8-86)

United States Department of the Interior
National Park Service

NATIONAL REGISTER OF HISTORIC PLACES
CONTINUATION SHEET

Section 7   Page   7   Boteler Cement Mill
                                                        Jefferson County, WV

of the remains.   No particular style could be attributed to the building;
because of its year of construction it can be called "Early Republic."

     There are no frames and many bricks are missing from the window sills.
The location of the frames can be estimated from the remaining plaster.
Nothing is left from the interior of the house, but holes on the walls,
indicating the position of joists and beams.   The interior was plastered,
though the exterior was brick.   The building is almost square (approximately
21'-2" x 21'-6").   At the back side there is a retaining wall of
approximately 5'-2" distance from the south wall, which curves on the east
side creating an earthen mound.   The building is made of bricks (common bond,
5 stretchers - 1 header).   The roof is missing, so are the lintels of the
windows and the walls above them on the third floor.   The lintels of the
first and second floor are also missing, but there is an indication of their
pattern (vertical bricks, oblique at each end).   On the west wall there was
a fireplace and chimney, that still exist.   The chimney was stepping down at
every floor, so was the thickness of the exterior walls.   The first floor was
probably supported by the shelf created by this difference in thickness.   On
the east and west wall of the first floor there is a long and narrow opening,
having the shape of a musket hole; their purpose is not clear.   The white
paint after the flood of 1889 is still apparent.   Of course, the fence does
not exist any longer.

     Through observation of the chemical characteristics of cement rock and
strenuous experiments, Dr. Boteler invented the method of calcining natural
cement.   The old grist mill ended up being a site of continuous
experimentation: from the water-driven mill to the experimental kiln, to the
"tramway," and the turbine-wheel.   That is why the mill complex represents a
significant and distinguishable entity of industrial, commercial and
inventive activities of the early 1800s.

     Its contribution to the production of natural cement, and thereof to the
construction of important engineering works, and its active role in the
materialization of the Chesapeake and Ohio Canal ranks it among the most
eminent, worth-preserving and registering complexes.

Canal and Dam System

     A crib dam was placed across the Potomac River just below the location
of the kilns to create a reservoir for power supply as well as a slackwater

NPS Form No. 10-900-a   OMB No. 1024-0018
(8-86)

United States Department of the Interior
National Park Service

NATIONAL REGISTER OF HISTORIC PLACES
CONTINUATION SHEET

Section 7   Page 8   Boteler Cement Mill
                                                       Jefferson County, WV

for transportation. The dam followed a natural rock ledge across the river,
and was built by fabricating open-topped crates of wood boards (also known as
gabions), pinning these into the rock sheet forming the river bottom with
long iron spikes, and filling the gabions with stone. They were then covered
with more boards to form a walkway. Currently, the wooden gabions have
rotted away leaving piles of stone to mark the alignment of the dam. As the
dam followed a natural ledge, it is not perpendicular to the river, but
crosses at an angle of 13 degrees downstream of the perpendicular.

The dam is abutted on the West Virginia side by a concrete pier, the
remains of which are still visible today. This abutment also formed the
beginning of a masonry river wall which extended downstream from the dam to
the mill building. This wall served to protect the canal from the periodic
flooding of the Potomac River. It is still in existence, although it shows
some deterioration.

A canal existed from upstream of the dam to the mill buildings, and ran
to the south of the river wall. It is conjectured that the canal itself was
of earth construction with a suitable sideslope, most likely 2:1. No widths
are known for the canal, but it was known to have transported scows with
cement rock from the kilns to the mill. It also served to channel water to
the headrace of the mill for power supply. It is further conjectured that
turning basins existed at the mill and the kilns to turn the scows about.
Present evidence suggests this, although the canal is completely filled in,
and the site is presently a bench area between the river and River Road.

==
8. Statement of Significance
==
Applicable National Register Criteria (Mark "x" in one or more boxes for the
criteria qualifying the property for National Register listing)

     x   A   Property is associated with events that have made a significant
               contribution to the broad patterns of our history.

   ____ B   Property is associated with the lives of persons significant in
               our past.

     x   C   Property embodies the distinctive characteristics of a type,
               period, or method of construction or represents the work of a
               master, or possesses high artistic values, or represents a
               significant and distinguishable entity whose components lack
               individual distinction.

     x   D   Property has yielded, or is likely to yield information
               important in prehistory or history.

Criteria Considerations (Mark "X" in all the boxes that apply.)

   ____ A   owned by a religious institution or used for religious
                  purposes.
   ____ B   removed from its original location.
   ____ C   a birthplace or a grave.
   ____ D   a cemetery.
   ____ E   a reconstructed building, object,or structure.
   ____ F   a commemorative property.
   ____ G   less than 50 years of age or achieved significance within the
                  past 50 years.

Areas of Significance (Enter categories from instructions)
                        industry
                        military
                        commerce
                        transportation

Period of Significance 1828-1861
                            1867-1901

Significant Dates 1828
                  1862

Significant Person (Complete if Criterion B is marked above): N/A

Cultural Affiliation N/A

                _____

                _____
Architect/Builder   unknown

                _____

Narrative Statement of Significance (Explain the significance of the property
on one or more continuation sheets.)

NPS Form 10-900-a
(8-86)

OMB No. 1024-0018

United States Department of the Interior
National Park Service

NATIONAL REGISTER OF HISTORIC PLACES
CONTINUATION SHEET

Section 8   Page   1

Boteler Cement Mill
Jefferson County, WV

    The Boteler Cement Mill site in Shepherdstown, West Virginia meets Criteria A, C and D for eligibility to the National Register of Historic Places. This site meets Criteria A as it is associated with the September 1862 Civil War battle of Shepherdstown. The Boteler Mill site lies below a high cliff which commands a view of the Maryland shore of the Potomac River and an important river ford adjacent to the mill. Although the mill was inoperative at the time, this site was geographically strategic location in what is sometimes referred to as "the battle of the cement mill," and served as a refuge for Federal troops during the battle. The Boteler Cement Mill site meets Criteria C as a site significant for association with industry, transportation and commerce. The site is significant to the history of the cement industry. The remains of the fourth-oldest cement plant in the country represent a cohesive complex including quarries, an office building, kilns of several sizes and designs, mill remains and buried water power and transport systems. This site is a distinguishable entity whose parts in combination and proximity remain an important example of the early cement industry in the limited states. The site also has significant associations with local, regional and intra-plant transportation. The Chesapeake and Ohio Canal Company erected locks across the river from the mill to facilitate slackwater navigation to and from the mill. Local railroads later played a part in shipment of the mill's products. Canal and cable-tramway transport systems were used to move raw materials on-site. The Boteler Cement Mill also played a significant role in local and regional commerce. The Norfolk and Western Railway was not only a hauler but a consumer of Boteler's cement which it used for railway construction.

    The cement from the Boteler Mill played a significant part in the construction of the C&O Canal, a transportation route which made Washington, D.C. an outlet for Boteler Cement, which was indeed utilized in the construction of numerous significant landmarks in the national capitol. The Boteler Cement Mill site meets Criteria D as a site with potential significance as a historic non-aboriginal archaeological site. The potential exists for gaining knowledge of Civil Way events, and also for exploring the processes and technology of natural cement production.

    Natural cement milling operations at the Boteler Cement Mill can be conveniently separated into two phases. The first began in 1828 when Henry Boteler discovered a large deposit of natural cement rock on the site of his new merchant grist mill on the Potomac River just east of Shepherdstown, West Virginia. Boteler spent the first few years of this period developing quarries and enlarging his battery of kilns. Boteler's Mill was the major

NPS Form 10-900-a   OMB No. 1024-0018
(8-86)

United States Department of the Interior
National Park Service

NATIONAL REGISTER OF HISTORIC PLACES
CONTINUATION SHEET

Section 8   Page 2   Boteler Cement Mill
                                             Jefferson County, WV

supplier of cement for the construction of the Chesapeake and Ohio Canal, and
in fact to the entire upper Potomac River Valley until the cement mill at
Round Top near Hancock, Maryland went into production in 1837. Boteler's
Mill continued to produce cement for canal and railroad construction,
although at reduced levels of production. Boteler enjoyed a stronger market
in the construction projects of growing Washington, D.C. In 1855, owners
Boteler and Reynolds leased the Potomac Mill, as it was then known, to Lerri
Moler and I. H. Taylor. The milling of grain assumed a new prominence during
this period of ownership. All work ceased on August 19, 1861 when federal
troops burned the mill to prevent it from falling into Confederate hands.
The mill was the focal point for the Battle of Shepherdstown on September 19,
1862, a skirmish associated with the larger conflict at Antietam.

     The hiatus in cement production caused by the Civil War marked the end
of the first phase at the Shepherdstown Cement Mill. The second phase of
production began in 1867 when James W. Barber organized the Potomac Mills,
Mining and Manufacturing Company. After unspecified repairs, the mill
resumed production and was running at "fullest capacity, and making an
excellent quality of cement..." in 1875 according to the Shepherdstown
Register. During the ensuing decades the mill changed ownership several
times and closed intermittently due to weather, low water, floods, or
transportation problems, but continued to produce cement at or near capacity.
The mill operated in this fashion until 1901 when a period of idleness
followed by the death of owner, Major Henry Woodward Blunt, put an end to the
production of natural cement in Shepherdstown.

     The Boteler Cement Mill satisfies Criteria A for its association with
military history. The mill site was involved in the September 19, 1862
Battle of Shepherdstown which occurred in the aftermath of Antietam. The
mill site affords an excellent vantage point from which to view the battle
scene, and is significant as troops took refuge in and directed fire from
structures which stand today. On September 19, 1862, Union troops entrenched
in the dry bed of the C&O Canal across the river from the mill began firing
at Confederate positions on the high bluff above the mill. On the next day,
union forces crossed the river and were repelled by the Confederate riflemen
atop the bluff. In a disorganized and deadly retreat many union soldiers
took cover inside the 6 kiln arches which stand today. Artillery fire from
the Union positions across the river, aimed at the Confederates atop the
fluff, exploded about the kilns, and many Union troops were wounded or killed
by their own sides fire. Many sought to escape this shooting gallery if

NPS Form 10-900-a
(8-86)

OMB No. 1024-0018

United States Department of the Interior
National Park Service

NATIONAL REGISTER OF HISTORIC PLACES
CONTINUATION SHEET

Section 8   Page   3

Boteler Cement Mill
Jefferson County, WV

friendly fire by crossing the stone crib dam, still visible in the Potomac River.

The Confederate sharpshooters shot many Union soldiers as they scrambled over the slippery dam. The Confederates took the mill site, using the mill buildings as emplacements to direct fire, and forcing the Union troops down off the cliffs and into the river.

The mill site encompasses the cliffs, trails and buildings involved in the skirmish, and affords a view of the dam, ford, C&O Canal and general area of "the Battle of the Cement Mill," making it a significant Civil War Battle site and a contributor to national history.

The Boteler cement mill meets Criteria C as the site represents a distinguishable entity whose components lack individual distinction. The site meets Criteria C for its associations with the history of industry, transportation and commerce.

The Boteler Cement Mill is the fourth oldest cement mill in the United States. The mill site is a cohesive, contained industrial complex surrounded by an otherwise natural setting. All of the features, structures or buildings associated with natural cement mills in general and this site historically are present in close proximity and in varying condition. The site is dominated by an 80 foot high bluff from which cement rock was extensively quarried for over 60 years. An unsuccessful kiln constructed in 1829 exists intact, as does a small kiln built to test the rock for suitability of composition. The main 6 kiln production battery stands near the largest of the quarry cuts. Foundations and walls remain from the main mill building and its subsequent additions. The shell of the mill office building still stands. These components, while not impressive individually, help to demonstrate the flow of materials involved in the manufacture of cement and some of the processes involved in natural cement production.

The Boteler Mill is also significant for its association with transportation from both an intra-plant and regional perspective. The power canal for the mill played an unusual dual role as it served as an intraplant water borne materials transfer route, along which scows moved cement rock to the mill. This system was later supplemented with a cable hoist system.

NPS Form 10-900-a
(8-86)

OMB No. 1024-0018

United States Department of the Interior
National Park Service

NATIONAL REGISTER OF HISTORIC PLACES
CONTINUATION SHEET

Section 8   Page   4

Boteler Cement Mill
Jefferson County, WV

The cement mill was a major customer of the Chesapeake and Ohio Canal across the Potomac River in Maryland. Boteler moved a great quantity of his produce via the canal for use in its construction between Washington, D.C. and Cumberland, Maryland, and for construction projects in Washington, D.C. The canal boats accessed the mill through a lock which entered the slackwater above a stone crib dam built above the mill site. The mill also relied on the nearby Norfolk and Western Railway for long-distance shipments and during times of low water when barges could not negotiate the river.

The Boteler Mill is also significant from the standpoint of commerce. The mill had a dual relationship with the C&O Canal and the N&W railway, relying on them not just for transportation of finished product, but as consumers of their natural cement. The C&O Canal purchased the lion's share of its construction cement from Boteler until the 1837 opening of the Round Top will near Hancock, MD. Although not always of superior quality, Boteler cement was favored locally due to its low transportation cost. Boteler's cement production enjoyed a market climate rife with construction and internal improvement projects. The Boteler Mill continued to ship cement via the C&O Canal, and large quantities of cement were delivered to Washington, D.C. where it was used as an integral component in the construction of numerous landmarks such as the Washington Monument. The Boteler Mill also established relationship with the N&W Railway, and supplied cement for the construction of railroad bridge piers and abutments, and other railway engineering structures.

The Boteler Mill is therefore significant as a contributor to local and regional commerce, much of which aided the construction of our national landmarks and regional infrastructure.

The Boteler Cement Mill site meets Criteria D as it possesses the potential to yield information important to several areas of history through archaeological investigation. The location of several structures in this complex on river terrace which is subjected to periodic flooding suggests that although smaller artifacts have likely been swept away, large features remain preserved under layers of alluvial silt. This consideration, combined with the presence of a busy, extractive industry which operated until the turn of the Century suggests that archaeological remains from the brief Civil War skirmish and occupation would be of a sparse and highly disturbed nature. However, archaeological investigation in the floodplain would yield information important to areas related in the section regarding Criteria C.

NPS Form 10-900-a   OMB No. 1024-0018
  (8-86)

United States Department of the Interior
National Park Service

NATIONAL REGISTER OF HISTORIC PLACES
CONTINUATION SHEET

Section 8   Page   5   Boteler Cement Mill
                                              Jefferson County, WV

     There is presently no above ground evidence for the cable tramway used
to transport raw materials between kilns and the mill. The power canal,
unusual for its additional role as a method of intra-plant transport of
materials lies completely buried by silt, as does the trailrace arrangement
of the mill. The likelihood exists of finding the remains of heavy machinery
within the mill foundations. Portions of the several kilns on site remain
partially buried. The office building has revealed a rich burn layer through
preliminary soil testing.

     The Boteler Cement Mill is eligible for listing to the National Register
of Historic Places as a site of archaeological significance. The known
subsurface features can yield important information pertaining to the history
of technology, specifically transportation, water power and cement
manufacture.

==
9. Major Bibliographical References
==
(Cite the books, articles, and other sources used in preparing this form on
one or more continuation sheets.)

Previous documentation on file (NPS)
___ preliminary determination of individual listing (36 CFR 67) has been
        requested.
___ previously listed in the National Register
___ previously determined eligible by the National Register
___ designated a National Historic Landmark
___ recorded by Historic American Buildings Survey   # _____
___ recorded by Historic American Engineering Record # _____

Primary Location of Additional Data
___ State Historic Preservation Office
___ Other State agency
___ Federal agency
___ Local government
 x University: West Virginia University
___ Other
Name of repository: Institute for the History of Technology and Industrial
                                Archaeology
==
10. Geographical Data
==
Acreage of Property _____

UTM References (Place additional UTM references on a continuation sheet)

        Zone Easting Northing   Zone Easting Northing
    1   3
    2   __ _____ _____   4 __ _____ _____
        _x_ See continuation sheet.

Verbal Boundary Description

     From a point, the northwest corner of the intersection of Trough Road
and River Road, North 10 degrees East for distance of 300 feet, to the
Potomac River. Thence with the south bank of the river North 88 degrees west
for a distance of 1,500 feet. Thence South 5 degrees West to the top of the
ridge, a distance of 600 feet, and returning to the point of beginning, North
76 degrees East, a distance of 1600 feet.

Boundary Justification

     This boundary is set to include all remaining buildings and industrial
works of the Shepherdstown Cement Mill site. Taking the boundary to the top
of the ridge will also include the quarries from which the raw cement rock
(limestone/silica) was taken. The river boundary includes the headrace for
the mill, the retaining wall and the south abutment for the crib dam which
supplied the mill.

NPS Form 10-900-a   OMB No. 1024-0018
 (8-86)

United States Department of the Interior
National Park Service

NATIONAL REGISTER OF HISTORIC PLACES
CONTINUATION SHEET

Section 9   Page   1   Boteler Cement Mill
                                                  Jefferson County, WV

Hahn, Thomas Swiftwater. "Cement Mills of the Potomac." Ed.D Dissertation,
     West Virginia University, 1982.

Kelly, Dennis P. "The Battle of Shepherdstown," <u>Civil War Times</u>, November
     1981, pp. 8-15, 32-35.

NPS Form 10-900-a   OMB No. 1024-0018
(8-86)

United States Department of the Interior
National Park Service

NATIONAL REGISTER OF HISTORIC PLACES
CONTINUATION SHEET

Section 10   Page 1   Boteler Cement Mill
                                                    Jefferson County, WV

Mill Site: Zone Easting Northing
             1   18   260820 4367820
             2   18   260350 4367900
             3   18   260300 4367720
             4   18   260800 4367780

Dam: Zone Easting Northing
             1   18   260490 4367890
             2   18   260200 4368090

```
===============================================================================
11. Form Prepared By
===============================================================================
name/title: Industrial Archaeology Field School Students

organization: West Virginia University    date: July/August 1992

street & number: 1535 Mileground        telephone: (304)293-2513

city or town: Morgantown                        state: WV zip code: 26505
===============================================================================
Additional Documentation
===============================================================================
Submit the following items with the completed form:
```

Continuation Sheets

Maps
    A USGS map (7.5 or 15 minute series) indicating the property's location.
    A sketch map for historic districts and properties having large acreage
        or numerous resources.

Photographs
    Representative black and white photographs of the property.

Additional items (Check with the SHPO or FPO for any additional items)

```
===============================================================================
Property Owner
===============================================================================
(Complete this item at the request of the SHPO or FPO.)
name _____

street & number_____ telephone_____

city or town_____ state_____ zip code _____

===============================================================================
```

CHAPTER 3

Federal Records/Federal Repositories

Ruth Ann Overbeck

INTRODUCTION

In the late eighth or early ninth century, A.D., the Welsh monk Nennius completed *Historia Britonum*. Nennius, who is sometimes referred to as the "father of British history," prefaced his chronicles with, "I have heaped together all that I have found."

Even if I wanted to emulate Nennius, I could not do so, especially within the confines of this book. After 25 years' use of federal records, I still have not plumbed the depths of all the records that are useful to industrial archaeologists. Thus, I agreed to write this chapter knowing that (a) identification of every federal government record group relevant to IA (Industrial Archaeology) site documentation is virtually impossible; (b) undertaking such a task within a reasonable time frame would require a sizable team of archaeologists, historians and archivists; and (c) the information collected could fill volumes.

This chapter is designed to stimulate interest in the records' relevance to IA projects; to encourage IA project teams to seek out and utilize a wider variety of federal records; and to provide general guidelines on methods to access those records.

To accomplish these ends, this chapter first gives a fleeting glimpse of the heritage of government involvement in industry. It then looks at some early federal documents that contain IA relevant information and moves forward to two abbreviated "case studies." The concluding section provides general information about some under-used record groups and suggests paths to take to find appropriate records.

HERITAGE

The reasons the U.S. Federal government has compiled an enormous amount of IA relevant information precede the government's formation. In large part, the roots are in English law and go at least as far back as the fifteenth century. During that century Parliament created a zone surrounding London in which wood could not be cut to fuel the smithies' fires. Other government actions in that pre-industrial age began to affect what would, in fact, become known as "industry." During the seventeenth century, for example, England's Court of Star Chamber extended the definition of criminal conspiracy to include acts in restraint of trade. English lawyers used this definition in 1717 to label labor's early attempts to organize and to strike as criminal acts.[1] Thus, well before the onset of the Industrial Revolution, the British government established the precedent of industrial and commercial regulations and laws ready to be adapted by the new U.S. Government and applied to the industrial age.

When the United States separated from England, the double yoke of being the supplier of raw materials to a mother country and the consumer of goods she produced was lifted from the new nation's shoulders. This opened the way for industrialization, but not all embraced it enthusiastically. Thomas Jefferson was perhaps the most vocal opponent. In 1781, he wrote, "While we have land to labor [on], then, let us never wish to see our citizens occupied at the workbench .... let our work shops remain in Europe...."[2]

EARLY RECORDS

Jefferson's philosophy notwithstanding, almost immediately upon creation, each of the U.S. Government's three branches, executive, legislative and judicial, became involved in industrial matters. Article 1 of the Constitution, Section 8 empowers Congress to "promote the Progress of Science and useful Arts." Intended to secure to the nation's authors and inventors exclusive rights to their writings and discoveries, the law encouraged ingenuity. As inventions succeeded, they in turn abetted American industry.

Almost as soon as the new government opened for business, inventors sought congressional approval of their creations. To cope with wonders such as nail-making machines and lightning-proof umbrellas, Congress established a patent board composed of three cabinet heads. Members of that first board were Secretary of State, Thomas Jefferson, Secretary of War, Henry Knox and Attorney General, Edmund Randolph. These three decided whether or not each invention was "sufficiently useful and important" to merit a patent. Files of this short-lived board and its successor, the U.S. Patent Office, are well known and are maintained by the National Archives.[3]

Even though Congress shifted the responsibility for patents to the executive branch, it did not free itself from the consideration of industrial matters. The first item published under "Finance" in the report of the first session of the first Congress was a petition written in 1789. Its signers were mechanics, tradesmen, etc., from Baltimore, Maryland, and they identified themselves by occupation as well as by name.

While it looks bland on first sight, the petition provides a significant amount of information about late eighteenth-century manufacturing in Maryland's leading industrial city. Its authors described the decline of American manufactures that they alleged occurred once the Revolution ended and foreign trade resumed. They asked Congress to limit importation of foreign manufactured goods because they adversely affected American-made items. Among the products they cited as made in or near Baltimore were a variety of papers and paper items such as blank books, mathematical instruments, window glass, loaf sugar, chocolate, bar iron and nail rods and "all kinds of iron castings."

The petitioners implied that during the Revolution, when imports of foreign goods to the United States fell dramatically, local manufactures grew significantly. They could obtain most of the raw materials for their products fairly close by. However, two industries that they wanted to protect, sugar refining and the production of chocolate, depended on the importation of foreign-grown raw materials. This raises the question of how the budding industrialists viewed the role of foreign trade and provides a possible context component for the industrial archaeologist. Did the Baltimore manufacturers really want the United States to allow only the exchange of raw materials? Or to follow the same policy of importation of raw materials and exportation of manufactured goods that the British colonial trading companies had practiced?

At its most specific, the petition demonstrates the diversity of local manufactures, but also confirms the importance of the city's nascent iron industry, one for which Baltimore became famous during the mid-1800s. In addition, the names and occupations of the petitioners were precise enough to determine that two of the men later moved to Washington, D.C. Once there, they manufactured items used in the construction of the Capitol and the White House.[4]

From this three and one-half-page document, written in laymen's language in 1789, an IA team can reap substantial information for a context. If one of the petitioners could be identified as the owner of the site under investigation, that would be a superb bonus.

Similar petitions from across the nation are scattered throughout the *American State Papers* and its successor, the *Congressional Record*. Still, petitions are not the volumes' only source of IA information. A random selection elicited the report of the Fourth Congress' Committee for Commerce and Manufacture. Contained in the report are some details of the textile industry in the Delaware River Valley: a man named Jacob Brown owned a cotton mill on Brandywine Creek in Delaware; and raw silk was a component of the bolting cloth which one Robert Damon manufactured in nearby Wilmington.[5]

The congressional speeches printed in these volumes are also sources of information. Speech after speech referred to Congressmen's home districts and its patent applicants, its roads that needed to be built or repaired, the attributes of its towns seeking industries, the names of the factories that were failing or prospering and the industrial successes and disasters. While many of their references were site specific, speeches made during debates about pending legislation often related to regional or industry-wide issues and as such were suitable for developing large scale industrial archaeology contexts.

The *American State Papers* and the *Congressional Record* are mandated to be included in the collections at every federally designated regional repository/library. At least one of each state's universities also has them. Although the quality of the indexes varies from volume to volume, the books are indexed by proper name as well as, by subject. Still, they are seldom used by IA researchers.

Also, *The New American State Papers, 1789–1860,* an edited collection published by Scholarly Resources, Inc., of Wilmington, Delaware, is a multivolume set that covers the following topics, with emphasis on those series of volumes most likely to be useful to industrial archaeologists: Agriculture (19 vols.), Commerce and Navigation (46 vols. of general reports and a 47th on tariffs, free trade, embargoes and internal commerce), Explorations and Surveys (7 vols. on continental North America, 7 vols. on overseas exploration, and a 15th vol. on surveys), Indian Affairs (13 vols.), Labor and Slavery (2 vols. on immigration and naturalization, 1 on slave trade, 1 on slavery in territories, and 3 on resettlement of free men), Manufactures (9 vols., described below), Public Finance (31 vols.), Public Lands (8 vols., including 1 on land revenues and mineral lands), Science and Technology (14 vols. described below), Social Policy (5 vols.), and Transportation (7 vols. described below). Volume 2 of the manufacturing series includes a "Report on Factories Incorporated in the U.S., 1800–1820," prepared by Secretary of State John Quincy Adams in 1824. Volume 3 of the same series includes "Documents Relative to the Manufactures in the United States Collected and Transmitted to the House of Representatives, In Compliance with a Resolution of Jan. 19, 1832, by the Secretary of the Treasury in 2 vols."

This covers states from Delaware to Maine, plus Ohio. The science and technology series includes volumes on national scientific institutions, astronomy and meteorology, weights and measures, patents, steam engines, telegraphs and military technology, special studies, and geology. The transportation series has a general volume followed by topical volumes on roads, canals, railroads, inland waters, and oceanic transport.

On the executive side, the federal government demonstrated its early interest in industry during the enumeration of the census. Beginning with the first census in 1790, the government instructed census takers to provide a count of the people in each household who worked in manufacturing as well as, those who worked in agriculture. By the mid-nineteenth century, mere counting did not provide the government with enough details. Therefore, in 1850 census takers asked for the occupation of each head of household. In 1860 they began collecting the occupation of every adult.

Additionally, in 1850 the Bureau of the Census implemented two special censuses, one for those who manufactured goods and one for farmers. Each manufacturer supplied the type of business, including specific items produced, the number of people employed, the total number of days worked during the year, the cost to produce the goods, and the amount of goods sold.

Thus, patterns of growth, changes in prosperity and even in goods produced can be determined by looking at a site specific manufacturer's census records across the decades, 1850–1880. Coupled with the household census, the owner's personal life can be determined and in areas with few industries, the occupations given in the household census can help the industrial archaeologist to recreate at least a partial roster of the manufacturer's employees.

Manufacturers' censuses also provide the data with which to enhance a broader industrial context for a neighborhood, a town or city, county or even a state. At the state level, the Bureau of the Census published a compendium of statistics for each decade, including 1890, most of whose raw census data was destroyed by fire.

The manuscript versions of the household census records are on file at the National Archives in Washington, D.C. These records are such a popular source for local historians and genealogists that the decades that are open to the public at the personal level, 1790–1920, including the extant fragments of the 1890 census, have been microfilmed. Many town and county libraries can supply the rolls that are relevant to the area they serve. State-wide collections are more apt to be housed at university and state libraries and archives. Some manufacturing censuses also have been microfilmed, but are generally found only at major repositories.

Over time the federal government has spawned countless other records that are useful to IA projects. In addition to those already cited, the records range from industry-wide regulations created by an executive department to cases tried in federal courts. Like the *Congressional Record,* they may be professionally printed and neatly bound. On the other hand, a record group may consist of a few pieces of handwritten paper or 600 rolls of microfilm. The records may be carefully indexed or loosely grouped together under an amorphous sounding title. They may be housed at institutions such as the Library of Congress, the National Archives and the Smithsonian Institution. Or, they may be housed in regional offices. The latter is especially true if the agency that generated the records is separated into geographic entities, i.e., the "districts" of the U.S. Army Corps of Engineers and the Federal Courts.

Even a fairly small-scale IA project could easily benefit from research in more than one federal record group. Consider, for instance, an abandoned rail line's tiny whistle-stop train station, complete with rusting mail bag stand. Census records would yield personal information about the stationmaster and the community that the station served. U.S. Postal Service records could provide names of postmasters and might establish familial links between the stationmaster and the postmaster. The Department's site location reports would yield the location and duration of the post office. Interstate Commerce Commission (ICC) files could contain a verbal and graphical description of every mile of tracks complete with materials used and profiles of the roadbed, justification for shutting down the rail service, and perhaps even illustrations of the train station itself. U.S. Geological Survey maps might pinpoint old place names and would illustrate any changes over time in terrain and in the station's location relative to the nearest main highway. The *Congressional Record* might contain speeches made by the local Congressman or Senator in objection to the abandonment of the rail line or to the station's closing.

REAL-LIFE EXAMPLES

The whistle-stop train station project is hypothetical, Anywhere, U.S.A. The next two examples are drawn from actual documentation projects. One is a U.S. Government early twentieth-century spillway, built and maintained under the aegis of the U.S. Army Corps of Engineers. The other was a privately owned river crossing that was part of an inter-governmental fracas that ultimately played out in federal courts.

Because it was a U.S. Corps of Engineers project, most of the primary documentation for the construction and maintenance of the Bonnet Carre Spillway on the Old River section of the lower Mississippi River has been generated by and is housed with the U.S. Government. Still, the documentation is scattered between Louisiana, northern Virginia, the Maryland suburbs of Washington, D.C. and Washington, D.C. itself.

As a project authorized by Congress, the spillway's purpose, funding and construction and completion reports were all submitted to Congress by the U.S. Corps of Engineers. Generally, these reports are smaller portions of larger documents that appear under variations on the title *The Improvement of the Lower Mississippi River for Flood Control and Navigation.*

Annex No. 9 is a good case in point. It was published in 1932 as part of a three-volume report on the improvement of the lower Mississippi River. Subtitled "The Bonnet Carre Spillway Hydraulics, Etc." the *Annex* provides background on the authorization of the project, complete with congressional citations. It then describes each set of tests that the U.S. Corps of Engineers conducted in its field laboratory during the three years prior to spillway construction. These consisted of borings for the foundation, hydraulic experiments that included models and tests for coefficients of discharge for weirs, velocity and scour experiments for weir discharge basins, riprap experiments for weir talus, backwater curves for flood ways and scour and deposit velocities for flood-way soils.

In addition to the specific information the *Annex* provides about the Bonnet Carre Spillway, it also provides a textbook case of the state of hydraulic engineering for medium sized projects in the late 1920s and early 1930s. It describes the project engineers' hypotheses based on preliminary research, gives formulas and test results, and states the rationale for decisions made.[6]

Like *Annex No. 9,* other primary Bonnet Carre reports to Congress were printed and bound and can be used at the U.S. Corps of Engineers Historical Center near Washington, D.C. or at the Library of Congress. Documents deemed essential for the spillway's on-going repair and maintenance are housed at the U.S. Corps of Engineers' New Orleans District Office. The district office's record group includes copies of older documents such as correspondence, field notes and photographs. At first, the research team thought that the document sets held by the U.S. Corps of Engineers and the National Archives would be virtually identical. Upon comparison, this was not true, so both record groups had to be examined thoroughly.

The photograph collection at the National Archives proved to be particularly beneficial. Because it was identified under an obscure name, both the IA team and the archivists almost missed it, but it was worth the persistence necessary to locate it. Photographs of the floodway before and after cutting showed the type and size of vegetation, including cypress, gum, ash and cottonwood trees and a dense semitropical undergrowth. They also showed goats munching away, instead of the dairy cattle that the U.S. Corps of Engineers had reported in *Annex No. 9* as the animal of choice for vegetation control.

Views taken during construction provided corroboration of written documentation and the 8″ × 10″ black and white completion photographs showed the needles of the spillway weir in various operating positions. By 1936, just eight years after Congress authorized the project, it was operational. When research in the documentation available through government sources was completed, the IA team had few technical gaps to fill.[7]

The trail through federal documentation for the private sector crossing of Red River was much more circuitous. Like

Bonnet Carre, it led through the Congress and the U.S. Corps of Engineers files. Other relevant data was located in records of the Bureau of Census and Bureau of Indian Affairs as well as, in the Confederate Army papers at the National Archives, and in two federal courts.

In 1854 Benjamin F. Colbert, a Chickasaw Indian who lived in Indian Territory, acquired the rights to a decade-old ferry that crossed the Red River between Indian Territory (now Oklahoma) and Texas. When Colbert sought in 1875 to build a toll bridge, his grant came from the federal government, via action of the Union Agency for the Five Civilized Tribes. Among his early patrons was the Butterfield Stage Coach line.

In 1886, Congress signed into law an act that authorized Colbert's successor, the Red River Bridge Company of Texas, to construct and maintain a railway and wagon bridge across Red River. Furthermore, it authorized the company to charge tolls. Details of this bridge and its successor appear in the transcript from the Red River Bridge Company receivership case. The case was heard in the U.S. Circuit Court of Appeals for the Tenth Circuit and records of the proceedings remain with the court.

Other information about the three bridges that ultimately occupied the site was published in reports of congressional hearings. The hearings related to the construction, in the 1930s, of a free bridge that was designed to link new national highway system roads in Texas and Oklahoma. The free bridge paralleled the toll bridge and was so close that the competing bridges could be seen from one another. Reports of hearings conducted by the U.S. Corps of Engineers and copies of the voluminous correspondence that flowed between the U.S. Corps of Engineers, the Oklahoma and Texas Highway Departments, interested members of Congress and the general public can be found in federal and both state repositories.

Because the U.S. Corps of Engineers is headquartered in Washington, D.C., the hearing scheduled on the toll rates of the bridge company was heard in the Supreme Court of the District of Columbia. Due to the non-state status of the District of Columbia, this was, in effect, the Capital's Federal Court at the time the case was heard. The bridge company filed for an injunction to prohibit the opening of the free bridge. When the judge of the U.S. District Court of the Eastern District of Texas granted the injunction, Texas Rangers barricaded the free bridge. The Governor of Oklahoma responded by setting up a road block at the toll bridge and manning it with the National Guard.

All together, the federal government generated a plethora of Red River Bridge documentation. Even so, deeds, newspapers, local histories, oral history interviews, private photograph collections and local and state archives were necessary to provide the complete context. From these sources came descriptions of the ferries, construction details about the bridges and their official openings, the impact of the disastrous floods that swept the bridges down river and biographical information about the owners. The toll bridge went out in a blaze of glory in 1961 when the gas line slung under it erupted and burst into flames. Its piers still lie beneath the water and the oldest trees along the banks bear the scars of the wagon wheels that got too close on their way to the ferry.[8]

SELECTED RECORD GROUPS

Other record groups bear close scrutiny as they are substantially under-used by IA teams. Two, which were created by the Interstate Commerce Commission (ICC), have been deposited with the National Archives in Washington, D.C. They are the 16,000 case files that the Commission heard between 1887 and 1924 and the 11,000 cubic feet of records created by the Railroad Valuation Board from 1915 to 1960. A third record group is the enormous folklore and oral history collection at the Library of Congress' American Folklife Center.

The ICC heard cases from all over the country regarding the inland transportation systems of the United States. The substance of the evidence presented in these cases is also the substance of industrial archaeology.

In 1887 the ICC became the first federal regulatory agency to utilize a court stenographer for its hearings, so records of the proceedings were taken verbatim. Since railroads were such prime transports that whole towns moved to be near the tracks, each case contains at least some local industrial history as well as, information about the operation of the railroad.

The industrial doings of Muskogee, Oklahoma, are chronicled in the Case of the Muskogee Commercial Club and Muskogee Traffic Bureau V the M. K. & T. Railway Company, which was docketed in December, 1906. Located in the heart of a cotton growing region, Muskogee and McAlester, which were 65 miles apart, were designated shipping points and the railroad wanted to discontinue the point at Muskogee.

During the hearing, 14 witnesses gave 450 typed pages of testimony. When cotton buyers, the president of the Muskogee compress company, handlers, merchants, and representatives of the railroad finished testifying, they had described almost every aspect of cotton growing in the area, from planting to putting the compressed bales on the freight cars. In addition, they gave information about the condition of local roads, the kind of compressing equipment used, and a map that depicted the cotton production in 13 surrounding counties during 1906. Information from the proponents of McAlester as a sole shipping point almost constitutes a local history by itself.[9]

The horror of this record group is that the case files have no single index by locality. There are indexes, however. Many larger libraries, especially law libraries at universities, contain the ICC's published *Reports*. These volumes report the findings of facts in cases and conclude with the Com-

mission's opinions. They are not to be confused, however, with the published reports that Congress required the ICC to transmit annually.

Beginning in 1916 with Volume 12 of the *Reports,* place names appear in each volume's index. A five-year index has been published for 1908–1913. From 1907 back, each volume of the *Reports* must be checked individually by subject of the case, then the determination must be made if the case's location is relevant.

The second group of ICC records arrived at the National Archives in 1992 and is an essential resource to document railroad structures and artifacts. These records also contain information vital to fleshing out context statements. Known as "valuation records," this voluminous record group was created by the ICC and railroad employees, often acting as a team, between 1915 and 1920. Periodic updates, which occurred until the 1960s, afford the researcher the opportunity to document change over time. By using the updates, the researcher can even determine the specific rolling stock that a railroad held from the date of the basic valuation to the 1960s. Notes of caution are necessary. The quality of the records varies from railroad to railroad; and long before the records arrived at the National Archives, the ICC destroyed documentation for short lines that were abandoned prior to 1950.

Railroad valuation records are divided into the general categories of land, engineering and accounting reports along with supporting documentation. They are arranged in sixteen subgroups whose titles include Engineering Field Notes, Equipment and Machinery Schedules, Detailed Land Maps and Final Reports. Accessing the records is comparatively easy, but the researcher must provide the specific location by state, county, town or other identifier such as railroad milepost number, the dates of interest and the corporate name under which the railroad was operating at that time and location. Before contacting the Archives staff, researchers should attempt to determine if more than one railroad maintained a legal interest in the site. "Shared" track, for instance, will probably be filed only under the owner/lessor's corporate name, not that of the lessee railroad company.

In spite of its title, the first record the researcher probably needs to see is the Final Land Report. The report summarizes some of the information in other subsets such as land acquisition. It also provides compilations of the value of land used by the railroad for common-carrier purposes. More important to IA teams, however, is the fact that the Final Land Report serves as a finding aid to the valuation records. It provides information that enables the researcher to identify the relevant engineering field notes, the maps, the land acquisition schedules, the grant schedules and the land appraisal report for a specific location.

The next subset to investigate depends on the information wanted. Those who prefer to be oriented graphically at the beginning of their search should turn to the Detailed Land Maps. Maps in this subset depict lengths of track that, depending on the complexity of the site, are drawn in one-half mile to four-mile increments. The smaller the area covered, the larger the scale, up to 1 inch per 100 foot. The maps cover engineering details such as track layout and the locations of buildings and bridges. Many of the details are assigned key numbers that are matched to information about the feature or structure in other subsets.

Representatives of the Railroad Valuation Board and employees of the railroad jointly chained every mile of railroad. Their Engineering Field Notes relate to grading, ballast, ties, track and every railroad structure. The notes describe all crossings, culverts, bridges and railroad track intersections. When the bridge and building notes are of high quality, they contain detailed descriptions of structures and often include photographs and/or blueprints and drawings. Frequently, however, the engineering team used a hard-lead pencil for noting information and reading those notations can be taxing.

By using the full spectrum of Railroad Valuation Reports, the IA team can build a virtually complete history of any given piece of track, including such information as the acquisition of each parcel of land that the railroad used for common-carrier purposes, the inventory of the equipment and fixed furnishings at a depot, and the names of the commercial and industrial buildings that lined the right-of-way.

Like the ICC Case Files, the studies filed at the American Folklife Center at the Library of Congress can be difficult to access. The Center's holdings are enormous and include projects undertaken both by the library and countless outside individuals and groups. These consist primarily of folk music and oral history tapes and transcriptions that have been gathered since the 1930s. The subject matter is international and broad ranging and encompasses the songs of the Great Depression as well as, stories of how the yellow ribbon became a national folk symbol.

Project index cards vary in quality and accuracy depending on when they were created. They consume drawer after drawer of cabinets. A friendly staff makes finding the information a little easier. An added attraction is that the Center maintains an updated list of cultural repositories throughout the nation and will refer the researcher to relevant organizations.

Still, even the work songs in the Center's collection reveal much about working conditions in the mines, about the crew killed in a train wreck and what it means to have lost an industrial job during the Great Depression. And what better way to find out how a job used to be performed than by listening while the person who did the work describes the techniques, dangers, hardships and pleasures.

A case in point is the 1991 survey the Folklife Center conducted jointly with the National Park Service on Acadian culture in Maine's Upper St. John Valley. Researchers gathered information on a wide variety of topics such as settlement patterns, farm life and local weaving that survives as a craft handed from generation to generation rather than learned in a class or from a book.

More important from the point of view of IA teams, is that they also obtained vivid word pictures of the changes in the valley's timber industry and how those changes have affected the workers' lifestyles. The old seasonal patterns dictated that the men move to lumber camps only after they finished their fall harvests. Once in camp they would lumber all winter, then float the logs down river to the mills during the spring flood. This rhythm persisted into the 1900s, but by the mid-twentieth century the lumber industry had converted to year-round operations. By the time the interviews were conducted, only a few men who were striving to be self-employed and independent partially followed the old seasonal pattern.[10]

With so many tantalizing possibilities and given the usual time and money constraints of an IA project, the question becomes not "Are there relevant federal records to the project?" Rather, it is "Which federal level information do we really need to complete this project successfully?"

By first investigating sources described in Barbara Howe's chapter on local and state resources, including locally available National Register and HABS/HAER reports, the IA team can develop a research design that will identify which federally held records are most needed. The obvious ones are census records and U.S. Geological Survey maps, both of which are relatively accessible.

Local histories and newspaper files may lead to records groups. Reading the index of every volume of the *American State Papers* and *Congressional Records* is probably not appropriate. Spot checks of the indexes during the years when a congressman or senator may have taken a local industrial topic to the Congress certainly can be profitable. Again, these records are relatively accessible. So are the federal court cases such as the ones used in the Red River Bridge research and they generally are held as part of the court's records.

Other files are more problematic, but it is worth conducting preliminary research nearer home because it can save a lot of time, frustration and money. For instance, a review of ICC *Reports* and appropriate indices at the nearest large library should determine whether or not research at the National Archives is warranted. The same holds true for the nearest large library's collection of U.S. military reference material. For example, although it lacks a good index, the *War of the Rebellion: Official Records of the Union and Confederate Armies* (U.S. Government, 1880–1910) sometimes can eliminate a trip to the National Archives.

ACCESSING RECORDS

Library of Congress

The American Folklife Center staff will take phone calls from researchers, but prefers letters of inquiries with as many specific delineations as possible about the information requested. Include your phone number and best time of day to reach you. The Center's staff is small and a response may take a month or more. Staff members advise that the best way for researchers to be certain that they get the desired information is to do the research on site themselves.

Other IA relevant divisions at the Library of Congress, such as Geography and Maps, give the same advice. Always provide as much information about your request as possible. The more specific the request, including such information as where a citation to a map was seen, the more likely the researcher is to receive the information requested. All mail should be addressed to the division, that is, "Geography and Maps" or "The American Folklife Center, etc.," where the resource is located, followed by, Library of Congress, Washington, DC 20540.

National Archives

For those who know the exact record they need and have learned through another source such as a footnote what the Record Group number is, a letter or phone call to the appropriate branch or division will bring help. For others, the process is more onerous. Then, the first line of attack is the Consultants' Office. Bear in mind that Washington phone numbers change frequently, but as this book goes to press the number for the Archives Consultants' Office is (202) 501–5400. The address is Consultants Office, National Archives, Washington, DC 20408.

Any researcher who plans to enter the Archives with equipment such as a PC, camera, etc., should check with the Consultants Office about the policy regarding use of the device. Also, reservations should be made in advance to use certain record groups at the Archives, especially the Photograph Collection where research space is at a premium. Reservations are not accepted for the Central Reading Room or the Microfilm Reading Room. Both of these fill to capacity when various national genealogy and history groups are in Washington for a convention. Moreover, a lengthy stay at microfilm readers and copying machines can be proscribed when other researchers are waiting.

On-site requests for records at the Archives are filled only at scheduled intervals and delivery time can take up to one and one-half hours. A management level senior staff member recommended in 1992 that anyone coming to the Archives for the first time or to use an unfamiliar record group should allow a week to become familiar with the system and the records.

Numerous record groups at the National Archives have been microfilmed. The Research Administrator/Historian for the Office of the Postmaster General, for instance, advises that all extant site location reports for post offices (1865–1946) are available through the Archives as Microfilm Publication M1126. Individual paper copies for a specific post office or a few offices can be purchased as well as, positive copies of an entire roll. Each roll generally contains

several counties within a state, so purchasing microfilm may be cost effective. Check with the Consultants' Office on costs to purchase paper copies or film.

U.S. Army Corps of Engineers

Most of the U.S. Corps Engineers' records are held in regional repositories. To learn their location contact the Records Manager at the U.S. Corps of Engineers' District Office which has responsibility for the state in which the project is located.

U.S. District Courts

The Clerk of the Court is the officer responsible for all records of a District Court and will be able to advise on the location of the court's records, both historic and current. Researchers should use the "blue pages" in the phone book or telephone the Information Operator to determine the phone number of the appropriate District Court. Knowing the number, title, and date of the case being sought will speed the response from the Clerk immeasurably.

Office of the Law Revision Counsel, U.S. House of Representatives

As of 1992, the Law Revision Counsel of the U.S. House of Representatives began releasing its annual compilation of all current Federal statutes on CD-ROM. This effort makes the Code affordable for those who have the hardware on which to run it. The Code contains all Federal laws in effect, some of which date back to 1791, at the time of its release. Use of the Code is one of the fastest means of accessing regulations affecting industry, so long as the law is current. The CD-Rom version allows for a thorough search of the code by words, by phrases, or by concepts and user manuals and retrieval software are available for both DOS and Windows. The CD-ROM is distributed as part of the Federal Depository Library Program, so researchers should check their local repository first. Otherwise, it can be ordered as stock number 052-001-00439-6 for $30.00 payable by check, VISA or MasterCard from: Superintendent of Documents, Government Printing Office, P. O. Box 371954, Pittsburgh, PA 15250-7954.

CONCLUSION

The fact that our forebears cared enough to create the records that are housed in federal repositories provides a barometer of the importance of the IA projects they cover. Whenever feasible, these records should be used and savored. Even if the project budget is small, for just the cost of postage or a telephone call, a federal record may be out there waiting. Spending the time and money to find it may bring significant rewards. Happy researching.

ENDNOTES

1. Morris, Richard B. *Government and Labor in the Early American Colonies.* New York: Columbia University Press, 1946. Throughout this work Morris traces the impact of British government laws and their interpretations on workers in colonial America.

2. Larson, Martin A. *Jefferson: Magnificent Populist.* Washington, D.C.: Robert B. Luce, Inc., 1981.

3. Note that many of the early patents records have not survived. Those that have are included in the Archives' holdings. Viola, Herman J. *The National Archives of The United States.* New York: Harry N. Abrams, Inc., Publishers, p. 205–206.

4. U.S. Congress, *American State Papers—Documents, Legislative and Executive, of the Congress of the United States, from the First Session of the First through the Third Session of the Thirteenth Congress, Inclusive: Commencing March 3, 1789, and Ending March 3, 1815,* Volume V. Washington, D.C.: Gales and Seaton, 1832, pp. 4–8.

5. *Ibid.,* p. 492.

6. U.S. War Department, Corps of Engineers, U.S. Army, *The Improvement of the Lower Mississippi River for Flood Control and Navigation,* Volume III, Annex No. 9. St. Louis: M.B.C. Print, 1932.

7. Later correspondence revealed that the goats, alas, wandered into the swampy areas of the floodway so often that their hooves picked up a fatal disease.

8. Overbeck, Ruth Ann. "The Red River Bridges: A Study in State- Federal Governmental Problems." M.A. Thesis, University of Texas at Austin, 1969.

9. Rapport, Leonard. "Sources at the National Archives for Genealogical and Local History Research: The Interstate Commerce Commission Formal Case Files: A Source for Local History," *Prologue: Journal of the National Archives,* Vol. 15: No. 4, Winter, 1983.

10. Brassieur, C. Ray. "The Long Hard Road to Madawaska: Acadian Cultural Retention in Maine's Upper St. John Valley," *Folklife Center News,* Vol. XIII: No. 4, 4–13, Fall 1991.

CHAPTER 4

Research in State and Local Archives for Preparing Histories of Specific Sites

Barbara J. Howe

INTRODUCTION

Researching the history of an industrial site means far more than recording its extant features. It also means using the manuscript and photographic resources that are available at local historical societies, state or regional repositories, or local courthouses. This essay, then, will address the types of documentation that industrial archaeologists might find useful and the most likely repositories for those sources.

PUBLISHED SOURCES

The first place to look might well be the local histories that have been written for communities large and small across the United States for almost 150 years. These will vary widely in quantity and quality, but there are some generalizations that can be made to guide researchers since local histories have been published in several rather distinct types.

Industrialists will be much more prominent than workers in the vast majority of local histories. In the nineteenth and early twentieth centuries, this was particularly true because the books were often published by subscription, and those whose biographical sketches were included in the back of the weighty tomes paid to be there. Thus, while one may find the names of businesses owned, dates of operation and key products, one is unlikely to learn about failures, unless they led to success in some other venture. Local histories published in the last fifteen years, often by national companies that work with historical societies to produce these volumes, have replaced the pages of paeans to businessmen with family histories supplied by members of the community. Here, it may also be possible to learn the same infor-

mation, but the emphasis is on genealogy and the sketches are short.

The nineteenth- and early-twentieth-century histories can also include chapters on early businesses and industries. For example, Henry Howe's *Historical Collections of Ohio in Two Volumes,* Vol. 1 (Cincinnati: C. J. Krehbiel & Co., 1907, c. 1988) includes an essay on the mines and mining resources of Ohio by Andrew Roy, late state inspector of mines; short biographical sketches of pioneer engineers; and an essay on the inspection of workshops and factories of Ohio by Frank Henry Howe from reports of Henry Dorn, chief inspector for the state.

Unfortunately, the authors of these volumes often assume that the reader has a great deal of familiarity with the community, and locations are not now readily identifiable from the text. In a state like West Virginia, where few buildings had identifiable street addresses because mail was collected at the post office, it can be very difficult to pinpoint a location for a rural industrial site like a grist mill. Even if an address were given, it would likely be a rural route address which would require that the researcher have a map identifying those routes in order to find the road on which the mill was located.

It may also be possible to find published accounts by travelers in the nineteenth century who toured industrial sites. Charles Dickens's account of his visit to Lowell, Massachusetts, is perhaps the most famous, but Dickens came away with a very rosy view of Lowell, because he compared it to the dreadful conditions in England's industrializing cities. These travelers, of course, may or may not have understood the processes that they were describing in their writings.

It was not until the 1930s that most historians began to be more conscious of our *industrial* past and industrial processes, as opposed to emphasizing the owners of important businesses and factories. The Federal Writers' Project (FWP) had an enormous influence in documenting the industrial past. The historians who prepared the various local histories published under the auspices of the FWP concentrated on the common man (and some women) for the first time in the historiography of local history.

They Built a City: 150 Years of Industrial Cincinnati (Cincinnati: *Cincinnati Post,* 1938) provides one example. The book is organized into fifteen chapters, including chapters on transportation, pork and beef packing, soap making, brewing, boots and shoes, heavy industry (metallurgical industries), carriages and wagons, graphic arts (newspaper publishing), printing industry, public utilities and radio broadcasting. Perhaps most important, photographs became a significant part of local histories. Gone are the lithographs of historic sites or prominent white men of earlier local histories. Instead, one finds interior photos that show male workers cutting beef and women slicing bacon; an aerial photograph of Ivorydale, home of Procter and Gamble; a photo entitled "kettle pattern," which shows the interior of a soap making kettle, etc.

Far more material was collected for these volumes than could ever be published, and industrial archaeologists should check to see if the manuscript versions of these histories are available. These can be located through the *Survey of Federal Writers' Project Manuscript Holdings in State Depositories,* by Ann Banks and Robert Carter (Washington, D.C.: American Historical Association, 1985). However, if the manuscript versions are like those for West Virginia, they are collections of the various versions of drafts prepared by the authors and may be confusing to use and cite.

Professional historians became interested in urban history in the 1930s and have continued that interest, with another surge in publishing in the 1960s. While these books may not focus on the industrial process, per se, they can provide a context for the development of urban industries in their explanation of the physical growth of a city or the development of a political climate that promoted or opposed industrial growth. Examples of this genre are Bessie Louise Pierce's 3-volume *A History of Chicago* (New York: Knopf, 1937–1957); Blake McKelvey's 3-volume Rochester (Cambridge: Harvard University Press, 1945–1956); and Stanley Buder's *Pullman: An Experiment in Industrial Order and Community Planning, 1880–1930* (New York: Oxford University Press, 1967). Unlike their predecessors, these volumes contain bibliographies and footnotes that allow industrial archaeologists to pursue additional research in the sources the author used. Perhaps Buder did not adequately cover the technical aspects of making Pullman cars, for instance, but one learns through his notes that the records of the Pullman Palace Car Company are at the Newberry Library in Chicago.

Local history publishing was revived in the 1970s and 1980s through the efforts of companies such as Walsworth

Publishing Co. These volumes, which resemble high school yearbooks in format rather than the "dry as dust" unillustrated volumes of the 1880s, are produced by local historical societies and local historians of varying degrees of ability. They also can be treasure troves of photographs pulled from the files of the local historical society or members' private collections for special publication.

These books will be the easiest resource to locate because they are available at local public libraries, local historical society or museum libraries, state libraries, the Library of Congress (probably), university and college libraries or through interlibrary loan. They can be accessed through the on-line catalogues at major libraries or through published bibliographies. Recent volumes are usually available for purchase through the local historical society that published the volume or, in large cities, through bookshops that specialize in regional history. Older volumes can be purchased through specialty used book stores.

Published sources also include volumes on industrial processes, natural resources or transportation systems. The West Virginia Geological Survey, for example, published an extremely useful series of county, natural resource and industry studies in the early twentieth century. The survey also provides a guide to places in *West Virginia Gazetteer of Physical and Cultural Place Names* (1986). Look for published bibliographies or on-line catalogues to these resources. In *Local Businesses: Exploring Their History* (Nashville: American Association for State and Local History, 1990), K. Austin Ker, Amos J. Loveday, and Mansel G. Blackford suggest Thomas Derdak's *International Directory of Company Histories* (Chicago: St. James Press, 1988); Henrietta M. Larson's *Guide to Business History: Materials for the Study of American Business History and Suggestions for their Use* (Cambridge: Harvard University Press, 1948); Robert Lovett's *American Economic and Business History: A Guide to Information Sources* (Detroit: Gale Research Co., 1971); and David O. Whitten's *Manufacturing: A Historiographical and Bibliographical Guide* (Westport, Conn.: Greenwood Press, 1990) as volumes that can guide researchers to published sources. Whitten's volume is the first of a projected three-volume series by Greenwood Press, with volumes two and three to be published in 1993 and 1994.

There may also be company histories or biographies of company founders available in regional and state archives (in the state capital). Company histories range from detailed and well-documented publications by professional historians to glossy, heavily illustrated anniversary histories produced by a company's public relations firm. Biographies of prominent company officials will range in quality to the same extent.

In addition to published works, master's theses and doctoral dissertations can be valuable resources for those studying local industries or transportation systems. These theses and dissertations may have been produced in departments of history, geography, geology, civil engineering, mechanical engineering, sociology, industrial relations, etc. It is important to remember that a thesis written by a sociologist in 1930, perhaps analyzing the labor-management issues at a work place, may document the industrial process in 1930. That is now a historical account. The most valuable part of theses and dissertations is probably not the analysis, which varies widely, but the usually enormous bibliographies and detailed footnotes provided by graduate students who feel it is important to check every possible reference for their topics.

Academic libraries keep copies of theses and dissertations produced at those institutions, and some may be available at libraries where the industry studied is located. For example, a doctoral dissertation on northwest Ohio's glass industry may be found at the university where it was produced as well as at the University of Toledo library or the Toledo-Lucas County Public Library. It is very difficult to identify master's theses because there is no national index to these works. They may be referenced in local publications or be indexed in regional archives (probably at a major university or college) or libraries. Most doctoral dissertations, on the other hand, are listed in *Dissertation Abstracts*. They are available on microfilm or in xeroxed form through University Microfilms, Inc. of Ann Arbor, Michigan, as well as through interlibrary loan or in libraries.

Periodicals

In addition to local histories, information on local industries and transportation systems may be found in journals published by local and state historical societies or by historical societies interested in a particular industry. One example of the latter type is the *Chesapeake & Ohio Historical Magazine*. Like books, these vary widely in quality and frequency of publication and in the amount of documentation required for articles submitted. They will also vary widely in the amount of context provided for an individual site or industrial process. For example, these locally published journals (and books) are probably the best places to find the ubiquitous claims of "birthplace of the Industrial Revolution." State history journals often have extensive book review sections that can provide leads to additional resources. History journals are indexed in publications such as *Social Science Index* or through on-line retrieval systems.

National and local professional journals for engineering, architecture, construction and real estate organizations also provide current information on those professions and advertisements from suppliers or goods and services relevant to the readers. Representative journals are those of the American Concrete Institute, American Society of Civil Engineers and American Society of Mechanical Engineers, and American Institute of Architects. Examples include *Scientific American, Engineering News Record* and *Philadelphia Real Estate Record & Builders' Guide* (PREBG). These, over time, become primary sources themselves, for they may dis-

cuss appropriate standards of practice, new materials on the market, and award-winning new construction. To illustrate, the PREBG reported on the Baldwin Locomotive Works in Philadelphia, announcing rumors in 1888 that the works would be leaving its Broad Street location and then noting the construction of a boiler house and spring "manufactory" in 1892.[1] These journals are available in libraries of universities that house colleges of engineering or architecture or in major public libraries.

Specialized journals for industries or labor unions can provide detailed information on the "state of the art" at the time of publication. Over time, these journals become important resources for industrial archaeologists. Examples of industry-wide publications include *Coal Age,* etc. Examples of periodicals by particular industries include *The Carbider* (Union Carbide) and *Consol News* (Consolidation Coal). The Chesapeake & Ohio Company published a national employees' magazine entitled *Chesapeake & Ohio Lines Magazine* and *Tracks*. These are most likely to be found in academic libraries that have a business school or engineering school. Relevant journal articles can be accessed through *Industrial Arts Index,* first published in 1918, or *Business Periodicals Index,* first published in 1958.

Archives and libraries may also house company annual reports or catalogues. Catalogues will list major products, while annual reports may also provide information about new machinery installed, expansion plans, and financial status. For example, the *Chesapeake & Ohio Canal Company Reports* are available in published format for much of the nineteenth century. The reports and proceedings of the stockholders of the James River and Kanawha Company, which tried to build a canal and later a turnpike from Richmond, Virginia, to the Ohio River, are also available for the mid-nineteenth century.

State governments also publish periodicals, and perhaps annual reports of government agencies, that may be useful for industrial archaeologists. These are likely to be available in major regional archives or academic libraries or in the state archives. It would be possible to document the development of West Virginia's road system, in part, through such official state publications as *West Virginia Highways: The State Good Roads Magazine, West Virginia Highways: Official Publication of the State Road Commission of West Virginia* and *First Convention of County Road Engineers of West Virginia* (1909).

City, business and telephone directories are another important source of periodical information for those studying industrial sites. City directories do not appear until cities become large enough to need a way to keep track of people, and they can be sporadic, especially for small towns. The directories usually include a business directory section, similar to that in a telephone directory's yellow pages. Businesses may also be identified in the main part of the directory, the alphabetical listing of individuals and businesses. There, listings will vary in detail, but the corporate name may be followed by a listing of principal partners and products, as well as the address. Businesses may also pay for advertisements to be placed on the covers of the directories or on the margins of pages throughout the directory. City directories also provide a way to examine the changing work force between the decennial censuses and to compensate for the missing 1890 census because they do identify individuals by name, address and occupation.

Some city directories also provide overviews of the city's economy in an attempt to lure new businesses to the city. For example, the 1879–80 Wheeling, West Virginia, city directory has a lengthy history of the city as an introduction. There, one can find a possible reference to the Wheeling Cotton Mill. This probably was the factory located at the site of the tack factory in 1879–80 because, in that year, the city directory referenced "the present TACK FACTORY [founded in 1866] . . . alluded to elsewhere as having been a cotton factory about the time to which I am referring. In the course of time, it stood idle for some years, and consequently a source of loss, most of the machinery of the same was sold to George T. Tingle, Esq., and put into operation on the creek bank, which in turn was afterwards used for the purpose of manufacturing Woolen Yarns by Mess. S. & J. Bradley, one of whom was killed by an accident on the Baltimore and Ohio railroad soon after it was opened in Wheeling" in 1853.[2]

City directories present some problems. Nineteenth-century directories may have required people or businesses to pay to be listed. Addresses for businesses and individuals may be imprecise, that is, "ss Jackson b Pine and Vine," meaning that the building is somewhere on the south side of Jackson Street between Pine and Vine streets. Street numbering systems have also changed over time, and older directory listings can be compared to Sanborn maps, discussed below, to identify current locations.

Business directories may be published for a region, metropolitan area or, in a small state, on a statewide basis. They range in size from small pocket directories published by a chamber of commerce to identify their members to large comprehensive statewide directories that may include every businessperson, regardless of how large or small the enterprise. Directories are organized by industry/business and by location. Examples include George D. Hall's *Directory of Central Atlantic States Manufactures* and specialized industry directories, such as the *West Virginia Sawmill Directory,* published in 1968 by the West Virginia Department of Natural Resources' Office of State Forester. National business directories include *Bradstreet's Book of Commercial Reports,* first published in 1857, and Dun & Co.'s *The Mercantile Agency's Reference Books,* first published in 1859.

Telephone directories include the yellow pages sections of business listings. Listings vary widely in detail, but they may identify principal products available for sale. The directories, like business and city directories, will also provide some information on the number of similar companies in a particular geographic area.

Newspapers are a widely available periodical source for industrial archaeologists, but a source that is difficult to access if the researcher does not know specific dates to examine. Newspapers include advertisements from businesses for their products as well as, feature stories, usually in a business section. Strikes, the introduction of new products or new machinery, layoffs and hirings, and plant openings and closings may merit newspaper coverage in daily or weekly papers or in special annual "Progress and Industry" editions. Obituaries may provide information on the work history of the deceased.

If the industry is particularly newsworthy, it will merit coverage on the front or editorial pages. For example, Morgantown Energy Associates built a co-generation plant in downtown Morgantown, West Virginia, in 1989–1991. The resulting controversy about the siting of the plant, the efficiency of the co-generation process to produce steam and electricity, and the possibility for air pollution generated front page coverage in the city's *Dominion Post* newspaper for over two years. Similarly, plans for a high-voltage power transmission line across southern West Virginia and Virginia generated the same level of controversy and public discussion in newspapers in that region.

This does not indicate that every published account in any newspaper will be completely accurate, but stories can provide leads to other documents or individuals who may collaborate the story or provide conflicting accounts of the coverage. In the process of following extended stories, one might find a series of photographs that documents the construction of an industrial site or the demolition of a site to make way for new construction. For example, in the Morgantown case, an old glass factory was demolished to make way for the co-generation plant, and the newspaper covered the progress made in cleaning up the hazardous waste deposited on the site over the decades as a result of the glass-making progress as well as the construction of the new facility.

The major disadvantage of newspaper research is that the papers often are not indexed. Local and state archives are most likely to have indexes for papers in their holdings, if available. Public libraries also often keep clippings files, which may provide some substitute for an index for recent years. If the industry has national significance, it may have merited articles in the *New York Times,* established in 1851 and indexed since that date; *Washington Post,* established in 1877 and indexed since 1979; *Christian Science Monitor,* established in 1908 and indexed since 1945; *Barron's; Wall Street Journal,* indexed since 1955; or *USA Today,* established in 1982 and indexed since that date. Regional newspapers that have been indexed for recent years are the Boston *Globe,* Denver *Post,* Houston *Post,* Los Angeles *Times,* New Orleans *Times-Picayune,* St. Louis *Post-Dispatch,* San Francisco *Chronicle* and St. Paul *Dispatch and Pioneer Press.*

In the 1980s, the National Endowment for the Humanities funded statewide newspaper projects to identify and microfilm newspapers, with the expectation that at least one repository in a state, either a major regional archives or state archives, would have a complete collection of all newspapers published in the state from the first to the most current. These should be available on interlibrary loan if it is not possible to visit the host archives.

VISUAL SOURCES

The earliest form of visual documentation that might be available for a historic site is the lithograph found in some nineteenth-century local histories or the "bird's eye" view of nineteenth-century towns. Lithographs may be extremely accurate or they may depict what the artist anticipates the factory will look like after, perhaps, an addition is made. For example, Henry Howe's *Historical Collections of Ohio in Two Volumes,* cited above, is illustrated with lithographs of the Ashtabula Bridge (p.273), a view at the quarries in Berea (p. 526), the Brush Electric Light Co.'s works (p. 507), and Cincinnati's Mount Auburn Inclined Plane (p. 783). The "bird's eye" view is likely to show a large geographical area and may be best used to identify the location of a factory or transportation line instead of trying to document the details of the building itself.

Industrial archaeologists clearly understand the importance of photographs in documenting industrial sites. Exterior photographs may be found from the mid-nineteenth century on, but interior photographs of large cavernous spaces like factories, taken by professional photographers, only date from the late nineteenth century and early twentieth century. Amateur interior photographs will date from the 1940s or later, when flash cameras became more popular for the public.

The most likely sources of historic photographs are local historical societies and museums, historic sites that focus on industrial processes, regional and state archives, public libraries with large local historical collections, the Library of Congress and the National Archives. Newspaper morgues are ideal, but public access may be very limited. Ask to see if the newspaper's photograph holdings have been transferred to a regional archives, as is the case with the photographs of the *Philadelphia Evening Bulletin* (1940s forward) and the *Philadelphia Inquirer* (negatives only, 1937–1987), which are now at the Temple University Urban Archives Center in Philadelphia. At the federal level, the National Archives and Library of Congress hold extensive photograph collections. The Farm Security Administration photographs at the Library of Congress, for example, document not only farm life in the 1930s, but also the factories built as part of the almost 100 New Deal homestead communities built throughout the country in that decade.

Unfortunately, one has to be prepared for the fact that these collections may not be well indexed and that many of the photographs may not be clearly identified. Look for categories such as "child labor" when using indexes because Lewis Hine produced a large number of photographs of factories to document the abuse of children as factory laborers in the 1910s.

In some cases, there may be postcards or stereocards showing industrial sites or particularly picturesque structures like covered bridges. Many small towns had extensive postcard documentation for the early twentieth century, perhaps even more than is available today for the same location. Early twentieth-century postcard producers also identified scenes we would not usually think of using today, so it may be possible to find factory scenes. For some reason, stereocards often showed buildings or bridges under construction. Regional and state archives usually have a postcard collection, and there may also be private collectors in the area who will share their findings.

Moving pictures can also be a source of documentation for industrial processes. If the photographer understood the process being documented, the film or video may be the only remaining record of that process, as is the case in "Allegheny Glass House," which documents glass making at Morgantown, West Virginia's, Seneca Glass Co. or "Coke Making at Bretz," which records the coking operations at Bretz, West Virginia. The Seneca film was made for the Historic American Engineering Record (HAER) in the early 1970s, and the company closed in 1983. The Bretz film was also made by HAER, and coking has since stopped there.

It may also be possible to find television news footage in a local archives. For example, Marshall University's James Morrow Library, in Huntington, West Virginia, houses the footage of a local television station's news programs, dating back to the early 1950s. Local television stations like to cover industrial accidents, anniversaries, and strikes—the unusual more than the mundane. While this sounds like a gold mine, one must also remember that local news stories are often very short.

HISTORIC SITES SURVEYS

Thousands of sites around the United States have been surveyed through programs conducted by local or state governments, the federal government, or historic preservation organizations. This is not the place to discuss the survey process, but the survey documents are available in the state historic preservation office, the office of the organization or government agency that sponsored the survey, or, perhaps, a major research library or regional archives. The Historic American Buildings Survey (HABS) program began in 1933, Historic American Engineering Record (HAER) in 1969 and the National Register of Historic Places, as we know it today, in 1966. State-level surveys began in the late 1960s and early 1970s. Usually, the surveys cover buildings, sites, districts, structures and objects that were fifty years of age or older at the time of the survey.

These survey forms will vary widely in quality of photographs and research and amount of documentation available. There should at least be a U.S. Geological Survey (USGS) topographical map, a sketch map showing the location of the building, and a photograph of the site. State inventory forms are often just one page of information, and there may only be 35 mm contact prints or 3″ × 5″ photographs attached.

National Register of Historic Places, HAER and HABS forms and accompanying reports for HABS and HAER buildings are available on microform through Chadwyck-Healey, Inc., while copies of National Register forms may also be available through state historic preservation offices or local historic preservation organizations. The nominations for the National Register include descriptions of the architecture of the building (section 7) and statements of significance (section 8) as well as, bibliographies of sources used and identifying information which includes historic names, addresses and UTM (universal transverse mercator) readings. Sketch maps and USGS maps must also be included. While these forms may be reproduced on a microform, the photographs are usually 5 × 7 or 8 × 10 inch photographs that will allow the researcher to see the building as it existed at the time the photos were taken. There may also be historic photographs with these nominations, although that is not a requirement. The quality of research and writing needed for nominations and the amount of accompanying documentation required, in most cases, increased dramatically during the 1980s, especially for the National Register of Historic Places.

Documentation for sites listed with HABS and HAER is much more substantial and can include numerous high-quality photographs, lengthy reports on the history of the building or industry studied and several pages of high-quality measured drawings to document the structure and industrial process. While a National Register nomination may include a few pages on the history of a particular building, for example, an area-wide HAER study may identify the local natural resources that led to the development of a specific industry, trace the development of a number of companies that utilized that resource and then detail the industrial process in a particular building and the evolution of that building and process over time. HABS reports on the homes of industrialists may provide background on the industry, or at least lead to sources about the industry, even if the industrial structures have disappeared.

In some cases, there are books that include HABS and HAER survey results. *Historic America: Buildings, Structures, and Sites* (Washington, D.C.: Library of Congress, 1983) catalogues properties recorded by HABS and HAER through 1983, while *Industrial Eye,* by Jet Lowe with editing by Diane Maddex (Washington, D.C.: Preservation Press, 1986) is a collection of photographs from HAER projects. The American Association for State and Local History, National Park Service and National Conference of State His-

toric Preservation Officers cooperated to publish *National Register of Historic Places, 1966–1988* (1989), with includes brief information on more than 50,000 properties nationwide.

Representative examples of local or statewide publications of HAER projects include Daniel M. Bluestone's *Cleveland: An Inventory of Historic Engineering and Industrial Sites* (Washington, D.C.: Historic American Engineering Record, 1978); Charles K. Hyde's *The Lower Peninsula of Michigan: An Inventory of Historic Engineering and Industrial Sites* (Washington, D.C.: Historic American Engineering Record, 1976) and *The Upper Peninsula of Michigan: An Inventory of Historic Engineering and Industrial Sites* (Washington, D.C.: Historic American Engineering Record, 1978); and Matthew Roth's *Connecticut: An Inventory of Historic Engineering and Industrial Sites* (Washington, D.C.: Society for Industrial Archeology, 1981).

In addition to *Historic America* and *National Register of Historic Places, 1966–1988,* there are numerous locally published architectural history books produced by commercial presses, local historical societies or local historic preservation organizations. These volumes may include information about factories or railroad stations, but buildings are usually included for their architectural merit instead of data that industrial archaeologists might find most useful, that is, manufacturing processes or products. These volumes are available in bookstores that specialize in regional books or in local, academic and state libraries and archives.

Finally, data from historic sites surveys is published through tour brochures or used in interpretive materials at historic sites. Current driving and walking tour brochures and promotional and interpretive materials for historic sites such as old grist mills or railroad stations can be found at the sites or at chambers of commerce, convention and visitor bureaus, local public libraries or travel agencies. Older similar materials may be found at a regional archives that keeps an extensive pamphlet collection. When searching for these materials in an archives, it is best to ask for assistance because indices to pamphlet collections do not necessarily follow standard rules of cataloging.

ORAL HISTORIES

Most major regional and state archives will have an oral history collection of some type. The subjects covered by the interviews, indexing of the tapes, and number of tapes transcribed will vary greatly, depending on the resources and collecting focus of the archives.

Industrial archaeologists may find these to be very useful, particularly if the interviews were conducted by individuals who understand the process being explained, or extremely frustrating if interviewees simply gave vague statements. It is often difficult to get precise dates in oral histories, although events may be related as being before or after the acquisition of a particular piece of machinery or expansion program. With that reference, industrial archaeologists can use other sources to pinpoint a date more precisely. There may also be photographs that accompany the oral history and which illustrate the processes being explained.

Those who will be relying heavily on oral histories as sources for the history of a particular site may want to read some of the vast literature that has been produced about the topic to help them evaluate the tapes that they are using. Two particularly useful sources are Barbara Allen and Lynwood Montell's *From Memory to History: Using Oral Sources in Local Historical Research* (Nashville: American Association for State and Local History) and Dunaway and Willa Baum's edited *Oral History* (Nashville: American Association for State and Local History), a collection of essays dealing with topics such as long-term memory and the relationship between oral history and folklore.

Researchers who will be doing their own oral histories for the first time can find information on procedures in Willa Baum's *Oral History for the Local Historical Society,* 3rd ed., rev. (Nashville: American Association for State and Local History, 1987). An external power supply or fresh batteries, an external microphone, a good recorder and good tapes are the basic necessities for conducting a decent interview—plus good questions and some knowledge of the topic to be discussed. When taping in an industrial setting, one interviewer found that the varying electrical current in the factory played havoc with the sound quality on his tape recorder and that a battery-powered recorder would have been more useful. Researchers should also be sure to get donor forms from interviewees to ensure their right to publish the information gathered. The best solution for the long-term benefit of other researchers is to work with an archives that collects oral histories and arrange to use its donor form and donate copies of the tapes to that archives.

LOCAL AND STATE GOVERNMENT RECORDS

County courthouses can contain a wealth of information, such as deeds, mortgages or deeds of trust, personal and real tax records, incorporation records, wills and probate records, county court (county commission) records for bridges and roads or even the licensing of taverns. Deeds are most easily available, but they were not always recorded immediately after a transaction because, in rural areas, the owner might keep the deed at home until he or she had time to ride into the county courthouse to file it. Researchers also need to know a little about nineteenth-century financing. Individuals could act as bankers/financiers so that finding property changing hands on a rapid basis may not mean any change at all in who operated the plant, just a way of securing financing for improvements. Deeds are usually well indexed by both grantor (seller) and grantee (buyer) and, in large cities like Philadel-

phia, may be abstracted on microform to help researchers. The deeds may provide a wealth of information about water rights for mills and equipment included in a sale of property, or they may just transfer the property from one individual to another with little or no detail. Mortgage records accompany the deeds and explain the financing for the property. Here, you can get a better idea of the price of the real estate when it sold, for deeds could simply have listed the price as "$1 and other good and valuable considerations."

Tax records may only provide the amount of tax levied on the land and buildings, or researchers may have access to the work sheets used by the assessor to determine the value or find the exact year when a change was made that explains why the tax book records "new addition" next to the higher value. An increase in taxes may mean that the owner made additions or other improvements to the building, or it may mean that there was a general reassessment or increase in the rate of taxation because of a new levy in that community. Checking assessments of surrounding properties should indicate if the increase on one property was in line with others or indicated something unique to that structure.

Look, also, for mechanics' liens that may have been filed because workers or suppliers were not paid; these may tell the researcher that the company did not pay for a certain piece of equipment when it was installed, and the supplier then has placed a lien on the property which will be the first item owed by the new buyer when the property is sold, if not paid off earlier. These liens are filed in the courthouse.

Other records from the courthouse may be more spotty. There may have been no legal requirement to record births and deaths in the county before the twentieth century. If the person did not die in the county, the will may not be probated there, but it also will not necessarily *not* be there! Perhaps surprisingly, people with many assets do not necessarily have wills or, if they have wills, they may be simple ones that say "I leave everything to my beloved wife," with no details about what "everything" includes. If the researcher is lucky, the individual being searched will have left a very detailed will or one that was challenged by heirs in a lengthy and detailed battle that reveals more about the person's assets.

County courthouses also house records of businesses incorporated within the county. These will give names of individuals who were incorporators and tell something about the purpose of the company. Records of corporations may be filed in separate volumes and be well indexed, or they may be filed in deed books for the early years of the county. Look, also, for volumes that indicated "fictitious or assumed names." These are not records of people doing business fraudulently but, rather, records of individuals who operate in partnerships or are in business for themselves. There you can find, for example, that "Joe Smith" is the person behind the business you see in the phone book as "Anytown Milling Machines."

Look, also, in the county offices which maintain the records of trials or other legal actions. Volumes with titles such as "chancery court index," "law court index," "criminal court index," or "civil court index" should contain references to lawsuits or arrests and prosecutions that may be important in the history of a business or its workers, in the case of a labor union struggle that involved local court action. Docket books should trace the case through the court system. If one is lucky, references from these indexes should give access to the actual trial documents themselves. These are most likely stored away in the mustiest, dirtiest part of the courthouse because only researchers like historians and industrial archaeologists will ever want to use them. If time is not too much of a factor, check every reference to the name you are searching, for, in one case in Tyler County, West Virginia, what looked on the surface to be a case about a child custody battle in the 1890s also included information on whether the husband or wife had provided the financing for a once jointly-owned business. If one is unlucky, however, the index references may refer to endless court actions that can no longer be fully explained because courthouse staff have legally emptied their files according to records retention schedules.

Because county governments have had an amazing range of responsibilities in American history, industrial archaeologists may find very scattered, or very detailed, records on topics such as building bridges and roads, laying sewers, providing landfills and promoting (or protesting) industrial developments. Deeds that indicate when a county government purchased land for a bridge can be correlated with minutes of a county commission meeting that awarded the contract for the bridge to be built. County governments establish industrial development agencies and are asked to go on record against land uses some citizens see as harmful. Those actions should be in the minutes of the county commission or the records of groups like those industrial development agencies or county planning agencies. The more contentious the issue being debated, the longer the paper trail is likely to be.

Records from county courthouses may be easily accessible in well-organized records rooms or stored in an attic for lack of space elsewhere. It is also useful to check at the state archives or a major university archives to see if these records have been microfilmed through an historic records survey such as those conducted during the 1930s. The Church of Jesus Christ of Latter Day Saints has also sponsored an extensive microfilming project of local county records, primarily for genealogical purposes, and made copies of these film rolls available to archives and state libraries around the country. Unfortunately, courthouses tended to burn down on a fairly regular basis throughout the nineteenth century, so some records may have been lost. During the Civil War, it is also possible that local governments had more important things to do than record deeds, and records may be spotty.

State governments have been involved in the development of industrial sites and transportation systems long before the late twentieth-century competition to locate major employers such as Tennessee's Saturn plant. For example, nineteenth-century Virginia used public-private partnerships to build its turnpike system, and the records of those partnerships can be found in the codified laws of the commonwealth and in the archives of the Board of Public Works. State governments also may produce documents through their departments of commerce or economic development agencies that provide an overview of the status of the state's industries at a particular time.

State governments also assumed responsibility for work place inspection in the late nineteenth and early twentieth centuries. Reports produced by officials such as the commissioner of labor or inspector of mines should be available at the state archives or major regional archives. Similarly, state boards of health may have produced reports useful to industrial archaeologists. While they were interested in stopping epidemics and licensing medical practitioners, they were also interested in the impact of health problems on society.

One example of this may be found in the first publication of the West Virginia State Board of Health. In 1883, the board published Dr. John L. Dickey's essay on " 'Nailers' Consumption,' and Other Disease Peculiar to Workers in Iron and Glass." Dr. Dickey, a Wheeling physician, began by noting the "ten large iron and nail concerns, employing in all the departments about five thousand seven hundred men and boys" and the "twelve glass works, in which are employed about two thousand six hundred and fifty persons"; Dickey's choice of language is a clear clue that women and/or girls were also employed in the glass works. Dickey then discussed the problems facing the nailers and nail feeders who spent their days "breathing in an atmosphere laden with minute particles of iron and steel. The nailer has charge of three or four machines, and much of his time is spent in the grinding room sharpening the knives of the nail machines on large, rapidly revolving sand-stones . . . ." In addition, the nailers had to "use, three or four times a day, the 'patent scraper' for leveling the face of the stone, which becomes worn in grooves and grows smooth and glazed on the surface with the particles of steel." Turning to the glass industry, Dickey reported that "the 'packers' use fine oat straw and prairie grass in packing the glass in boxes, barrels and crates for shipment. They are exposed to the dust and chaff from this material, which is very irritating and sets up nasal catarrh." The women and girls who washed the glass suffered from rheumatism because their hands were always in water and their feet often wet.[3]

In the last decades of the twentieth century, planning has become more complex, with increasing numbers of environmental issues to be addressed, and regional and state government agencies, usually through the use of consultants, produce often lengthy planning documents and environmental impact statements about proposed projects. These identify historic and archaeological sites in the path of the proposed development but also become historical documents themselves. Often, these are produced in draft form to solicit comment from agencies and the public. While drafts may be useful, researchers must be sure to find the final version of these reports, because they can change substantially in response to these comments. The reports may be available through a state or regional archives, the agency requesting the report, or the firm that produced it.

Manuscript Sources

Manuscript sources can vary widely, from a few ledger books to hundreds of feet of materials. Similarly, they may be found stashed in a closet in a company or in a well organized corporate archives such as those found at the Wells Fargo Company or Coca-Cola. Records still in the possession of the company may or may not be available to the public, and researchers should call the company for information on access before planning research trips. The whole problem of access to company records and additional information about them is available in *Corporate Archives and History: Making the Past Work,* edited by Arnita A. Jones and Philip Cantelon (Malabar, Fla.: Krieger Publishing Co., 1993).

Records of defunct companies or even old records of existing companies may be found in a state archives or regional repository. These may have been systematically deposited over the years or, all too often, they are rescued at the last minute when the company closes. In the case of one Martinsburg, West Virginia, textile mill, a researcher happened to find the new owner of the closed plant, only to learn that the new owner had indeed inherited the plant's records, but they were of no use to him in his new endeavor and were being pitched out. Whatever is rescued will be saved through a salvage operation—what is left that fits into the vehicle available at the time to go get them. The records may be so overwhelming that, even if available, they are, like federal records, often not useful without an index. A case in point is a warehouse-type room full of ledger books for the Pocahontas Operators Association, which began mining coal in southern West Virginia and western Virginia in the late nineteenth century. The financial records, company store records, doctors' records and other materials, including numerous photographs, are an invaluable source but are only really useful for someone with enormous amounts of time.

Harvard University's Graduate School of Business Administration houses the records of the R. G. Dun & Co. The collection consists of 2,500 manuscript volumes of credit reports dating from the 1840s through the 1880s. The records were kept after the 1880s, but they were kept in a different format, and no one knows what has happened to these. The collection has an alphabetical index of business and personal names for each county or major city of each state or territory. To search the collection, you will need names and locations of the entries by state and county. It is important for Baker Library staff to know the patron's research topic and purpose (dissertation, article, book, historic structures report, etc.). The collection is not available for genealogical purposes. The staff of the Historical Collections Department at Baker Library can conduct a one-hour search for materials for a fee

if the researcher submits a written request. Permission to publish, to exhibit quotations, or to use information from the collection must be obtained from Dun & Bradstreet through the Historical Collections Department of Baker Library. As an alternative or supplement, there are also small pocket-sized directories that Dun & Bradstreet published, but these are very sketchy compared to the manuscript versions.

The manuscript credit records include reports for all sorts of businesses, from women working alone as milliners to large factories. They can explain whether a husband was really running the business in his wife's name, or vice versa, to avoid creditors; whether the business may have failed eventually because the owner was an alcoholic; whether the owner of a business moved out of town or turned over ownership to a son, etc. In one case, the R. G. Dun & Co. reports explained an unusual deed transaction in which a nineteenth-century Kanawha County, West Virginia, woman purchased a saw mill from a man who, from the deeds, did not appear to be a relative. The local investigators reporting to the R. G. Dun & Co. explained the change in ownership by saying that the woman's husband had worked for the saw mill owner; when he was ready to sell, she had purchased it for her husband to run.[4]

Manuscript records in other locations may be identified through sources such as the National Union Catalog of Manuscript Collections. Also, of course, it is useful to check bibliographies of printed histories of various industries to see where researchers found sources that may also be useful for a particular company. Local historical societies and museums, however, may also have records that are not identified in national catalogues or other publications.

Maps can also be considered as primary sources for industrial archaeologists, and most major archives will have a collection of maps for the area whose history is documented in the archives. Maps can range from sketches of an early town plan to detailed topographical maps made by the most modern equipment. The maps may be filed separately in the archives, folded in the back of geological survey volumes, or be "stored" on microfilm, as are the Sanborn insurance maps. Maps of land subdivisions, which can show the locations for factories if they were sited when the plan was drawn, can be found in the county courthouse where the deeds were recorded, either bound in the volumes that contain the relevant deed or indexed and filed separately for easier reference. Maps are discussed in more detail in Robert Vogel's essay elsewhere in this volume.

CONCLUSION

The above is only a brief summary of the types of records available at the state and local level for those interested in industrial archaeology. As for all historical research, the resources can range from frustratingly scattered and small collections to overwhelmingly vast and complex collections. In any case, researchers face the challenge of compiling as much evidence from these sources as possible to help document the resources found on site.

ENDNOTES

1. These announcements were in *Philadelphia Real Estate Record & Builders' Guide,* 3 (20 February 1888): 77; and Ibid., 7 (3 February 1992): 924.

2. Wilde, Joseph L. *The "Leader" Wheelinq City Directory for 1879–80* (n.p.: C. C.Johnson, n.d.), 51; date of tack factory given on p. 96.

3. Dickey, John L. " 'Nailers' Consumption,' and Other Disease Peculiar to Workers in Iron and Glass," in West Virginia State Board of Health, *First, Second and Third Annual Reports of the Secretary of the State Board of Health of West Virginia For the Years Ending Dec. 31, 1881, 1882, & 1882* (Wheeling: Chas. H. Taney, State Printer, 1883), 149–154.

4. The Ella Moulton and Henry Clarke deed transactions are in Kanawha County (West Virginia) Deed books, vol. 33, p. 629; vol. 37, p. 332; and vol 49, pp. 58, 389, Kanawha County Clerk's Office, Kanawha County Courthouse, Charleston, West Virginia. The relations between the Moultons and Clarke are explained in Virginia, vol. 21, p. 111, R. G. Dun & Co. Collection, Baker Library, Harvard University Graduate School of Business Administration.

CHAPTER 5

Quadrangular Treasure: The Cartographic Route to Industrial Archeology

Robert M. Vogel

Most industrial structures and sites are by their very nature and location difficult to study systematically. In some instances they are too remote or too concealed to be discovered first-hand. Some are difficult to photograph or measure because of their physical condition, configuration, scale, or setting. Moreover, while industrial archeologists may carefully record and document a site, seldom can they afford to do the same for its larger setting—even though this may be essential to a full understanding of the specific site. Because of the precise and detailed information included on quadrangle maps, these have special value to industrial archeologists. Indeed, as information sources, quads often are more than merely valuable, they are indispensable.

The map as a means of locating places, natural features, and a limited range of cultural features such as railroads and highways needs no further comment. Less universally recognized, though, is the value of the *large-scale* map as a source of information on a vastly enlarged world of man's additions to and alterations of the earth's surface. Without question, the most informative and generally useful large-scale maps of the United States are the "quads" or "topo" maps published by the U.S. Geological Survey (to which we will henceforth refer as the Survey).

These maps are sold by the millions to local governments, utility companies, planners, scholars, hikers, and a wide variety of other organizations and private citizens having an even wider variety of other interests. The Survey points with justifiable pride to the immense range of purposes to which its maps can be turned. What it has been unaware of is their singular value to the industrial archeologist, for they comprehend astonishing amounts of information relating to historic industrial structures and sites, information that is as readily available in no other form.

It probably is fair to say that while many of the people concerned with industrial archeology—geographers, engi-

neers, and excavating archeologists, for example—have long been familiar with these maps and their value for locating sites and analyzing material evidence, the interdisciplinary nature of the field leads to the suspicion that there are many others to whom these wonderfully useful documents are either unknown or mysterious. To none should they be either.

To industrial archeologists of whatever background quads are useful at all stages of investigation—preliminary identification of sources, gathering of evidence, and interpretation and analysis. Quads are especially helpful for preliminary inventory work, for determining how to gain access to a site, and even for ascertaining the best time and vantage point for taking photographs (see Figures 3-B, 7-A, and 7-B). Quads also are useful once in the field—for preparing site plans and identifying structures, and for providing a solid base for inference about sub-surface remains (see Figure 4-B). Last, quads embody information concerning broader contexts—geographic, topographic, and, often, social and economic. They reveal precise spatial relationships between structures on a site, and between sites and their markets and resources. And—if maps of different publication dates are compared—they reveal changes over time (Figure 1-8). It is the intention here to explore the sort of information that can be obtained from these maps, how it may be interpreted for use in industrial-archeological investigation, and one technique for the handling of maps in the field.

The Basis of the Quads

The reference to "quads" in most cases is to a series of "general-purpose" maps published by the Survey since the early 1880s. They are the largest-scale maps routinely published by the government, and show an astonishing variety of natural and cultural (man-made) features. Since they indicate the configuration or relief of the earth's

(Reprinted from *IA*, The Journal of the Society for Industrial Archeology; Volume 6, Number 1, 1980 with permission from the Society for Industrial Archeology)

surface—the topography—by a variety of conventions such as elevation figures and contour lines, they are, generically, "topographic" maps. But so are any maps that show relief. The peculiarity of this series is that they cover only a small section of ground—far less than the area of most political units (such as counties or townships) that are the common basis for maps. Having no other basis for their boundaries, and to provide a degree of uniformity in size, the maps are bounded on their four sides by parallels of latitude and meridians of longitude producing a near rectangle called a *quadrangle.*[1] Hence, generally speaking, these are topographic maps, but more specifically quadrangle maps or, in the parlance of the field, simply "quads."

The quads originally were published at a scale of 1:62,500 (1 inch = nearly 1 mile) and covered ¼ degree of both latitude and longitude. One-quarter of a degree = *15 minutes* of arc, and the series was so known. The 15-minute series prevailed through the 1950s, and many areas of the country—particularly those where the feature density is light—have been mapped only in that series. Beginning in the 1960s demand for more detail caused a shift to the larger scale of 1:24,000. A map at that scale (1 inch = 2,000 feet) embracing an area 15 minutes by 15 minutes would have been unwieldy, so the coverage was quartered to 7½ by 7½ minutes. The resulting *7½-minute* series is the standard today, with most of the densely populated areas of the continental U.S. covered.[2] Many of the older 15-minute quads have been remapped into four 7½-minute sheets. All that follows relates to this series.

Here a word about scale size, a commonly-misunderstood concept. *Large scale* = large amount of detail and small area covered; *small scale* the reverse. At the 1:24,000 scale of the 7½-minute quads, 2½ map-inches = slightly less than a mile on the ground.

The quads are identified solely by *name.* The quad name usually is that of the most prominent city or town shown. If a large city is covered by two or more quads, each or all may take the city name with directional distinctions added (WASHINGTON EAST, WASHINGTON WEST). Where no cultural feature is present, the name of a natural one may be taken (BALD MOUNTAIN). *Occasionally* a quad is named for an engineering feature (CONOWINGO DAM). In ordering and referring to quads the state also is specified, as many names are duplicated among states. When a quad covers more than one state, all are shown in the title, the state with the greatest area on the sheet being given first (WHEELING, WEST VIRGINIA-OHIO). For each state and Puerto Rico an index map is published with the quads

shown as a grid overlay. For each quad the name and date of publication are shown. Both 7½- and 15-minute quads are identified, as available at the time of the index map's publication.

The date of quad publication varies widely. The Survey attempts to keep the maps current but the term is relative. A major revision of a given quad rarely occurs at less than 20-year intervals, even in dense areas where the rate of change is apt to be great. Minor revisions are made more frequently, however, by aerial survey (the principal method by which most Survey mapping is done anyway), the revisions being shown on the earlier edition by a purple overprint indicating features new or changed since original publication.[3] These revisions are regarded as interim, and are not field checked.

The Quad as an Industrial-Archeological Key

The allusion to astonishing amounts of information contained in the quads is no idle comment. There are three fundamental classes of information shown on the quad: natural features; cultural features; and relief, both natural and cultural. It is the demonstrated aim of the Survey to pack the quad format with as much data as humanly possible, the apparent limits being only the cost of information gathering and map legibility. In each class the information content is both verbal and graphic/symbolic, in various combinations. Graphic conventions are used so far as possible, often supplemented by lettering to specify the particular feature or give its name. Railroads, for example, are shown by the familiar single or double line with "crossties," the name of the particular railroad lettered along it.

A fundamental element of the quad format is the use of color indications. BLACK is employed for all cultural features and lettering (except contour numbering); RED for major roads and certain lesser land boundaries; BLUE for all hydrological features (from oceans and rivers to swamps and marshes); and GREEN for wooded areas, orchards, and certain natural growth, but not for "low" growth such as fields and meadows.

All land-relief features—principally contours—are shown in BROWN, as are a few special land configurations, both natural and man-made, such as mine tailing heaps, dunes, and unusual surface conditions. These are the principal colors used. Additionally, PINK (actually a screened red) is used in urban areas where the building density is too high to show individual structures with any degree of legibility.[4] The other secondary color is the already-mentioned PURPLE used to indicate interim revisions by overprint.

A principal value of the quads is the wealth of information that can be packed in (or *on*) by reducing features—especially cultural features—to symbols, of which a wide variety is used. Say, for example, that the researcher is faced with the task of locating a factory known to be near a certain town. The name of the respective quad is identified from the index map for that state, and from the quad the factory probably can be found. How? Because of another helpful quad convention. The scale of the 7½-minute quads is large enough that literally every building but the smallest out-buildings can be shown. Structures of about the size of a single residence are indicated symbolically (in black) by a square that more or less approximates the size of a typical house. But anything much larger is shown by a block that quite closely represents it in both scale and plan shape. This, of course, includes most industrial buildings, making a factory relatively easy to spot. It does not, however, permit distinction between a medium-sized factory and a super-market. Other clues help, though: If the block is on a railroad or stream, it is more likely to be industrial than commercial. Thus, if there is a single factory in the town, it probably is the one sought. If there are several, at least the search is narrowed.

It is in the area of discovery of unexpected industrial-archeological remains, however, that the quad is at its most spectacular. To examine one for an area that is to be visited for whatever purpose is almost inevitably to discover things unknown and unexpected. Letting the eye range along a line of railroad may reveal bridges (fixed or draw), tunnels, directly railroad-related structures such as stations and shop buildings, and indirectly associated ones such as factories. Along waterways can be found dams, bypass canals, falls with mills, more bridges, and pumping stations. In mineral-rich areas are likely to be deep and open-pit mines and related installations. A public institution such as a large hospital with a chimney shown adjacent probably means an isolated power plant that may be old enough to contain steam engines. Other examples of the myriad ways by which the quads can be "read" for industrial-archeological purposes are given by the accompanying illustrations.

While the most valuable use of the quads from our standpoint is in site location, there are other, related ones. The maps are documents of genuine worth in the teaching of technological, industrial, and cultural history. For example, the quad of Lowell, Massachusetts, or one of the other highly concentrated textile centers ranged along the Merrimack River makes clear the reasons why these particular places initially were selected for industrial development (Figure 1). The difference in elevation of the river above and below the impounding dam, shown both by the contour lines and the figures at bench marks and "spot elevations," is direct evidence of the waterpower available as the water falls through this vertical distance. The system of power canals built to distribute the water is vividly shown. The mills ranged along the canals are seen in some cases (most being absorbed in the pink of built-up area) in contrast to the later steam-powered mills. These, erected after the waterpower capacity at each site was exhausted, were located not on the canals but on the railroads that came later.

Relationships between industrial and town development often can be traced, as can transportation corridors and the development of all cultural manifestations in terms of the hydrology and topography. While such relationships as these can, of course, be shown on other maps of an area of study, these often are difficult to obtain. The quads are ubiquitous and readily available for any and all regions of the U.S.

From the most pragmatic standpoint, the quads have a considerable use in traveling by car, foot, or any other means. *All* roads are shown, from interstate highways down to "jeep trails," as the Survey likes to designate something passable only by four-wheel-drive vehicle. Anything shown of an order above the jeep trail usually is entirely negotiable by conventional car—even though it may be unpaved—opening up a wonder-world of shortcuts, site access, and vistas that is closed entirely to those common folk reliant on the traditional oil-company map. The large scale of the quad provides so many landmarks that only the most hopelessly inept map reader should manage to become lost when navigating by this means.

A final supplementary use of the quad is as a log sheet in site inventorying. Their relatively low price makes it entirely feasible to use the quad itself for directly marking sites and structures. The margins are generous (the more so the more northerly, as noted) providing ample room for notes. The indications of latitude and longitude, Universal Transverse Mercator (UTM) coordinates, and on some maps of state grid systems along all borders make it possible to designate the precise location—in any system—of any structure or area.[5] From the profusion of data on the quad, location descriptions may be made in terms of proximity to roads/streets and landmarks as well, of course—all this in the comfort of the home base.

Handling the Quads in the Field

The 7½-minute quads are about 27 inches high by 22 inches wide overall. Two schools of thought appear to exist on the most practical method of physically handling the sheets, especially in the field. The most simple method consists simply of folding them into quarters, first with a vertical fold and then a horizontal, which causes the quad name to show on both exposed quarters of the folded map. This method has the advantages of simplicity, of showing the entire quad when opened up, and of leaving generous margins for annotation. There are several disadvantages. The maps being loose, they tend to get jumbled when covering a good sized area involving many sheets. Unless a clipboard is used, there is no inherent writing surface under the map, while with a clipboard—if traveling—it is necessary constantly to shift from one quarter of the sheet to another by unclipping and refolding, and probably even to shift sheets.

The other principal method for dealing with the quads is to use a loose-leaf binder. This involves moderate expense and has one or two deficiencies of its own, but offers the serious quad user some overwhelming benefits. The system is based on filing the maps in standard four-ring legal binders (Boorum & Pease S-356, for example) which both keeps them in place and in an established order. The order may, of course, be tailored to fit a particular project. They may be arranged regionally, in tiers, to cover an area; or the sheets may be set in the sequence of a route of travel, or of a waterway; or they may cover the major cities of a region; or any other arrangement.

Finding the sheets in the binder, and relating them to the ground, is best guided by the state index map. This can be made the first sheet and its quad squares numbered in some convenient sequence; covering the entire state if small, or regions if a large one. The quads themselves then are numbered to correspond, and filed in numerical order. Quads present in the album (or in other albums) can be indicated on the index map by diagonal slashes or filling in with light-colored magic marker.[6]

The method of binding the quads consists of:

1. Cutting the sheet exactly in half horizontally, giving a lower and an upper half. Each half thus is 13½ inches high, just under the legal-sheet length of 14 inches. If this will do violence to some important feature or town that ought to be kept whole, the cut can be made slightly above or below it and the top or bottom sheet margin cut down to keep the longer

half-sheet within the 14-inch limit of the album. Or, a flap can be folded over. The other half-sheet will be short, of course, but no matter.

2. Each half-sheet is then folded exactly in half on a vertical line, impression out. Note that the impression is not always centered on the sheet left-to-right. Therefore it is best not to make the fold by bringing the sheet edges together, but by lining up the *printed borders* of the quad itself by holding it against a window (or light table). When lined up, the fold can be creased.

3. The excess of the side margins is then trimmed off. A slight problem arises here. The maximum width of a sheet that will fit entirely within the album covers is nine inches. Trimming the half sheets to that width not only removes nearly all the available note-taking margin, but encroaches to some extent on the figures indicating the various coordinates. The effect naturally becomes the more pronounced the further south the coverage. A solution is simply to trim wider—say to 9½ inches (for a 19-inch unfolded sheet width) which for most areas leaves the critical figures untouched. This does mean that when the album is closed the bundle of maps projects about a half-inch beyond the covers, but that makes little difference with normal handling.

4. Finally, the half-sheets are punched for the four-hole spacing and inserted. As the map name on both sheets is now on the back side of each half-sheet, it is necessary to write it on the upper right-hand corner of each, along with the numbers of any indexing system used. The top and bottom half-sheets of a given quad are easily distinguished by the location of the top and bottom margins.

A disadvantage of the system is that only a quarter of the quad is visible at a time. The "pages" can, of course, be pulled out at will and unfolded exposing the full quad width, and tops and bottoms held together if needed. The various advantages and disadvantages of each system can be weighed with respect to individual needs.

Other Maps Available

While the 7½-minute quadrangle maps (and to a lesser extent the old 15-minute series) are the last word for site location, there are other useful maps in the Survey's arsenal. For broader, less-detailed coverage the 1:250,000-series quadrangle maps are very good. Each map in this family of 473 covers an area two degrees of longitude (the boundaries on even-number degrees) by one degree of latitude, except for some for coastal areas. At this scale one map-inch = about four ground-miles. Shown in the same color convention as on the large-scale quads are major water features, major roads and many lesser ones (with route numbers), state and county boundaries, contours, woods cover, places down to fairly small hamlets, and, most useful, railroads, rendered sufficiently heavy and black as to be thoroughly followable. These maps are named for a major place within. Puerto Rico is covered by a single topographic map at a scale of 1:240,000. For Hawaii there are five and for Alaska 153 1:250,000-scale quads in this series. Index maps for Alaska, the Continental U.S., Hawaii, and Puerto Rico are available.

The National Ocean Survey (NOS)[7] publishes a splendid series of nautical charts for all the U.S. coasts and navigable rivers. One index map covers the Atlantic and Gulf coasts, Puerto Rico, and the Virgin Islands; another the Pacific Coast and Alaska. While intended mainly for navigation, much of industrial-archeological interest is shown, and these charts are particularly useful for work in harbor areas.

Beyond the Survey's maps, most states publish map series of their own, some of them at large scale and full of detail. These generally cover counties or other political units rather than quadrangles, and in many cases are at the same scales used by the Survey.

The Canadian equivalent to the U.S. Geological Survey quads are the National Topographic System maps. Most of the country is covered by quadrangles at a scale of 1:50,000 (one inch = nearly 0.8 mile). The more densely-populated areas are mapped by detailed, large-scale quads at 1:25,000 (one inch = 2,000+ feet or nearly 0.4 mile), while the Arctic areas and much of the West are covered only by 1:250,000-scale maps. Indexes to all maps are published.

Availability

Complete information on the availability of USGS quadrangle and other map series may be obtained from the U.S. Geological Survey, Distribution Section: 1200 S. Eads St., Arlington, Va. 22202, for areas EAST of the Mississippi River, Puerto Rico, and the Virgin Islands; and from Federal Center, Denver, Colo. 80225, for areas WEST of the Mississippi including Alaska and Hawaii. An index map for each state and for Puerto Rico, and a pamphlet describing the various topographic map series are available gratis. Each index map lists a variety of state and U.S. maps also available plus map reference libraries and private dealers within the state, and contains detailed ordering

information. The 7½- and 15-minute quads currently are $1.25 each, the 1:250,000 quads are $2.00.

NOS index maps and charts may be ordered from National Ocean Survey, Distribution Division, C44, Washington, D.C. 20235. Chart prices vary according to scale and coverage.

Canadian maps, indexes, and information on all map series available may be obtained from the Canada Map Office, Department of Energy, Mines & Resources, 615 Booth St., Ottawa, K1A 0E9. Map prices vary from $.75 to $1.50. Requests for indexes or information should specify the area of interest.

Further References

The ultimate exposition on the Survey's quadrangles and other maps, the origins of the Survey itself, its mapping programs, and on current cartographic technology is a *tour de force* by Morris M. Thompson, *Maps for America: Cartographic Products of the U.S. Geological Survey and Others* (xiv + 265 pp.). This was published by the Survey on the event of its centennial in 1979, and contains a glossary and index. Most of the many illustrations are in full color. It is available from the Survey's Arlington Distribution Center noted above for $11.00. The bibliography will lead the serious student as far into this area as wished. Also available is a free pamphlet on the quads for general public use.

Listings of new maps, revisions, and other up-to-date information is contained in the monthly *New Publications of the Geological Survey,* available on request from the USGS, MS 329, Reston, VA 22092.

A fine work on Canadian mapping is L.M. Sebert's *Every Square Inch, the Story of Canadian Topographic Mapping.* Ottawa: Surveys & Mapping Branch, Department of Energy, Mines & Resources, 1970; address as above.

The origin of topographic mapping in both North American countries is found in the renowned Ordnance Survey maps published by the British government since the 18th century. The interesting history of this service is told by G.B. Harley in his *Ordnance Survey Maps, A Descriptive Manual.* Southampton: Ordnance Survey of Great Britain, 1975.

The Selective Bibliography accompanying Stott's article cited in note 5 provides other references of both interest and usefulness.

Notes

1. A *near* rectangle, for of course while lines of latitude are parallel and therefore so are the top and bottom—north and south—boundaries of the map, meridians of longitude are parallel only at their intersection with the equator. At all other points north and south they are convergent. Thus the east and west boundaries of all U.S. quads lean inward to the top, the quad in reality being barely-perceptibly trapezoidal. The one tangible effect of this is that the quads for southern areas are considerably wider than for northern, as squareness is approached going south.

2. Puerto Rico is covered by 7½-minute quads but at the scale of 1:20,000 (one inch = about 1,667 feet). Alaska coverage is by a quadrangle series at 1:63,360 (slightly smaller than the 15-minute series mentioned in the text) at which scale one inch = exactly one mile. The quadrangles in this series cover 15 minutes of latitude by 20 to 36 minutes of longitude.

3. In these interim revisions, demolished structures are not always removed from the map.

4. This is, of course, a drawback from the standpoint of locating structures in these areas, but there is some mitigation in the fact that certain "landmark" structures *are* shown, such as public buildings, schools, churches, and, occasionally, factories. (See Figures 1 and 2-A.)

5. A highly informative and practical essay by Peter H. Stott on the basis and use of the UTM grid system of coordinates is in *IA* 3 (1977): 1-9.

6. An alternate indexing system that maintains a geographical relationship of the quads is suggested by SIA member William E. Davies of the Survey. The quads are keyed to the 1:250,000-scale quad (this series is mentioned later in the article) of which they are part by ruling it into its 128 7½-minute areas, each of which will represent a 7½-minute quad. The rows are numbered 1 through 16 horizontally and the tiers lettered A through H from bottom to top. Each quad then can be designated by its appropriate number and letter plus an abbreviation of the large quad's name. The CHERRY RUN, MD-WV-PA quad, for example, would be designated CUMB 16-F, for it falls in the 16th vertical row and the 6th tier from the bottom of the CUMBERLAND 1:250,000 quad.

7. Formerly the U.S. Coast & Geodetic Survey.

Reading the Quads for Industrial-Archeological Sites

All map details are taken from USGS 7½-minute quadrangle maps, and are shown at the full scale of 1:24,000. One inch thus represents 2,000 feet on the ground. The quad from which the detail is taken is indicated below, with its dates of publication and photorevision, as: 1964/72.

The construction-date of the structures in the photographs is given in parentheses; the date of the photograph at the end of the caption.

Because of the black-and-white reproduction of the quad details shown here, their legibility—compared to that of the original full-color maps—is considerably diminished. The following notes will help in making the translation from the original form to the reproduction.

GREEN—Entirely absent

BLUE—Entirely absent. The dark-blue borders of ponds, lakes, reservoirs, and rivers, and the single line of small streams, have been over-drawn in black. The light-blue screen representing the body of these water features within the borders has been rendered here with a coarse screen as:

BROWN—This color has reproduced with varying degrees of strength, depending upon the intensity of the original. The index contours appear in nearly every case; the intermediate contours faintly or not at all.

PURPLE—These photorevised features appear as black.

RED—Has reproduced as black.

PINK—The (red) screen indicating urban areas has reproduced very weakly or not at all. These areas, where germane to the detail, have been outlined with a heavy dashed line.

Figure 1. URBAN INDUSTRIAL ARCHEOLOGY. The amount of industrial-archeological information to be found on the quads of the major industrialized cities is nearly boundless. The historic textile city of Lowell, for example, contains industrial remains both unique and typical, much of it reflected on its quad. Evident first is the Merrimack River and the 19th-century system of power canals fed by it, the most extensive such arrangement in the world. At 1. are shown most of the system's hydraulic structures: the principal dam (identified by name) at the head of the falls, and the various locks, weirs, and other control elements. (The quad is not infallible—several are not shown.) At 2. are a number of railroad bridges over the canals (curiously, no railroads cross the river in the immediate vicinity). Highway bridges over the river, railroads, and canals abound at 3.: large and small; modern, early (the Aiken St. or Ouelette Bridge of 1883 is a five-span parabolic truss bridge by the Berlin Iron Bridge Co.), and of all intermediate ages. At 4. is a foot bridge. A pair of local water-supply structures is seen at 5., either one of which might be early enough to be of interest.

In looking for the famed mills of Lowell the principal failing of the quad as an industrial-archeological locator becomes immediately apparent. Where are they? Without much doubt the two buildings at 6. are factories or mills. The long, narrow building on the Concord River (southeast corner) suggests a water-powered mill (or formerly so), the

Figure 1. *LOWELL, Mass. 1966/79*

more so because of the adjacent railroad siding, while the small L-shaped block on Pleasant St. (north edge) could be an early water mill that expanded into a later structure represented by the squarish block on the opposite side of the brook. Or it might be another pumping station. Or something entirely different. And the four structures shown at 7. might or might not be factories or mills; lacking positive knowledge only a visit would reveal that to the explorer. But the great cotton mills (and the Lowell Machine Shop) that brought Lowell its fame are swallowed up in the cloak of invisibility that is the Survey's "urban area." While the pink area (seen here as a screen) gives up its schools, churches, and public buildings, it effectively hides from us most of the array of industrial buildings ranged along the east reach of the river and in several clusters on the canals. The two large structures at 8. are in purple and thus must be new, erected between the quad's publication and its photorevision in 1979.

At 9. are apparent railroad structures—perhaps freight houses. Finally, at 10. are what probably are simply oil storage tanks but which might be gas holders, on the basis of the rail siding that suggests the one-time delivery of coal for gasmaking.

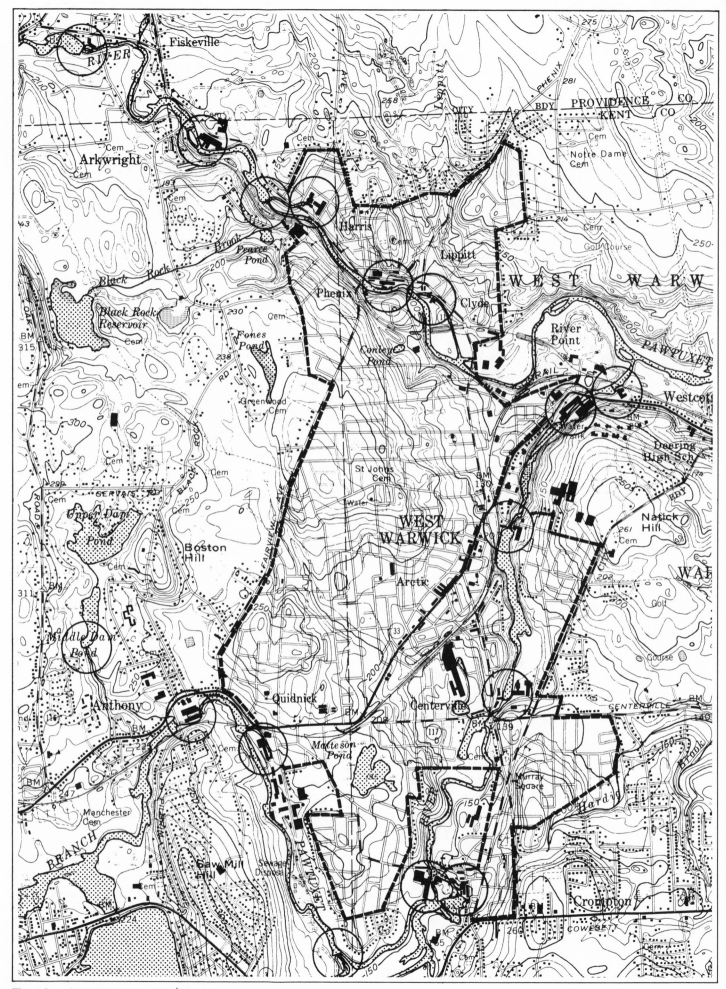

Figure 2-A. *CROMPTON, R.I. 1955/70 & 75*

Centerville Mill (mid-19th century). Works Progress
Administration, *1940*

Figure 2. HYDRAULIC POWER STRUCTURES. A) No
better example exists of the 19th-century practice of utiliz-
ing the descent of a single stream to produce power for a
number of manufactories than the harnessing of the falls on
Rhode Island's Pawtuxet River and its main branches. The
series of dams, pools, races, and cotton mills that appeared
between about 1808 and the 1860s largely survive and are
strikingly reflected on the CROMPTON quad. That these
are 19th-century mills is clear not only from the evidence
that they are water-powered but by observing that they are
long and narrow, the ruling configuration of that period of
inadequate artificial lighting, when it was essential that no
machine be far from a window. (Note a certain inconsis-
tency from quad to quad in what constitutes "landmark"
buildings in the screened urban areas. While the mills of
Lowell were not shown, here mills are the most prominent
of the landmark structures.)

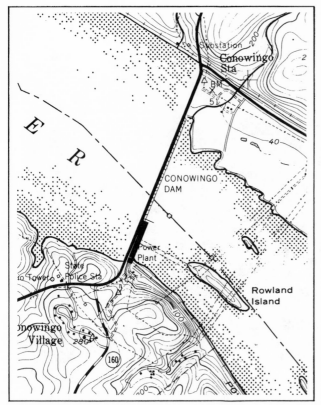

Figure 2-B. *CONOWINGO DAM, Md.-Pa. 1953/70*

B) The necessity of subdividing the drop of a river among a number of waterpower sites in the 19th century (each with a fall of some 10 or 15 feet) is contrasted with the capability a century later of extracting the energy of even a major watercourse in a single, huge, high-head installation, made possible by hydro-electric generation. Conowingo Dam and powerplant on the Susquehanna River (1927; enlarged 1964) is a good example of a large plant of its time. Head: about 90 feet (discoverable from the pool-elevation and contour-line figures). Capacity: 718,000 horsepower.

Conowingo Dam and hydroelectric station (1927).

C) Both the graphic and the verbal evidence of an intermediate-capacity hydraulic power site springs from the SHEPHERDSTOWN quad. As it is set in Roman type, we see that "Dam No 4" is, in fact, a place name, and an absolutely descriptive one. There is no canal leading from above the dam and the contour-line figures indicate a difference in river level above and below the dam—or head—of about 20 feet. Thus: a medium-head hydroelectric installation, fairly small so probably early 20th century. The photo shows the Dam No 4 hydroelectric station, built in 1909 with two units, the turbines driving the generators above through rope drives (see the SIA *Newsletter*, March-May 1975:3). What cannot be deduced from the quad is that Dam No 4 itself was built in the mid-19th century to supply water for the Chesapeake & Ohio Canal—the abandoned trace of which is indicated on the north bank—and that electricity generation is a later byproduct. Note also that the transmission lines leading from the station are on such a small scale that they are not shown on the quad, as are the prominent ones at Conowingo.

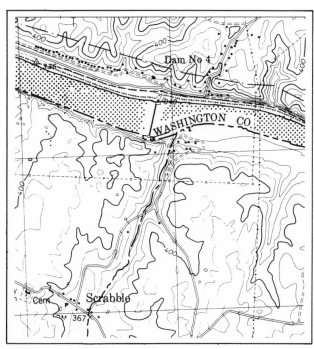

Figure 2-C. *SHEPHERDSTOWN, W.Va.-Md. 1978*

Dam 4 and hydroelectric station (1842 and 1909). 1975   Photos by author unless otherwise noted.

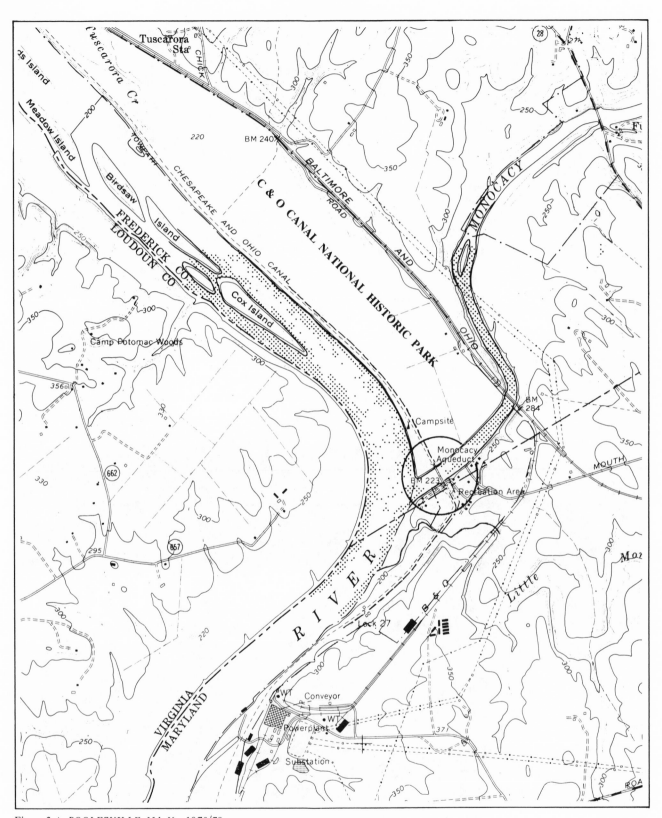

Figure 3-A. *POOLESVILLE, Md.-Va. 1970/78*

Monocacy Aqueduct (1833), Chesapeake & Ohio Canal. National
Capital Parks, National Park Service, *c1950*

Figure 3. BRIDGES. A), B) Bridges are perhaps the most
readily discovered structures on the quads. Every road and
railroad that crosses a watercourse means a bridge (except
in the case of ferries, which are clearly indicated). From the
quad several things can be learned directly about a bridge:
its name, when shown (A); its total length, which can be
scaled between the abutment symbols (the wide "V" at
each end, pointing toward the opening); its height above
the ground or water, which usually can be read from the
contour lines and any bench marks or other elevation
figures that may be given; the means of access to either end
or the area below, by noting roads and trails; the suitability
of photography (or simply viewing), by noting the topography and the amount of woods growth at the site; and
whether or not there is a draw span, by noting the presence

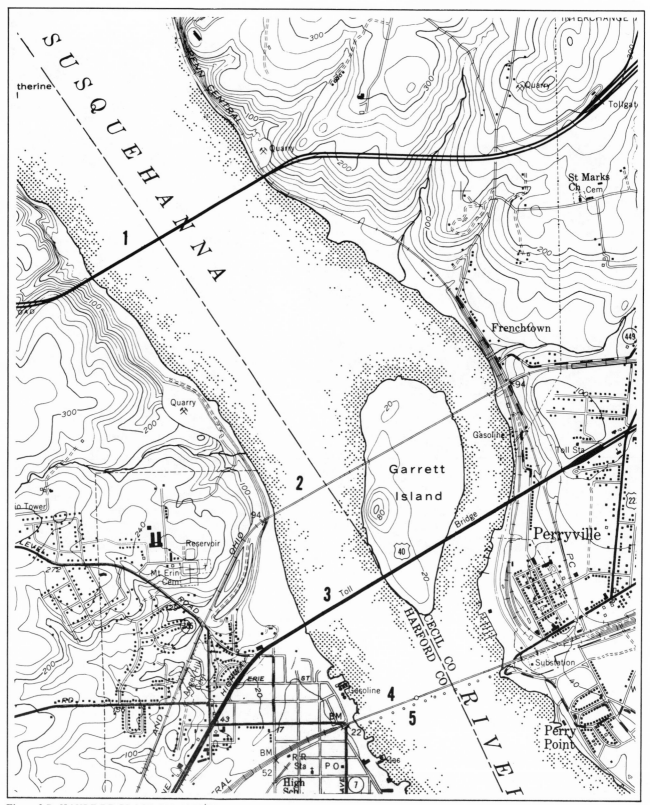

Figure 3-B. *HAVRE DE GRACE, Md. 1953/70 & 75*

Susquehanna River Crossings between Havre de Grace and Perryville, Md., looking north. Jack E. Boucher for the Historic American Engineering Record, *1977*

of the symbol (B-4). Furthermore, a number of additional things can be inferred. One such is the approximate age of a bridge. A span carrying an Interstate highway (B-1) generally can be no more than 15 years old, the approximate age of the Interstate system. But the span on U.S. Route 40 (B-3) probably is considerably older and of possible interest (a steel arch of 1940, in fact).

The bridges carrying the Baltimore & Ohio and Pennsylvania railroads (the latter now Conrail) (B-2; B-4) might be of any age, but, as few major railroad bridges have been built since the early years of this century, these might be of historical worth. Actually, both are, having been built in 1909 and 1905 respectively. The B&O crossing is at a high level with through truss spans over the channels; the PRR structure at a lower level, accounting for the swing draw span over the main channel. The line of circles at B-5 implies the extant piers of a former bridge. (These supported the timber-truss bridge of the Philadelphia, Wilming-

ton & Baltimore, a PRR predecessor, and, after the present bridge was built, a steel highway bridge that served until erection of the Route 40 bridge.) Finally, it can be seen from the quad that the proximity of the members of this large family of bridges makes possible the photographing of any bridge from its neighbor to the south, but not the north, without shooting into the sun.

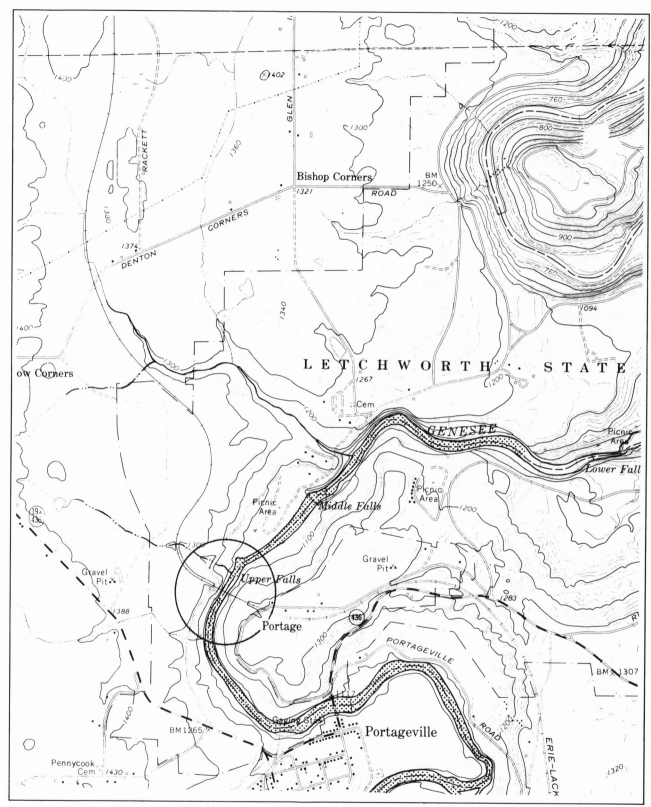

Figure 3-C. *PORTAGEVILLE, N.Y. 1972*

C) Although the only direct clue to a bridge's structural type found on the quad is the drawbridge symbol, again, some inferences can be drawn. Viaducts, for example, are clearly indicated when a railroad (or occasionally a highway) crosses a deep gorge containing a relatively narrow watercourse. The Erie Railroad's celebrated Portage Viaduct, though not named on the quad, can be located with absolute certainty by observing that there is a place (consisting, apparently, of five houses and perhaps a barn) called *Portage* at a point where the Erie (at the time of the quad's publication the Erie-Lackawanna, now Conrail) crosses the Genesee River, and that the contours indicate clearly a very steep, narrow gorge. The height of the rail above the river, read from the contours, is about 240 feet; the length of the viaduct, scaling between the abutments, is about 820 feet. And so it actually is, within a few feet.

Portage Viaduct (1903), Erie Railroad. Jack E. Boucher for the Historic American Engineering Record, *1971*

Figure 4. MINING & MINERALS. A) Many signs of mines and other workings and structures related to minerals extraction—both active and abandoned—are present on the quads. Open-pit mines are plainly shown symbolically, verbally, and usually by the contours. Deep mines are indicated by a pair of unique symbols. A "Y"—the stem pointing into the opening—indicates a drift (side-hill) mine, and a half-solid square a shaft. The abandoned coal mine tunnel in the photograph was found from the symbol (circled). (Note that the place names on quads are themselves often clues to the presence of industrial-archeological sites: Eckhart Mines as here; just south of which [not shown] is Borden Shaft. There are countless "Mills," "Factories," "Falls," "Furnaces," and like suggestions of human industries, as well as a variety of other indicative names such as Ironton, Glassboro, Coke Oven Hollow, Graniteville—to draw the explorer on.)

Figure 4-A. *FROSTBURG, Md.-Pa. 1949/74*

Entrance to abandoned coal mine (1916). 1975

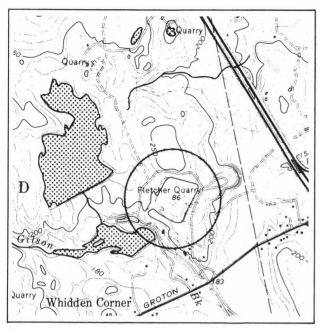

Figure 4-B. *NASHUA SOUTH (formerly TYNGSBORO),*
Mass.-N.H. 1965

B) Quarries, too, are well marked, always by the contours (note that the contour lines for depressions or pits bear ticks pointing downhill, differentiating them from hills), and usually by a verbal designation and symbol. Large, well-established workings occasionally are named, as in the case of Fletcher's granite quarry. The presence of a rail siding at a quarry implies that it might be active (at least that the rails still were in place at the time of the quad's publication), and that it is (was) a fairly large operation.

The familiar crossed-picks symbol is a somewhat ambiguous one, used to indicate any sort of surface mineral working, and thus is only moderately useful.

Fletcher's granite quarry. 1976

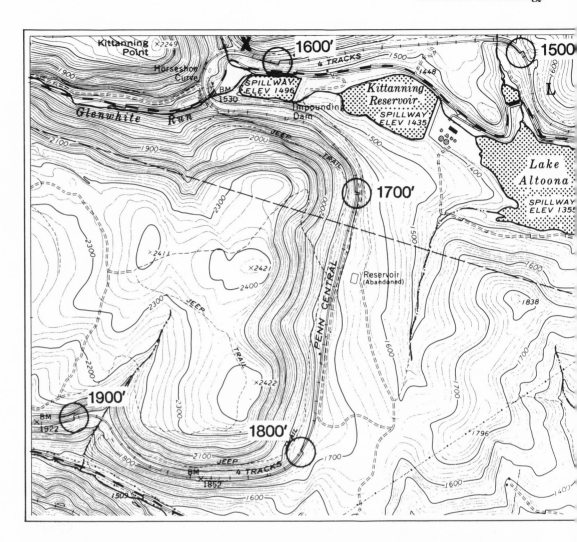

Horseshoe Curve (1853), Pennsylvania Railroad. Cheney Collection, National Museum of History & Technology, *1920*

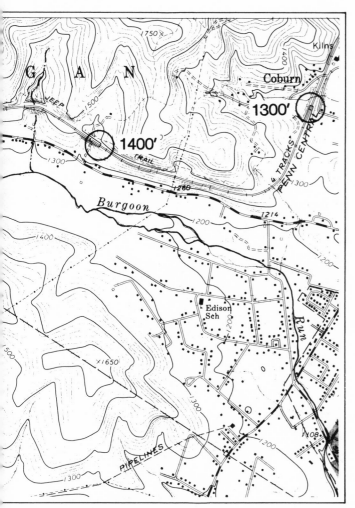

Figure 5. *HOLLIDAYSBURG, Pa. 1963/72*

Figure 5. RAILROAD ENGINEERING. The means by which rail lines traverse irregular terrain while maintaining a grade that rarely exceeds two percent (a rise of two feet in a run of 100 feet) is vividly shown on the quads. It is quite as interesting to "read" a rail line in a mountainous section as to walk it on the ground. It is perfectly clear how railroads in such regions follow the contours by side-hill cuts or benches where possible, and how, where the line cannot follow the contours, it must cross them. When the crossing is made through solid material, the result is a cut if the obstruction is minor, or a tunnel if major. If the obstruction to a level line is the "absence" of material—a depression or valley—the line is carried on a solid earth fill or embankment, or a viaduct if the opening is a significant one. All of these features are plainly visible on the quad.

One of the most interesting examples of heroic railroad engineering in the East is the celebrated Horseshoe Curve on the Pennsylvania Railroad's main line west of Altoona. The problem and solution it represents can be read directly from the quad. The problem was to connect the line in its march over the Alleghenies at a point south of Coburn, where its elevation was 1,340 feet (above sea level) with the pass formed by the valley of Sugar Run to the west. There it was to follow the valley's north wall in a side-hill cut at an elevation starting at about 1,800 feet. To join those points as the crow flies would have involved immense quantities of fill and a colossal viaduct over Burgoon Run south of Coburn. But worse, the difference in elevation between the two points is some 460 feet. To overcome that rise in the straight-line distance of 2.5 miles would have resulted in an unacceptably steep gradient of some 3.3 percent. The solution was to lengthen the run by an amount that would bring the grade down to the design maximum of something under two percent. The line, accordingly, was continued westward up the north side of Burgoon Run valley on a fairly easy route along the natural contours to the point where the valley divided at Kittanning Point. The route then was doubled back eastward along the south side of the valley in a perfect "horseshoe" 1,100 feet across. Then it followed the contours south and west around the base of a steep-sided hill, passing through the range via the Sugar Run valley on its way west.

The distance between the two points via the Horseshoe Curve was some 5.3 miles. A climb of 460 feet in that distance resulted in a relatively easy grade of about 1.9 percent. Apart from the great quantity of benching, the only heavy earthworks involved in the project were embankments some 100-feet high where the route crossed the prisms of the two streams flowing from around Kittanning Point, and a deep bench cut into the Point itself. This work is seen on the quad and the photograph, which is taken from point X on the quad looking about south-by-west. The line's rate of climb can be determined from the values of the index contours that cross it. These lines, representing levels of elevation at 100-foot intervals, intersect the tracks about one-mile apart; in other words, the railroad climbs the mountain at the rate of just under 100 feet per mile.

Figure 6. LOCATING MISCELLANEOUS STRUC-
TURES. Many unsuspected structures of industrial-
archeological interest can be discovered by examining the
quads for suggestive verbal descriptions sometimes, but not
always, accompanied by symbols.

    A) The WT designation at a solid black dot, indicating a
water tank, usually represents a garden-variety elevated
tank or a standpipe of no particular age or interest. That

Figure 6-A. *CURTIS BAY, Md. 1969/74*

such seemingly mundane clues can, on occasion, lead to
sites and structures well beyond the ordinary is seen in the
case of the Curtis Bay (Baltimore) Tank, a large above-
ground reservoir in a striking masonry casing. While the
expectations of such discoveries normally will not justify
field explorations on their own, if in an area on other
business it can be rewarding to wander a bit off course to
see just what certain suggestive map indications actually
represent.

Curtis Bay Tank (1931). 1975

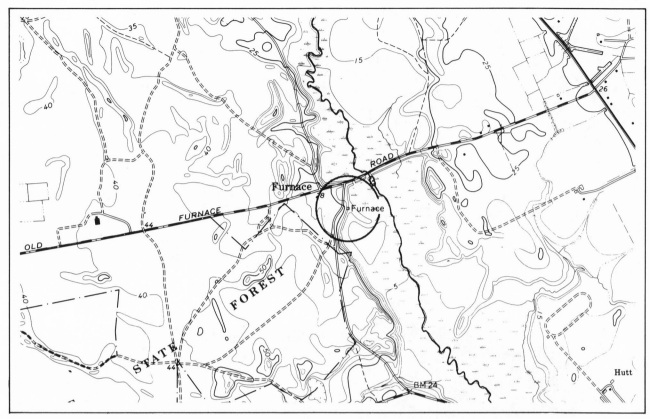

Figure 6-B. *SNOW HILL, Md. 1966*

B) Certain types of "non-building" industrial structures are so rarely occurring that they do not warrant a symbol of their own, but nevertheless are of a large enough scale that they must be indicated in some way. The Survey's convention in such cases is to show them as open squares or rectangles roughly to scale, and label them appropriately. These designations can bear wonderful fruit. The Nassawango blast furnace is one instance of this. The symbol and label confirm that a furnace of some type still exists in an area where one could be anticipated on the basis of the place-name *Furnace* (in which no buildings at all seem to survive), and the presence of *Old Furnace Road* and *Furnace Creek* (not shown on the detail).

Nassawango blast furnace (1830). 1977

Figure 6-C. *ESSEX JUNCTION, Vt. 1948/72*

*Racks for air-drying green brick, and coal-fired beehive kiln
(1920s?), Drury brick works. 1972*

C) An unusually interesting example of an obscure
structure is shown here. The rather large open rectangle
suggests a sizable building of some sort. But what are
"Racks?" Investigation produced a set of the now-rare
racks used for the open-air drying of green bricks prior to
their firing. At this site, too, appeared a slight lapse in the
quad, for while the "Brick Kiln" indicated was indeed
present, not shown is a far more interesting predecessor
beehive kiln—abandoned—the more significant for retaining
the coal-firing grates that in most of these kilns have been
removed during conversion to gas or oil firing.

Figure 7. ACCESS AND VANTAGE. When exploring in strange territory, absolutely nothing—not even local inquiry in most cases—can take the place of the pertinent quad for both reaching a site and determining how best to see it or photograph it from a distance.

A) Take, for example, the famed Staple Bend (or Portage) Tunnel, the first railroad tunnel in the U.S. It is across the river from the slag dump of the Bethlehem Steel Co's. Johnstown plant. It is readily located on the quad, being directly labeled and shown by symbol. If to be photographed, the south portal obviously is the one of choice because of the light. But as there is no access road in the immediate vicinity how to reach it? The quad tells all. From the town of Franklin a "light-duty" road departs to

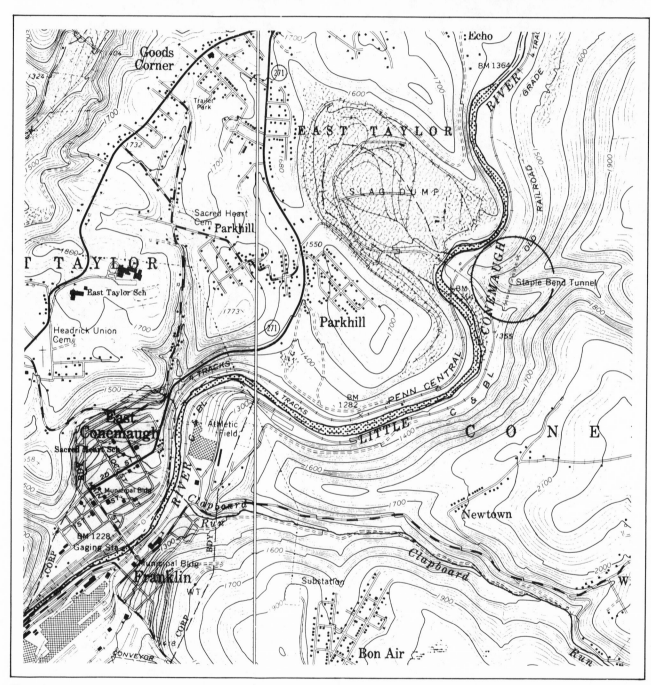

Figure 7-A. *JOHNSTOWN and GEISTOWN, Pa. 1964/72*

the northeast, climbs a moderate hill (as shown by the number of contour lines crossing it at short intervals), makes a sharp bend to the southeast and immediately becomes an "unimproved" road through the woods, well above and paralleling the river and the C&BL Railroad (Bethlehem's works line). This road continues along the river heading directly for the tunnel, but before reaching it it heads down hill, leaves the woods, and stops dead at the railroad. The would-be visitor apparently must count on going the rest of the way on foot, for about ¾ of a mile. So it is in practice. The unimproved road indeed is passable by car to about the point shown, and the tunnel easily reached by walking along the tracks, thence along the abandoned roadbed right up to the portal itself. Visualize trying to get clear oral instructions for all that from someone in Johnstown or even Franklin.

Staple Bend (Portage Railway) Tunnel (1832), south portal. 1962

B) Vantages for observing or photographing long structures such as major bridges frequently can be located from the quad by reading the contours for high, open ground that might not be evident from the structure's immediate vicinity because of obscured sight lines. The Baltimore & Ohio Railroad's crossing of the Ohio River south of Wheeling involved a magnificent stone approach viaduct, on a curve, at Bellaire, Ohio. Although all of the original iron work in the bridge has been replaced, the viaduct remains unaltered, in full service. The sweep of the structure and the trusses of the land and river spans can be fully seen and photographed only from the west, and from a considerable elevation. The quad indicates that the ground rises quite sharply on the west side of the city, just beyond the viaduct, and that the hillside is laced with small streets and buildings, presumably houses (from the pink "urban" screen). From this area–between the houses–any number of suitable vantages are, in fact, available. (The quad shows also the means by which the railroad gained the necessary elevation for the crossing on the Benwood, W. Va. side, within the narrow confines between the river's edge and the steep rise of the hill, by making a three-quarter loop on a [steel] viaduct.)

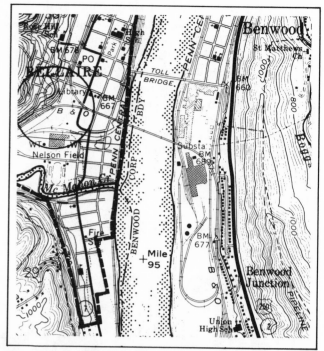

Figure 7-B. *WHEELING, W.Va.-Ohio 1968/78*

Stone viaduct (1870) of the Bellaire, Ohio approach to the Ohio River Bridge, Baltimore & Ohio Railroad–view from hillside west of the city. 1979

CHAPTER 6
The UTM Grid Reference System

Peter H. Stott

The Universal Transverse Mercator ("UTM") metric grid system is a worldwide geographical reference system, which, like latitude and longitude, provides a unique coordinate reference to any point on the earth's surface.[1] The paper which follows describes the UTM grid system and its important applications to and advantages for historic site research. To encourage some facility with maps—which is an important first step in understanding the grid system—the article is introduced with the concepts of topography and map scale.

"Topography" takes its derivation from two Greek words, "topos" (meaning "place") and "graphos" (meaning "record"). Consequently, a "topographic map"—literally a "record of the place"—is "a detailed representation on paper of natural *and artificial* features."[2] Popular misconceptions to the contrary, a "topo map" is not simply a map using contour lines to show elevations above sea level; the identification of buildings, railway lines, civil boundaries, and other artificial and natural features are also important elements of topography.

In its fullest applications, the topographic survey is an inventory of all cultural and natural resources commensurate with the scale of the map. Although historic material is not always given a prominent place, topographic maps frequently note abandoned canal or railway routes and established historic sites. Less directly, contour and fence lines, limits of vegetation, and other map features will often provide evidence of the past use of a site.

Topography is a very integral part of archeology—whether above or below ground. Like topography, archeology provides a record of a place—a place that is drawn, photographed, and studied, not in isolation, but in the social and topographical context of its surroundings. To the archeologist the topographic map should be an indispensable tool: it aids him in finding a site; it allows him to study a site within the context of the natural and artificial features affecting and affected by it; and it allows him to record the location of a site for his future study and for permanent record.

The degree of detail on a topographic map is usually defined by the scale of the map. Scale is the relationship between "ground distance" and "map distance." This is represented most obviously by the simple statement "1 inch equals 2,000 feet." A more convenient form, and one not limited to conventional units of measure, is the representative fraction, written as a fraction (e.g., 1/24,000), or now more usually as a proportion or ratio (1:24,000). Both examples explain that one unit of map distance is equivalent to 24,000 of the same units on the ground. In other words,

$$1 \text{ inch} = 24,000 \text{ inches} = 2,000 \text{ feet}$$
$$\text{or}$$
$$1 \text{ cm} = 24,000 \text{ cm} = 240 \text{ meters}$$

[1] A number of people have very kindly agreed to review informally the text and offer their comments. Among those to whom I am particularly grateful are Alden Colvocoresses and Bill Jones of the USGS Topographic Division; David Bouse of the Canadian Office of Restoration Services, Dept. of Indian and Northern Affairs; and Wilford Cole of the National Park Service's Office of Archeology and Historic Preservation.

[2] Emile D. Chevrier and D. F. W. Aitkens, *Topographic Map & Air Photo Interpretation* (Toronto, 1970), p. 3. (Emphasis added.)

Peter H. Stott is Research Assistant for the Division for Historic Preservation, New York State Office of Parks and Recreation.

(Reprinted from *IA*, The Journal of the Society for Industrial Archeology; Volume 3, Number 1, 1980 with permission from the Society for Industrial Archeology)

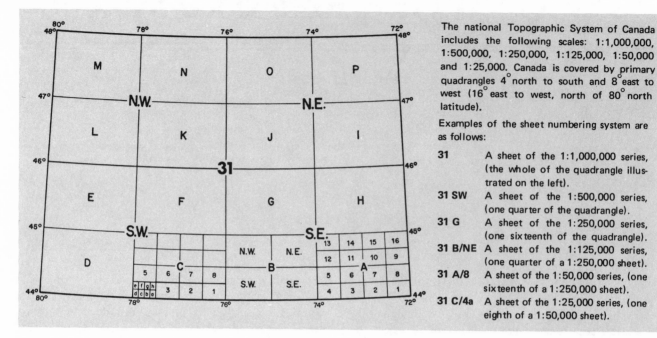

The national Topographic System of Canada includes the following scales: 1:1,000,000, 1:500,000, 1:250,000, 1:125,000, 1:50,000 and 1:25,000. Canada is covered by primary quadrangles 4° north to south and 8° east to west (16° east to west, north of 80° north latitude).

Examples of the sheet numbering system are as follows:

31	A sheet of the 1:1,000,000 series, (the whole of the quadrangle illustrated on the left).
31 SW	A sheet of the 1:500,000 series, (one quarter of the quadrangle).
31 G	A sheet of the 1:250,000 series, (one sixteenth of the quadrangle).
31 B/NE	A sheet of the 1:125,000 series, (one quarter of a 1:250,000 sheet).
31 A/8	A sheet of the 1:50,000 series, (one sixteenth of a 1:250,000 sheet).
31 C/4a	A sheet of the 1:25,000 series, (one eighth of a 1:50,000 sheet).

Figure 1. *Sheet numbering system of Canadian "NTS" maps. (From L.M. Sebert,* Every Square Inch. *Courtesy of the Surveys & Mapping Branch; Energy, Mines & Resources Canada)*

Small-scale maps (those which depict a large portion of the earth's surface) include the 1:1,000,000-scale International Map of the World[3] (about 16 miles to the inch); and 1:250,000-scale maps (about 4 miles to the inch), the largest scale at which both Canada and the U.S. are completely mapped. Most large-scale mapping in Canada is at 1:50,000 (about .8 miles to the inch). At this scale most of the country's settled areas have been completely covered, as well as certain strategic areas of the far north. Mapping at a scale of 1:25,000 is limited to densely settled areas.[4] Figure 1 portrays the system of sheet lines used in Canada's National Topographic System (except in the far north), based on quadrangles 8 degrees wide by 4 degrees high.

In the continental U.S. the equivalent mapping scales are 1:62,500 (about 1 mile to the inch) and 1:24,000 (1 inch = 2,000 feet). Maps at the smaller scale are 15 minutes (one quarter of a degree) on a side; larger-scale maps at 1:24,000 are 7½ minutes on a side. These "quadrangles" are usually

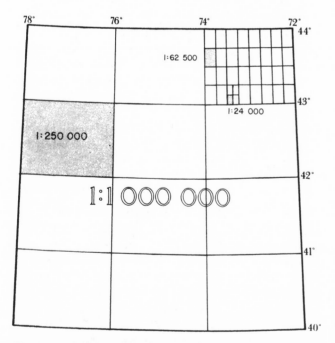

Figure 2. *Relationship of principal map scales in the National Topographic Map Series of the U.S. Geological Survey.*
– *1:1,000,000 International Map of the World series, 6° x 4°*
– *1:250,000, 1/12th of the IMW series, 2° x 1°*
– *1:62,500, 1/32nd of the 1:250,000 series, 15 minutes on a side*
– *1:24,000, 1/4th of the 1:62,500 series, 7.5 minutes on a side*

[3] The "IMW" is an international map series first proposed in 1891 by the German geographer Albrecht Penck (1858-1945) to map completely the land areas of the world to internationally controlled cartographic standards at a scale of 1:1,000,000. The program is today administered by the United Nations Cartography Section. North American maps in the series may be obtained from the agencies discussed below; most others may be obtained through the Defense Mapping Agency Topographic Center, 6500 Brooks Lane, Washington, D.C. 20315.

[4] L.M. Sebert, *Every Square Inch: The Story of Canadian Topographic Mapping* (Ottawa, 1970), p. 12.

designated as being either 7½-minute or 15-minute. Figure 2 illustrates the relationship between these two scales and the smaller scales.

In the United States the agency charged with the production of a topographic survey is the U.S. Geological Survey.[5] Large-scale topo maps are available directly from the USGS for $1.25 each (and from many booksellers and stationers for somewhat more). The USGS Branch of Distribution for maps east of the Mississippi is at 1200 South Eads Street, Arlington, VA 22202; the branch for maps west of the Mississippi is at Federal Center, Building 41, Denver, CO 80225. State indexes to mapping (gratis) may be ordered from either office.[6]

In Canada the corresponding agency is the Surveys and Mapping Branch (Dept. of Energy, Mines, and Resources). Public inquiries and sales are handled though the Canada Map Office, 615 Booth Street, Ottawa, Ontario K1A OE9. Prices range from 75 cents to $1.50 for large-scale maps. Index maps (gratis) are arranged according to lines of latitude and longitude; requests should specify the locality desired.[7]

Referencing systems—the way of communicating a particular location—may take any number of forms. A street address is one form; so is an atlas or road-map grid, by which, for example, the reader is referred to "A-3." Much of the U.S. and Canada is covered by a series of township and range lines developed for the disposition of government lands; these lines are still widely used as a referencing system. Various organizations have developed other systems.

For practical reasons, however, we limit the discussion which follows to those systems compatible with all topographic maps.[8] These include non-cartographic systems such as street addresses (e.g., 31 Mulberry Street) or landmark orientation (1500 feet west of the railway station). The disadvantage of these systems is that they provide convenience and precision only in proportion to the user's familiarity with the area. These systems are also virtually impossible to standardize either for computerization or general inventory purposes.[9]

On U.S. topographic maps[10] there are three cartographic referencing systems in general use: geographic coordinates, in degrees, minutes, and seconds; state plane coordinates, in units of feet; and UTM coordinates, in metric units. Modern Canadian topographic maps show geographic coordinates and full UTM grid.

Geographic, or spherical, coordinates were a direct consequence of the first attempts to visualize the shape and size of the earth. Eratosthenes (c.276-195? B.C.), Curator of the Library at Alexandria, is generally credited with their first application, later refined by the 2nd-century A.D. geographer Ptolemy.[11] In principle the system of geographic coordinates is the simplest of systems since its three-dimensional network of grid lines (the "gratticule") conforms neatly to the shape of the earth. But even aside from the ancient problems associated with transferring a global image to a plane surface without distortion, the nonrectilinear configuration of the grid makes the coordinates unwieldy both in computation and in print.

The state plane and UTM coordinate systems are both examples of a two-dimensional rectangular grid of evenly spaced lines superimposed on a map surface. Every point on that surface then has an identity determined by its distance from two major "axes." This concept, sometimes called Cartesian coordinates after its inventor, the philosopher/mathematician René Descartes (1596-1650), is now a familiar feature of elementary mathematics.

The development of the present plane coordinate system coincided with the development of long-range artillery.

---

[5] The term "Geological Survey" may be misleading. Although the organization was founded in 1879 to facilitate the exploration of mineral and water resources, it was quickly realized that a topographic survey should take precedence, and today, of the various mapping programs undertaken by the Survey, the National Topographic Mapping Program is by far the most extensive.

[6] A request for "Special Handling" generally assures a response within one week.

[7] Four to six weeks should be allowed for delivery.

[8] For an examination of other referencing systems see Alden P. Colvocoresses, "A Unified Plane Co-ordinate Reference System" in *World Cartography* 9 (1969): 9-65. This article provides a very thorough argument for the use of plane coordinate systems by national topographic surveys throughout the world.

---

[9] An exception to this statement, David Bouse has pointed out to me, is provided by the "geocode" of the Canadian Inventory of Historic Buildings. Fifteen digits are used to break down a site's location according to province, town, street, and number according to an intricate coding scheme. The system has also been adapted for rural sites, with a corresponding increase in complexity.

[10] The Canada Map Office has for some years given the UTM a prominent place on its maps and in its publications. See particularly Sebert, above.

[11] G. C. Dickinson, *Maps and Air Photographs* (London, 1969), pp. 2-3.

Figure 3. *Plane coordinate axes laid out over topographic map detail. Distance "c" computed from Pythagorean Theorem as* $\sqrt{(5-1)^2 \times (4-1)^2} = 5$.

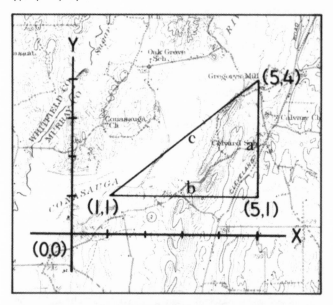

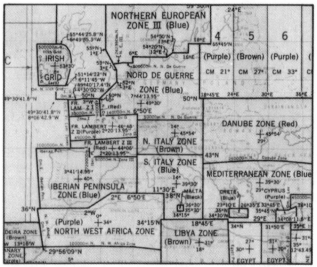

Figure 4. *Plane Coordinate grids in use during World War Two.*[14]

Until World War I, heavy ordnance was generally aimed by a system of trial and error known as "shooting in." In 1914 the use of the "French 75" with a firing range of 5 miles made this impossible; it was no longer possible to see the target.[12] Using the geographic coordinates of the gun and the target to determine distance and angle proved excessively complicated and time-consuming, and the French General Staff turned to rectangular coordinates. By superimposing a plane coordinate grid on military field maps, each point could be given coordinates which expressed its horizontal and vertical distances from the origin of the grid. (See figure 3.) Using the Pythagorean Theorem (that the square of the hypoteneuse was equal to the sum of the squares of the other two sides), it was a simple matter to determine the distance between any two points on the grid. The angle of fire could be determined from elementary trigonometric functions. The grid developed by the French General Staff became famous as the *Nord de Guerre* and was in service until the end of World War II.

With high expectations, similar grids were proposed for civil use after the war. Suggested one geographer in 1924:

> The ordinary citizen will not get use to it all at once of course, and he may even look askance at it to begin with. It will be some time, I think, before the soldier can with confidence invite his young lady to meet him at 206.793 at 2020 hours. But that will come in time.[13]

The problem with rectangular grids, however, was that it was impossible to extend a grid very far without creating serious distortion in the planar grid over the curved surface of the earth. (Try wrapping graph paper around a grapefruit.) So a multitude of grids proliferated, and by the opening of World War II, the medium and small-scale maps of Europe were a mass of conflicting grids (figure 4). At the conclusion of the war the U.S. Army Map Service assembled

[12] Jacob Skop, "The Evolution of Military Grids," *The Military Engineer* 43 (1951): 15-18.

[13] Sir John T. Burnett Stuart, at a session of the Royal Geographical Society "The Choice of a Grid for British Maps," *Geographical Journal* 63 (1924): 105. At another meeting in 1933 an advocate confidently predicted the day when grid references would be on everyone's notepaper and visiting cards. The noted geographer A. R. Hinks suggested that the time was not far off "when every lamppost in London would have on it its rectangular coordinates, so that if one was lost in a fog or anything of that sort, one would be enabled to discover one's exact locality." *(Geographical Journal* 82 [1933]: 43-44, 51.)

[14] From "Index of American and British Mapping, March 1945." U.S. Army Map Service, *Grids and Magnetic Declinations. AMS Memorandum 425* (4th ed., Washington, D.C., 1945).

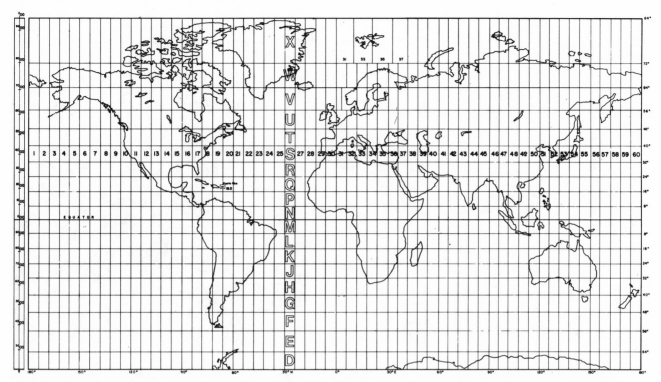

Figure 5. *Map of the world showing zones and rows. An additional zone is shown at left marked with the 500-km central meridian and 1000-km ticks.*

a task force to examine and evaluate all grids then in use and make recommendations for a single unified system. Their recommendation, now adopted by most of the world for military purposes, was the Universal Transverse Mercator grid system, based on the international unit, the meter.

The U.S. experience followed a similar pattern. At the end of the first World War, a yard grid using overlapping zones was established for military maps of the U.S. It was not until the 1930s, however, that civil grids were established. The foot grid developed by the U.S. Coast & Geodetic Survey was not quite as rational as the Army grids. Separate zones were established for each state, and it often happened that some states had three, four, or sometimes five distinct zones. While these state plane coordinate grids provided a perfectly acceptable way for local surveyors to tie in to the national triangulation, the use of the myriad irregular grids was unacceptable for national or international use, where the maps usually cross many of these grid zones. The state foot grids are still in wide use, though the UTM has entirely replaced the old yard grid.

The smallest-scale map in general use was the Millioneth-Scale International Map of the World. To keep zone lines from appearing on this series required that the zones be at least 6 degrees in width, the width of the IMW sheets. This meant that 60 zones were required to circle the earth completely. The zones also took over the numbering of the IMW sheets, with Zone 1 at the International Date Line, and progressing eastwardly around the world until reaching Zone 60 on the other side of the date line. Figure 5 illustrates this progression of zones. Zone 18, for instance, between the 72-degree and 78-degree meridians, covers much of the U.S. east coast and Ontario. Because the grid system, based on the Transverse Mercator map projection, covered the entire earth (except for the polar zones), it was called the Universal Transverse Mercator grid system.[15]

How It Works

Like the simple geometric X and Y axes alluded to above (and in figure 3), each grid reference has both an X coordinate (the "easting") and a Y coordinate (the "northing").

[15] The grid was established only for the non-polar regions. North of the 84° N parallel and south of the 80° S parallel the Universal Polar Stereographic (UPS) Grid is used. The only major land mass to which the UPS is applicable, however, is Antarctica. It is discussed in full in the U.S. Army's Field Manual, *Map Reading* (FM21-26), available from the U.S. Government Printing Office, Washington, D.C. 20402.

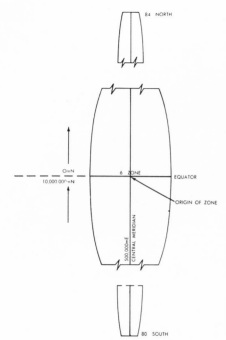

Figure 6. *A grid zone illustrated with reference to its major axes, the equator and a central meridian. At the equator each zone is approximately 668-km wide. (From U.S. Dept of the Army Field Manual,* Map Reading, *(FM 21-26)*

Delaware Aqueduct, Lackawaxen, Pa. (1847-1848). The longest of the four suspension aqueducts built by John A. Roebling for the Delaware & Hudson Canal Co. (SHOHOLA, PA 012921). (Library of Congress photo by Jack E. Boucher for the Historic American Engineering Record, April 1971)

The origin of each zone's grid is on the equator on the central meridian of each zone. Because this would mean that references to the left or below the axes would have at least one negative number for a coordinate, the central meridian was given an arbitrary value of 500 kilometers (500,000 meters). In the northern hemisphere the equator was given a value of 0 km; in the southern hemisphere it assumed a 10,000-km value. Thus coordinates to the left of the central meridian would have a value less than 500 km, while those to the right would have a value greater than 500 km.[16] (See figure 6.) Because the central meridian and the equator are the major axes of the grid, they are also the *only* grid lines which coincide with meridians and parallels.

For example, the central meridian of Zone 18 is the 75-degree meridian.[17]

Now turn to figure 7, a corner from a U.S. Geological Survey quadrangle. In one corner is a grid reference box, which schematically diagrams the process of determining a grid reference. It has been devised for this example for the sake of clarity, but it is absent from most USGS maps. It is frequently included, however, wherever grid lines are printed in full, as in Canada. On the large scale maps of the U.S. and Canada (1:24,000 and 1:25,000 scales) grid lines are each one kilometer apart (1000 meters, or approximately 3280 feet). Where they are not shown in full, grid lines are located in the margin by blue "tick" marks. UTM figures labeling the ticks or grid lines are composed of one or two small superscript digits (called "anterior digits") and usually two "principal digits."[18]

---

[16] Some values of course are impossible. The maximum width of a zone (at the equator) is approximately 668 km, giving a maximum range of approximately 165 to 834 km. A noticeable exception is when the width of a zone is artificially broadened. The New York State Transverse Mercator System is an example of such a zone extension, in use on maps issued by the State Department of Transportation. Though western New York normally lies in zone 17, to keep the state entirely within one zone, the grid lines of zone 18 were simply mathematically extended to the western edge of the state. Consequently, all grid lines and grid coordinates west of the 78-degree meridian on NY DOT quads bear no useful relationship to standard UTM coordinates.

In certain circumstances, maps will show two or more zones, sometimes overlapping. When determining coordinates under these circumstances, it is important to choose the grid zone in which the site would *normally* fall. Otherwise the reference will not be easily adaptable to all map series.

---

[17] This particular central meridian happens to be the west edge of the SHOHOLA, PA quadrangle (figure 7). The figure [5]00 is not shown on the quad because of congestion at the corner, but the figure [5]01 is exactly one kilometer east.

The material in this paragraph is thoroughly and clearly discussed in *Map Reading* (note 15).

[18] It is the practice of U.S. and Canadian map agencies (and many others as well) to give the full meter readings–6 or 7 digits–only at the northwest and southeast corners of the map. In addition, grid ticks are unlabeled where the digits would conflict with other lettering.

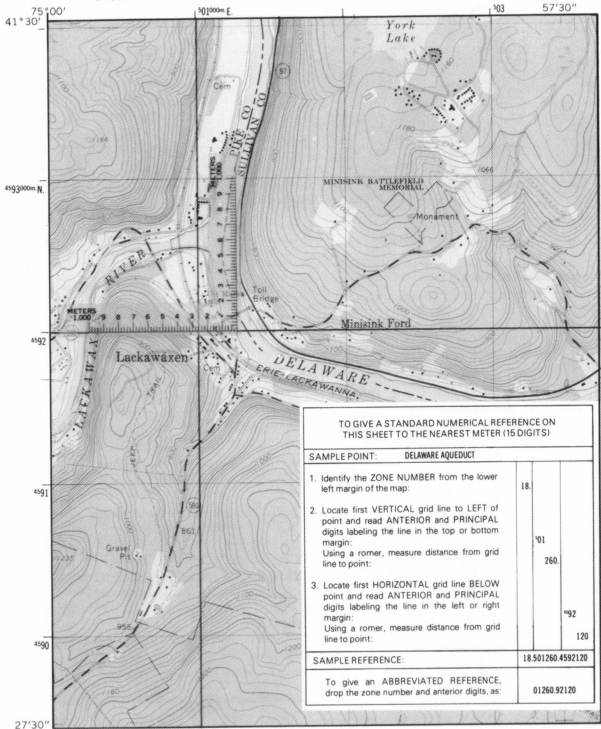

UNITED STATES
DEPARTMENT OF THE INTERIOR
GEOLOGICAL SURVEY

TO GIVE A STANDARD NUMERICAL REFERENCE ON
THIS SHEET TO THE NEAREST METER (15 DIGITS)

SAMPLE POINT:	DELAWARE AQUEDUCT	
1. Identify the ZONE NUMBER from the lower left margin of the map:	18.	
2. Locate first VERTICAL grid line to LEFT of point and read ANTERIOR and PRINCIPAL digits labeling the line in the top or bottom margin:	⁵01	
Using a romer, measure distance from grid line to point:	260.	
3. Locate first HORIZONTAL grid line BELOW point and read ANTERIOR and PRINCIPAL digits labeling the line in the left or right margin:		⁴⁵92
Using a romer, measure distance from grid line to point:		120
SAMPLE REFERENCE:	18.501260.4592120	
To give an ABBREVIATED REFERENCE, drop the zone number and anterior digits, as:	01260.92120	

Figure 7. *A corner of the U.S. Geological Survey 7.5-minute quadrangle SHOHOLA, PA (1965 edition, photo revised 1973). Thousand-meter grid lines have been added. The Delaware Aqueduct is marked by the words "Toll Bridge."*

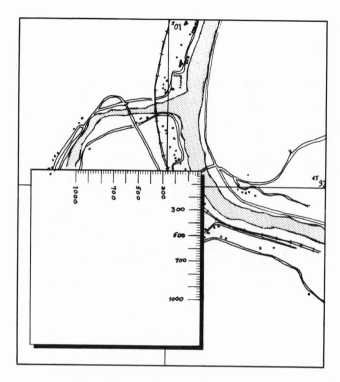

Figure 8. *Use of a handmade paper romer to determine coordinates to the nearest meter.*

Known Surviving Examples of Bowstring-Truss Bridges Following the 1841 Whipple Patent (All New York State)			
Date	*County*	*Quadrangle*	*Grid Reference*
1867	Albany	ALBANY	98330/20860
1870	Columbia	CLAVERACK	04880/74230
c.1860	Fulton	PECK LAKE	50370/60980
?	Lewis	BRANTINGHAM	70080/33080
?	Lewis	PORT LEYDEN	70195/20075
1869	Montgomery	RANDALL	50110/55860

Figure 9. *Example of abbreviated references used in an inventory of Whipple Bowstring-Truss Bridges.* [21]

In the example illustrated by figure 7 we wish to determine the grid reference for the Delaware Aqueduct, built by John Roebling for the Delaware and Hudson Canal, 1847-1849. To do so we must identify the southwest corner of the kilometer square in which the aqueduct lies. This corner is bounded by the grid lines labeled $^501^{000\,m.}$ E. (501,000 meters east of the "false" origin of the zone's grid) and ^{459}2 (4,592,000 meters north of the origin). Horizontal coordinates (the eastings) are always read first, followed by the vertical (northing) coordinates. The military mnemonic expression is **"read right-up."** [19]

It then simply remains to measure the distances north and east from the grid lines to the point and add these values to those of the grid lines. This may be done either by estimation (using the metric scale in the margin as a guide) or by measuring. The grid reference box in this example uses a measured distance. To measure the distance accurately requires a tool called a "romer." Transparent romers are available commercially, [20] but they can also be very simply drawn on the corner of a 3x5 card. To use a romer, place the upper right corner on the point whose reference is to be

determined and read the values where the romer crosses the grid lines. (See figure 8.)

The coordinates are then assembled into a full numerical grid reference by separating the two parts with a decimal point (sometimes a slash), and prefixing the pair with the zone number, derived from the bottom left-hand margin of the map—e.g.,

zone easting northing
18.^{501260}.^{459}2120

It is this 15-digit form that is at the moment most common in the U.S., having been adopted by the National Park Service's Office of Archeology and Historic Preservation as well as each of the State Historic Preservation Offices. It is difficult, however, to determine from the grid reference the approximate location or map name, and there is a variety of established means of including this information and shortening the grid reference. In the abbreviated form noted in the grid reference box, both the zone number and the anterior digits have been dropped—e.g.,

$01260.$$92120

---

[19] *Map Reading* (note 15), p. 12.

[20] They are available for $5.25 each from the Keuffel & Esser Company, 1521 North Danville Street, Arlington, VA 22201 (Attn: Vince Cascio), with discounts for bulk orders. The romer was named after its inventor, Capt. Romer of the British army.

---

[21] From Chamberlin, W.P., "History of Road and Bridge Building Technology in New York State," A Report of Progress on Research Project 80-14 through March 31, 1975, Engineering Research & Development Bureau, NYS DOT, Albany; and from Division for Historic Preservation, NYS OPR.

Although this figure is not unique,[22] it is a very useful form for local inventories or other circumstances where the quadrangle name or approximate locality is known. (See figure 9.) By prefixing this reference with the quadrangle name, uniqueness is restored, with the added advantage of the map name built into the grid reference—e.g., SHO-HOLA, PA 01260/92120.

For large unmistakable structures, an estimated reference to the nearest 100 meters is sufficient, shortening the grid reference still further. Following the practice of the alphanumeric form (see below), short references are usually run together—e.g., SHOHOLA 012921. Similarly, a reference to the nearest 1000 meters would be only 4 digits long (SHO-HOLA 0192).[23]

Alphanumeric Form

The above descriptions outline what is known as the numerical or "civilian" form of grid reference. However, the recommendation of the Army Map Service, and the form adopted by military and many civilian mapping agencies (including the Canada Map Office), is the alphanumeric, "military" form of grid reference. In this usage the abbreviated reference is run together without break and prefixed, not by the map name, but by a letter code derived from the anterior digits. The grid reference box on each map indicates the correct letter codes (figure 10). Each pair of letters designates a square 100 kilometers on a side.[24] The zone number is retained and followed by a "row number," designating one of several strips, each usually eight degrees in latitude as shown in figure 5.

Thus translated, the military grid reference for the Delaware Aqueduct would be 18T WA 01260/92110 (though the standard grid reference box would give only the estimated reference to the nearest 100 m, 18T WA 012921).

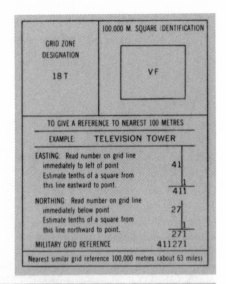

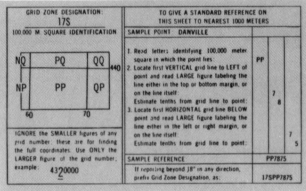

Figure 10. *Grid reference boxes used (above) on the Canadian 1:50,000 series and (below) on the U.S. 1:250,000 series. Both examples use the alphanumeric form of grid reference. Note that the right example, covering a much larger land area than that on the left, uses grid lines that are 10 km apart. The lines are indicated by coordinates with* single *principal digits (*$^{43}2$, $^{43}3$*) instead of the more usual double digits (*$^{43}20$, $^{43}30$*).*

---

[22] This grid reference will be repeated at 100-kilometer intervals (about every 62 miles) in four directions.

[23] This is often the best estimated accuracy obtainable on a medium-scale map series, like that at 1:250,000. Figure 10 shows a grid reference box at that scale.

[24] The first letter is derived from the easting anterior digit; the second from the northing anterior digits. The appendix gives instructions for calculating one form from another.

Construction of the Winnipeg Aqueduct, Shoal Lake to Winnipeg, Manitoba (1913-1919). The Water District Railway paralleling the water-supply aqueduct was completed in 1914 for construction and maintenance of the aqueduct, which is 110 miles in length [EAST KILDONAN (62H/14h) 368278 to WAUGH (52E/11 east) 414987]. (Photo courtesy of Canadian Engineering Heritage Record)

Who Should Use Grid References and Why

The universal use of a grid reference system is an important element in furthering public awareness of industrial archeology, and indeed of historic sites in general. Journal or newsletter articles may proliferate about a site but the greatest obstacle to public visitation (and hence a demonstrable popular preservation cause) is the lack of a precise location. All have experienced the frustration of trying to locate a relatively obscure site in a small town, and spending perhaps half a morning wandering local roads. Unfamiliar territory is made no more familiar by the addition of a street name.

Now, provided with a grid reference and map (even the 1:250,000-scale is often sufficient, and these can be purchased for large areas of the country without enormous expense), the enthusiastic archeologist can head directly for the Coke Ovens of Cascade, WV (MASONTOWN 010795), the ruins of the Harmony Borax Works in Death Valley, CA

(FURNACE CREEK 113370), or the Baillie-Grohman Canal in Canal Flats, British Columbia (CANAL FLATS 82J/4W840554).[25]

Here, then, is a popular need. But the need is equally present for professional historians and archeologists. The site (an artifact located in space) is the primary document of a particular aspect of cultural history. As such it demands the same rigorous documentation given to a primary bibliographic source. A precise grid reference guarantees that when all other landmarks have been demolished, hills laid

---

[25] Those who collect topographic maps for field trips and other uses may find a 4-hole, 14-inch ring binder convenient, an idea for which the author is indebted to the SIA's Robert M. Vogel, Curator of Mechanical and Civil Engineering, Smithsonian Institution. Quadrangles for northern latitudes will conveniently fit if trimmed, cut in half horizontally, and each half folded. The 1:250,000-scale maps may also be stored in this fashion, though the cut should be a vertical one.

Silver King Coalition Mines Co. Ore Loading Station, Park City, Utah (1900-1901). Terminus for an aerial tramway which transported silver ore from the Silver King mine to tracks of the D&RGW RR in Park City (PARK CITY EAST 579995). (Photo by Jack E. Boucher for the Historic American Engineering Record, August 1971)

E.B. Eddy Digester Tower, Hull, Quebec (1901). Possibly the first vertical digester applied to the sulphite pulping process, permitting the economical manufacture of a higher quality paper [OTTAWA (31G/5) 446305]. (Photo courtesy of Canadian Engineering Heritage Record)

plain, streets discontinued, and buildings replaced, the site is still retrievable.

With these thoughts in mind, the following guidelines are proposed for citing grid references of U.S. and Canadian sites:

For the main subject of a journal article:

Topographic map name + full grid reference to nearest meter

SHOHOLA, PA 18.501260.4592120
CANAL FLATS, BC (82J/4W) 11U NF 84000/55400

For less important sites in the same article, newsletter references, and photograph indentifications (where not mentioned in text): [26]

Topographic map name + abbreviated estimated reference to nearest 100 meters

SHOHOLA, PA 012921
CANAL FLATS, BC (82J/4W) 840554

USGS topographic maps should be cited by name only; Canada Map Office maps should include the map number in parentheses. Where the locality is the same as the map name, and has already been mentioned in the text, the map name need not be repeated in giving a grid reference.

Full grid references should be placed in footnotes, but abbreviated references may often be conveniently placed within the text in parentheses.

In April 1975 the U.S. Geological Survey announced that in the future all maps at scales of 1:1,000,000 (the IMW) and larger would carry a full fine-line UTM grid. The grid has already appeared on specialized maps and many of the 1:250,000-scale maps. However, it will be some time before

---

[26] Not all sites mentioned in an article need be referenced, of course. It will generally be unnecessary to reference familiar landmarks, noted only in passing.

each large-scale map can be reprinted. Some old quadrangles printed before 1959[27] and all of them published
before 1953 lack the blue UTM ticks. In this case there are
several possible remedies. The easiest solution is to determine the coordinates of the corners of the map using the
U.S. Army's Technical Manual TM 5-241-11, "Coordinates
for 7½-minute Intersections," and by having those, establish the location of critical ticks. Coordinates may also be
determined directly from geographic coordinates by using
Technical Manual TM 5-241-4/1, "Transformation of Coordinates from Geographic to Grid."[28]

There are areas of the U.S. and Canada where no large-scale
mapping has been completed. Although 1:250,000-scale
maps will exist for the area, that scale may well be insufficient. The next-best resource is generally the state or pro-
vincial mapping agencies. In the U.S., "General Highway
Maps" are published by each state's transportation or highway department under federal guidelines, usually at a scale
of 1:62,500 on a county-by-county basis.[29]   Some states
also publish other map series and inquiries should be directed to those offices.

[27] The printing date of a map is marked in the lower right hand
corner, just below the neatline (the line bordering the map proper).
The date included with the map name is the edition date.

[28] Both technical manuals are available from the U.S. Army A G
Publications Center 1655 Woodson Road, St. Louis, MO 63114.

[29] Maps of the New York State Dept. of Transportation are an
exception. That office produces USGS-based quadrangle maps in
black and white at 1:24,000 and other scales, but see above, note
16.

Appendix

Determination of 100-kilometer Square Designations for the UTM Kilometer Grid System

The designation for each 100-kilometer square is a two-letter combination determined from zone number and the anterior digits of eastings and northings. Using the tables below, it will be seen that an EASTING value of 500 km (i.e., anterior digit "5" in the top margin) in zone 18 will become "W." A NORTHING value of 4500 km in the same zone will become "A."

Like the full grid reference itself, the easting value must always precede the northing value; thus the 100-km square for the Delaware Aqueduct is designated by the two letter combination "WA."

Table A: Easting Values

Hundreds of km	Zones: 7,10 13,16,19,11...	Zones: 8,11 14,17,20,23...	Zones: 9,12, 15,18,21,24...
1	A	J	S
2	B	K	T
3	C	L	U
4	D	M	V
5	E	N	W
6	F	P	X
7	G	Q	Y
8	H	R	Z

Table B: Northing Values

Hundreds of km	Even Nbr'd Zones	Odd Nbr'd Zones
...	...	...
60	R	L
59	Q	K
58	P	J
57	N	H
56	M	G
55	L	F
54	K	E
53	J	D
52	H	C
51	G	B
50	F	A
49	E	V
48	D	U
47	C	T
46	B	S
45	A	R
44	V	Q
43	U	P
42	T	N
41	S	M
40	R	L
39	Q	K
38	P	J
37	N	H
36	M	G
35	L	F
...	...	...

Selective Bibliography

Chevrier, Emile D., and Aitkens, D.F.W. *Topographic Map and Air Photo Interpretation.* Toronto: Macmillan, 1970.

Cole, Wilford P. *Using the UTM Grid System to Record Historic Sites.* Washington, D.C.: Office of Archeology and Historic Preservation, National Park Service; advance edition, March 1977. Provides a detailed explanation of grid references computed in a variety of situations.

Colvocoresses, Alden P. "A Unified Plane Co-ordinate Reference System." *World Cartography* 9 (1969): 9-65. *World Cartography* is the journal of the United Nations Cartography Section, Department of Economic and Social Affairs.

Dickinson, G.C. *Maps and Air Photographs.* London: Edward Arnold, 1969; New York: Crane, Russak & Co., Inc., 1970. This is both an authoritative reference tool and a thoroughly readable text. It provides a good introduction to the history and use of topographic maps.

Harley, G.B. *Ordnance Survey Maps, A Descriptive Manual.* Southampton: Ordnance Survey, 1975. A magisterial manual to the world's premier mapping agency, the Ordnance Survey of Great Britain.

Keates, J.S. *Cartographic Design and Production.* New York: John Wiley and Son, 1973. Advanced-level cartography.

Raisz, Erwin. *Principals of Cartography.* New York: McGraw-Hill, 1962. One of several good introductory texts to maps and map making.

Sebert, L.M. *Every Square Inch, the Story of Canadian Topographic Mapping.* Ottawa: Dept. of Energy, Mines, and Resources, 1970.

Skop, Jacob. "The Evolution of Military Grids." *The Military Engineer* 43 (1951): 15-18.

U.S. Department of the Army. *Map Reading.* FM 21-26. Washington, D.C.: U.S. Government Printing Office, 1969.

U.S. Department of the Interior. Geological Survey. *A Brief History of the U.S. Geological Survey.* Washington, D.C.: Government Printing Office, 1974.

CHAPTER 7

The Photogrammetric Recording of Historic Transportation Sites

Paula A. C. Spero

INTRODUCTION

The purpose of this chapter is to examine the applicability and accuracy of documentation drawings prepared from close-range terrestrial photogrammetry and to compare them with the results of traditional documentation techniques. Research upon which this essay is based was organized to coincide with specific equipment and software resources available within operating divisions of the Virginia Department of Highways and Transportation in order to examine the feasibility of carrying out such recordations when federal mandates require them.[1] The equipment and software used for this study should be available to most state departments of transportation. The only equipment not already available was the camera which was purchased by the state subsequent to the recommendations of this research project. Photogrammetric fieldwork was conducted under the direction of Fred Bales, Photogrammetric Engineer. In addition to the production of documentation drawings from photogrammetric methods, the potential for additional applications of photogrammetric data such as condition assessment, determination of member sizes, etc., were examined. This secondary phase of the study focused particularly on the potential to measure cross-sectional dimensions from the photogrammetric models.

ESSENTIALS OF PHOTOGRAMMETRIC DOCUMENTATION

Photogrammetry is defined as the science of taking measurements from photographs. The term "photogrammetry" was first used in 1855 by a European geographer.[2] The naming of this science coincided with the beginning of rapidly accepted photogrammetric experimentation in Europe.

Although photogrammetric applications were not widely used until the late nineteenth century, the principles involved were understood during the Renaissance. Practical field applications awaited the development of photographic equipment. In the 1800s optical prisms replaced the pinhole camera, fixing solution was found to keep photographic images from fading, light sensitive negatives were used and a stereoscope was made.[3] With the capability to reproduce permanently an image photographically, photogrammetric field applications quickly emerged, both on land and in the air.

The field of photogrammetry is still broken down into two broad divisions: aerial photogrammetry and terrestrial photogrammetry. The most commonly recognized modern use of photogrammetry traditionally has been topographic mapping. In the past few decades, however, the application of photogrammetric techniques has ranged widely from macroscopic to microscopic measurements. A division within the terrestrial photogrammetry category has developed to accommodate the need for microscopic measurements. Close-range terrestrial photogrammetry applies to objects up to 300 meters (984 feet) from the camera station, while terrestrial photogrammetry handles distances greater than 300 meters.[4]

Within the last several decades many research projects have shown the feasibility of using close-range terrestrial photogrammetric techniques to measure such things as widely varied as rock deformations in mines and craniofacial mapping of bones, teeth and soft tissue. In general, there are three broad categorizations of close-range applications: architectural, biomedical and industrial photogrammetry.[5] Architectural photogrammetry can be traced back to the beginning of the discipline; the others are new developments.

Close-range terrestrial photogrammetry has been satisfactorily used to study architectural monuments throughout Europe from the mid-nineteenth century. Among the numerous modern European studies is a French project of the 1970s in which the extremely detailed facades of historic churches were closely examined through stereophotogrammetry. Within the past few decades, documentations of architectural monuments have been made in the United States. In 1977, the National Park Service Office of Archeology and Historic Preservation produced a guide to photogrammetric recording of resources.[6] Several examples of photogrammetrically recorded architectural sites are illustrated in that publication. More recently, 25 structures were photogrammetrically documented in Charleston, South Carolina, by the Historic American Buildings Survey. The Virginia Department of Highways of Transportation has published information on the use of photogrammetry for recording bridges.[7]

The use of close-range photogrammetric procedures for architectural surveys, then, is widely recognized. The 1980 edition of the American Society of Photogrammetry's *Manual of Photogrammetry* states: "More recently, the field of architectural application of photogrammetry has undergone considerable expansion both in scope and diversity." Types of architectural surveys possible using these techniques are listed as

1. rapid and relatively simple
2. accurate and complete
3. very accurate[8]

The rapid and relatively simple surveys provide sufficient information for historical inventories and other preliminary studies. Accurate and complete surveys provide information that is much more detailed than the first type. This type of information would be necessary to document intricate details and areas of deterioration on historical structures. Very accurate surveys require accuracy in the order of 0.1 mm (3.9 $\times$ 10^{-3} inches) to 1 mm (3.9 $\times$ 10^{-2} inches). Only very close investigation of surfaces or movement would warrant such detailed study.

Producing Photographs of the Sites

The photographic work for nontopographic, architectural or structural photogrammetry projects can be done with either metric or nonmetric cameras, the difference being that metric cameras are designed specifically for use in photogrammetry. Metric cameras can be either single or stereometric. The former is composed of two main parts, a mount to support the camera and a tilting metric chamber, which are separable for ease of transport and designed for easy attachment to a tripod. The stereometric camera consists of two cameras separated by a bar and attached to a tripod as a unit. The camera available for this project was a Zeiss Jenoptik UMK 10/1318, a single metric type. The focal length of this camera is 99 mm (3.90 inches) and the film used is 13 cm (5.1 inches) $\times$ 18 cm (7.1 inches) $\times$ 1.5 mm (0.06 inch) glass plates, type B Kodak tri-x panchromatic plate. Glass plates are used to avoid the image distortion, through temperature changes and shrinkage, associated with film.

Three types of photographs are used in photogrammetric studies, as defined by the camera and object orientation. When the optical axis, or camera axis, is vertical, the photographs are vertical, and when the optical axis is horizontal, the photographs are horizontal. When the optical axis deviates from being either horizontal or vertical, the photographs are oblique; they can be low oblique (small angle) or high oblique (large angle) photographs.

All three types of photographs were made in this study. Vertical photographs taken from a "cherry picker" were used for plan views and horizontal photographs on the ground were used for elevation views. The several oblique photographs taken while documenting elevations would require restitution using special universal or analytical stereoplotters to make accurate representations of the objects photographed. The restitution process was outside the current equipment capabilities of the department. A limited number of oblique photographs were taken in the event that such equipment might subsequently become available. All vertical and horizontal photographs, however, were easily handled on available equipment.

Stereoplotting the Sites

The delineation of the objects from these horizontal and vertical photographs is executed from a mechanically reproduced, three-dimensional image of the object. In order to create a three-dimensional model of the object to be studied, a pair of photographs, or stereopair, of the object is taken. When these two photographs are aligned in the stereoplotting machine in a way that reproduces the relationship of the camera field stations precisely, the object can be viewed in three dimensions and an accurate reproduction can be made. To align the photographs correctly it is necessary to know where the optical axis for each photograph was located at the time of photography. The optical axis passes through the center of the lens and is perpendicular to the image plane. This point of intersection between the optical axis and the image plane is the principal point. It is not automatically obvious on the negative or film positive. For this reason four fiducial marks are photographically recorded on the image at the moment of exposure, and the principal point is the intersection of these four marks when opposite marks are connected.

When film positives, or diapositives, of the object are used, as was the case with the system available for this project, the principal points are located and centered on the plate holders, the focal length of the camera is reproduced in the instrument and the space coordinates of the two camera stations are reproduced on the instrument.

For this project the plotting of the objects was done on a Galileo Officine Stereosimplex G5 stereoplotting instrument. A "freehand" planimetric compilation from the model was executed by means of a linear pantograph operated by the stereoplotter while examining the model through the binocular viewer. The pencil on the pantograph is automatically depressed and moved by controls on the main body of the instrument. Various scales of drawing which magnify the photograph scale are possible by manipulation of the pantograph triangulation.

When viewed through the binocular viewer of the stereoplotting instrument a three-dimensional image of the object is observed. Within the field of vision of each eyepiece is a black dot. When the controls are manipulated to fuse these two dots, both dots mark precisely the same point on the respective photographs and the dot that results appears to float as it is moved over the surface plane. It is the movement of this floating mark over the object plane that is recorded on the plotted drawing. The point of the pantograph and the floating mark correspond to the same point on the object mode. In the same way spatial coordinates on surfaces of the model can be determined by manipulations of the mark.

Just as binocular vision allows depth in the field of vision when compared with monocular vision, stereophotographing an object allows three-dimensionality in the image reproduction. This is accomplished by fusing two separate but overlapping perspective images into one three-dimensional representation of the object. Thus, to reproduce a three-dimensional image of the object photographed it is necessary to overlap photographic coverage of the object. A model of the object, or portion of the object, is then created in the stereoplotter using the two overlapping photographs. Generally, there is a 60% overlap of the areas on sequential photographs. This requirement for overlapping photographic coverage determines the number of photographs necessary at each site.

EXECUTED DOCUMENTATION DRAWINGS

As stated previously, the techniques used for this study were confined to those which could be accomplished using equipment and expertise available within the Virginia Department of Highways and Transportation, and by implication with other state departments of transportation.

Although a variety of structure types and site conditions were chosen for the study, the reduced drawings which follow illustrate structures only. The other resources and information sheets discussing the peculiarities of photographing each site are available in a report by this author, "The Photogrammetric Recording of Historic Transportation Sites."[9] The drawings are of the planimetric rather than the topographic type. Because the type of photogrammetric projects was quite different from that required for topographic mapping, the resourcefulness of the stereoplotting technicians was important. It was necessary for the research personnel to work closely with the stereoplotting technicians to communicate what the drawing should illustrate and how they should delineate certain portions of a few structures. The preparation and plotting time for these drawings was affected considerably by the unfamiliarity of the technicians with close-range mapping techniques.

It was decided to document the existing condition of the structures involved in this study to test (1) the resulting documentation of material deterioration and structural condition, and (2) the limits of the accuracy of the photogrammetric method. In the event that "as-built" drawings of a structure were preferred rather than "present condition" drawings, the documentation drawings produced to show existing condition could be altered. It would be an easy task to remove documented knicks and bends and replace missing material on the accurately dimensioned photogrammetric drawing.

The drawings included in this essay illustrate various stages in the compilation of the documentation drawings. The structure documentation first emerges in roughest form from the stereoplotter's delineation of the three-dimensional photographic model. Several drawings illustrate this initial stage. The very light pencil lines made by the stereoplotting instrument are defined next by the simple application of an ink outline. Some drawings need to have surfaces clearly delineated with a straightedge at this point. Several drawings illustrate this intermediate stage. Finally, the stereoplotted drawing goes to the draftsman for refinement. Several drawings illustrate this final stage. A case-by-case evaluation of these drawings will show advantages and disadvantages of this system.

CASE STUDY APPROACH

Case studies of a variety of resources were made. The specific resources examined were chosen to represent the following:

1. a cross section of transportation sites likely to be impacted by highway projects;
2. a selection of various types of materials and construction techniques which would test plotting capabilities; and,
3. a wide range of field conditions which would test the photogrammetric procedure.

Numerous sites were visited and studied, and the structures and objects listed in Table 7.1 and Table 7.2 were chosen to satisfy these requirements.

Phases of Research

The research was divided into several phases:

1. Data Acquisition
   a. reconnaissance
   b. photographic field work
   c. field measurement
2. Data Reduction
   a. photographic laboratory work
   b. stereoplotting

Table 7.1 *Transportation Structures*

Material	Type	County/City	Route	No. Spans	Length, Ft.
Metal	Pratt Truss	Nelson	653	1	138
Metal	Thacher Truss	Rockingham	1421	1	133
Metal	Pratt Truss	Shenandoah	758	3	359
Concrete (arch Spans)	Arch	Richmond	1 &301	16	3,290
Wood	Covered Truss	Alleghany	Nr. 60	1	108
Metal	Bedstead Pony Truss	Augusta	683	1	75
Concrete	Arch	Frederick	608	1	50
Metal	Bascule	Portsmouth		1	56
Brick & Wood	Beam	Nansemond	634	1	30

*1ft.= 0.3048m.

3. Data Analysis
   a. comparative documentation
   b. dimensional information

Data Acquisition

Initially, it was necessary to find sites within the state which were appropriate for the study. Each of the numerous sites visited had to be evaluated before the photogrammetric field work was done. Considerations were

1. accessibility of site,
2. visibility of site, and necessity for preliminary preparation,
3. orientation of site, and determination of optimal photography time,
4. requirements for special equipment, and,
5. determination of desirable views to be photographed.

The second phase of data acquisition was the photographic field work. This part of the study was under the direction of Fred Bales of the Location and Design Division of the Virginia Department of Highways and Transportation and employed a state-rented metric terrestrial photogrammetric camera. Only the camera would not normally be available in a modern transportation department. The essential steps in the field were

1. placing targets (reference points) on the object,
2. setting up camera stations on a line parallel with the object,
3. photographing the object, and,
4. recording distances between targets and elevations of discrete points on the object.

(Field information on individual sites is available in "The Photogrammetric Recording of Historic Transportation Sites" by the author, published by the Virginia Highway & Transportation Research Council.[10])

The third phase of data acquisition was the field measurement of several structures. The structures chosen were representative of the problems encountered in this type of field work. Areas to be measured were, for the most part, inconvenient to reach; sometimes it was impossible to reach an entire portion of a structure. Wading through streams, climbing on bridge members and abutments, and precariously positioning one's self for reading a dimensional measurement add time and the potential for inaccuracy to these measurements. Sites located in urban areas add the additional inconvenience and danger of vehicular traffic. Standard tools were used for these measurements, namely, rulers, steel tapes and calipers.

Data Reduction

Exposed photographic plates were taken to the lab for development. The results were positive prints on transparent material, or diapositives, which were positioned between two glass plates for use on the stereoplotter. The objects were delineated from a three-dimensional model created by viewing the two images simultaneously.

Data Analysis

Drawings emerged from the stereoplotter in rough form. Some were left in this rough stage and some were sent to the drafting section for refinement. The drawings were prepared to illustrate the development of a photogrammetric drawing. Each stage in the drawing process is represented in this essay.

Table 7.2 *Industrial and Historic Road Sites*

Type	Material	County
Industrial Sites:		
Mill	Brick, stone,concrete	Prince George
River navigation lock	Random stone	Fluvanna
Crozet Railroad tunnel	Cut stone	Augusta
Railroad culvert	Cut stone	Augusta
Historic Road Sites:		
Road trace	Earth	Albemarle
Road marker	Stone	Fluvanna
Bremo rest area	Stone	Fluvanna
White Post	Wood	Clark

Several site drawings were then chosen to be closely studied and compared with results of the traditional hand measured method. In addition to examining the potential for accurately and acceptably documenting structures by photogrammetric techniques, the potential to make broader applications of the photogrammetric field work was examined. Once the field work was completed, a three-dimensional record of the structures studied was on file for reference. Additional information which might be needed in the future could potentially be derived from the photogrammetric plates. For example, an extremely time-consuming element in the field inspection of structures, particularly of metal truss bridges, is measuring the cross-sectional area of individual members. To test the potential of using the photogrammetric method for this type of measurement, several sites were chosen for close analysis of the dimensional accuracy. The thickness of random areas of the structures was measured photogrammetrically and by hand. The photogrammetric dimensions were obtained from the same models used for the documentation drawings, with no additional preparation of the sites. Elevation readings of the points in question were made and compared with hand measurements of the same points to determine the accuracy of reading dimensions of depth from photogrammetric models.

ADDITIONAL APPLICATIONS OF THIS RESEARCH

While in the evaluation emphasis was placed on structures and objects of the type likely to be impacted by proposed transportation projects, the concept is applicable for many other types of structures, such as dams, power plants and buildings, and has in fact been used for such documentation of a variety of objects.[11,12] Recordation is only a small facet of potential photogrammetric applicability; not only is it possible to document existing intact structures but damaged structures of potential historic significance can be accurately recorded without resorting to approximate methods. This is particularly significant for structures made of nonstandard components. Several of the sites chosen for this study verify this assumption.

Of course, photogrammetric study is not restricted to historically significant sites. The present emphasis on bridge replacement and rehabilitation forces examinations of the load-carrying capacity of older bridges which may not necessarily be historically significant. The photogrammetric acquisition of data essential for structural analysis would have numerous advantages over tedious field measurement.

Close-range terrestrial photogrammetry can also have obvious uses in modern structural failure analysis. Since measurements are not restricted to a finite number of points moving only in one component of direction, it is possible to measure deformation in walls or individual members from the perspective of the whole structure. Suspect structures could be monitored without the use of strain gages. Also, initial field examination of damaged structures due to be reconstructed could be supplemented in the office with detailed examination of the photogrammetric studies. These additional applications were beyond the scope of this research project.

CASE STUDIES

Luten Concrete Arch Bridge

This simple, one-span concrete bridge, located in Frederick County, is of a type designed by Daniel Luten, and is typical of a number of small span highway bridges built throughout the United States in the early years of the twentieth century.

The structure is clearly delineated. Projecting surfaces are obvious from the perspective of the model view and the relationship of angled wing walls to the bridge structure is clear.

The Luten arch bridge drawing is an example of a well developed intermediate phase drawing (see Figure 7.1). Surfaces have been very clearly delineated in the application of ink outlines. Differentiation of planes and surfaces by varying line weights would be executed by the draftsman in the final refinement stage.

Pratt Truss Bridge

This bridge was built in 1882 and is one of the oldest metal truss bridges in Virginia and is listed on the National Register of Historic Places. It is located in Nelson County over the Southern Railroad. Metal truss bridges are composed of steel or iron components riveted together to make individual members, which are often connected at the panel joints by nuts and bolts. Because of this intricate configuration the advantages of photogrammetric documentation of structures can be seen clearly in metal truss bridge examples. In this drawing the location of all rivets and the configuration of all joints is delineated precisely.

The Pratt truss bridge drawing is an example of an early final stage drawing (see Figure 7.2). All truss members have been delineated, and the process of edge definition has been started. Additional definition by varying line weights would next be added by the draftsman.

Thacher Truss Bridge

This bridge, built in 1898, is the only Thacher truss in Virginia and is listed on the National Register of Historic Places. It is located in Rockingham County over the Linville Creek.

Several views of this bridge were photographed: a side elevation, an elevation of the portal end, and a close-up detail

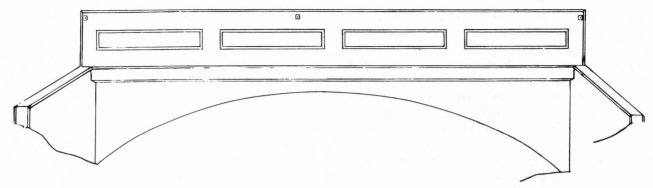

Figure 7.1. A late stage photogrammetric documentation drawing of a Luten concrete arch bridge.

of the L-3 joint connection. (This joint designation uses the conventional engineering system of numbering where U = upper chord connections, L = lower chord connections, and the sequence begins with 1 at the left side.) Each is presented at a different scale, showing the amount of structural detail possible by varying parameters in the field and in the lab. The decision as to how much detail is necessary depends on the requirements of the documentation. The advantages of photogrammetric documentation of historic structures are highlighted after close examination of these three views. All cables, rivets, pins and other components are precisely located on the structure. Locating all these by hand would take far more time, ingenuity and agility than was required for the photogrammetric field work on this bridge.

This site required clearing foliage in order to expose end posts and bearings; it also required maneuvering around barbed wire fences and through a shallow stream to set up the camera stations. All of these are typical problems encountered when documenting historic transportation structures.

The Thacher truss drawings represent different stages in the photogrammetric documentation process (see Figures 7.3, 7.4 and 7.5). The elevations of the side and portal have been defined with a straightedge and outlined with ink. A further refinement of these two views by a draftsman would be required. The joint detail drawing is a final stage documentation drawing which has been refined by a draftsman. The level of detail illustrated on this view (threads are visible on bolts) would be especially helpful in the rehabilitation analysis of a bridge or the reconstruction of transportation structures.

Bedstead Pony Truss Bridge

The Augusta County bedstead pony truss bridge is one of the few remaining true bedstead truss bridges in Virginia. The date of its erection is undocumented since the bridge date plate is missing, but the manufacturer is identified as the Champion Bridge Company of Wilmington, Ohio.

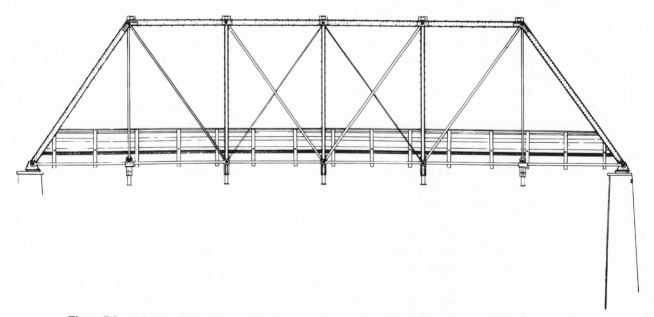

Figure 7.2. A late stage photogrammetric documentation drawing of the Nelson County 1882 Pratt truss bridge.

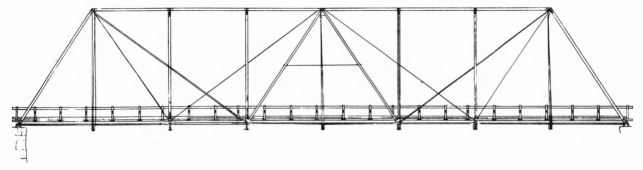

Figure 7.3. An intermediate stage photogrammetric documentation drawing of Virginia's only Thacher truss bridge, built in 1898.

Two elevation views and a very close-range joint detail view of L-1 were photographed. As with the Thacher truss bridge documentation, each view was presented at a different scale, showing the potential for illustration of detail by this method. All components of this bridge are accurately represented as they appear; that is, the rivets, turn buckles, and bolts are exactly located. An attempt has been made on the portal view elevation drawing to illustrate the precise location of corroded areas. The photogrammetric method of documentation has the advantage of not only pinpointing these areas and details but of storing this information for future reference. A detail which might seem irrelevant at the time of field inspection may be overlooked on first inspection. With photographic plates storing all views of the structure, necessary details can be recovered by a stereoscopic inspection in the office.

The bedstead truss documentation drawings illustrate intermediate stages of the photogrammetric documentation process (see Figures 7.6, 7.7 and 7.8). The elevation of the entire structure represents a slightly more refined stage, where the structure has been delineated in ink and further defined with a straightedge, and some line weight variation has begun. The portal elevation and the joint detail views are ex-

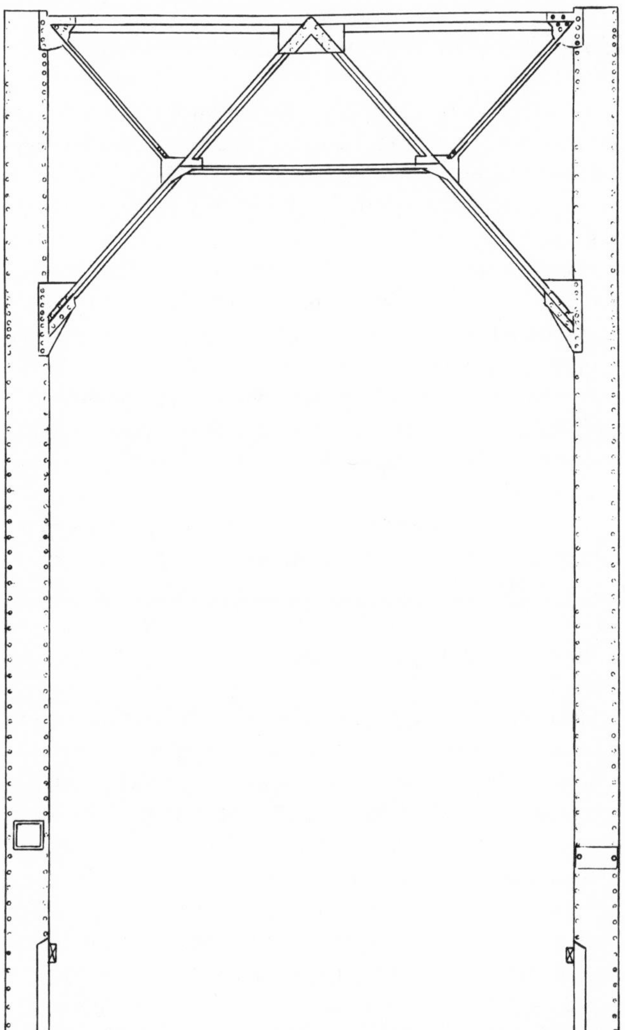

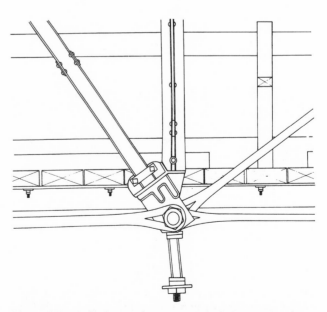

Figure 7.4. An intermediate stage photogrammetric documentation drawing of the portal view for the Thacher truss in Figure 7.3.

Figure 7.5. A final stage photogrammetric documentation drawing of a joint detail from the Thatcher truss in Figure 7.3.

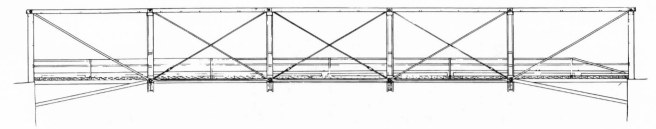

Figure 7.6.   An intermediate stage photogrammetric documentation drawing of a bedstead pony metal truss bridge.

Figure 7.7.   An intermediate stage photogrammetric documentation drawing of the portal view of the bedstead truss bridge in Figure 7.6.

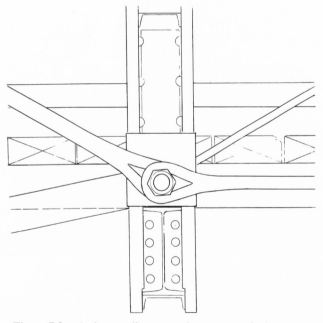

Figure 7.8.   An intermediate stage photogrammetric documentation drawing of a joint detail from the bedstead truss bridge in Figure 7.6.

amples of drawings which have been delineated by a straightedge and ink, with no accentuation treatment by a draftsman, as was done in Figure 7.5.

The bedstead truss bridge was chosen for the comparative analysis and will be discussed in greater detail in the next section.

Hodge's Ferry Bascule Bridge

The Hodge's Ferry bridge is located in Portsmouth, Virginia. It comprises beam spans and one bascule span which is one of the few remaining movable spans in Virginia. It is also the only Scherzer rolling lift highway bridge known to remain in the state.

The Scherzer rolling lift portion of the Hodges Ferry bridge was chosen for the photogrammetric study. Two views of the bascule are illustrated. Figure 7.9 is an elevation of the entire lift span photographed from a boat at rest in the river. Figure 7.10 is a close-range view of the moving portion, which consists of a circular, segmental, built-up girder, a counterweight, track, gears and chain. It was photographed from the bridge deck.

Both drawings illustrate the second stage of photogrammetric documentation drawing, where edges have been outlined and clearly defined with straightedges. The drawings would be given to a draftsman for further refinement as the last stage in the documentation of this portion of the bridge.

Site conditions are hazardous for this bridge, which is located in a congested suburban area. The dangers are twofold: vehicular traffic is heavy and areas of this section of the bridge are difficult to reach. The photographic field work was completed within one-half hour. Hand measurements of all the intricate details of this mechanism would be far more precarious and time-consuming and probably impossible. Consider what would be involved in order to obtain hand measurements information to produce a dimensionally correct drawing such as the end elevation of the Humpback Covered Bridge shown later in this essay. The Hodges Ferry bridge rocker arm portion (Figure 10) was chosen for comparative analysis and will be examined in greater detail in the following section.

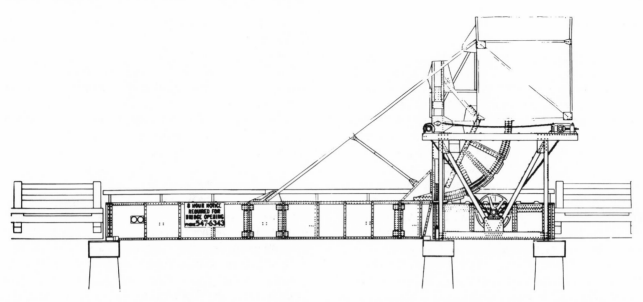

Figure 7.9. An intermediate stage photogrammetric documentation drawing of the Hodge's Ferry bridge bascule span, photographed from the water.

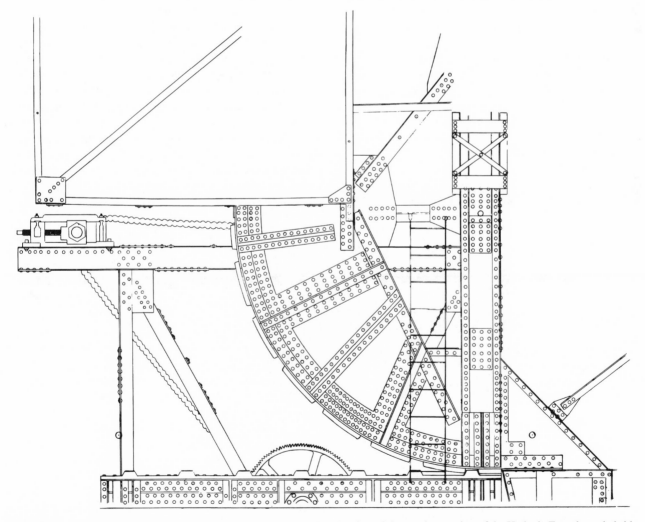

Figure 7.10. An intermediate stage photogrammetric documentation drawing of the moving portion of the Hodge's Ferry bascule bridge, photographed from the bridge deck.

Lee Bridge

The Robert E. Lee bridge is located in Richmond, Virginia. It is a concrete arch structure, built in 1934, which spans the James River, two railroads, two streets, and a canal. There are 16 open spandrel, double ribbed, reinforced concrete arches whose total length is 3,209 feet (978 m), and a series of concrete beams on the approach ends of the bridge. The entire Lee bridge is 3,710 feet (1,131 m) long.

The James River consists of two channels separated by Belle Isle at this site. The length of Lee bridge and the conditions of this site made it one of the most difficult sites to document. The depth of the James River prohibited the use of waders and forced manipulation in a boat. Portions of the bridge were obscured by very large trees and buildings, particularly on Belle Isle. Because of the experimental nature of this report it was decided to document nine of the arches in two parts. A portion of the four-arch section of Lee bridge north of Belle Isle is reproduced here as Figure 7.11, which is a well developed intermediate stage photogrammetric documentation drawing. All edges are clearly defined and the bridge's profile is well represented. The pierced parapet wall made this drawing a tedious and time-consuming subject for the stereoplotting technician. The end result, at this stage, is satisfying in quality and economy of time as hand measurement of this long span bridge would have been far more time consuming. This drawing would be further refined by a draftsman to complete the final stage documentation drawing.

Humpback Covered Bridge

The Humpback covered bridge near Covington is one of the few remaining covered wooden truss bridges in Virginia and reportedly one of only two "Humpbacks" in the United States. It was the only wood structure chosen for this study.

The documentation of the Humpback Bridge focuses on the three views which were photographed and drawn: an elevation of the portal end, an elevation of the entire structure and a close-range detail of the interior. Each view is shown in sequence, with the photogrammetric delineation following the traditional one. Figures 7.12 and 7.13 illustrate the portal end elevation. Figures 7.14–7.17 illustrate the structure elevation and interior detail.

The site conditions were typical of the bridges studied for this project. Several trees obstructed the view of the entire structure and it was necessary to cut away foliage which covered portions of the bridge. One camera station required maneuvering in a shallow stream to set up the equipment. Weather conditions were good and the photographic work was straightforward. The interior view was experimental, no additional lighting was introduced and the interior was quite dark. The interior photographs were exposed for 5 seconds and the resulting model produced a very good representation of the structural components of the wooden truss.

The documentation drawings of this bridge are very successful in illustrating the advantages of the photogrammetric documentation of historic structures. First, they illustrate the extensive coverage possible in one day of field work. Second, they illustrate the detail which can be accurately shown without precarious and time-consuming field measurements. Third, they document the existing condition of the structure and show all areas of deterioration. This last observation is only necessary in an accurate and complete survey or for rehabilitation or restoration purposes. It does, however, show the capacity for study and documentation of details by close-range terrestrial photogrammetry.

Figure 7.11.   A refined intermediate stage photogrammetric documentation drawing of a portion of the Robert E. Lee Bridge in Richmond, Virginia.

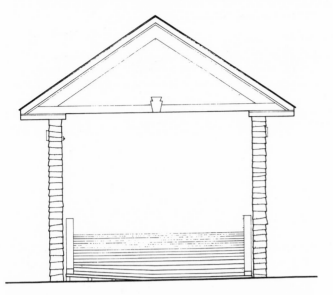

Figure 7.12. The HAER documentation drawing of the Humpback Covered Bridge, portal view, executed by the traditional technique using hand measurements.

Figure 7.13. The documentation drawing of the Humpback Covered Bridge, portal view, executed by the photogrammetric technique. This is a late stage photogrammetric documentation drawing.

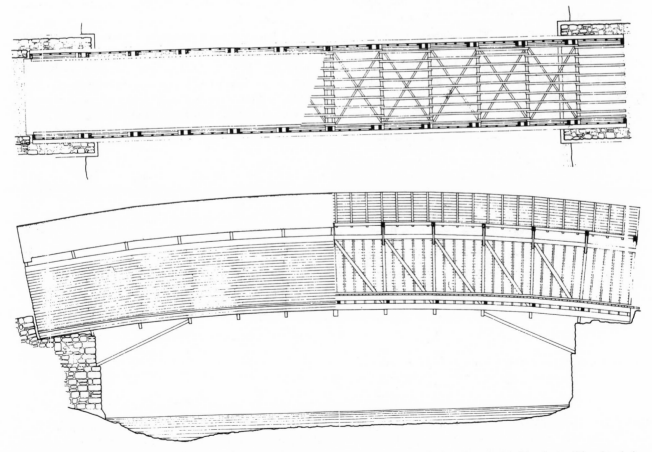

Figure 7.14. The HAER documentation drawing of the Humpback Covered Bridge, south elevation, executed by the traditional technique using hand measurements.

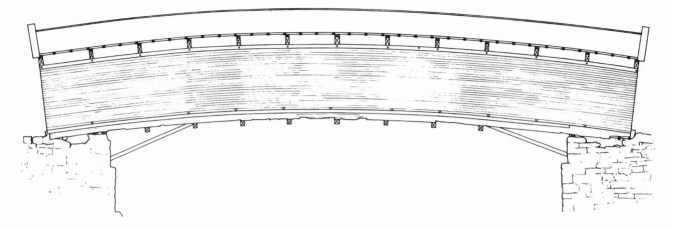

Figure 7.15. The documentation drawing of the Humpback Covered Bridge, south elevation, executed by the photogrammetric technique. This is a late stage photogrammetric documentation drawing.

The three views of the bridge also illustrate different stages in the process of delineating photogrammetric documentation drawings. Both the portal and side elevations are in the beginning of the refinement stage. Surfaces and edges are very clearly defined by the use of ink and straightedge, where appropriate. A more refined rendition of these two views would require greater definition of surfaces and a clearer distinction in line weight qualities. The interior view of the truss structure is just barely beyond the initial stage in the documentation process. It is a literal representation of the object as seen in the three-dimensional model viewed in the stereoplotter. The light pencil lines of the drawing have been outlined and a few edges of members have been clarified with the use of a straightedge. All gouges and rough edges in the wood are apparent.

The Humpback covered bridge was chosen for comparative analysis and it will be discussed in greater detail in the following section.

COMPARATIVE AND DIMENSIONAL ANALYSIS

The results of the photogrammetric documentation technique used in this study were analyzed from two perspectives. First, a comparison was made between documentation drawings produced by the photogrammetric method and the traditional hand measured method. Then, an analysis was made of the dimensional accuracy of the photogrammetric results. In this dimensional analysis comparisons were made between photogrammetric and hand measurements, both in the photographic plane of the object and perpendicular to

Figure 7.16. The HAER documentation drawing of the Humpback Covered Bridge, interior structural detail, executed by the traditional technique using hand measurements.

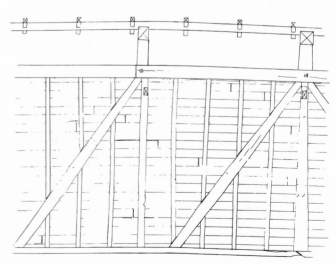

Figure 7.17. The photogrammetric documentation drawing of the interior structure of the Humpback Covered Bridge. This is an early stage photogrammetric documentation drawing.

that plane. A few photogrammetric models were studied in this manner to determine what types of dimensional information could be obtained from the steroscopic models of these sites. The results of these detailed analyses are presented in the following two sections.

Comparative Analysis

In the previous section examples of documentation drawings were illustrated. These examples showed the progression of stages in the production of photogrammetric documentation drawings.

A single site was chosen for a comparative analysis of photogrammetrically and traditionally produced drawings. The traditional drawings were produced by Historic American Engineering Record (HAER) of the Humpback Covered Bridge. Three views of the Humpback covered bridge (side elevation, portal elevation, interior structure) were compared.

The Humpback Covered Bridge: Portal/West Elevation

The most striking difference in the two drawings of this view is that the traditionally drawn view (Figure 7.12) portrays the structure as it was built, newly completed and in perfect condition, while the photogrammetrically drawn view (Figure 7.13) documents the structure in its present condition, which can be verified by a photograph. The present condition includes missing shingles and molding, large deteriorated areas of wood and termite damage in the lower left corner. The detailed documentation possible on a drawing of this scale (1″ [25 mm] = 1′ [300 mm]), with photographs taken from a distance of approximately 25 feet (7.6 m), is illustrated particularly well by the termite damaged area of the left end post and the nailhead positions shown over the entire structure.

This type of drawing probably would be considered too literal a representation of the structure by HAER, an organization whose responsibility is to document important historic American engineering and industrial sites. This agency uses traditionally produced drawings. The January 1981 *HAER Field Instruction Manuals* states:

> . . . drawings are generally considered to show the "as is" condition of a structure when it is drawn. Consequently, any portion of a drawing that fills in missing parts of a structure, or which partially reconstructs or restores a structure to anything other than its present condition, should be clearly noted, and the source or basis of such a construction should be cited as a footnote printed directly on the drawing.

These instructions are qualified later in the Manual with comments on several drawings:

> Precisely delineated, but too literal in recording the existing state of the structure. It's safe to assume the building wasn't built with holes in the floor and nothing important to the structure is communicated by recording the dilapidation in drawings (photographs can do that). One of the advantages of a measured drawing is the ability to "restore a site to its full integrity using adequate evidence and/or common sense. . . . Avoid the "Romantic Ruin" syndrome. Don't be so literal in recording a site that you end up drawing in broken windows, blown shingles and piles of junk. If the mullions remain in the window sashes, put the glass back in them in the drawings, etc. More extensive "restorations" should only be done where clear evidence can be cited. . . .[13]

Thus, if highway department mitigation agreements for impacted historically significant transportation sites required documentation to HAER standards, delineation of the structures in question would require some cosmetic restoration or replacement of deteriorated or missing materials on the drawing. This would demand far less time from the draftsman than drawings like this Humpback covered bridge portal drawing demanded. It would be a simpler task to delineate the structure in perfect condition than to show the precise location of damage and the exact size of irregularly shaped materials, like shingles, as was done in the execution of this drawing. The capability to produce either literal or nonliteral drawings is certainly available with the photogrammetric method. For example, most of the metal truss bridges and the concrete arch bridge in this study were delineated as they were built, since deterioration was minimal. (See previously described illustrations.)

The Humpback Covered Bridge: Side/South Elevation

The advantages of the traditional hand measured drawing method are more clearly illustrated by this comparative example. With the siding removed on half the bridge the truss structure is exposed on the traditionally produced drawing (Figure 7.14). Since this drawing is a compilation from hand-measured field notes, the combination of these two views into one drawing is only slightly more time-consuming than would be a single view. On the other hand, a composite view like this would require far more work from the photogrammetric method, and the photogrammetric drawing shows only the exterior (Figure 7.15). The only way to photograph the truss structure is from the interior (see Figure 7.17). Figure 7.17 illustrates barely two truss panels. This small model required two photographs because the camera-to-object distance was only 11 feet (3.4 m) and the camera coverage was, therefore, restricted. Documenting half the structural system would necessitate many setups, both with the camera in the field, and on the stereoplotter with stereopair photographic plates. In addition, a composite drawing made from models at the different scales which would result from differing object-to-camera distances would be very confusing and difficult to execute.

The plan view shown on the hand measured sheet would present the same problems in the field as documenting the interior structure would. The camera-to-object distance (this time to the bottom of the bridge from the water, with a vertical view) would be small enough to require numerous setups for documenting the Humpback covered bridge floor plan. Although the elevation of the entire bridge would necessitate far less field work by the photogrammetric method than by the traditional method, the nature of this site would require a combination of both methods for the efficient recording of the floor plan and half the truss structure.

The Humpback Covered Bridge: Interior Structural Detail

The interior structural detail comparative example shows disadvantages in the photogrammetric method, as did the previous view. The portions that are illustrated are very well documented in the photogrammetric drawing (Figure 7.17), but because the deck obscured the view below and the camera view prohibited including the roof structure, the structural detail is far more complete in the hand measured drawing (Figure 7.16). It would be necessary to supplement the photogrammetric field work with hand measurements to document the portions of the interior structure which could not be covered by photogrammetry alone.

The advantages of structural detail documentation produced by the photogrammetric method are better realized with analytical use than for archival purposes. To correctly analyze a truss the area of least cross section must be known. With the bird's eye view available on an executed photogrammetric drawing, the smallest cross-sections can be quickly and accurately pinpointed and the structural analysis can proceed with significantly less field time than traditional hand measurement would require.

The advantages of the photogrammetric system, however, are illustrated again by this example in the quality of the detail which can be precisely reproduced on a drawing. This can be seen in the nailheads protruding from members and in the gouges shown in the wood. The irregularity of the hand-hewn members also shows in the photogrammetric drawing.

Dimensional Analysis

The dimensional accuracy of the photogrammetric documentation method was examined on a case-by-case basis. Measurements of portions of the structures were compared both in the photographic, or surface plane of the objects and perpendicular to this plane, in the depth of the objects. The photographic plane dimensions were scaled directly from the photogrammetric drawings and compared with hand measurements taken in the field. The perpendicular plane dimensions were read from the photogrammetric models as elevation readings and compared with the hand measurements. These perpendicular dimensions were studied to check the accuracy of depth measurements taken from the photogrammetric models. The capacity to accurately measure depth, in this perpendicular plane, from stereopair photographs would allow member thickness, in addition to lengths and widths, to be measured from the stereoscopic models rather than from hand measurements taken in the field. Representative bridge sites were chosen for the case-by-case study of dimensional accuracy.

Photographic Plane Dimensions

The photographic plane dimensional analysis was an examination of the dimensional accuracy of the drawings themselves. This segment of the study compared measurements in the photographic plane of the objects. The sites chosen for analysis of accuracy in the photographic plane of the structure are listed below:

1. Bedstead pony truss bridge, side elevation and joint detail,
2. Luten concrete arch bridge, elevation.

The comparative results for these site measurements are found in Tables 7.3 through 7.5. Hand measurements taken in the field are listed in the first column of Tables 7.3 through 7.5, scaled measurements taken from the completed photogrammetric documentation drawings are listed in the second column. The difference in dimensions derived by both techniques was also viewed as a percentage of the total dimension for each measurement taken. It was necessary to consider this relative error in measurement since there was a large dimensional differential among these sites. As with the perpendicular plane measurements, a 1/4 inch (6 mm) error in a 2 inch (50 mm) measurement is far more significant than a 1/4 inch (6 mm) error in a 300 inch (7.6 mm) measurement.

The data from the photogrammetric documentation drawings were obtained directly with an engineer's scale. A problem encountered in this dimensional analysis and not in the following perpendicular dimensional analysis was due to the different scales at which the drawings were executed. Scaled measurements from a large structure, drawn at a scale to accommodate the structure on a standard drawing sheet, could be in error due to the thickness of a drawn line. This factor is probably the most significant cause for error in the following results, which are discussed site by site.

Augusta County Bedstead Pony Truss, Table 7.3

Table 7.3 shows the comparative results from hand and scaled measurements on the side elevation of this truss

Table 7.3 *Hand Measurement vs. Scaled Dimensional Comparison Augusta County Pony Truss (Figure 7.6)*

Hand Measurement, (feet)	Scaled Measurement (feet)	Difference (inches)
1. 5.948	5.95	0.024
2. 0.932	0.90	0.384
3. 7.51	7.50	0.120
4. 7.52	7.55	0.360
5. 7.54	7.50	0.480
6. 7.51	7.45	0.720
7. 7.54	7.475	0.780
8. 0.526	0.50	0.312
9. 0.422	0.40	0.264
10. 0.531	0.550	0.228
11. 0.599	0.575	0.288
12. 0.797	0.80	0.036
13. 0.500	0.475	0.300
14. 4.740	4.725	0.180
15. 15.290	15.300	0.120

NOTE: 1 ft. = 0.3048 m
1 in. = 25.4 mm

Table 7.4 *Hand Measurement vs. Scaled Dimensional Comparison Augusta County Pony Truss Detail (Figure 7.8)*

Hand Measurement, (in.)	Scaled Measurement (in.)	Difference (in.)
1. 2.3125	2.3	0.0125
2. 3.9375	3.9	0.0375
3. 0.2500	0.3	0.0500
4. 1.7500	1.7	0.0500
5. 5.1875	5.3	0.1125
6. 2.375	2.3	0.0750
7. 9.500	9.45	0.050
8. 6.000	6.05	0.050
9. 0.375	0.40	0.025
10. 14.500	14.5	0
11. 5.625	5.4	0.225
12. 2.167	2.05	0.117

NOTE: 1 in. = 25.4 mm

bridge. The initial reaction to the large errors, in contrast to the errors found in the perpendicular dimensions, is that the results show large inaccuracies in the drawings. Some of the hand and scaled measurements differ by as much as 3/4 inch (19 mm), as compared with the largest error of approximately 1/4 inch (6 mm) in perpendicular plane dimensional comparisons. When the larger difference of 3/4 inch (19 mm) is considered as a percentage of the total dimension, and in light of the scale at which the drawing was executed, the results are better.

This elevation was drawn at a scale of 1″ = 3′ (25 mm = 900 mm). At this scale the thickness of a pen line can measure as much as 1 inch (25 mm). This single factor could certainly account for the larger order of error found in these dimensional comparisons.

From an error percentage perspective, the results are also favorable. Nine of 15 measurements (60%) show errors of less than 2%; 13 of 15 measurements show errors of less than 5%. The two measurements with errors greater than 5% are measurements of very small dimensions and could be in error due to the thickness of a pen line. The errors in this comparative dimensional analysis would probably be reduced if the bedstead truss elevation drawing was executed at a larger scale, as is the detail drawing in the following example.

Augusta County Bedstead Pony Truss Joint Detail, Table 7.4

The order of error in the Augusta County joint detail view is less than in the Augusta County bedstead truss side elevation drawing. These results are listed in Table 7.4, which shows that differences in hand and scaled measurements ranged from no difference to the largest at 1/4 inch (6.35 mm). The only inordinately large difference is a 20% error,

although it appears insignificant (0.05 inch [1.27 mm]) in the Table 7.4 listing. As discussed in numerous examples, measurements of the order of this one, that is, less than 1 inch (25.4 mm), were not reliably determined by the photogrammetric technique with the equipment used in this project. In other examples this error was primarily due to corrosion and paint build-up of up to 3/8 inch (9.5 mm). For this site detail drawing, small measurements are also unreliable due to reading error from the thickness of the line that defines the detail. The scale at which the joint detail is drawn is 2″ = 1′ (50 mm = 300 mm). At this scale, the thickness of a pen line can measure as much as 0.15 inch (3.8 mm). Thus, the potential for error in a small dimension is obvious.

For measurements of larger dimensions the results are good. The portion that measured 14.5 inches (368 mm) registered as precisely 14.5 inches (368 mm) in both hand and scaled measurements. Sixty-seven percent of the errors in measurement were less than 1/8 inch (3.2 mm).

The dimensional comparative results from hand and scaled measurements were favorable in this case, even though the photography was poor due to weather conditions. The documentation drawing produced by the photogrammetric method, then is as accurate as a hand measured documentation drawing, given a reasonable scale drawing and a small camera-to-object distance.

Luten Concrete Arch Bridge, Table 7.5

The camera-to-object distance at this site was significantly larger than the distances in the previous few examples. The field work was done 48 feet (14.6 m) from the bridge. Because of the small span of the bridge, it was plotted, or drawn, at a scale of 1″ = 1′ (25 mm = 300 mm).

Comparative results for hand and scaled measurements were good, except for the measurement of a very small dimension (less than 1 inch [25.4 mm]). This 3/4 inch (19 mm) measurement was in error by 20%, while the other measure-

Table 7.5 *Hand Measurement vs. Scaled Dimensional Comparison Luten Concrete Arch (Figure 7.1)*

Hand Measurement, (feet)	Scaled Measurement (feet)	Difference (in.)
1. 27.86	27.80	0.72
2. 3.04	2.98	0.72
3. 26.25	26.14	1.32
4. 0.70	0.56	1.68

NOTE: 1 ft. = 0.3048 m
            1 in. = 25.4 mm

ments compared at less than 2% error. As cited many times in the discussion of dimensional accuracy, for measurements of such small dimensions the error inherent in the system is far too great to give reliable results. Errors in the field can result from large corrosion and paint build-up, while errors from the photogrammetric drawing can result from the scale of the drawing and the thickness of a drawn line. A higher accuracy would certainly be expected for small dimensional measurements, if the range of photography were much closer.

Perpendicular Plane or Cross-Sectional Dimensions

The sites chosen for analysis of accuracy in the perpendicular plane tested the capacity to obtain depth, or thickness, dimensions. Ultimately, this technique would be used to measure cross-sectional areas of members. The two sites used for this perpendicular plane portion of the study are listed below:

1. Bedstead pony truss bridge, side elevation and joint detail,
2. Hodge's Ferry bascule bridge, rocker arm detail,

The comparative results for these site measurements are found in Tables 7.6 through 7.8. Photogrammetric data are listed in the second column of the tables as machine elevation readings. Hand measurements are listed in the third column, and the differences between the two are listed in the last column as fractions of inches.

The photogrammetric data were obtained in the lab with the photogrammetric stereopair models of the sites located in the stereoplotting machine. The method used was an adaptation of the techniques used by the Virginia Location and Design Division for the production of topographic maps. Simplistically described, this technique records height differences among discrete points with respect to a referenced low point or zero elevation.

After the documentation drawings were completed the designated stereopair photographs used for that process were reoriented in the stereoplotting machine. No additional field work was necessary for this phase of the study. Thickness dimensions were derived from the stereoscopic model of the structure established by the stereopair photographs in the stereoplotting machine. The thickness of carefully specified components of the chosen structure were determined from relative elevation readings between the high (or front) and low (or back) surfaces of each designated component. These precisely located points were then measured by hand on the structures and the results were compared.

Problems were encountered in obtaining both photogrammetric and field measurements. Since the photogrammetric method is a photographic process, the quality of photography was very important for this detailed analysis. Poor conditions included overcast and rainy weather and grainy photographs resulting from a large camera-to-object distance. In some cases shadows were cast in the photographs and elevation readings were partly obscured because there was no definite point in the background to which the technician could reference. The deteriorated state of the structures was another problem. In many areas the corrosion and rust buildup was such that it was extremely difficult to get accurate readings either on the stereoscopic model or in the field. Additional problems in the field included the inaccessibility of some areas and hazardous conditions at the site.

Augusta County Bedstead Pony Truss, Table 7.6

The limits of the photogrammetric method were tested most by this site. Field conditions for the photogrammetric work were poor. The sky was very overcast during the photographing of the side elevation; the photographs suffered from a dark sky and from a large object-to-camera distance. These side views were photographed from 55 feet (16.8 m). The result was a stereoscopic model on which detailed read-

Table 7.6 *Cross-Sectional Dimensional Comparison Augusta County Pony Truss (Figure 7.6)*

Location No.	Machine Elevation Reading. (in.)	Hand Measurement (in.)	Difference, (in.)
1.	2.172	2.187	0.015
2.	1.692	1.813	0.121
3.	1.224	1.375	0.151
4.	2.328	2.313	0.015
5.	2.292	2.250	0.042
6.	1.296	1.359	0.063
7.	4.260	4.250	0.010
8.	3.528	3.469	0.059
9.	3.960	3.750	0.210
10.	2.040	2.000	0.040
11.	0.972	1.000	0.028
12.	2.316	2.375	0.059
13.	12.000	12.016	0.016
14.	0.888	0.906	0.018
15.	2.772	2.875	0.103
16.	1.620	1.688	0.068
17.	6.792	6.875	0.083

NOTE· 1 in. = 25.4 mm

ings were difficult. Elevation readings were taken to 1/1000 inch (0.0254 mm), but the reading for the last decimal place was largely estimated. Comparative measurements were made at 17 randomly distributed locations.

Considering the field conditions, the results were quite good. Four of the 17 readings were difficult to read in the lab and in the field due to rust and paint buildup. These were at locations 2, 3, 9, and 15. The largest error in this group is almost 1/4 inch (6.35 mm), which is a considerable error on a measurement of 3-3/4 inches (95.25 mm). Aside from these 4 erratic readings, all other errors are below 1/8 inch (3.18 mm), or 0.125 inch (3.18 mm). On a structure which has areas of corrosion buildup over 1/4 inch (6.35 mm), it would be unreasonable to expect greater accuracy. The very best readings on this site were accessible and easy to read both in the lab and in the field. These were for locations 1, 4, 7, and 14, with errors of about 1/64 inch (0.40 mm). These 4 readings cluster near 1% error, when the difference in dimensions derived by both techniques is considered as a percentage of the total dimension. Fourteen of 17 (82%) of the readings were below 5% in error and 11 of 17 (65%) of the readings were below 3% in error.

Augusta County Bedstead Pony Truss Joint Detail, Table 7.7

The problems encountered during the field work for the side elevation discussed above were compounded in the joint detail by a rainstorm which began as setup for the detail view started. Despite the fact that the camera-to-object distance was significantly smaller (12.72 feet [3.88 m]), the weather conditions were worse and resulted in very poor quality photographs. The readings on a site with such a small camera-to-object distance should have been extremely good. Obscured areas on the detail accounted for one very poor reading, which was off by almost 22%, and some otherwise erratic readings. Since this was a close-up of a truss joint detail, dimensions considered were generally far smaller than in the

Table 7.7 *Cross-Sectional Dimensional Comparison Augusta County Pony Truss Joint Detail View (Figure 7.8)*

Location No.	Machine Elevation Reading, (in.)	Hand Measurement (in.)	Difference (in.)
1.	1.032	1.000	0.032
2.	1.944	1.969	0.025
3.	0.456	0.375	0.081
4.	2.1096	2.2125	0.015
5.	7.2876	7.250	0.0376
6.	1.4496	1.406	0.0436
7.	0.336	0.3125	0.0235
8.	0.462	0.500	0.038
9.	2.352	2.375	0.023
10.	8.844	8.875	0.031

NOTE: 1 in. = 25.4 mm

previous example. Some measurements were as small as 3/8 inch (9.52 mm). Thus, errors of 1/8 inch (3.18 mm) are significantly greater in this example than in the side elevation of the truss. On first inspection, Table 7 shows excellent comparative results, with all but one difference in measurements being less than 1/16 inch (1.59 mm). From a strictly analytical perspective, these results are less acceptable when considered as error percentages. One reading is 22% in error, two others are approximately 7% in error. At the same time, 70% of the readings are 3% or less in error. With field conditions at the Augusta County bedstead truss site presenting the problems described above, the results of the comparative dimensional analysis, although complicated by erratic readings, show that the photogrammetric technique has promise in its potential for taking cross-sectional area measurements.

Hodge's Ferry Bascule Bridge, Table 7.8

The rocker arm detail of the Hodge's Ferry movable bascule span was selected for the dimensional analysis because it is an example of a site which would be prohibitively time-consuming to hand measure. This view was illustrated in Figure 7.9. This section of the bridge is made up entirely of riveted components and would involve many tedious hand measurements.

Field conditions for the photogrammetric work were good. The weather was perfect and camera-to-object distance was only 24.6 feet (7.5 m). The major problem was that the bridge was heavily traveled by vehicular traffic and the work required setting up the camera on the span itself. This

Table 7.8 *Cross-Sectional Dimensional Comparison Hodge's Ferry Bascule Bridge (Figure 7.10)*

Location No.	Machine Elevation Reading, (in.)	Hand Measurement (in.)	Difference, (in.)
1.	4.488	4.5156	0.0276
2.	4.872	4.875	0.003
3.	0.384	0.375	0.009
4.	0.696	0.750	0.054
5.	0.372	0.375	0.003
6.	3.192	3.250	0.058
7.	2.700	2.6875	0.0125
8.	5.616	5.625	0.009
*9.	2.496	Impossible to reach	
*10.	5.064	4.84375	0.22025
11.	9.036	9.0625	0.0265
12.	5.604	5.5625	0.0415
13.	4.848	4.750	0.098
14.	59.964	59.96875	0.00475
15.	5.520	5.500	0.020
16.	2.736	2.6875	0.0485
17.	0.300	0.3125	0.0125
18.	0.408	0.375	0.033
19.	0.684	0.6875	0.0035
20.	1.092	1.125	0.033

*data rejected
NOTE: 1 in. = 25.4

heavy traffic also posed additional problems in the field work for the hand measurements. Hand measuring this site required maneuvering on beams with no bridge deck cover, as well as being on the bridge with fast moving, frequent vehicular traffic. Also, corrosion build-up was a problem in some portions of the bridge.

From a strictly technical perspective, the photogrammetric field conditions were excellent and resulted in very good quality photographs and accurate readings. Because the model was so clearly defined it was easy to specify the precise points to be measured and compared. Just as the Augusta County pony truss tested the limits of the system under poor conditions, this example tested the limits under good conditions.

As seen in Table 7.8, data points from two locations were rejected: one because it was impossible to measure by hand as the member projected over the water with no support near it (9) and the other because the point was in shadow and so difficult to read on the stereopair model that the reading was unreliable (10).

Table 7.8 lists comparative results in measurements. The hand and photogrammetric measurements are very close. Using the valid data points, all measurements show under 1/8 inch (3.18 mm) difference between hand and machine measurements. Of these 18 data points, 8 show less than 1/64 inch (0.40 mm) difference, 3 show less than 1/32 inch (0.79 mm) difference, and 6 others show less than 1/16 inch (1.59 mm) difference between field measurements and machine readings.

An examination of the data on an error percentage basis shows 16 of 18 (89%) of the data points below 4% error in measurement. The two points which are over 4% error are measurements of very small dimensions 3/4 inch (19.05 mm) and 3/8 inch (9.52 mm) and the fractional errors are considerable, even though they are only 0.054 inch (1.37 mm) and 0.033 inch (0.84 mm), respectively. The comparative measurements for components on the Hodge's Ferry bridge show that the photogrammetric method is potentially a reliable technique for making cross-sectional measurements on structures.

SUMMARY AND DISCUSSION

The documentation drawings illustrated in this essay clearly show that the ability to produce documentation drawings by a photogrammetric procedure is within the capability of the Department of Highways and Transportation if a proper camera is available. These drawings of representative historic structures demonstrate all stages in the photogrammetric drawing production technique by illustrating varying degrees of refinement in the drafting process. Several drawings show literal representations of the photogrammetric models of the structures. These drawings were reproduced as they were completed from the stereoplotting machine, with no attempt to make them into presentation drawings. The documentation drawings of other sites were delineated by a draftsman to varying degrees of refinement, thus demonstrating the process from beginning to end.

This study has shown numerous advantages of the photogrammetric method. Information recorded on photographs is stable and comprehensive. Since the method is a precise photographic technique, all the information ever potentially desired from a site is permanently stored with the exposed photogrammetric plates. This fact would allow flexibility in the planning of a survey or documentation program for historic highway structures since the drafting and other labor intensive operations could be scheduled to avoid peak work loads. With minimal field work, rapid and relatively simple inventories of structures can be completed while storing the potential to document or analyze in detail the structures inventoried. Traditional methods for inventories and documentation drawings require many person-hours of field work initially to obtain hand measurements of the structures. In a climate of reduced staff, this capability is particularly significant. Also, the supplementary photographic coverage normally used in the traditional hand measured methods can be minimized.

The discussion of the executed documentation drawings in the previous two sections set forth a satisfactory comparison between photogrammetrically and traditionally produced documentation drawings. It was shown in these comparisons that the recordation of a structure in whatever form desired is possible. Examples like the Humpback covered bridge portal elevation illustrate literal "as is" representations of a structure. Although this literal form of recording may not be desirable from an aesthetic point of view, from an engineering perspective and for highway department use, the ability to document the literal condition of a structure would be very valuable. A literal representation of the three-dimensional photogrammetric model allows damaged areas to be precisely pinpointed with minimal field work.

The dimensional comparison in the last section showed that additional information can be obtained from the stereoscopic models created from stereopair photographs. In that section a preliminary analysis of the potential for reading cross-sectional areas of members from these models showed positive results. For highway department use this damage and dimensional information would be valuable in the analysis and maintenance of historically significant sites, as well as for other types of structures. On the other hand, if the documentation of a deteriorated structure required an "as-built" drawing, delineation of the structure in question would not be literally recorded from the photogrammetric model. Instead, deteriorated or missing materials could be modified on the drawing by the draftsman, while the information of the literal condition of the structure would remain in storage on the photogrammetric plates. In cases of extreme historic significance, the photogrammetric delineation could certainly provide the skeleton for a more aesthetically pleasing and sensitive drawing, if required.

The question of which type of documentation is preferred is tied to philosophical issues in the field of historic preservation. On one side of the issue is the desire for a strong, well articulated, and aesthetically pleasing representation of the historic site in question. On the other side of the issue is the need for absolutely accurate representations of structures for analytical and rehabilitative purposes. It has been the frustrating experience of more than one engineer working on historic sites to have to return to the site to remeasure dimensions because of inaccurate or illegible hand notes of the "cosmetic" restoration in a drawing.

Because the engineering community appears to be awakening to the need to preserve its heritage, an understanding of the valid requirements of both sides of the issue is necessary and a compromise is possible. Certainly the potential for both accurate and aesthetically pleasing renditions exists using photogrammetric recording techniques.

This study has shown that with minimal time in the field the photogrammetric method produces the ability to document structures in a very precise and detailed manner, and potentially of a quality acceptable to the agency which requires the documentation.

However, in order to be able to work within the existing structure of a highway department, several problems inherent in the use of the photogrammetric method must be addressed. These can be mitigated with additional experience, equipment and training. Three types of problems emerged as this research progressed: those in the field work, those in the lab and those in the structures themselves.

The sites were chosen to include a range of field conditions that would test the photogrammetric procedures. Imagination and ingenuity were required to record a number of sites. It was necessary to set up in streams, on boats, on structures accommodating heavy vehicular traffic, above the sites in cherry pickers and in remote and inaccessible places. Obstructions often required spending time clearing a site before the photogrammetric setup could begin. The demands of the field conditions in this study could certainly coincide with field conditions in any typical survey or documentation program. Therefore, it would be extremely difficult to follow one specific procedural guideline for documenting historic sites. Flexibility in the approach to various sites would be necessary. Clearly, the ability to rectify oblique photos would mitigate this situation to some extent.

This study also showed that the photogrammetric method is weather dependent. The quality of photography was very important, particularly at close range, for the technicians to be able to delineate the photogrammetric model. Lab work on the Augusta County bedstead truss bridge site, for example, was tedious and more time-consuming because the photographs were exposed in dark, rainy weather and were not of as good quality as the photographs at other sites. This can be overcome with proper scheduling.

Additional problems became apparent in the lab. The stereoplotting technicians were unaccustomed to executing planimetric renditions of structures. It was necessary to supplement the photogrammetric coverage with close-up standard photographs of details of the sites in order for the stereoplotting technicians to delineate the structures accurately. These supplemental detail photographs were essential for successful recordation.

The last problem encountered is inherent in the nature of historic sites. Some of the structures studied were badly deteriorated. Rust and paint build-up on the metal structures were severe in areas. Stone structures were chipped and cracked and wooden structures were rotted or missing parts. This factor complicated gathering the data for the comparison of dimensional accuracy in photogrammetric and hand-measured methods. Despite this, the potential to accurately obtain dimensional data from photogrammetric models, both in the photographic and perpendicular planes, was demonstrated.

It was impossible to obtain elevation readings for some metal truss members which were thin and contrasted against the sky. In order to read cross-sectional data for metal truss bridges in future uses of the photogrammetric method, black targets ought to be attached to the backs of members. This is necessary to give a reference point for reading elevations on the backs of those members with only sky behind them; it is otherwise very difficult to tell where the member ends in the perpendicular plane. These black targets could be magnetized, as could those used on the face of the structure, and the setup for photogrammetric recording would proceed with little additional work.

The precision of measurements was limited because of structural deterioration. To determine stringent limits of the dimensional accuracy in the photogrammetric method, additional tests should be conducted on nondeteriorated sites where rust and paint build-up would not complicate the determination of accuracy. Good comparative results were also limited by the size of the measurements used; very small measurements should always be supplemented by a check with hand measurements, as accuracy with measurements under 1 inch (25.4 mm) was very poor with the type of equipment used in this project. If more sophisticated, microprocessor digitizer equipment had been available, results would have been more reliable.

In some cases, the unfamiliarity of the stereoplotting technicians and the draftsmen with this type of rendering made it necessary to work closely with them to communicate what the drawings should illustrate. The skills of the technicians were challenged by this project. In a few instances the standard procedures used in ordinary work, for example, standard use of ballpoint pens, were unacceptable for the purposes of this study. For these reasons it is strongly recommended that procedural guidelines and drafting requirements be established and appropriate training be executed for the personnel executing photogrammetric documentation drawings, should additional photogrammetric recordation of historic sites be desired.

This study has shown that it is feasible to document historic structures by use of close-range terrestrial photogrammetry. This method of documentation can be successfully applied within the capability (assuming a proper camera) of local highway departments to produce very precise documentation drawings and, with little additional work and some modification of drafting guidelines, renderings acceptable to other agencies can be produced. If desired, the results of the photogrammetric documentation fieldwork can provide additional information about the structures. Thus the applicability of the photogrammetric documentation procedure is broader than solely the production of documentation drawings.

CONCLUSIONS

Based upon this study the folllowing conclusions have been reached:

1. Documentation by photogrammetric methods is applicable to, and of sufficient accuracy, for a wide variety of structures and sites and is very cost-effective by reducing person-hours required for hand measurements, traffic control, and scaffolding.

2. With the exception of the camera and rectifying equipment, the production of documented drawings photogrammetrically is within the capacity of currently available equipment in most, if not all, departments of transportation.

3. A major advantage of the photogrammetric method is that the most critical phase (obtaining the field data) is the least labor intensive phase. By traditional methods this is the most labor intensive operation.

ENDNOTES

1. U.S. Department of Transportation, Federal Highway Administration, "Memorandum HNG-30," unpublished memorandum dated Sept. 5, 1980.
2. Slama, Chester C., ed., *Manual of Photogrammetry*. 4th ed. Falls Church, VA: American Society of Photogrammetry, 1980, 5.
3. Gomer T. McNeil, *ABCs of Photogrammetry, Part I: Fundamentals*. Ann Arbor, MI: Edwards Brothers, Inc., 1950, 1.01–1.02.
4. Slama, *Manual of Photogrammetry*.
5. Ibid.
6. Borchers, Perry E., "Photogrammetric Recording of Cultural Resources." Washington, D.C.: Technical Preservation Services Division, Office of Archeology and Historic Preservation, National Park Service, U.S. Department of the Interior, 1977.
7. Hilton, Marvin H., and Fred B. Bales, "Application of Close-Range Photogrammetry to Bridge Structures," Virginia Highway and Transportation Research Council, in preparation.
8. Slama, *Manual of Photogrammetry*.
9. Spero, Paula A. C., "The Photogrammetric Recording of Historic Transportation Sites. Charlottesville, VA: Virginia Highway and Transportation Research Council, June 1983.
10. Ibid.
11. Agnard, Jean-Paul and Sanfacon Roland. "Photogrammetric Study of French Architecture." Proceedings of the Symposium on Close-Range Photogrammetric Systems. Falls Church: American Society of Photogrammetry, 1975, pp. 1–3.
12. Borchers, Perry E., "Photogrammetric Recording of Cultural Resources." Washington, D.C.: Technical Preservation Services Division, Office of Archeology and Historic Preservation, National Park Service, U.S. Department of the Interior, 1977.
13. Historic American Engineering Record, Field Instructions. Heritage Conservation and Recreation Service. Washington, DC: U.S. Department of the Interior, 1981, pp. 34–35.

CHAPTER 8

Remote Sensing Technology Applied To Site Documentation

Ronald W. Eck

INTRODUCTION

Remote sensing can be defined as the detection, recognition or evaluation of objects or features without actually being in contact with those objects. Our eyes are remote sensors, as are telescopes and cameras mounted underneath an aircraft. Sensors can be further subdivided into photographic sensors, cameras and nonphotographic sensors, thermal scanners and airborne radar. In this chapter, emphasis will be on the use of aerial photography as the principal type of remote sensing imagery because of its availability and widespread use. However, some of the other types of imagery will also be discussed.

Remote sensing is an important tool for engineers, archaeologists, geographers, planners and others concerned with discovery, evaluation and preservation of historic sites or environments. Remote sensing provides a systematic means of seeking out features that previously were discovered only by accident. In addition, the photographs or images themselves become historic documents representing conditions that existed at a particular point in time.

The purpose of this chapter is to provide an overview of the capabilities, limitations and the basic principles of remote sensing data collection and interpretation as applied to the field of industrial archaeology. The chapter is not intended to be an in-depth treatment of the rapidly evolving discipline of remote sensing. References are provided for readers seeking more detailed information.

The chapter is organized into three main sections. The first section describes some common remote sensors and their characteristics. The second section discusses interpretation techniques with particular emphasis on human modification of the natural environment. The third section describes some applications of remote sensing to industrial archaeology, including two case study examples.

SENSORS AND THEIR CHARACTERISTICS

Aerial Photography

The oldest, and by far the most widely used remote sensor, is aerial photography. Aerial photographs have special potential as a source of historical information because of the detailed and exact record of the site that they can provide. Aerial photographs are complementary to maps but have a number of advantages not shared by them:

1. Aerial photographs are often available for many dates while maps are usually available for only a few dates.
2. Aerial photographs are true to the date of photography while maps may not have been fully revised to their nominal dates.
3. Aerial photographs show all visible features from the air, including buildings, structures and the character of the ground surface and its vegetation. Maps are selective and usually give little information on the character of the ground and its vegetation.
4. Aerial photographs show features as they actually were, with some information on the elevation of buildings and structures. Maps show them by conventional representation, in plan only.

Types of Aerial Photographs

There are several different types of aerial photographs. Vertical photographs are photographs taken with the axis of the camera held in a vertical or near vertical position, that is, perpendicular to the surface of the earth. Because such images are so useful for mapping and interpretation, the term aerial photo is usually, (at least in U.S. practice), assumed to mean a vertical photograph. Overlapping exposures in a flight line allow an interpreter to study vertical photographs three-dimensionally with a stereoscope (to be discussed in more detail later in this chapter).

Oblique photographs are images taken with the camera angle intentionally tilted from vertical. An image containing the horizon of the earth is termed a high oblique. One that does not contain the horizon is called a low oblique. While an oblique photograph covers a larger area than a vertical photograph from the same altitude, its usefulness is limited. This is because the scale varies throughout the image and because images do not readily lend themselves to stereoscopic viewing. Since the vantage point is readily identifiable, oblique photos are useful in orienting laypersons to particular projects or locations.

A mosaic is an assembly of individual photographs that are cut, matched and pasted together to form a single large print. A mosaic assembled by reference to known points on the ground is called a controlled mosaic. If there is not ground control of linear distances, the mosaic is said to be uncontrolled. When carefully assembled, both types of mosaics provide good map approximations. Controlled mosaics are expensive and cannot be studied three dimensionally. However, they are useful for plotting site locations, for settlement pattern analysis and for vegetative zone studies.

Scale of Aerial Photographs

Lillesand and Kiefer[1] note that the amount of detail shown in an aerial photograph depends, among other things, on the scale of the photograph. They point out that a photographic

scale, like a map scale, is an expression that states that one unit of distance on a photograph represents a specific number of units of actual ground distance. It is important to remember that the same objects are smaller on a "smaller" scale photograph than on a "larger" scale photograph (1:50,000 is a smaller scale than 1:10,000).

When the objectives of a particular aerial survey have been clearly defined, the choice of image scale will depend on allowable expenditures, minimum resolution requirements and desired area coverage per frame. In general, photographic imagery provides ground resolution that is superior to other types of remote sensing imagery.

Photographic resolution has been defined[2] as the capability of an entire photographic system (lens, film, processing, etc.) to render a defined image. The ground area covered by a given exposure or frame is a function of the negative format size, the camera focal length and the flight altitude above the ground. Figure 8.1 illustrates ground coverage for a 9 x 9-inch negative format at three different altitudes above the ground.

Films

The tone and quality of an image depend on the spectral reflectance of the objects being photographed and the sensitivity of film emulsions to varying wavelengths of reflected light. Light wavelengths are measured in micrometers; the portion of the electromagnetic spectrum visible to the human eye encompasses wavelengths of about 0.4 to 0.7 micrometers as shown in Figure 8.2. To discriminate between features

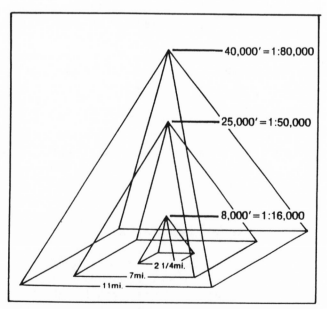

Figure 8.1. Ground coverage as a function of altitude for a 6-inch camera focal length. (Lyons, T.R. and Avery, T.E. Remote Sensing: A Handbook for Archaeologists and Cultural Resource Managers. Washington, D.C.: National Park Service, 1977).

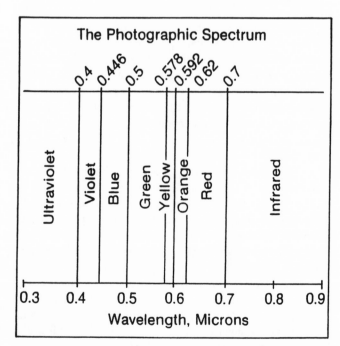

Figure 8.2. Photographic portion of the electromagnetic spectrum. (Lyons, T.R. and Avery, T.E. Remote Sensing: A Handbook for Archaeologists and Cultural Resource Managers. Washington, D.C.: National Park Service, 1977).

having different reflectance characteristics, a film can be selected in advance that will produce the desired result. Archaeologists typically rely on two types of black and white film: panchromatic and infrared, and two types of color films: normal color and infrared color.

Panchromatic films have about the same sensitivity as the human eye. They are regarded as the standard films for aerial mapping and photography. Images on panchromatic film are rendered in varying shades of gray, with each tone comparable to the density of an object's color as seen by the human eye. Panchromatic film is a superior black-and-white film for distinguishing objects of truly different colors. "Pan" film is recommended for projects such as highway route location, urban planning, archaeological mapping and locating property ownership boundaries. Lyons and Avery[2] note that since old roads and trails are easily seen, panchromatic images are also useful as field maps for archaeological surveyors who must find their way through unfamiliar terrain.

Black-and-white infrared film is sensitive to infrared radiation as well as to the blue, green and red portions of the visible spectrum. It is sometimes exposed through red or dark red filters so exposures can be made for red and infrared wavelengths only. Such photography is said to be "near-infrared" because most exposures utilize only a small band of radiation ranging from about 0.7 to 0.9 micrometers. Gray tones on infrared film result from the degree of infrared reflection of objects rather than from their true colors. For example, broadleaf vegetation is highly reflective and, therefore, photographs in light tones of gray. Coniferous vegetation tends to be less reflective in the near infrared portion of the spectrum and consequently registers in much darker tones.

Bodies of water absorb infrared light to a high degree and therefore register quite dark on film unless heavily silt-laden. This is useful for determining the extent of river tributaries, canals, tidal marshes, swamps and shorelines. Infrared materials are superior to panchromatic materials for penetration of haze.

Normal color film is daylight-exposure film that is sensitized to all visible colors. Such film has proven especially valuable for identifying soil types, rock outcrops and industrial stockpiles. Normal color can also penetrate water well. Correct exposure requires conditions of bright sunlight.

Infrared color film is a false-color film that differs from normal color in that the three emulsion layers are sensitized to green, red and infrared radiation instead of the usual blue, green, and red wavelengths. When the film is correctly exposed, the resulting transparencies display colors that are false for most natural features. The film was originally designed to emphasize differences in infrared reflectance between live, healthy vegetation and visually similar objects camouflaged with infrared-absorbing green paints.

It should be apparent that no one film serves all purposes. The varied tones and patterns produced by differing ranges of film sensitivity complement each other. The maximum amount of information can be extracted only when several types of imagery covering the same area are studied simultaneously. Photographic coverage representing two or more regions of the electromagnetic spectrum is known as multispectral sensing.

Nonphotographic Sensors

The ability of the eye to see and the mind to interpret imaged phenomena is restricted because only limited portions of the electromagnetic spectrum are detectable, that is, the visible and near visible portions.[3] However, many natural and cultural phenomena which are not recognizable within these ranges can be identified when their characteristic emissions from other regions of the electromagnetic spectrum are recorded. This is accomplished through the use of nonphotographic sensors which consist of devices or instruments which record energies reflected or emitted from the earth's surface in either pictorial or nonpictorial form without the use of optical lenses. Devices which record naturally emitted or reflected energies are said to be "passive." An available-light camera is a passive photographic sensor. Devices which generate and transmit energies and record reflected returns are said to be "active." A camera with a flash attachment is an active photographic sensor.

The data collected by either passive or active systems may be recorded on magnetic tape, viewed on a television monitor or CRT or converted into electrical impulses which, in turn, through a photoelectric cell, expose a negative film thus producing an image comparable to a photographic picture. Although the resolution is typically poorer and they are more complex, (and, therefore, more expensive), nonphotographic imaging systems are advantageous in a variety of situations. Through the detection and measurement of radiation, a great deal of information can be obtained from the natural and cultural environments.

Imaging Sensors

In addition to photography, there are systems for sensing and recording radiation reflected or emitted from a target which convert the energies into an image which the eye recognizes in visual forms. Such systems operate across the portion of the electromagnetic spectrum that includes the microwave, far and near infrared, visible and ultraviolet regions as shown in Figure 8.3. Instruments used include video cameras, active radar and passive scanning instruments.

Thermal infrared imagery (thermography) provides a representation of differences in object temperatures. Gray tones show relative temperatures. Thermal radiation may result from the reflectance of solar energy or from internally generated heat. Regardless of cause, the recording of this energy can provide significant cultural resource information. For example, moist soils have a greater capacity for heat radiation than dry soils and, therefore, different patterns of emissions. This contrast results in spectral differ-

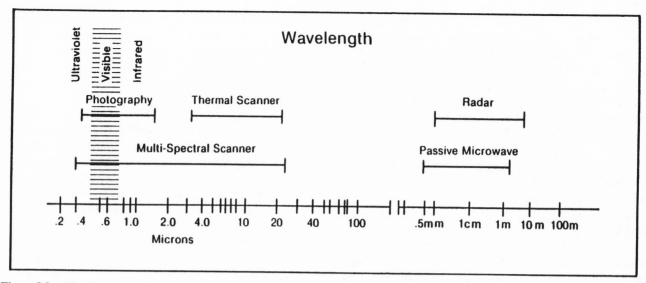

Figure 8.3.   The electromagnetic spectrum—microwave to ultraviolet regions. (Lyons, T.R. and Avery, T.E. Remote Sensing: A Handbook for Archaeologists and Cultural Resource Managers. Washington, D.C.: National Park Service, 1977).

ences between old irrigation ditches, dormant springs, soil depressions and similar features and drier surrounding areas. It is important to note that thermal infrared imagery has relatively low resolution compared with conventional aerial photography.

Multispectral scanning, like multiband photography, has potentially great applicability to archaeological studies. The scanning instrument consists of an array of detectors, each of which is designed to be responsive to a different discrete portion of the electromagnetic spectrum. The number of spectral bands can range from fewer than 10 to more than 20. By providing synchronous filtered records of the feature of interest, its different characteristics are revealed. In addition, multispectral scanning lends itself to automatic methods of analysis and interpretation since it images a scene in several spectral regions and automatically makes these data comparable in terms of densities and patterns through the use of specialized equipment.

Radar is an active remote sensing device which transmits a pulse of microwave energy and then receives reflections of the signal from a target. Radar devices operate in the microwave portion of the electromagnetic spectrum; wavelengths range from a few millimeters to more than a meter. Since it provides its own energy (illumination), radar can function without sunlight which means missions can be conducted day or night.

Long-wavelength radars are not affected by clouds or precipitation. Avery and Berlin[4] note that the angle and direction of microwave illumination for radars can be controlled to enhance features of special interest.

Some of the National Aeronautics and Space Administration's (NASA) manned spaceflights (Gemini, Apollo and Skylab) have collected photographs of the earth. However, most of the data obtained from space has been from unmanned satellites. The sensor systems which collect this satellite imagery are, except for military reconnaissance systems, nonphotographic.

As described by Avery and Berlin,[4] the United States LANDSAT represents the first spacecraft program designed specifically for collecting multispectral data from a vertical perspective at moderate resolution for monitoring and managing natural resources. The LANDSAT satellites that have been launched have acquired over one million images systematically and repetitively covering most of the earth.

One of the sensors carried on LANDSAT is a multispectral scanner (MSS) which collects reflected radiation in four discrete spectral bands ranging from 0.5 to 1.1 micrometers. The principal sensor carried by the more recent LANDSATs is the Thematic Mapper (TM). Avery and Berlin[4] note that the TM collects radiance data in seven discrete spectral bands ranging from 0.45 to 12.5 micrometers. Except for band 7, the bands were specifically selected for vegetation analysis; band 7 was intended for geological applications. Ground resolution for the TM is about 100 feet except for the thermal infrared band which has a resolution of about 370 feet.

Although, in general, the resolution from LANDSAT sensors is too poor for detailed archaeological study, the imagery does have value in regional analysis. For example, archaeologists in Delaware[5] used LANDSAT data to unearth 10,000-year-old Indian artifacts that lay in the path of a planned highway. The archaeologists knew that the study area had been populated by Indians who subsisted on hunting and gathering. Thus, they tried to identify habitats suitable for settlement by hunters and gatherers. The objective with LANDSAT was to identify wetland areas, especially those close to sources of fresh water. The reasoning was that such areas are typically lush with vegetation and also appeal to animals, that is, an ideal setting for someone who wants to hunt or gather fruits and berries. A classified LANDSAT image of the corridor was created. The potential for Indian settlement within particular areas was indicated in zones of high, medium or low likelihood. This information helped transportation agency officials select the route's final alignment, modifying the alignment where possible to avoid high-potential sites.

Nonimaging Sensors

Nonimaging sensor instruments measure the quantity and rate of radiant energies and store the recovered data in the form of traces such as an electrical resistivity curve or as data on magnetic tapes.[6] A high degree of measurement accuracy is obtained but at the expense of a relatively low yield of information. This becomes apparent when the data quantity from such systems is compared with the amount of data contained in a photo image. However, a principal advantage of nonimaging sensor products is that they are in a form readily adaptable for computer analysis.

Several types of nonimaging systems are useful in archaeological studies. Nonimaging radar systems are employed to penetrate soils and rock in search of buried structures. Electrical resistivity devices and magnetometers have been successfully used for the same purposes. Other nonimaging electromagnetic recorders include radiometers, spectrometers and scatterometers. Discussion of these devices is beyond the scope of this chapter; interested readers are referred to the *Manual of Remote Sensing*.[7]

INTERPRETIVE TECHNIQUES

Aerial photographs represent a detailed record of features on the ground at the time the image was taken. Airphoto interpretation is defined as the art and science of identifying features on aerial photographs and determining the meaning or significance of these features. As stated by Lillesand and Kiefer,[8] a photo interpreter systematically examines the photographs and other supporting materials such as maps and reports of field observations. Based on this analysis, an interpretation is made as to the physical nature of objects appearing in the photographs, (making inferences about the type of soil in a particular area of a photograph). The degree of success in photo interpretation varies with the training and experience of the interpreter, the nature of the objects being interpreted and the quality of the photographs being used. For more detailed information on the elements, techniques and visual requirements of airphoto interpretation, the *Manual of Photographic Interpretation*[9] should be consulted.

Elements of the Photo Image

A number of image characteristics are important in identifying features on aerial photographs. The more important of these will be reviewed briefly below.

Both the relative and absolute size of objects are important. The scale of the aerial photograph must first be noted. The size of features can be measured, or roughly estimated by comparison with identifiable objects such as houses, roads and vehicles. For example, comparison of the various sizes of buildings in a given area, in relation to their surroundings, assists in determining probable usage. Commercial and industrial areas tend to contain large buildings in close proximity. Small buildings with more room around them mark the usual pattern of residential areas and villages.

Many objects possess characteristic shapes that help to identify the features. Man-made features appear as straight or smooth curved lines, while natural features appear to be irregular.

Prominent man-made features on an aerial photograph include highways, railroads, bridges, canals and buildings. The regular shapes of these features contrast sharply with the irregular shapes of streams, rock outcrops and timber stands.

All objects in relief will cast shadows when there is a directional source of light. A great deal can be learned about the overall shape of an object by studying its shadows. For example, the profile of a building may be identified from the characteristic shape of its shadow. Mounds can be distinguished from depressions and tanks from lined pits of the same form. The general type of construction may be determined from object shadows. Sometimes, the number of spans, cable suspension and/or abutments are often reflected by the shadow of a bridge. The long shadows that occur early and late in the day and in the winter months may enhance relief, pattern and texture but they may also obscure detail in valleys, depressions and excavations.

Surrounding objects (topographic location) can be important clues in interpreting an aerial photograph. The existence of archaeological sites can often be predicted by knowing the topographic conditions in which they occur.

Texture, the degree of coarseness or smoothness exhibited, can be useful in identification of images. Texture is the pattern produced by the arrangement of features that are themselves too small to be resolved individually. It reflects the roughness of a surface; smooth surfaces such as roads and undisturbed water may have a featureless texture. Cultivated vegetation usually has a smoother and more regular texture than that of rough uncultivated land, which is again different from that of woodland. Texture is directly related to photo scale.

Some features may exhibit an arrangement or pattern on the aerial photograph. Historic roads, ruins or fields can often be recognized by the distinctive patterns they leave behind. Typical patterns include trees regularly arranged in orchards, crop and harvest patterns, land drains, houses, roofs of industrial buildings, raw materials or products stored in yards, spoil patterns from mining, wheel tracks and marks left by buried pipelines. A pattern is often more easily noticed than the elements forming it, which can then be inferred or examined more carefully to make an identification.

Objects of different tone and texture have different qualities of light reflectance and, therefore, register in varying shades or tones on a photograph. Tones can aid in the discrimination of objects. For example, smooth paved roads, especially those constructed of concrete, show as light bands on photographs. Earth and rough-surfaced roads often appear much darker in tone. The ballast between railroad ties shows a sharp tonal contrast to the metal rails on large-scale photographs. Airport runways and surfaced parking areas reflect light and, consequently, are much lighter in tone than the darker ground that surrounds them.

Factors affecting interpretation that vary with time of year include the following:

1. Sun height and hence shadow length
2. Leaf fall of deciduous trees (revealing features beneath)
3. Soil moisture and plant growth (soil and crop marks) snow and thaw
4. Flows in rivers, streams and ditches; water levels in reservoirs and flooded pits; flooding and tides
5. Seasonal practices; stockpiling, earthmoving, agriculture

Soil tone differences and patterns are caused by local differences in soil color, texture, depth or moisture condition. The difference can be either natural or due to disturbance, such as trenching or pipelines, or buried structures, such as foundations or archaeological remains. Soil tone differences and patterns are best seen in winter and spring when there is the greatest area of bare soil. In spring, the water table is highest which brings out tonal contrast between coarse and fine-grained soils, and feeds springs and seeps which reveal critical zones in slopes.

Procedure for Interpreting Photographs

Discussion so far has focused on identifying objects based on two dimensions, length and width. Viewing a single photograph is like seeing with a single eye; the distance from the observer can be judged only with great difficulty. Depth perception is nonexistent compared to that achieved with stereoscopic vision.

Binocular or stereo vision is the ability to see depth or relief with the human eyes. When an object is photographed from two different points in space, the dual images that result can be viewed three-dimensionally with a simple and inexpensive stereoscope. The two photographic images, consisting of a left-hand and a right-hand view, are arranged under corresponding lenses of the stereoscope; the instrument forces the left eye to look only at the left-hand photograph, while the right eye sees only the right-hand view. The result is a somewhat vertically exaggerated three-dimensional image.

Figure 8.4 illustrates a simple folding, pocket-size lens stereoscope which is commonly used in airphoto interpretation work. These inexpensive devices can be obtained from suppliers of forestry or photographic equipment.

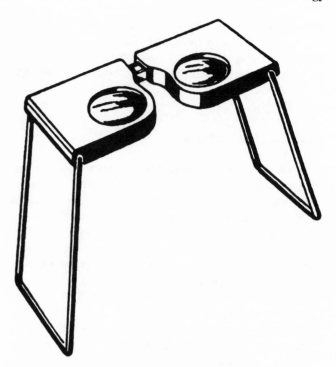

Figure 8.4. Folding pocket-size lens stereoscope.

The following step-by-step instructions outline a quick technique for obtaining a stereoscopic view from two aerial photographs:

1. Locate an obvious feature that appears in both photographs, for example, a farm field, highway intersection or some prominent man-made feature.
2. Align the photographs side-by-side so that the chosen feature is "lined up."
3. Overlap the photographs so that the images of the same ground objects are about 2 to 3 inches apart.
4. Place the stereoscope over the photos so that the images of the same feature (selected above) are centered under each lens.
5. Look through both lenses at the same time, eyes focused on infinity, as though looking at a distant object. Some users see stereo the first time they try; others need more practice. Most first-time stereoscope users initially see two distinct images, which gradually fuse creating the impression of a third image in between the two pictures seen initially. The third image is usually stereo. With a little practice, the two images will fuse into stereo effortlessly.

For interpretation, aerial photographs should be scanned stereoscopically and note made of tones, shadows, shapes, sizes, patterns and textures that can give clues to the location, identity and extent of structures and evidence of the character of the ground and the presence of disturbances and buried structures. Familiar or easily recognized features are first identified and then unrecognized features are considered. Table 8.1 lists some of the features that may interest the ar-

Table 8.1 *Natural and Man-Made Site Features and Associations and Possible Changes and Developments with Time.*

GROUND SURFACE
Bare Ground
　Infertile Rocks and Soil, Contaminated Ground
　Eroding and Accreting Surfaces
　Plowed Land
　Land Cleared for Construction
　Recently Filled Areas
Vegetation
　Natural
　Woodland; Cleared Strips (transmission lines, pipelines)
　Hedges, Crops and Pasture
Crop and Soil Marks and Low Relief Features
　Cultivation and Harvesting Marks, Land Drains, Old Hedge Lines and Field Boundaries
　Contaminated or Enriched Ground, Disturbed Drainage, Geological Effects
　Filled Trenches and Ditches, Pipelines, Buried Foundations
RELIEF
Slopes
　Natural Slopes, Cliffs
　Cuttings, Quarry and Pit Faces
　Embankments, Spoil Piles
　Developments and Changes with Time (e.g., surface erosion, water seepage, disturbed drainage, fallen material, revegetation and re-
　　medial works)
Depressions
　Collapse and Solution Features (e.g., swallow-holes, subsidence due to underground extraction, associated flooding)
　Settlement and Consolidation of Fill
Excavations
　Permanent (e.g., benches, road or rail cuts, basements and mineshafts)
　Long Term (e.g., pits and quarries)
　Temporary (e.g., foundations, trenches and mining)
　Developments and Changes with Time (e.g., progress in extent and depth, water levels, instability of sides and infilling)
Fill to Surrounding Level
　In valleys, low ground, excavations, dumping, sanitary landfill, reclamation, landscaping
　Developments and Changes with Time (e.g., location, original ground surface level and site features, progress in extent and thickness,
　　materials and soil and crop marks)
Fill Above Surrounding Ground Level
　Terraces
　Embankments (e.g., road, rail, dams and coastal structures)
　Spoil Piles (e.g., mine waste, dredgings and spoil from road and railroad cuts)
　Development and Changes with Time (e.g., location, original ground surface level and site features, progress in extent and thickness,
　　revegetation, landscaping and instability of slopes)
WATER AND DRAINAGE
　Seeps, Springs, Wells, Pipelines
　Ponds, Lakes, Reservoirs, Dams
　Streams, Rivers, Seasonal Watercourses, Ditches (e.g., erosion of banks, breaches, changes of course, abandoned channels)
　Bridges, Culverts, Weirs, Sluice Gates, River Works
　Canals (banks, locks, docks, tunnels and reservoirs)
　Land Drains, Sewer Lines, Outfalls
　Vent Pipes, Manholes, Inspection Covers
　Wet Ground, Marches, Bogs and Mudflats (e.g., channels, drainage and reclamation)
　Coastline (beaches, sand dunes, rock outcrops and coastal structures)
BUILDINGS, STRUCTURES AND INSTALLATIONS
Infrastructure
　Roads, Railroads, Canals, Bridges, Cuts and Fills
　Water Supply, Drainage, Sewage Treatment Facilities
　Electricity (power plants, fuel stacks, cooling towers, power lines, transformer stations)
Urban
　Residential, Public Buildings, Commercial, Manufacturing
Industrial (characteristic requirements, varying with each industry)
　Water Supply (rivers, streams, channels, reservoirs, cooling towers, settling tanks)
　Power Supply (electric lines,, pylons, transformer stations, coal piles, oil tanks)
　Raw Materials (mineral and metal ore mines, storage yards, extraction and handling equipment)
　Buildings (workshops, drying and processing sheds)
　Process Plant (kilns, coke ovens, furnaces, fractionating towers)
　Product Storage (storage tanks, parking areas for vehicles, bricks, pipes, coal, etc)
　Product Distribution (power, oil and gas lines, road vehicles, railway sidings, canals, wharves)
　Waste Products (coal refuse, slag, ash, landfills, salvage yards, slurry lagoons)
　Developments and Change with Time (e.g., foundations, new construction, modifications, extension, change of use or procedure, de-
　　molition, site clearance, filling of pits and removal or landscaping of waste heaps).

chaeologist, and changes and developments that they may show with time. The slightest detectable variations in tone may be significant, as with shadows, that can indicate variations in surface relief and soil or crop marks that can show differences in soil drainage, fertility or thickness that may be natural or related to past disturbances or buried features.

When several sets of aerial photographs exist for a site, taken at different dates, they will allow natural changes and previous use of the site to be examined. Such a series will also show the site under different altitudes and directions of the sun and hence of shadow length and direction, and different seasons of the year and hence of different states of crops, and of dryness and wetness of the soil. Careful search for differences in tones may reveal details on some of a series of photographs that may only become evident under particular conditions. It will often be possible to select sets that show particular features of interest to the best advantage, or show the development and demolition of an industrial complex or the excavation and filling of mine workings.

The aerial photographs should not be used in isolation, but rather interpreted along with evidence from other sources. Some features of the site may be named on old or current maps. Any available ground-based photographs or oblique aerial photographs of the site can be compared with vertical photographs to establish their viewpoint. Study of local geography, old and current topographical maps and maps of land use, geology and soils and familiarity with the occupational and industrial history of the area and with the terrain on the ground will all make interpretation easier and allow features to be recognized and identified that would otherwise have been overlooked. The site should be inspected on foot, if possible, to confirm interpretations made and to allow interpretation of those features that are recognized in the photograph but cannot at first be identified.

A clue to interpretation may be obtained by noting the associations between the various features of the scene. An example of association between natural features is that of floodplains, terraces and abandoned channels with rivers. Man-made features are often associated with natural features, for example, weirs, locks, wharves and power plants with rivers and gravel pits with river floodplains and terraces. Industrial facilities usually consist of a number of associated elements that characterize the particular industry, for example, in the case of brick manufacturing, clay pits, drying sheds, kilns, chimneys, fuel and brick storage yards and railroad sidings or truck loading docks.

Interpretation may be aided by the preparation of an "air photo key" or by the use of an existing one. An air photo key is a device designed to aid photo interpreters in the rapid and accurate identification of objects from a study of their photographic images. It includes a word description of each object in the key and a photograph illustrating each of these features. Photo keys have been prepared for features related to industrial archaeology.[10,11]

ARCHAEOLOGICAL APPLICATIONS

In the United States, with its history of industrial and natural resource development, there are many sites that have been affected by past development. There may be buried masonry, former transportation rights-of-ways, voids or contaminating substances present which affect the uses of the site. For example, coal may have been mined, leaving voids that are liable to cause subsidence. There may be extensive buried foundations remaining, for example, from demolished coke ovens or basements of buildings, or a former chemical plant may have left hazardous chemicals.

Information on past use may be difficult to obtain because of the ignorance or reticence of owners or occupiers. Inspection may be impractical for the same reasons, or may not reveal past use from ground level. Aerial photographs then have a special potential as a source of historical information because of the detailed exact record of the site that they provide, which may be difficult to obtain by other means.

For assistance in recognizing features and analyzing the photographic record, there is a relatively large amount of published information available. Wallwork[12] outlines the historical development of industries and their effect on the landscape, especially that of the extractive industries which produce the largest amount of derelict land. He provides many aerial photographs and maps illustrating the development of industrial dereliction, including that due to coal mining, brine pumping and salt works, iron ore mining and clay workings. Chisnell and Cole[10] explain how each type of industrial complex has a unique sequence of raw materials, buildings, equipment and products and waste materials, many of which can be identified on aerial photographs, directly or by inference. Recognition of industrial features is also discussed by Avery and Berlin.[13] An air photo key for identifying 31 classes of industrial sites has been developed by Collins and Bush.[11] Each class of site is described and six aerial photographs were selected to illustrate all 31 classes using annotated overlays.

Examples of Photographic Interpretation

The usefulness of aerial photographs for studying the present condition of a site and its history of changes depends on the range of dates of the aerial photographs available and their characteristics, including emulsion type, camera focal length, time of year and time of day. As examples of the types of information that might be obtained, stereopairs are presented for two sites in West Virginia. Note that the photographs represent single points in time; no attempt was made to obtain all existing photo coverage of the sites.

One site, shown in Figure 8.5, is adjacent to the Morgantown, West Virginia, urban area. The black-and-white circular features represent the remnants of a petroleum tank

Figure 8.5. Stereopair showing remnants of petroleum tank farm adjacent to the Morgantown, West Virginia, urban area. (Agricultural Stabilization and Conservation Service).

farm. The white dots indicate locations where the steel tanks had been recently removed. Circles with gray color tone indicate the sites of tanks which had been removed some time ago since vegetation has grown up at those locations. The two dark circular features, casting shadows, near the lower left portion of the tank farm represent two steel tanks which are still standing. The larger dark circles surrounding the tanks (and tank sites) indicate vegetation which has grown up on the earth impoundments constructed around each tank to contain leaks or spills. Also clearly visible is the network of unsurfaced service roads providing access to the individual tanks. The relatively straight cleared areas criss-crossing the tank farm site are most likely the right-of-ways associated with the pipeline system serving the tank farm.

CONCLUSION

There are a number of ways in which information can be obtained on the history of a site. The site may be inspected; however, access may not be possible at the time in question. Evidence of natural changes or past use may not longer be evident from inspection at ground level. These problems can be overcome by using a variety of historical sources of information, including written records, maps and remote sensing imagery.

Remote sensing imagery has special potential as a source of historical information because of the detailed and exact record of the site that it can provide. Ebert and Lyons[14] note that archaeology demands accurate and justifiable measurement and documentation methods. In addition to traditional, discovery-oriented remote sensing applications, remote sensing methods and data have been used for other important purposes. These include designing and collecting samples and precisely measuring and monitoring structures and sites. For example, remote sensing can be used at the planning stage of the project to divide the survey area into zones for sampling. Or, images can be taken into the field and used as maps to lay out sample areas. In addition, images can be used in the field as aids in locating the position of sites which are encountered.

Remote sensing methods, primarily those involving photography, provide a more comprehensive means of recording data at a site than drawing methods, because remote sensing records a range of information, much of which is not even considered or understood at the time a site is recorded. Another important capability of remote sensing is that series of images may allow natural changes affecting the site and its development, use and abandonment to be followed over time.

BIBLIOGRAPHY

Avery, T. E. and Berlin, G. L. *Interpretation of Aerial Photographs,* 4th ed., Minneapolis: Burgess Publishing Co., 1985.

Chisnell, T. C. and Cole, G. E. "Industrial Components-A Photo Interpretation Key on Industry." *Photogrammetric Engineering* 24 (1958), pp. 590–602.

Collins, W. G. and Bush, P. W. "The Use of Aerial Photographs in the Study of Derelict Land-An Airphoto Key," *Journal of the Town Planning Institute* 55 (1969): 246–255.

Colwell, R. N., ed. *Manual of Photographic Interpretation.* Falls Church, VA: American Society of Photogrammetry, 1960.

Colwell, R. N., ed. *Manual of Remote Sensing Second Edition,* Vol 1, 2, Falls Church, VA: American Society of Photogrammetry, 1983.

Dumbleton, M. J. "Air Photographs for Investigating Natural Changes, Past Use and Present Condition of Engineering Sites," *TRRL Laboratory Report 1085.* Crowthorne, Berkshire, United Kingdom: Transport and Road Research Laboratory, 1983.

Ebert, J. I. and Lyons, T. R., eds. "Archaeology, Anthropology, Cultural Resources Management," Chapter 26, *Manual of Remote Sensing, Volume II,* 2nd ed., Falls Church, VA: American Society of Photogrammetry, 1983, pp. 1233–1304.

EOSAT: "Highway Planners Find Pre-Historic Artifacts with LANDSAT," *LANDSAT Data Users Notes* 6 (Spring 1991), 3–6.

Lillesand, T. M. and Kiefer, R. W. *Remote Sensing and Image Interpretation.* New York: John Wiley & Sons, 1979.

Lyons, T. R. and Avery, T. E. *Remote Sensing: A Handbook for Archaeologists and Cultural Resource Managers.* Washington, D.C.: National Park Service, 1977.

Wallwork, K. L. *Derelict Land Origins and Prospects of A Land Use Problem,* Newton Abbott, United Kingdom: David and Charles, 1974.

ENDNOTES

1. Lillesand, T. M. and Kiefer, R. W. *Remote Sensing and Image Interpretation.* New York: John Wiley & Sons, 1979.
2. Lyons, T. R. and Avery, T. E. *Remote Sensing: A Handbook for Archaeologists and Cultural Resource Managers.* Washington, D.C.: National Park Service, 1977.
3. Lyons, T. R. and Avery, T. E. *Remote Sensing: A Handbook for Archaeologists and Cultural Resource Managers.* Washington, D.C.: National Park Service, 1977.
4. Avery, T. E. and Berlin, G. L. *Interpretation of Aerial Photographs,* 4th ed., Minneapolis: Burgess Publishing Co., 1985.
5. EOSAT: "Highway Planners Find Pre-Historic Artifacts with LANDSAT," *LANDSAT Data Users Notes* 6 (Spring 1991), 3–6.
6. Lyons, T. R. and Avery, T. E. *Remote Sensing: A Handbook for Archaeologists and Cultural Resource Managers.* Washington, D.C.: National Park Service, 1977.
7. Colwell, R. N., ed. *Manual of Remote Sensing Second Edition,* Vol 1, 2, Falls Church, VA: American Society of Photogrammetry, 1983.
8. Lillesand, T. M. and Kiefer, R. W. *Remote Sensing and Image Interpretation.* New York: John Wiley & Sons, 1979.
9. Colwell, R. N., ed. *Manual of Photographic Interpretation.* Falls Church, VA: American Society of Photogrammetry, 1960.
10. Chisnell, T. C. and Cole, G. E. "Industrial Components-A Photo Interpretation Key on Industry." *Photogrammetric Engineering* 24 (1958), pp. 590–602.
11. Collins, W. G. and Bush, P. W. "The Use of Aerial Photographs in the Study of Derelict Land-An Airphoto Key," *Journal of the Town Planning Institute* 55 (1969): 246–255.
12. Wallwork, K. L. *Derelict Land Origins and Prospects of A Land Use Problem,* Newton Abbott, United Kingdom: David and Charles, 1974.
13. Avery, T. E. and Berlin, G. L. *Interpretation of Aerial Photographs,* 4th ed., Minneapolis: Burgess Publishing Co., 1985.
14. Ebert, J. I. and Lyons, T. R., eds. "Archaeology, Anthropology, Cultural Resources Management," Chapter 26, *Manual of Remote Sensing, Volume II,* 2nd ed., Falls Church, VA: American Society of Photogrammetry, 1983, pp. 1233–1304.

CHAPTER 9

Field Work and Measured Drawings

Richard K. Anderson, Jr.

INTRODUCTION

There are three goals for measured drawings as defined by the *Secretary of the Interior's Standards for Architectural and Engineering Documentation:*

1. Focus on significant facts and conditions about the site being documented.
2. Strive for accuracy and verifiability in dimensional and representational information about significant features. Drawings should be accurately scaled and delineated, and should contain a *verbal accounting* for field procedures, error factors, secondary sources, speculative reconstruction, incompleteness, etc.
3. Strive for clarity and concise "readability" in presentation. Drawings should be designed so that they guide the user visually and verbally to significant information about a site.

Measured drawings and their attendant field work are only required for Level I or Level II documentation, according to the *Secretary's Standards*. The level of documentation selected is governed by what kinds of media (drawings, photos, written histories) it will take to "adequately explicate and illustrate what is significant or valuable" about a site (Standard I). These levels assume that accurate, reliable, verifiable *dimensional* information is significant and is required in order to fulfill Standards I and II. They also assume that pictorial, diagrammatic, and schematic views (whether to scale or not) may be required in order to "explicate and illustrate" significant features, over and above photographic or written data. Other factors, such as project schedule, staff expertise and funding, are dependent on the level chosen.[1]

Types of Drawings

A measured drawing set may include a wide variety of drawing views and types. Commonly, a title sheet is first, followed by site plans, plans and elevations of the structure and one or more cross-sectional views of the structure to show significant internal relationships of parts, spaces or structural details. Some sections may be done as one-point perspectives where this technique improves the content and clarity of the documentation, aiding interpretation of the resource. Specialized drawings may be required to clearly show how significant features are constructed or operated. These may encompass views such as topographic maps, axonometrics, cutaways, perspectives, exploded assembly views, schematic process diagrams, force diagrams and the like. Axonometrics are excellent for showing how a structure is assembled; parts of an object may be deleted for clarity, cutaway to show internal structure or drawn as though disassembled. Process diagrams range from the pictorial to the schematic, and may or may not be done to a scale, depending on how significant scale is for interpreting the process. They may follow a literal site layout or be arranged in a manner that best accommodates logic and explanation. Force diagrams are used to depict and analyze stresses in members of bridge trusses or other structures. Axonometrics and process diagrams are discussed in more detail later in this chapter.

Production Sequence

Production of measured drawings occurs in four successive phases: research preparation, field work, preliminary drawings and final drawings. This chapter outlines what preparations to make, how to use appropriate field techniques, make field notes, take field photographs and prepare your drawings so that each of the four Secretary's Standards is met. Think of the Standards as objectives: you need to do enough research and site reconnaissance to focus on what is specifically significant and valuable about your site, prepare your drawings from accurate field work and/or other verifiable sources and finish your drawings so that they present the significance of your site "clearly and concisely" in standard sized records.

A chart published by HABS/HAER shows the relationships between the Standards and these phases (Figure 9.1). These phases overlap somewhat in application. Field work is not truly finished until preliminary drawings have been completed. Frequently conflicts in measurements or gaps in data may send a team member back to the site or to a historian to resolve measurement or identification and presentation problems while drawings are "on the boards." Contemporaneous historical research may also redirect the focus of a drawing before the preliminary drawing is completed. Formal photography is best done after the documentation team has decided how to coordinate documentary media to record particular significant features.

PHASE 1: PREPARATION

Documentation is a selective process, ideally driven by significance. Why should your site be recorded? Engineering and technological significance? History of industry and invention? Building technology? Architecture? Famous persons, business and political events? Or some combination of these? The answer to these questions will decide where to focus your efforts and what media to choose for clear and concise documentation. To help you answer these questions, you will need to know the general history of your site and what specifically makes it remarkable enough to record. You should know its historical context—find out where it fits into the regional and national history of similar sites—so you can zero in on what is particularly significant about your site and what parts merit documentation with drawings.

You should explore the site itself. Go over it in detail with other members of the recording team and examine it carefully for signs of its use and physical evolution. Make notes of features that confirm old records, raise questions or require further investigation. The recording team should also make a reasonable effort to review existing published materials, company records and preexisting engineering drawings, site maps, written and oral accounts, old photos, area maps, business directories, courthouse records and related sources. You may find that the site's importance revolves around a person, or a particular mechanical invention, or an industrial process, or the way unusual engineering and siting problems were solved. It may be that your site is the best representative of a typical one of its kind. You may be led to record a single building's floor plan or an entire industrial complex that includes a number of notable features, processes and types of machinery.

Determine A Plan of Action

Having done this, what drawings must be made in order to "explicate and illustrate what is significant or valuable" at your site? Drawings have the ability to communicate in ways impossible for photography and impractical for writing. Drawings can be far more selective and to the point than photographs, and they can include verbal information to aid interpretation. Keep in mind that some aspects of your site may be better recorded verbally, or photographically, or in some combination with drawings. Histories and photographic documentation must be considered and developed along with the drawings to form an integrated documentation package. Cross-referencing specific drawings, photos and written data in a documentation package can greatly enhance the documentation's impact and usefulness.

A site map of your industrial complex may be required because the industry's process or development is reflected by the layout or growth of its physical plant (Figure 9.2). Floor plans of a building may be required because the arrangement of rooms and machinery reflects the use of a certain kind of power system, labor organization or process. (No photograph could do this without cutting the top of the building off.) Elevations of buildings or bridge trusses may be important for dimensional, structural or aesthetic data. A cross section of your site, or building, or significant machine may be critical to showing relationships of important functions or the key feature to an invention or process. Selected architectural details might be needed, or even exploded isometric drawings to show how a significant structural joint or machine is assembled or operated. An industrial process might be "clearly and concisely" documented by a simple series of pictorial drawings or a schematic chart far better than by photographs or long verbal passages. Some of these types of drawings may already exist as engineering drawings, maps, company records and charts, or published diagrams; in these cases you should consider photocopying applicable works to save time and money instead of tracing them anew. Sometimes it may be necessary to redraw such materials in order to emphasize historical features and delete irrelevant, distracting information. Occasionally you may find it sufficient to produce an illustration or diagram of a particular feature for inclusion in the historical report rather than create a measured drawing sheet.

Once you have a reasonable grasp of existing records and the field data recoverable at the site, you will need to decide what the bases for your drawings will be (Standard II). Which sources and methods are appropriate to the significant things you are documenting (taking into account such factors as time, money, safety and quality)? Rigorous field measurements and photography? Reliance on preexisting drawings, historical photos and publications? Written descriptions? Disassembly of particular elements? Long-range data collection (photogrammetry, electronic distance measurement and surveying work)?

SUMMARY

PERFORMANCE STANDARDS OF THE HISTORIC AMERICAN BUILDINGS SURVEY/HISTORIC AMERICAN ENGINEERING RECORD (HABS/HAER)

(SECRETARY OF THE INTERIOR'S STANDARDS FOR ARCHITECTURAL AND ENGINEERING DOCUMENTATION, *FEDERAL REGISTER*, SEPTEMBER 29, 1983, PP. 44730-44734)

STANDARDS	I. CONTENT	II. QUALITY	III. MATERIALS	IV. PRESENTATION
REQUIREMENTS	"DOCUMENTATION SHALL ADEQUATELY EXPLICATE AND ILLUSTRATE WHAT IS SIGNIFICANT OR VALUABLE ABOUT THE HISTORIC BUILDING, SITE, STRUCTURE OR OBJECT BEING DOCUMENTED."	"HABS AND HAER DOCUMENTATION SHALL BE PREPARED ACCURATELY, FROM RELIABLE SOURCES WITH LIMITATIONS CLEARLY STATED TO PERMIT INDEPENDENT VERIFICATION OF INFORMATION."	"HABS AND HAER DOCUMENTATION SHALL BE PREPARED ON MATERIALS THAT ARE READILY REPRODUCIBLE FOR EASE OF ACCESS; DURABLE FOR LONG STORAGE; AND IN STANDARD SIZES FOR EASE OF HANDLING."	"HABS AND HAER DOCUMENTATION SHALL BE CLEARLY AND CONCISELY PRODUCED."

CRITERIA (by LEVEL I / II / III / IV)

CRITERIA	I. CONTENT	II. QUALITY	III. MATERIALS	IV. PRESENTATION
A. MEASURED DRAWING	I: FULL SET OF MEAS. DWGS.; II: SEE PHOTOS BELOW; III: SKETCH PLAN; IV: INVENTORY CARD	MEASURED DRAWINGS ARE TO BE PRODUCED FROM RECORDED, ACCURATE MEASUREMENTS. THOSE PORTIONS DRAWN FROM EXISTING DRAWINGS OR OTHER SOURCES SHOULD BE SO IDENTIFIED AND SOURCES LISTED.	I: INK ON TRANSLUCENT MATERIAL (19x24" OR 24x36"); II: 8x10" PHOTOCOPY; III: INK ON BOND PAPER (8½x11"); IV: INK ON INVENTORY CARD	ADEQUATE DIMENSIONS ON ALL SHEETS. I: MECH. LETTERING OR EQUIVALENT; III: SKETCH PLANS SHALL BE NEAT AND ORDERLY
B. PHOTOGRAPHS	LARGE FORMAT PHOTOGRAPHS EXTERIOR & INTERIOR; LARGE FORMAT PHOTOCOPIES: – SELECT EXISTING DWGS – SELECT HISTORIC VIEWS; IV: 35mm B&W	PHOTOGRAPHS SHALL CLEARLY DEPICT THE APPEARANCE OF THE PROPERTY AND AREAS OF SIGNIFICANCE. ALL VIEWS ARE TO BE PERSPECTIVE-CORRECTED AND FULLY CAPTIONED.	PRINTS SHALL ACCOMPANY ALL NEGATIVES. MUST BE ARCHIVALLY PROCESSED, NO R/C PAPER. 4x5" OR 5x7" OR 8x10". 35mm FILM.	DUPLICATE PHOTOS WITH A SCALE STICK. MIN. OF ONE PHOTO WITH A SCALE (PRINCIPAL FACADE)
C. WRITTEN DATA	HISTORY AND DESCRIPTION IN NARRATIVE OR OUTLINE FORMAT; III: ONE PAGE SUMMARY; IV: INVENTORY CARD	BASED ON PRIMARY SOURCES. INCLUDE: – METHODOLOGY – NAME OF RESEARCH & DATE OF RESEARCH – SOURCES – FRANK ASSESSMENT OF SOURCES AND THEIR LIMITATIONS. SECONDARY SOURCES MAY PROVIDE ADEQUATE INFORMATION.	CLEAN COPY FOR XEROXING. ARCHIVAL BOND REQUIRED. 8½x11".	TYPEWRITTEN ON BOND; IV: TYPED ON INVENTORY CARD
D. OTHER	OTHER MEDIA CAN AND HAVE BEEN USED. CONTACT HABS/HAER OFFICE BEFORE EMPLOYING A MEDIA OTHER THAN THOSE SPECIFIED ABOVE.			

TESTS	
INSPECTION BY HABS/HAER OFFICE STAFF. DOCUMENTATION NOT MEETING HABS/HAER STANDARDS WILL BE REFUSED.	

COMMENTARIES	I. CONTENT	II. QUALITY	III. MATERIALS	IV. PRESENTATION
	KIND AND AMOUNT OF DOCUMENTATION SHOULD BE APPROPRIATE TO THE NATURE, AND SIGNIFICANCE OF THE BUILDING, SITE, STRUCTURE OR OBJECT BEING DOCUMENTED.	THE PRINCIPLE OF INDEPENDENT VERIFICATION IS CRITICAL IN ASSURING HIGH QUALITY OF HABS/HAER MATERIALS.	BASIC DURABILITY PERFORMANCE STANDARD IS 500 YEARS.	HABS/HAER ARE MOST WIDELY USED OF SPECIAL COLLECTIONS AT THE LIBRARY OF CONGRESS.

Figure 9.1. Summary of performance standards for HABS/HAER documentation. (U.S. Department of the Interior, National Park Service, Cultural Resources Program, Historic American Buildings Survey/Historic American Engineering Record, *Secretary of the Interior's Standards and Guidelines for Architectural and Engineering Documentation: HABS/HAER Standards*, Washington, D.C.: U.S. Government Printing Office, 1990, p. 15. Chart originally prepared by Robert J. Kapsch, Chief, HABS/HAER.)

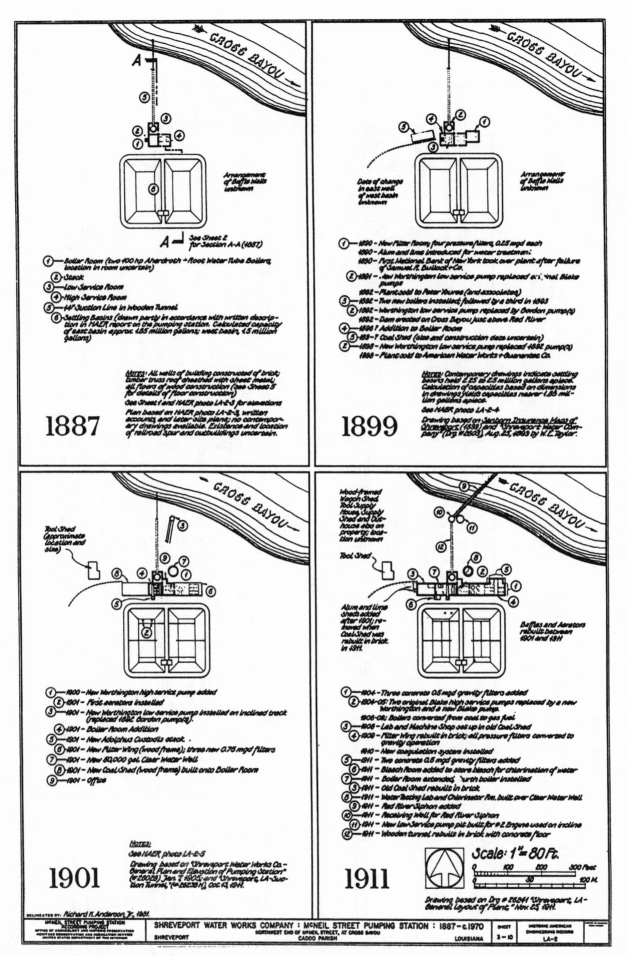

Figure 9.2. Site evolution of the McNeil Street Pumping Station, Shreveport, Louisiana, from 1887 to 1911. The expansion of this plant reflects industry-wide improvements in water treatment methods, as well as growth in the plant's service area. (Historic American Engineering Record, Heritage Conservation and Recreation Service; historical research by Terry S. Reynolds, 1980; delineation by Richard K. Anderson, Jr. 1980.)

Combinations of sources such as the above are common in good measured drawing documentation, and preexisting sources may save you some time in the field. However, don't take preexisting information at face value! Carefully check out written and oral data, and old drawings and photos *against each other and the site itself.* Old photos have occasionally been misidentified, and you may find that a building or complex wasn't built to or no longer conforms to the surviving drawings. Site maps from various sources may present contradictions, omissions or dimensional and representational inaccuracies. Sometimes these sources are the only clues to preexisting features at a site, and conflicts may lead a recording team to focus on specific documentary research or field work to try to determine what actually happened on site. In your final drawings you will need to cite the specific sources on which the drawings were based, or include annotations explaining how you resolved conflicting data, or filled in information no longer at the site itself. Such annotations will be vital to your work's accuracy and verifiability (Standard II). (Figure 9.3)

Begin Drawing Development

Once a plan has been developed, it is time to select the sheet size and scales for the drawings. Site plan scales may range from 1″ = 10 feet (small sites) to 1″ = 100 feet or more (for large industrial complexes). Building plans, elevations and sections are normally done at a scale of 1/4″ = 1′-0″; larger or smaller scales may be used depending on the size of the building, the significance of assembled details, and whether the view drawn will fit on a sheet along with annotations, scales and dimensions. Some views may take two or more sheets where too much detail would be sacrificed to draw the views at a scale small enough to fit one sheet. Individual details may appear at scales of 3/4″ = 1′-0″ and larger. Axonometrics and exploded views are laid out and drawn at scales sufficiently large to clearly show significant features, whether these be views of a site, or how a bridge panel point is assembled.

Thumbnail sketches, "cartoons" or "story boards" of proposed measured drawings are very useful in discussion for the development of a drawing set and for establishing the content of each drawing. As the cartoons evolve, write down on them notes to yourself about things to highlight, annotate, check in the field, research, etc. Review and revise the sketches critically as you go and imagine them as finished drawings—will they "clearly and concisely" show what is significant at your site? A flexible list of drawings should be made, keeping in mind that further research and field work may dictate revisions or additions to the list.

Schedule

Set up a realistic schedule for field work and drawing production. Time estimation will require some experience. No two sites are exactly alike, either as physical entities or in terms of available preexisting written and photo data. Hence it is impossible to set down an abstract formula for accurate estimation. As a general rule of thumb, a third of the project time will be spent in research and field work, a third producing preliminary drawings and sheet layouts, and a third inking and lettering finished drawings. These activities will overlap rather than occur in discrete phases.

PHASE 2: FIELD WORK

Field work encompasses all tasks performed at the site, such as sketching and physically measuring structures, taking field photographs and comparing preexisting drawings and other sources against the site remains. It usually does not involve excavation, as in classical archaeology, but archaeological exploration and analysis may be required in some instances.[2]

(Verification for the existence of subsurface features can be accomplished by probing soil with a thin steel rod, or using georadar equipment.) Destructive testing is not undertaken unless all other reasonable means of obtaining significant data have been exhausted. Field work should be directed toward significant features that will appear in your drawings and not scattered indiscriminately at everything (Standard I). The tools and methods you employ should be appropriate to the accuracy of drawings required, the field conditions and the type of resources you are recording.

Field Equipment

Below is a list of common hand tools and accessories used in the field for hand measurement work:

Datum Reference Devices
string/line (braided, not twisted)
plumb bobs
chalk line
chalk refill
carpenter's square
combination square
12-inch torpedo level
48-inch mason's level
protractor-level
water level
transit
stadia rod
tripod
stakes
compass

Tapes
100-foot tapes, 1/8-inch graduations
50-foot tapes, 1/8-inch graduations
6-, 12-, 16-, and 25-foot tapes, 1/16 inch graduations

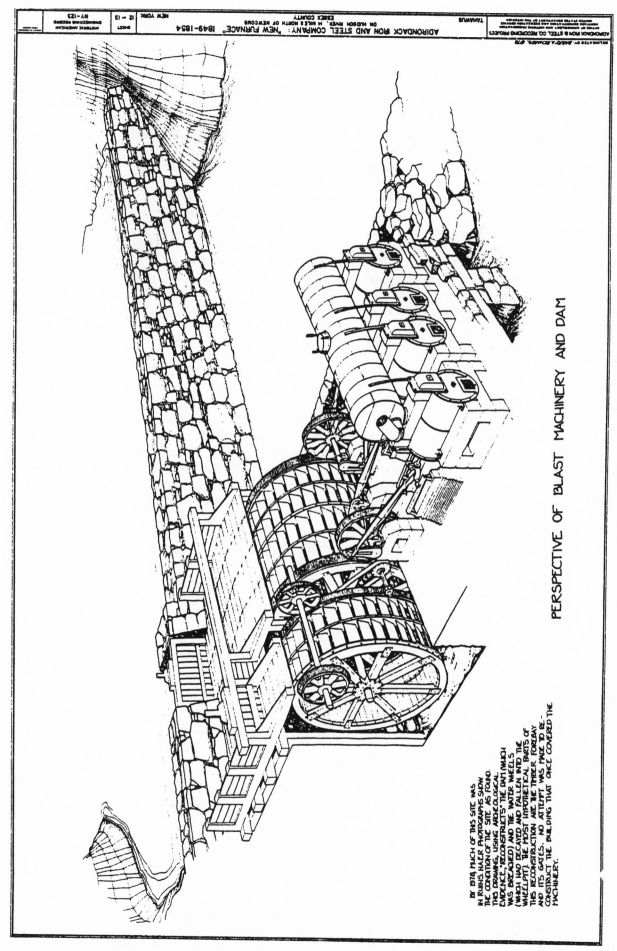

ADIRONDACK IRON AND STEEL COMPANY: "NEW FURNACE" 1849–1854

ON HUDSON RIVER, 14 MILES NORTH OF NEWCOMB
ESSEX COUNTY
NEW YORK

TAHAWUS

HISTORIC AMERICAN
ENGINEERING RECORD
NY-123

SHEET
12 OF 13

BY 1974, MUCH OF THIS SITE WAS
IN RUINS. HAER PHOTOGRAPHS SHOW
THE CONDITION OF THE SITE AS FOUND.
THIS DRAWING, USING ARCHEOLOGICAL
EVIDENCE, "RECONSTRUCTS" THE DAM (WHICH
WAS BREACHED) AND THE WATER WHEELS
(WHICH HAD DECAYED AND FALLEN INTO THE
WHEELPIT). THE MOST HYPOTHETICAL PARTS OF
THIS RECONSTRUCTION ARE THE TIMBER FOREBAY
AND ITS GATES. NO ATTEMPT WAS MADE TO RE-
CONSTRUCT THE BUILDING THAT ONCE COVERED THE
MACHINERY.

PERSPECTIVE OF BLAST MACHINERY AND DAM

Figure 9.3. The pictorial perspective view of this water-driven blowing machinery was developed from subsurface archaeological data as well as measurements of surviving dam and blow-ing cylinder parts. No historical photos were discovered which replicated this view, and no similar modern photos could be produced of ruins. (Historic American Engineering Record, Na-tional Park Service; delineated by Barry A. Edwards, 1976. Adirondack Iron and Steel Company: "New Furnace" 1849–1854, sheet 12 of 13.)

Scales
6- or 8-foot folding carpenter's rules, 1/16 inch graduations
6- and 12-inch machinists' scales (graduated in 1/10ths and 1/100ths, 1/32nds and 1/64th of an inch)
hook rule
depth gauge

Holding Devices
hammer and nails
magnets
C-clamps
nylon filament tape
weights (bricks, cans of sand, etc.)

Gauges
bevel gauge
thread gauge (National Fine and National Coarse series)
radius gauges (set, 1/32″ to 3/4″)
molding comb
insulated copper wire

Calipers
5-inch jaw calipers
6-, 12- and 20-inch outside calipers
12-inch inside calipers

Drawing Implements
pencil compass
mechanical pencils
leads (black, red)
stick erasers
graph paper sheets (17″ × 22″)
graph paper roll (24 inch width)
glue
scissors
clipboard (artist's size, 20″ × 24″)
extra clips
field note pouch

Markers
crayons (yellow, black)
chalk (white, red)
felt marker
masking tape

Accessories
toolbox
hand mirror
whisk broom
wire brush
dust mask & extra filters
work gloves (welder's)
goggles
paper towels
prepackaged hand wipes
heavy-duty hand cleaner (creme)

solvent (spot remover or lighter fluid)
cotton gloves (for negatives and old papers)
luggage cart
binoculars
magnifying glass
ladders and/or scaffolding
rope
insect killer (wasp spray)

Hand Tools
hammer
pliers
slot screwdriver
Philips screwdriver
WD-40 or other rust preventative lubricant
wire
scissors
utility knife
saw
cat's paw
crowbar
wedges

Reference materials
HABS & HAER manuals
geometry tables (formulas for various figures and functions)
handy references like Oberg, Eric and Franklin D. Jones *Machinery's Handbook: A Reference Book for the Mechanical Engineer, Draftsman, Toolmaker and Machinist.* (New York; Industrial Press Incorporated, 1973), and Knight, Edward H. *Knight's New Mechanical Dictionary* (Boston: Houghton, Mifflin and Company, 1884)
calculator (with trigonometric functions)

Lighting
flashlight (with magnetic holder)
extra flashlight batteries and bulbs
120v drop lights
extra 120v bulbs
3-to-2 prong plug adapters
light-socket-to-plug adapters
extension cords (3-wire grounded)

Work Clothing
hard hat
carpenter's overalls
long underwear
sweaters
windbreaker
field boots
rubber boots
rain gear

First Aid
insect repellent
sunscreen

antiseptic and bandages
snake-bite kit

Safety Precautions

Working around operational or abandoned industrial sites presents safety hazards which awareness and common sense can mitigate. In most cases, it is your responsibility to look around, think ahead and be wise. Safety equipment and signs will not prevent injuries from just plain carelessness.

Apparel: Work clothes such as carpenter's overalls, jeans, sweatshirts and sturdy shoes are usually sufficient for protection from dirt and abrasion. Do not wear long sleeves, long hair, neckties, bracelets or rings around operating machinery or belting. Shorts and T-shirts may be more comfortable in hot climates. Work gloves should be worn when handling things that are unusually abrasive, sharp, splintery, hot (as from sun exposure) or cold. Hard hats and heavy steel-toed boots should be worn at sites where there is considerable debris and recorders risk stepping on nails or working under falling materials (plaster and lath, rust and dirt). Sneakers and street shoes are acceptable for sites in good condition.

Buddy System: Never go into abandoned structures or remote places alone—always use the "buddy system" so that help can be obtained if someone is injured. Don't go out onto structures that are potentially or obviously unsound from dilapidation, rot or rust. Check out floors, beams, walls, trusses, catwalks, stairs and other items in abandoned buildings before using them. If necessary erect safety lines, scaffolding or ladders. If a rusted iron or steel structure is beginning to collapse, you may receive prior warning by a flurry of rust flakes or unusual noises. Beware of wet, slippery steel plate floors, oil on concrete surfaces and fine particulates or gravel that can act like roller bearings under your feet. Avoid the leaning sides of bowed masonry walls and chimneys. Doin't assume old wiring is "dead."

Exposure: At overgrown or neglected sites, be alert for irritating plants (such as poison ivy and poison oak), thorns, stinging insects (bees, wasps) and snakes. It is wise to take along sunscreen, insect repellent and a good brand of wasp killer. Wear a hat if you are outdoors a lot. Drink plenty of fluids to avoid dehydration.

Animal Droppings: If you encounter accumulations of bird droppings, avoid contacting them or breathing dust stirred up from them. Illness from these is rare, but cryptococcosis and histoplasmosis are potentially disabling or fatal diseases of the lungs and nervous system. Mouse, rat and bat droppings may also carry diseases. Wear a dust mask and protective clothing if you will be in fouled areas for extended periods. Local health authorities can conduct tests on droppings and suggest any necessary further precautions.

Asbestos: Asbestos is a white, fibrous, incombustible mineral that was widely used as an insulation and building material up into the 1960s. When inhaled it has been known to cause various degenerative lung diseases, including cancer, and it can also be absorbed through the skin. Historic industrial sites may contain pipes, boilers, ducts and other heated equipment insulated with asbestos as well as asbestos-bearing building materials (cements, mortars, gaskets, shingles). Normally, these present no danger, especially if the site is well maintained and insulation jacketing is intact. Loose asbestos is not hazardous unless it is handled or made airborne. Gently wetting loose asbestos and keeping it soaked with water will prevent airborne dust sufficiently for short-term recording activities. Do not attempt to remove loose asbestos yourself without proper protection; contact local health authorities for hazard evaluations if loose asbestos is extensive.[3]

Materials for Field Drawings and Notes

Field notes should be made on 17″ × 22″ sheets of 8 × 8 gridded bond paper (Standard III), which is available in pads from art supply stores. Adequate room for legible sketches, dimensions and annotations makes this size much better than smaller formats, and it folds to 8 1/2″ × 11″ size for standard file storage. The grid guides the hand in laying out neat notes and in drawing straight lines and square corners in plans and elevations. Don't be tempted to use "handy" paper scraps, since these can be lost easily, and they make for a disorganized set of records. Sheets larger than 17″ × 22″ are sometimes an advantage—they can be cut from rolls of 8 × 8 gridded stock or can be made by gluing 17″ × 22″ sheets at the edges with white glues (such as Elmer's Glu-All).

The paper base for gridded paper need not be acid-free for longevity, since field work at industrial sites usually contaminates the notes to some extent with dirt, perspiration and other substances. For long-term preservation, archival color electrostatic copies of notes should be made onto archival paper.

Use only one side of a sheet in order to reduce handling abrasions and contamination. Since field records are one of the primary means of verification for measured drawings (Standard II), their clarity and preservation is important. Paper is extremely cheap compared to the cost of labor making field records. Single-sided field notes also permit easier retrieval of information in the drawing room. Tears and holes in field notes should be repaired by gluing patches of gridded paper to the affected areas; tape of any kind should be avoided because it is not archivally stable.

It is very strongly recommended that sketches be drawn in No. 2 pencil (not ink) in order to make corrections easily. Dimension strings, arrows and dimensions should be done in a strong color, preferably red, so that they are plainly distinguishable from linework describing your structure (Standard IV). Verbal notes and annotations may be done in black or some color other than red. The use of drawing instruments is strongly discouraged (with the exception of a cheap drugstore compass for circles) because of the time lost handling, using and keeping track of such tools in the field.

Field Data Recording Methods

The field methods described below presume that hand measurement complemented with selective field photography is the predominate data recording method used. Various photographic, electronic and computer-assisted data gathering techniques and instruments have been developed for field and office use, and more sophisticated systems will inevitably appear. Most of these methods rely on line-of-sight data gathering, and they must be supplemented by hand measurement where line-of-sight is obstructed, or where access is too inconvenient and expensive to achieve with methods other than hand measurement. Much more data can be gathered more quickly by sets of photogrammetric negatives than with hand measurement, and the photographic data can be analyzed for other than purely dimensional information.

As with hand measurement, however, "high tech" data collection methods have steps where human input, judgment and notation are required, and significant errors can result when the advantages and limitations of the methods and equipment are not thoroughly understood. Error in some degree occurs in both "high tech" and hand-measured drawings. Whatever the error range is, it should be discerned and reported on the drawings, however the drawings are produced. Where "high tech" equipment and computer programs are used, these should also be annotated on the drawings for future reference and re-analysis (Standard II).[4]

Field Note Drawing Style and Content

Field notes should be executed free-hand with simple, clean lines free of ambiguous overruns and excessive starts and stops. Rendering ("artiness") is discouraged except where it is essential to clarity of interpretation, such as indicating materials, distinguishing parts of a complex cross section or preventing confusing figure/ground effects. In cases of great complexity, shoot numerous field photos to fill in details that would otherwise be too time consuming to sketch and measure. Conserve time in the field for later use in rendering final drawings. There are times when verbal notes save considerable time (e.g., write down the number of teeth on a gear rather than draw all of them as in Figure 9.5).

Notetakers should break each view they record down into a hierarchy of "scales" or "layers" which progress from schematic overall views to details. Sketch size should be large enough to legibly record appropriate dimensional data without crowding. All too often it will seem most efficient in time and paper to treat a view with one sketch and fill it with dimensions from the length of a building to the size of a doorknob, only to discover later that it is a mass of confusing lines and symbols (see Figure 9.4). Instead, notetakers should endeavor to put no more lines into a sketch than the number of features that can be dimensioned without crowding (Figure 9.5). For example, if you are sketching the elevation or plan of a factory building, start with a simple schematic overall view for recording datum lines, surveying points, major over-

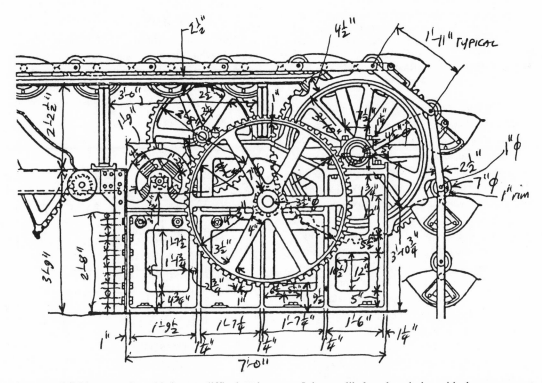

Figure 9.4. A cramped field note such as this is very difficult to interpret. It is very likely to be missing critical measurements, because of its unsystematic approach to recording this machinery. As a check, see if you can recreate this image using only the dimensions given! (Linework adapted from portion of Fig. 134 in E. B. Gebhardt, *Steam Power Plant Engineering.* New York: John Wiley & Sons, Inc., 1905, p. 226.)

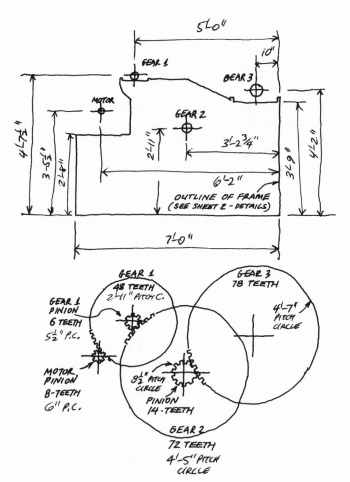

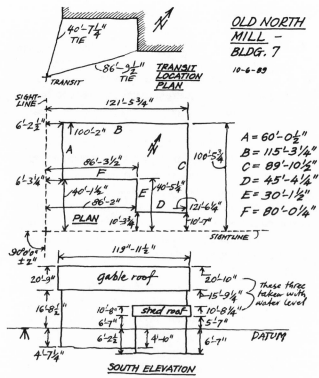

Figure 9.5. Simplified notes of the machinery in Figure 5 promote clarity and ease of use. Annotations prevent confusion, and only one type of information is recorded per sketch—(1) gear shaft centerlines and (2) gear teeth and pitch diameters. Details should be separately recorded. (Field notes by Richard K. Anderson, Jr.)

Figure 9.6. Basic field note sketch that records overall dimensions and shape of a building, including the transit station and horizontal datum plane locations, prior to more detailed notes of the structure. (Field note by Richard K. Anderson, Jr.)

all dimensions and check measurements such as diagonals; leave out such details as machinery, doors and windows, fire escapes and architectural details (Figure 9.6). The vertical and horizontal dimensional location of windows, doors and similarly sized features should be delegated to a second "layer" of sketches where these elements are drawn as simple boxes in a schematized elevation. What these boxes represent should be verbally defined in the notes, such as "outer edges of masonry openings," so that later users will know that they do not represent the inner edges of wooden window and door casings, or anything else (Figure 9.7). Details of machinery, construction and architectural details such as window casings, riveted joints, ironwork and other details should be left to a third "layer" of sketches (Figure 9.8). Even here it may be advantageous to record some items full size in a fourth "layer" of sketches, such as sections of moldings and structural members or rubbings of lettering cast into machinery frames. Similar principles apply to recording bridge trusses, machinery and other industrial structures. At times, it is advantageous to exaggerate arrangements schematically, or draw them deliberately out of proportion in order to call at-

tention to a detail or provide space for clarifying where critical dimensions end (Figure 9.9).

Another way to think of this system is by imagining to yourself what dimensions are needed and in what order as you progress in making a measured drawing at the drawing board. Usually one starts with datum lines or other principal references. Then the overall size and shape of the subject is

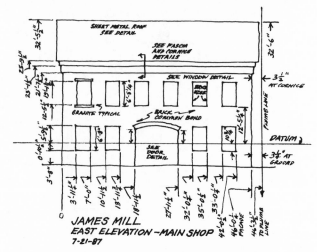

Figure 9.7. Sample of a field note illustrating how to begin recording an elevation; location of major openings is all that shoulld be covered in the first "layer" of notes. (Field notes by Richard K. Anderson, Jr.)

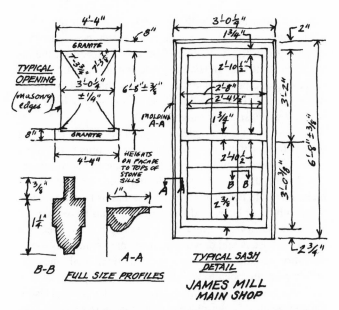

Figure 9.8. Large sketches for details allow room for dimensions and notes. Note the progress from general overall dimensions of a typical window opening to full size sections of window moldings. (Field note by Richard K. Anderson, Jr.)

drawn and confirmed before progressively smaller details are filled in.

Look for sensible "short cuts" that save sketching or measuring time. For example, if the elevation proposed above contained three different sizes of nine-over-nine light windows that differ in few other ways but casing size, draw a single sketch, designate principal dimensions with letter keys and create a table or chart to record dimensions specific to each window size. This method could apply as easily to mo-

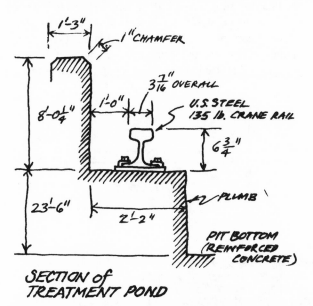

Figure 9.9. Distortion or foreshortening in a note may be used to promote efficiency, clarity and accuracy. Note how long dimensions are foreshortened where there are no details to record. (Field notes by Richard K. Anderson, Jr.)

tors, pulleys or I-beams of various sizes. Also, be aware that good field photographs will save sketching or measuring time when they can be used to record complex ironwork, surface features and detail too time consuming to sketch and measure.

Annotations and Dimensions

It is critical that notetakers label every sheet with the site name, view recorded, date and names of those making the notes. View labels should be fully descriptive, specific and unambiguous, for example, "North Elevation of Laboratory," rather than saying simply "Elevation" and leaving it to teammates or future users to puzzle over which side of which building it is.

The importance of recording annotations, dimensions and other data *clearly in the field* cannot be overemphasized. Haste creates confusion, and it is very unwise to rely on memory to remind yourself later what or why you drew or dimensioned something unusual. Write things down!

The functions of spaces should be labeled, as should names of any technological features. Materials should be noted, along with any other information significant to your project, even down to builder's plate data or markings stamped in pipes or parts. Be sure to record in your notes any measurement "short cuts," unusual conditions, inaccessible areas and dimensional error estimates where they are larger than might be reasonably expected. Reliance on other sources (Standard II) should also be noted. It may save time to make an electrostatic copy of an existing but outdated drawing and use it as a base to sketch and dimension changes and additions to the site or structure. Also, if you anticipate needing to redraw a field note several times in order to accommodate numerous layers of dimensions, consider making electrostatic copies of the original note sketch as a timesaver.

Set Reference Points

Before beginning measurements of a site or structure, reliable references for horizontal and vertical dimensions should be established. Do not assume that a building's floor is level or its walls plumb. Do not assume that line shafting is level, or that piping or any other feature conforms to a level or plumb alignment. While existing structure can be checked for plumb and level alignment, it is always best to set independent horizontal and vertical datum planes from which all dimensions are taken. This way you will not be blinded by false assumptions to site conditions such as structural deformations, irregularities, deliberate alterations or design subtleties.

Machinery and bridges are designed and built differently from buildings in many respects. Sketches and measurements of such resources should denote the *centerlines* of shafts, gears, levers, pulleys, pins, bolts, frames and structural members (Figures 9.5). Symmetry can be an ally in saving time, since only half of a symmetrical feature need be drawn to record principal data. Bridge members should be carefully studied because their centerlines are really "lines of action" or "neutral axes" which are not necessarily the geometric centers of members! Frequently machinery castings are "split" and bolted together about the centerline of a shaft, or you may find the parting line in a casting (created where two halves of a sand mold joined) denotes the centerlines of rounded features. Shafting and other rotating parts often have centering holes drilled in the ends. Diameters of pulleys, pipes and tanks are easily found by taking their circumferences with a tape and dividing by π (3.1416). Never try to "eyeball" the diameter of a round object—parallax error usually results in considerable underestimation of the true diameter.

Datum Planes

Datum planes are casually referred to as "datum lines" because they are usually marked as lines on structures. However, what these lines represent is the intersection of a level or plumb datum plane with the physical fabric of the site. A horizontal datum can be set by a transit, a water level, a string level or laser level.

With a transit, spots may be marked in the transit scope plane on features such as walls, piping, foundations, etc. These spots may be connected by chalk lines or strings in order to establish reference lines (spots should be no more than 15 feet apart to minimize error introduced by string sag). However, the transit is limited by sight lines as to where it can lay reference marks from any one station. The instrument must be moved in order to carry the datum plane around corners, buildings, exteriors to interiors, etc. The original datum plane can be maintained by measuring how far above or below the new plane is from the original with a

tape measure, recording this dimension on field notes and continuing new marks at the recorded difference dimension (Figure 9.10). It is a waste of field time to try to set the instrument itself in an old datum plane at a new location, since surveying equipment is not designed for this kind of adjustment. (See also Chapter 11, *Land Surveying Methods Employed by Industrial Archaeologists*.)

A water level is a simple instrument consisting of a long hose with a sight glass in each end, the assembly being filled with a colored liquid such as automobile radiator coolant (see Figure 9.11). A clear vinyl tube will serve also, and make it easy to ensure that the fluid contains no air bubbles. Vinyl tubing or hoses and sight tubes should have plugs or valves at the tops in order to prevent fluid from escaping when the hose is laid down. The principle behind this tool's operation is simply that water seeks its own level when the tubing ends are open to the atmosphere. (It is possible such a system may use two or more interconnected hoses.) Using a water level, a datum plane can be transferred around corners, and over or under obstacles that are impenetrable by lines of sight. The range of the water level is limited only by its length.

A string level is expedient for setting datum lines over short distances. To level a string, the string level instrument (or "line level") is hung at the midpoint of a string stretched between two points (see Figure 9.12). The string ends are then raised or lowered until the bubble in the level lies between the innermost marks. The string level is then removed from the string (its weight causes a sag), and the datum marked in several places along the string (including the ends) for future reference. If there is any doubt about the accuracy of the instrument (which depends on a precise dimension between the bubble tube and the string hooks), the instrument can be reversed on the string to see if the bubble returns to the same central reading point. If not, adjust the string until the bubble rests in the same place relative to the tube center (left or right) regardless which way the instrument is hung from the string (see Figure 9.13). Taking heights or depths to features that are

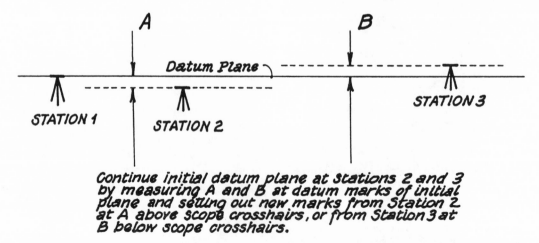

Continue initial datum plane at Stations 2 and 3 by measuring A and B at datum marks of initial plane and setting out new marks from Station 2 at A above scope crosshairs, or from Station 3 at B below scope crosshairs.

Figure 9.10.   Continuing a datum plane from a new transit station. (Drawing by Richard K. Anderson, Jr.)

Using a Water Level

Figure 9.11.   While not absolutely foolproof, there is little in the way of technology or moving parts to hinder the accuracy of a water level. (U.S. Department of the Interior, National Park Service, Historic American Buildings Survey/Historic American Engineering Record, Richard K. Anderson, Jr., *Guidelines for Recording Historic Ships,* Washington, DC. 1988, Fig. 4.2.32, p. 4.2.40., Illustration by Richard K. Anderson, Jr.)

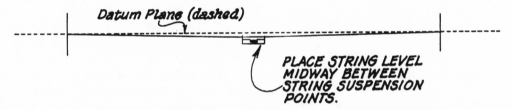

Figure 9.12.   Set-up and use of a string level. (Drawing by Richard K. Anderson, Jr.)

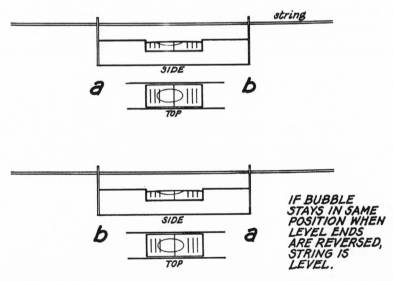

Figure 9.13.   A string level should be checked for accuracy by reversing it to see if the bubble centers in the tube in both positions. Should the bubble not center properly in both positions, merely adjust the string until the bubble shows the same position relative to the bubble mark centerline in both positions. The string is now level. (Drawing by Richard K. Anderson, Jr.)

not plumb to a marked datum line can be carried out by swing ties and a transit (Figure 9.14), or by simply measuring from the feature plumb to a mason's level which has one end leveled and aligned with the marked datum line.

In some situations, a laser level may be advantageous. This instrument projects a visible red (or invisible infrared) laser beam in a plane (horizontal or vertical) via a spinning mirror. It requires batteries or an external power outlet to operate, and its capacity to project a line on walls or other features is limited to straight lines of sight from the instrument's location. (Pipes, machinery, columns and other features will cast shadows on walls or other objects beyond.) However, time can be saved making measurements from the laser plane, since the laser beam will directly indicate measurements on a tape. Swing ties can be more quickly taken than with a transit telescope, and there is no danger of accidentally disturbing a transit setting.

Vertical datum lines are best set with a plumb bob, though a specially equipped laser level or a transit telescope's vertical circle can also be used to establish a vertical line or plane. From such references measurements may be made to check the inclination and offset of walls or other portions of structures and machinery. Neither a transit nor a laser level is as subject to winds as a plumb bob is. Plumb bob oscillation can be dampened by suspending the plumb bob in a bucket of water. Fine wire and heavy, vaned plumb bobs suspended in water can dramatically reduce wind effects (Figure 9.15).

Dimensions from Datum Planes

Dimensions should always be taken from a feature to the datum line in a direction perpendicular to the datum line (or,

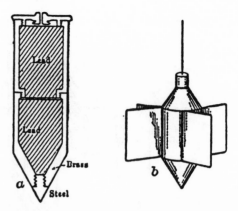

Figure 9.15. Plumb bobs for use in drafty circumstances. Suspension of the vaned plumb bob in water would dampen oscillations considerably. (Robert Peele, *Mining Engineer's Handbook*, New York: John Wiley & Sons, Inc., 1927; Fig. 22, p. 1438.)

more correctly, normal to the datum plane), in order to obtain the proper dimensions for constructing correct orthogonal projections in drawings. A simple way to assure a proper dimension is to place a measuring tape end at the feature being located (plumb to the datum), and swing the tape by the datum line—the minimum measurement must lie along a line normal to the plane. This rule applies whether making swing ties to heights above or below a datum line set on a plumb wall, or to heights above or below a plane sighted with a transit. When using the transit, merely look for the minimum reading at the crosshairs as a tape or stadia rod is moved around in the telescope field of view. (It may save time in some cases to have a vertical bubble level attached to a measuring rod [see Figure 9.16] in order to minimize "hunting.")

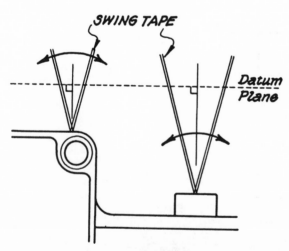

Figure 9.14. The shortest distance from a point to a datum plane or reference line is always the "true" measurement; it also happens to be along a line normal to the plane or perpendicular to the reference line. Such dimensions are found by swinging a tape (hence the term "swing tie") from the point to be located to the datum plane or reference line and reading the minimum measurement. (Drawing by Richard K. Anderson, Jr.)

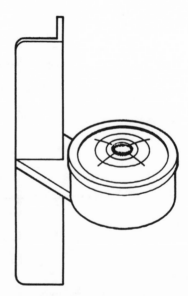

Figure 9.16. A vertical bubble level or rod level is used for plumbing stadia rods or other vertical measuring devices. When user has centered the bubble within the series of concentric circles in the vial, the instrument arm is vertical. (Drawing by Richard K. Anderson, Jr.)

Dimensions should be taken in the system in which the recorded structure was designed and built (usually English feet and inches in the United States, except for optical and scientific equipment which are metric). All dimensions and dimension strings should be clearly noted in red so they are easily distinguishable from black lines denoting structure. To be unambiguous, use foot and inch tick marks to distinguish between foot and inch numerals, and take time to letter your numerals clearly. Dimensions such as 5 feet and 3/4 of an inch should be noted as 5'-0 3/4" rather than 5'-3/4", since this provides assurance that an inch numeral has not been inadvertently left out; similarly there are times when something 7 1/4" wide should be recorded as 0'-7 1/4" so that users will be assured that no foot numerals have been accidentally omitted.

Accuracy

Taking measurements has its pitfalls as well as its rules. Accuracy is a matter of definition, tape graduations, purpose of your drawings and the precision to which the structure or object was built. As a matter of definition, "accuracy" really refers to the error tolerance permitted or realistically achievable in the field. There is a point beyond which narrow error tolerances become counterproductive in terms of time and information content. Common sense indicates that you would not try to measure a 50-foot high pumping engine to the nearest millionth of an inch, or the length of a rough stone wall to the nearest sixteenth of an inch. But neither should you settle for simply the nearest inch or foot when conditions permit and demand finer work, especially where precision has some bearing on the significance of the object or structure being recorded.

Normally, sufficient accuracy for HAER work is defined as a +/− error over a dimensional range for certain conditions:

0"–12": +/− as little as 1/64" for machined parts where fit and dimension is critical to operation; there may be occasions where micrometer measurements to +/− 0.001" are appropriate
+/− 1/16" for normal structural elements, machinery castings, etc.

1'–10': +/− 1/8" for smooth edges and structures in good condition
+/− 1/2" for rough stone; as much or more for structures in deteriorated condition

10'–100': +/− 1/4" for smooth edges and structures in good condition
+/− 1 1/2" for rough stone; as much or more for structures in deteriorated condition

100'–250': +/− 1/2" for smooth edges and structures in good condition
+/− 1 1/2" to 2" for rough stone; as much or more for structures in deteriorated condition

+/− 6" for site plans to be drawn at a scale of 20 feet to the inch or smaller.

250'–∞ +/− 1 part in 5,000 for hand measurement

In many cases you will be recording dimensions at a precision far greater than you can draw them to scale at a drawing board, but this observation is not an encouragement for sloppy measurement. Field notes are primary reference materials and should contain the greatest reasonable accuracy at full size—some future research or project may require the precise dimensional data in the notes. Wherever unusual conditions must allow for larger than normal errors, be sure to verbally note the estimated error/accuracy in your field notes with a +/− notation and include an explanation for it. The clarity and thoroughness of your notes are essential to the verification of your work (Standard II) by your professional peers, project superiors, clients and future researchers.

As for the instruments used for measuring—tapes, stick rules, machinists' scales, transit verniers, etc.—the accuracy can be no better than 1/2 of the smallest graduation on the instrument. In other words, if you are using a tape graduated only in 1/4ths of an inch, your accuracy can be no better than +/− 1/8 inch. The accuracy of Electronic Distance Measurement (EDM) equipment is dependent on several things such as the interval being measured, and the temperature, density and humidity of the air; EDM operators' manuals should be consulted for specific conditions and applicable corrections. Similar compensation conditions and error ranges should be considered when using "high tech" data gathering systems.

The purpose of dimensional information can have a bearing on field accuracy. For example, a site plan to be drawn at a small scale or used for a schematic drawing need not be measured in the field within fractions of an inch (assuming aerial mapping techniques or preexisting drawings are not used). Measurements of individual structures should be to within fractions of an inch. Finer precision should only be attempted where it has a significant bearing on the function or nature of the structure or object. You may also need to take into account ambient temperatures—a 100 foot bridge truss or steel building frame will expand and contract depending on time of year, direct sunlight versus cloudy day, etc.

Consideration for the purpose of a structure or the nature of its construction materials may have great bearing on the measurement precision used. Machinery, even very large examples (turntables, machine tools, pumping engines), are built to much finer tolerances than brick buildings, simply because machinery contains parts that mate, slide, rotate or mesh, and must do so accurately for the machine to function properly. Whether a stone wall is 102'-3" long or 102'-4" on the average has little significance in terms of its ability to function as a building.

Similarly, cross-sectional dimensions of rolled or extruded structural elements and parts should be taken carefully, since they are critical for the elements' ability to resist stresses and carry loads.

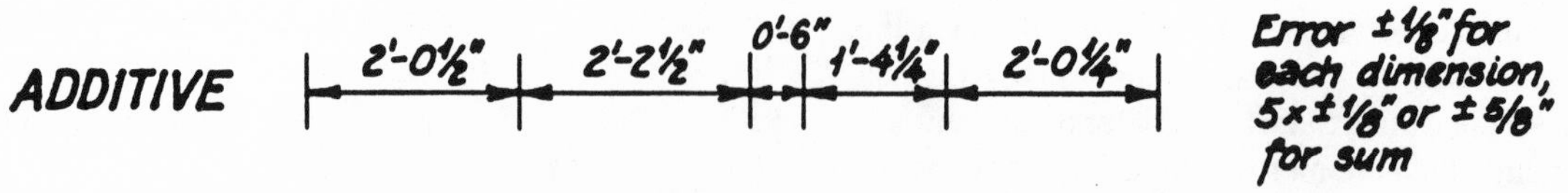

ADDITIVE |— 2'-0½" —|— 2'-2½" —|0'-6"|—1'-4¼"—|— 2'-0¼" —| *Error ± ⅛" for each dimension, 5 × ± ⅛" or ± ⅝" for sum*

Figure 9.17. Cumulative or additive dimensioning multiplies errors with each dimension. (Adapted from U.S. Department of the Interior, National Park Service, Historic American Buildings Survey/Historic American Engineering Record, Richard K. Anderson, Jr., *Guidelines for Recording Historic Ships,* Washington, D.C.. 1988, Fig. 4.2.1, p. 4.2.5.)

Taking Measurements

Measurements to datum lines and datum planes are easily made by swing ties, as described above. When making a series of measurements along a wall, truss or machinery, it seems natural to measure from window to window, panel point to panel point or bolt to bolt (see Figure 9.17). However, such incremental or additive measurements accumulate errors rapidly. In a chain of 10 dimensions made to +/− 1/8 inch, the final overall accuracy of the summed dimensions is 10 × 1/8 inch or +/−1 1/4 inch—such error can be significant, even at the drawing board. Whenever additive dimensioning is necessary the use of overlapping and checked measurements avoids cumulative errors (see Figure 9.18). For this reason, attempt to keep the zero end of the tape at the original starting point for all measurements, and take the dimensions down in a running series (see Figure 9.19). This method avoids cumulative errors, minimizes the error of any one dimension and prevents one erroneous measurement from upsetting the overall sum as well as, every other measurement beyond. Running measurements should be used unless obstructions or misalignments preclude completing an accurate series.

Be sure you know where the zero end of each tape is! In most products, it lies at the very tip of the end loop. On some tapes made for surveyors' use, the zero may be three or four inches from the tape end.

Be careful when reading a tape. Common errors are reading to the wrong side of an inch or foot mark, for example, 8 1/2 inch may be recorded as 9 1/2 inch if one is associating the numeral 9 incorrectly with the 1/2 inch mark between 8- and 9-inch graduations. If the tape is upside down, this kind of error is more likely, as is confusion of the numerals "6" and "9" in inch or foot readings. As discussed above, fractional dimensions less than 1 inch or 1 foot should be written as 0 3/4 inch so that it is clear no integer inch is omitted.

Tape sag or deflection can introduce negligible or significant errors, depending on the deflection's size and location.

Error is dependent on the amount of sag over a given distance. Tape materials are such that a 20-pound pull on a tape yields an accurate measurement despite the small sag in the tape resulting from the tape's weight. Large sags can have surprisingly small effects over long distances—a 9-inch sag in 150-foot horizontal measurement yields a difference of less than 1/8 inch between a measurement made along the sag and one made in an optically straight line between the two points.

Deflections caused by obstructions may or may not be significant. A 4-inch deflection at the midpoint of a 50-foot measurement causes an erroneous increase in length of about 0.043″ (less than 1/16″). But as that deflection is moved closer to the tape end, the error introduced becomes considerable. If the 4-inch deflection is 1 foot from either tape end, an error of more than +5/8 inch is introduced.

For measuring large sites a transit and stadia rod are highly recommended. Electronic accessories may substitute a laser and reflective target for a stadia rod in distance measurement. More information on the set-up, use and care of various transits and related equipment can be found in Chapter 11 and in surveying texts listed in the bibliography.

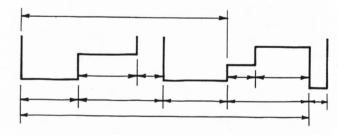

Overlapping and Check Measurements

Figure 9.18. Whenever additive dimensioning is mandatory, use of overlapping and check measurements is good practice for isolating errors and correcting them. (Adapted from U.S. Department of the Interior, National Park Service, Historic American Buildings Survey/Historic American Engineering Record, Richard K. Anderson, Jr., *Guidelines for Recording Historic Ships,* Washington, D.C.. 1988, Fig. 4.2.2, p. 4.2.7.)

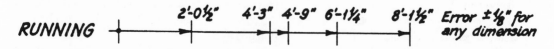

RUNNING |—— 2'-0½" 4'-3" 4'-9" 6'-1¼" 8'-1½" *Error ± ⅛" for any dimension*

Figure 9.19. Running dimensions minimize errors. (Adapted from U.S. Department of the Interior, National Park Service, Historic American Buildings Survey/Historic American Engineering Record, Richard K. Anderson, Jr., *Guidelines for Recording Historic Ships,* Washington, D.C.. 1988, Fig. 4.2.1, p. 4.2.5.)

Diagonals, Trilateration and Reference Grids

Never assume that a rectangular room has square corners. When measuring plans, always measure room diagonals as well as sides in order to establish correct room geometry at the drawing board (see Figure 9.20). Diagonals can also be used on facades, openings or in other planes where correct geometry must be established. Be aware that walls between corners may be bowed or kinked rather than straight.

Diagonals are a special case of trilateration, a long-established surveying technique that has numerous applications in hand measurement work. Small site plans can often be recorded and laid out by using trilaterations among corners of structures, geographic features and lot corners (see Figure 9.21), provided these measurements are made in level planes. Trilateration is also useful for establishing the size and location of irregular openings or objects in plan and elevation (Figure 9.22). Archways and curved features can also be recorded by trilateration from two or more known points (Figure 9.23); the measurement pairs or "coordinates"

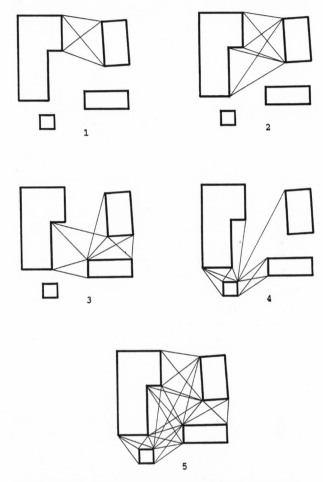

Figure 9.21. These diagrams show progress in trilateration of building corners in a small site plan (building sides should be measured as well). At the drawing board, a compass, scale and straightedge should lay out this plan easily. (Drawings by Richard K. Anderson, Jr.)

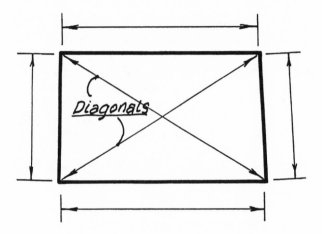

FIELD MEASUREMENTS

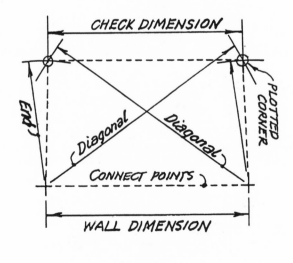

PLOT

Figure 9.20. Diagonals are the simplest and most direct means for accurately recording and plotting the actual shapes of rectangular rooms. (Drawings by Richard K. Anderson, Jr.)

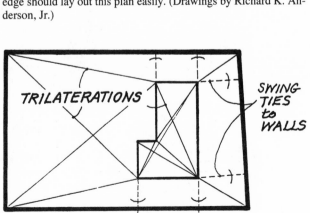

Figure 9.22. Trilaterations and swing ties from corners and walls of a room can locate internal features and describe their shape with ease. (Drawing by Richard K. Anderson, Jr.)

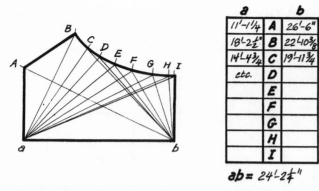

Figure 9.23. A diagram for trilateration of curved features is best accompanied by a table in which measurements are recorded for easy reference at the drawing board. (Drawing by Richard K. Anderson, Jr.)

for a series of points along a curve are best recorded in tabular form in field notes.

At times, a complex building plan such as this portion of a cyanide process gold-extraction mill may best be recorded by laying out a rectilinear grid at intervals convenient to the plan features. Features may then be located by trilateration from grid intersections (Figure 9.24). A single field note should show just the grid layout, dimensions and some diagonal ties used to check and establish the grid geometry. Separate reference strings are useful in recording misalignments and irregularities in plan or elevation. Swing ties taken from

features to such a string help locate the features accurately, as long as the endpoints of the string are at known locations (Figure 9.25).

Rubbings

Occasionally detailed castings, gear teeth profiles, builders' plates, ironwork, architectural or decorative detail and the like are easily recorded by making rubbings of them (full size) with tracing paper and a graphite stick or crayon. This kind of field note can be photographically reduced to the scales chosen for the drawings or input into a CAD system.

Profile Gauges

Useful for recording the forms of irregular shapes full size, a profile or contour gauge consists of a series of slender rods bound tightly together in a plane. These gauges range in length from 6″ to 12″. A profile is picked up by adjusting the rods until they are in direct contact with the shape to be recorded. The rods are then locked in their holder, and the profile traced from the ends of the rods onto a field note sheet. For curves and shapes between 12″ and 24″ in length, a piece of 12 gauge insulated copper wire can be bent to conform to the shape, then the profile of the wire can be traced onto a field note sheet.

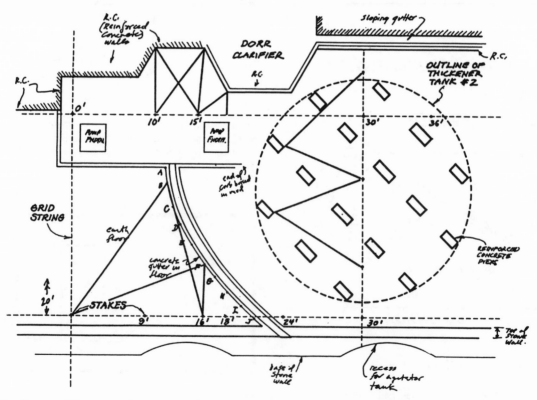

Figure 9.24. Once a grid is set up, trilaterations to site features can be made from stakes set out along the grid lines. (Drawing by Richard K. Anderson, Jr.)

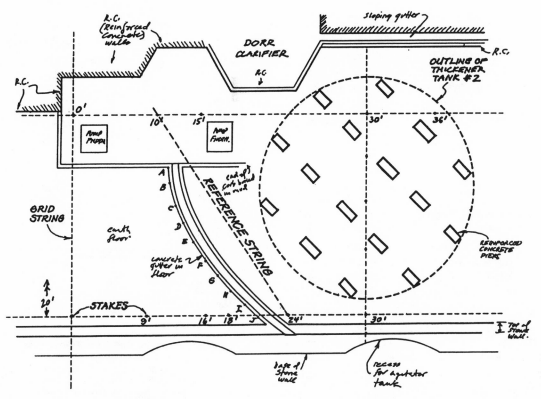

Figure 9.25. Curved features and other oddly located objects may be most easily recorded by an offset or angled reference line tied to a grid. (Drawing by Richard K. Anderson, Jr.)

Tips for Recording Machinery

Nearly all machinery comes with basic information cast or stamped into frames, or presented on builder's plates mounted in prominent places. All such information should be recorded in field notes for later inclusion in historical report appendices or ink drawings. Builder's plates give data such as manufacturer's names, addresses, dates, patents, model numbers and serial numbers. They often display further important information such as cylinder diameters and strokes, horsepower, speeds, capacities, pressures, temperatures, voltage, amperage, wattage, lubrication requirements, safety precautions, operating instructions and the like. Be sure to check over assemblages of machinery for equipment from more than one manufacturer, and record appropriate builder's plate data. Letters or numbers cast or stamped into parts may turn out to be part numbers, match numbers, assembly numbers or other relevant information showing how parts should be reassembled after disassembly for repair. Some casting numbers may coincide with part numbers listed in surviving engineering drawings or parts catalogs.

Many kinds of equipment parts and structural members come in standardized sizes (nuts and bolts, pipe diameters, fittings and valves, sections of structural wrought iron and steel, etc.) Consult handbooks and other references contemporaneous with your site for tables and diagrams that can provide dimensional data without requiring extensive measuring time in the field. In some cases this may require re-

search in libraries retaining "out-of-date" texts, or else consulting used and antique book dealers.

Industrial Processes

Investigation of industrial processes may require careful site investigation in addition to studying company records or contemporary professional textbooks, trade publications and handbooks in order to piece together significant information. You may have to carefully note steps in the manufacture of a product, and the way equipment is oriented and operated. You may have to record routes of tubing, piping, wiring, belts, chains, chutes, shafting, control cables, tracks and the like in order to understand how materials, energy, products, by-products and wastes are handled on site and why. Points of wear in floors, structures and equipment should be noted, as should holes in walls, "ghosts" on walls and floors revealing structural alterations or locations where machinery once stood. These observations may be essential for historians to "reconstruct" and interpret how processes worked on site at one time or another. The age and kind of equipment, manufacturing methods and working conditions will be of great interest to future users of the documentation.

Unusually complex processes that carry materials and products through three dimensions (diagonally, skewed or vertically, as well as horizontally) may be better comprehended if a rough scale model is built emphasizing the process machinery and components over against building structure. Simple materials such as cardboard and balsa wood sticks are all that are needed. The model could be built from preexisting drawings, field measurements or a combination of the two. Such models may help delineators to better visualize the process and link together significant steps and machinery for production of accurate process drawings.

Buildings

Industrial buildings range from small sheds to multistory mills, factories and other structures. Higher features of smaller buildings can be reached with ladders, or on elevations, long poles to which the ends of tapes are attached can be used for reaching soffits, window lintels and the like. Larger buildings can be tackled by several means that do not involve erection of scaffolding or renting "cherry pickers." Fire escapes give access to vertical zones of a facade for measurement. Team members might also climb to the top floor of a building and lower a tape which can then be read by team members at each floor or by someone outside using a pair of binoculars. For measuring heights, angles measured with a transit can be used in conjunction with trigonometric calculations, but the distance of the instrument from the facade and any projections or recesses must be known, as must the distance of the instrument above or below the datum plane (Figure 9.26). Counting repetitive elements, such as brick and stone coursing, siding and other materials, may also be used to arrive at vertical measurements. Directly taped measurements are preferable, but there are times when safety is paramount and the significance of the dimensions is not high enough to warrant use of scaffolding or cherry pickers. Error factors in such an approach should be accounted for in final drawing annotations.

Identifying Woods and Metals

At times, wood species may be significant and require identification. This may require a university specialist or someone from a state or federal agricultural agency. Wrought iron, cast iron and steel are separate alloys of iron with distinctive corrosion and deformation patterns. In cast iron, iron and a high percentage of carbon have separately crystallized. Cast iron rusts little, but it is brittle and commonly breaks under tension or impact without elongation, bending or other evidence of overstress. It is usually found serving where compression stresses are carried. Ductile iron castings are more malleable, as the name implies. Wrought iron is much more ductile than cast iron and is also rust-resistant. Corroded wrought iron will appear to have striations like wood grain running in the direction of the member's length. This "grain" results from the inclusion of slag strings during the production process. Wrought iron was commonly

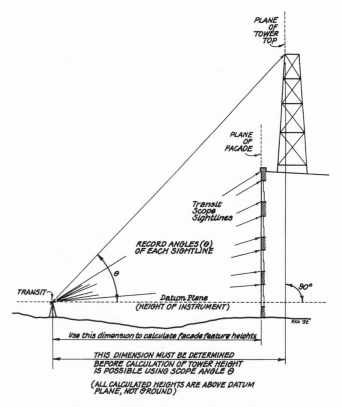

Figure 9.26. Successful use of a transit for recording inaccessible heights is dependent on knowing the projected horizontal dimension from the instrument to the feature whose height is being measured. (Drawing by Richard K. Anderson, Jr.)

used as a structural metal (especially in tension) from the 1860s to 1900, and it was used in machinery for bolts, shafts and other parts which endured tension or torsion stresses. Steel is decarbonized iron, often alloyed with other metals. While stronger than wrought iron or cast iron, steel is more corrosion-prone. It will pit and exfoliate more quickly than the other irons under similar conditions and time periods. Steel's strength and ease of manufacture eventually drove wrought iron off the market after 1900 for all but specialty applications where wrought iron's corrosion resistance was desirable. Cast iron, wrought iron and steel are magnetic, which permits easy separation from nonferrous metals like copper, zinc, lead, aluminum and various alloys where metal parts are painted. Most stainless steels are nonmagnetic, however. Copper alloys, brasses and bronzes, come in many colors from the familiar golden yellow, to pink or pale yellow, depending on the alloy composition. Brasses are basically alloys of copper and zinc, bronzes alloys of copper and tin, though there are copper alloys with both zinc and tin in their composition. Brass and bronze were frequently used for bearing liners, plumbing valves, lubricators, oil cups and decorative materials in older machinery. Aside from windows, glass may have been used as liners for pipe or machinery where corrosive chemicals were used. The glass composition itself may be critical.

In cases of great significance, analyses of metals, alloys, slags and minerals may be necessary in order to securely identify features, support or clinch hunches, etc. It may be necessary to include reports in footnotes or appendices, or indicate if costs or other matters limited or interfered with certain investigations.

Field Photography

Field photography is used to supplement field sketches and measurements. Photography should range from an overall survey of the site to specific significant details whose images can be referred to at the drawing board. Bear in mind that field photographs are primary resource materials just like field notes, and they are vital to the verification of your documentation (Standard II). Film and prints should be archivally processed and handled with care, especially since they will be of use to future researchers.

Photographs can be used cautiously as a substitute for field notes where access, safety of team members and sturdiness of a structure are issues, but all attempts should be made to obtain direct overall measurements of the structure to "bracket" the image scale of the photographs, and thus reduce scaling errors. Where accurate measurement of a large, high, inaccessible or unstable structure is required, photogrammetry should be considered.

Field photography is easiest with 35mm film and equipment (including a flash), though larger formats are acceptable (Standard III). Usually black and white films are employed, because they are cheaper and more archivally stable than color prints. After the film is processed, contact sheets of negative strips are made for use at the drawing board where they can be comfortably examined with an eye loupe. Photographs can frequently settle confusion caused by conflicting or ambiguous dimensions and thus save time-consuming trips to the structure to remeasure something or fill in data gaps. Specific photos can be selected for enlargement when detail can be distinguished, measured or traced from the photograph. The photo records should be organized, and every contact sheet, film strip and print should be properly numbered, labeled and captioned for use by the team and future researchers (Standards II and IV). Descriptive and thorough captions are extremely important. Point out such things as compass orientation, significant conditions, objects, features and process steps.

Measuring and checking dimensions from photographs is considerably assisted by including in each view a black-and-white scale stick of suitable length for each view (see Figure 9.27). The sticks are made from 1 1/4″ × 1/4″ pine lattice molding and range in length from 1 to 10 feet, depending on convenience and suitable size in photographic views. Each stick should be graduated in feet, with at least one foot further graduated into inches. Drill holes in the sticks so scales can be nailed to walls, hung from strings, etc. It may be useful to mount scales behind [white] datum line strings so that they show against the black fields. The bottoms or tops of the scales can also be aligned with datum strings.

It is best to attempt "rectified" photographs if you plan to derive a lot of dimensional data from particular field photos. A rectified photo image is created when the camera lens axis is normal to the plane of a wall or feature in which you place a scale stick and from which you plan to make measurements. Avoid using lenses with focal lengths shorter than 35mm—such wide angle lenses introduce image distortions at edges that make views undesirable for measurement; a 55mm lens is best for a fairly distortion-free image. Features which project forward or recede from the plane of the scale stick will have different image scales, and this must be taken into account when attempting to scale anything in any plane other than that in which a scale stick lies. This rule can be relaxed somewhat for telephoto views, since telephoto lenses compress image depth as focal lengths increase. The longer the focal length and the further the camera is from the subject, the more recessions and projections in the image are "flattened out" and appear at nearly the same scales in the photograph (see Figure 9.28). A tripod and higher shutter speeds are necessary for lenses longer than 200mm in order to avoid blurred images.

Set-up Tips for Rectified Photographs

Before positioning a camera for a rectified photograph, it must be understood that the film plane of the camera *must* be positioned parallel to the plane of the structure's facade, or a rectified photo *cannot* result. There are several ways to go about setting the camera up geometrically. Placing a torpedo (8″) level against the back of the camera can plumb and level the camera. While this may insure a level *horizontal* plane for the lens axis, it does not insure that the lens axis is square to the structure's facade in plan view, and it assumes that the facade itself is plumb. One could go to the trouble of using tapes or a transit to precisely lay out a station for the camera such that you know the lens axis will be square to the facade in plan by centering the camera's viewfinder on a certain

Figure 9.27. A typical four foot scale stick used by the author; nail holes permit attachment of the stick to structures for photographs. The reverse side of the stick is painted in a reverse black and white pattern, thus allowing one side of the stick to be used against light backgrounds, the other against dark ones. (Drawing by Richard K. Anderson, Jr.)

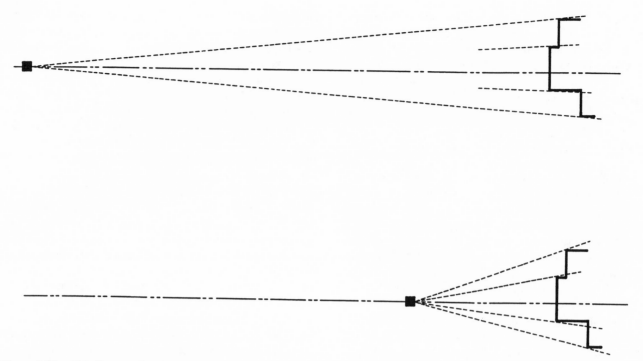

Figure 9.28. This diagram shows the reduction in parallax error with increase in camera distance from a subject and the use of telephoto lenses. (Drawing by Richard K. Anderson, Jr.)

predetermined feature, such as the edge of a window casing. However, a much simpler and faster method requires nothing more than a mirror. If you attach the mirror to the facade and position the camera so that the center of the image of the camera lens reflected in the mirror is also centered in the camera's viewfinder, the camera lens axis must be normal to the mirror plane, and the camera must be in the correct geometric location for a rectified photograph (Figure 9.29). This method automatically takes care of all positioning problems, including walls or features that are out of plumb. However, care should be taken to insure that the mirror is set correctly in the plane of the feature, and that it is not mispositioned due to bumps and dirt between it and the feature to which it is mounted. The smoother the surface, the better this trick works; the larger the mirror, the less little irregularities will introduce errors. If the reflected image of the camera is difficult to determine due to camera distance, temporarily mounting a telephoto lens will magnify the image sufficiently to align the lens axis before taking the photograph with a 55mm lens.

Rectified photographs can be enlarged to a specific scale for tracing significant features such as complex stonework, architectural iron castings, or other detail. Series of overlapping photographs can be made to document larger areas and preserve detail; it will speed photography and enlargement work if the camera is kept the same distance from the subject in overlapping views (use a measuring tape, knotted string or stick to control distance). It may be less trouble to trace an enlarged view and have the line tracing enlarged or

reduced to a desired scale. Photos may even be traced with a mouse and input into a CAD program on a computer; however, as with hand methods, accuracy of photo set-up and skill in tracing will be essential to the final accuracy of the drawings. (See Chapter 10 for information on large format photography.)

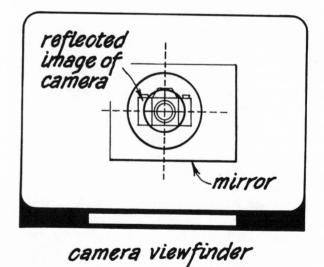

Figure 9.29. This is how the image of an SLR (single lens reflex) camera reflected in a mirror should look in the camera's viewfinder for the mirror to be normal to the camera's lens axis. If the mirror obscures detail, it can be removed after the camera is in position. (Drawing by Richard K. Anderson, Jr., 1989.)

Scaling from Photos

There are two ways to scale dimensions from a photograph:

1. Rely on a scale stick in the photograph, and use a pair of dividers to transfer the distance between two desired points to the scale stick for a reading.
2. Use a known dimension in a photograph (width of a window, length of a machine bed as recorded in field notes) to find the image scale by simple proportions. Suppose you must find a dimension because it was erroneously measured or omitted in field records. In a photo image, this dimension is 2.21 inches. Using simple proportions, this dimension is to 12″ as 2.21 is to 3.43″ (X ÷ 12″ = 2.21 ÷ 3.43″), or about 7 3/4″. The length of the valve chest top is similarly derived: length = 12″ × (3.80 ÷ 3.43) = 13 1/4″ or 1′–1 1/4″.

Photos taken at oblique angles can be used for dimensioning, but they are more suited for vertical measurements and qualitative information. Sometimes with added analysis and comparisons between known and unknown dimensions, oblique photos can yield reasonably accurate drawings.

Repeated elements of known size, such as steps, bricks, stone courses, railing stanchions, beam dimensions and the like can be good constants from which to derive measurements of other features in a photograph. While not as accurate as direct measurement with a tape, it is better than sheer guesswork or no information at all.

PHASE 3: PRELIMINARY DRAWINGS

Once basic field dimensions and secondary source information have been collected, preliminary drawings should be started as soon as possible. Either *Mylar*[5] or vellum should be used as the drawing base, although Mylar is more dimensionally stable because of its resistance to temperature and humidity changes, and it is easier to erase ink or pencil lines from its surface. Consider using ink (3×0 or 4×0 lines) for preliminary drawings since the contrast is much stronger than with pencil, and lines are less likely to smudge or fade (see Phase 4 for tips regarding ink-on-Mylar). See Figure 9.30 for examples of line widths. Phase 3 is where dimensional information from all sources is synthesized, and where conflicts in field work sources and presentation issues are discovered and resolved. The final graphic and verbal content of each sheet should be established at this phase, referring to earlier "story boards" or cartoons, and revising them as necessary.

Preliminary drawings should be regarded as though they were scaffolding or concrete formwork. Scale, accuracy and correct projections are important, but the drawing does not

6 x 0	——	(0.13mm, 0.005 in.)
4 x 0	——	(0.18mm, 0.007 in.)
3 x 0	——	(0.25mm, 0.010 in.)
2 x 0	——	(0.30mm, 0.012 in.)
0	——	(0.35mm, 0.014 in.)
1	——	(0.50mm, 0.020 in.)
2	——	(0.60mm, 0.024 in.)
2½	——	(0.70mm, 0.028 in.)
3	——	(0.80mm, 0.031 in.)
4	——	(1.20mm, 0.047 in.)

Figure 9.30. Line widths used in measured drawings.(Adapted from U.S. Department of the Interior, National Park Service, Historic American Buildings Survey/Historic American Engineering Record, Larry D. Lankton and Richard K. Anderson, Jr., *Historic American Engineering Record Field Instructions,* Washington, DC. 1981)

have to be pretty or drawn on a single piece of drawing material. Freely make verbal notes to yourself on the drawing surface, write down dimensions, jot down notes that should appear in the final drawings to clarify conditions, describe materials and processes, identify parts, show directions of motion or flow, etc. Have no hesitation to cut up and move parts of drawings if necessary to correct errors or change composition. Repetitive elements can be drawn once, electrostatically copied, then taped or glued to the drawing base to save time. A drawing can also be produced as separate pieces which are later brought together with lettering for final compositional arrangement. Where a given view will require two or more sheets for final inkwork, it may be wise to create the original view as a single assemblage before cutting it apart, in order to ensure that divided lines and features are continuous and match from one sheet to the next. Preliminary drawings can also serve as an experimental stage in which to work out appropriate and effective inking and presentation techniques. Keep in mind that the final drawings should be capable of reduction to 25 percent or even 15 percent of original size and still retain reasonable legibility. Fine lines should not disappear, pochés (see Figure 9.31) should not "block up" (turn solid black) and text should be readable.

It is important to maintain consistency throughout the drawings. Treating the same type of information the same way from sheet to sheet, in linework and lettering, allows a user to more easily see what is different from sheet to sheet. Repeated drawing elements, such as titles, graphic scales and notes should follow a consistent format and be consistently located in the same or similar positions sheet to sheet. This also reinforces the set as a unity. If hand-lettering is used, only team members with the same lettering style should letter sheets, or else the team should rely on a mechanical lettering system (such as Keuffel & Esser's Leroy system). See "Phase 4: Final Drawings" for more detailed guidelines.

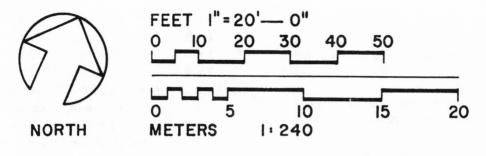

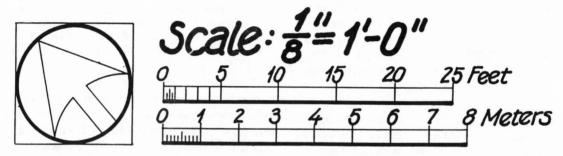

Figure 9.31. Some sample graphic scales and north arrows from HABS/HAER drawings. (Drawings by Richard K. Anderson, Jr.)

Lettering

Draft lettering for notes, blurbs and other text can be done by hand, by a mechanical lettering system, or printed out from a word processor equipped with fonts compatible with hand or mechanical lettering systems, unless an entire drawing is being drawn and lettered with a CAD system. Lettering should be of such a size, weight and style that it can be clearly read, even at 15 percent of original drawing size (as they will appear when published in books). Ersatz, exaggerated and trendy lettering should be avoided as less legible to users than established serif and sans serif styles. Calligraphy is not encouraged.

Preliminary drawings should include certain essential graphic elements such as a sheet and view titles, graphic scales and north arrows. Often preliminary drawings do not need to include every label and spot of text, since there is enough maneuvering room to position these in the final drawing phase. Blocks of text or keys that significantly affect sheet composition should be composed and finalized at this stage, however.

View titles (e.g., "Plan—Second Floor") should be in lettering large and heavy enough to draw the eye first and identify the drawing clearly to the user. Drawing title blocks (incorporated into sheet borders) should clearly identify the site by its historic and contemporary names, dates of construction, address (or location), including city, county and state.

Viewer Aids: Graphic Scales and North Arrows

A graphic scale provides the user with a way to check dimensions and make measurements from a drawing regardless of the scale of its reproduction. Since the graphic scale is enlarged or reduced with the drawing itself, both remain consistently proportional, thus meeting Standards II and IV. A useful scale will extend from 1/4 to 1/2 the length of the drawing—or longer. Greater length reduces the chances of multiplied errors made by scaling with much shorter scales. Both English and metric system scales should be included and labeled in the original scale of the drawing they accompany. Ideally, both vertical and horizontal scales should be provided as checks against distortion in reproduction, but horizontal scales are commonly used alone.

North arrows provide another aid to the user. They ordinarily appear on maps and on plan views of sites, structures and objects to give a user clear orientation (see Figure 9.31).

Using Preexisting Drawings

New copies of preexisting drawings may be used as base data for preliminary drawings. These copies can be made the same size, enlarged or reduced to scale as needed, but all copies should be checked for scale distortion along their lengths and widths. Photocopies done with a lithographic camera are least likely to introduce distortion, whereas diazo ("blueprint") and electrostatic copies commonly are stretched along the direction of travel through the copying machine. Drawings which require two or more sheets to complete a particular view should be equipped with "match lines" which can be used to correctly align and assemble reproductions of the drawings into a single scale view.

PHASE 4: FINAL DRAWINGS

The ultimate end of a documentary drawing is to store and communicate information. The idea is to help a user see relationships between important historical, technological, structural, visual and archaeological information your project brings together. Each drawing should communicate clearly and concisely—that is, positively, without ambiguity, confusion or unidentified "loose ends" and gaps, and that at several sizes of reproduction. This should be true both visually in linework and verbally in notes, whether the drawing is produced solely by hand, by computer or by any other means. Perhaps no drawing accomplishes these goals perfectly, but the following pages outline principles and procedures that will go far to attaining these goals. Phase four does not address content—that is an issue that should have been settled by the end of the third phase. Instead, *presentation* of content will be addressed, largely in the context of hand-drawn drawings. Principles discussed apply equally well to CAD drawings, however.

Archival Drawing Materials

Documentary drawings in industrial archaeology are usually created for archival records, either for HAER or for another repository. For this reason, archivally stable, durable materials and media should be used throughout a final drawing. Drafting vellum is acceptable as a base, but it is harder to correct ink mistakes on than Mylar materials, and unlike vellum, mylar is not easily torn, nor does it go through dimensional changes as a result of changes in moisture content. Mylar drafting film consists of a polyester base with a matte drawing surface applied to one or both sides of the film. The film is available in several thicknesses from 3 mils (0.003", very light) to 10 mils (0.010", very heavy); 4 or 5 mil thicknesses serve well for measured drawings. The drawing surface can be etched into the polyester base, or applied to it as separate layers. Double-matte films are preferred to single-matte, because linework and rendering can be done on separate sides, saving labor if a mistake should occur in one or the other technique.

Standard III of the Secretary's Standards require that durable standard-sized materials be used for ease of storage and future use. HAER uses three sheet sizes with preprinted borders and title blocks:

1. 19" × 22" (15 3/4" × 20 1/8" drawing area)
2. 24" × 36" (21 3/4" × 31 3/4" drawing area)
3. 33" × 44" (31 7/8" × 40" drawing area)

The smallest size is rarely used today. The second format is most common; the largest was recently adopted because the sizes of many industrial sites being recorded by HAER are larger than will fit conveniently on a 24" × 36" sheet. Because of the range of sheet sizes, line widths and lettering sizes are different for each format (see Figure 9.30). Other sheet sizes are of course permissible for non-HAER documentation, but the use of standard sizes is the point.

It is highly recommended that CAD drawings always be stored primarily as printouts, not on disks or in other digital forms. Disks are easily lost, can be erased or damaged and are subject to technological obsolescence so far as programming and hardware are concerned. A "low-tech" printout is always accessible to a future user without the complications or barriers of some electro-mechanical interface.

Drawing Tools

Technical pens smaller than #2 (0.30mm) used on Mylar should have jewel or tungsten carbide points. Steel points in these sizes wear out very quickly on Mylar.

Black ink is specified instead of pencil, because it has a higher contrast to the drawing background and produces lines of more uniform width than pencil, and it does not smudge—characteristics that are essential to good reproductions, durability and clarity. Mylar takes ink readily from drawing instruments, plotters and laser printers, and images can be photographically printed on it. Drafting inks used on Mylar should be specifically rated as "film" or "acetate" inks, not india ink, "drawing ink" or writing inks. India inks and writing inks do not perform properly in technical pens or plotter pens used for drafting, and they do not respond to a Mylar surface correctly or adhere to it properly. Inks such as Pelikan-FT and Pentel Ceran-O-matic film inks have passed accelerated aging tests by the Library of Congress for 500-year durability on Mylar. Inks should not be diluted for use, because diluted lines do not reproduce well. Color is never used at present because of problems with archival stability, assurance of color accuracy and costs of faithful color reproduction.

Body oils from hands will repel ink from vellum and Mylar surfaces. For vellum, troublesome spots can be removed with a chamois cloth, kneaded eraser or products such as Scum-X. On Mylar, oil spots can be removed with lighter fluid or a spot remover[6] without damaging ink linework. These solvents will also clean up minor pencil marks and they do not leave grit behind to accumulate on or clog pen points. Dried ink lines can be removed from Mylar with a slightly moistened vinyl eraser. Dried ink itself can be removed from drawing instruments and Mylar sheets with isopropyl ("rubbing") or ethyl ("grain") alcohols, however, the surfaces of some brands of Mylar whiten and deteriorate upon exposure to alcohols. Your Mylar product can be tested by dipping a small strip of it in alcohol and watching for any reactions.

Because adhesives are not archivally stable, dry transfer lettering, tape based lettering, adhesive film rendering and similar products should never be used on an archival drawing. Textures, lettering and rendering should be done in ink using templates, stippling or airbrush techniques, unless the drawing is printed out from a laser printer or plotter. If use of nonarchival media is essential to the clarity or conciseness of a final drawing, the finished nonarchival drawing should be photographically copied onto Mylar for preservation. In cases where funds and equipment are available, time may be saved by producing all lettering via laser printer, affixing it along with any rendering films to the linework of a drawing, and then photographically copying the assemblage onto Mylar. Photomylar copies should only be made of complete drawings, since the photomylar surface can be difficult to ink on. Some CAD programs will plot PostScript or TrueType fonts in addition to linework and pochés.

Title Sheets

Title sheets for drawing sets typically lay out the name of the site in bold lettering, and may include a reproduced engraving, historical drawing or attractive company logo. Location maps for the site are included at various scales from regional, state and local scales, frequently using U.S. Geological Survey 7.5 minute topographic maps as a base. A small site should be pinpointed with UTM coordinates (see Chapter 6); larger sites should have boundaries or endpoints established with two or more UTM coordinate points. Title sheets should also contain a statement of significance, a paragraph crediting team members, funding sources, owners and significant assistance, as well as the dates the project was undertaken. In some cases it is useful to report contract numbers or other administrative data that may be historically significant to future users. If the drawing set is a large one (more than 15 sheets), an index should be included for users who are seeking specific views (plans, elevations, process diagram) so their time is not wasted flipping sheets to find what they want. Sometimes the amount of significant information outlined above will require more than one drawing sheet to record.

Drafting Techniques: Linework, Pochés and Rendering

Clarity (Standard IV) inherently requires reasonably trained graphic and intellectual skills, whether generating a drawing by hand or by computer. Several texts are cited in the chapter bibliography which carry instruction and examples of good drafting and graphic techniques. (Computer hardware, programs and texts have not been included because of their relatively rapid development and obsolescence.) A documentary drawing should visually prioritize information by appropriate scales and line widths; by appropriate lettering sizes, styles and weights; and by good composition. Confusing figure-ground effects, feeble or sloppy linework, inconsistencies in repeated or concentric features and inappropriate detail are proscripted. Badly composed, sized and placed verbal information is also discouraged as not meeting Standard IV.

Numerous templates and drafting aids are available which make good drafting easier to achieve. At times it is productive to make a specialized template if a feature is repeated numerous times throughout a drawing set. Such templates can be cut with an X-Acto blade and needle files from sheets of 15 or 20 mil thick clear vinyl or styrene (available at hobby supply stores). As you cut the pattern, trace a pen through it occasionally to check for accurate shape and smoothness. Repetitive elements can be generated by a CAD system, filed and recalled to easily repeat an element in any orientation or location throughout a CAD drawing set.

Drawings should employ a variety of linewidths from 4×0 (0.18mm) to #4 (1.20mm) depending on sheet size (see Figure 9.30, suggested line width ranges for sheet sizes). Lighter widths are assigned to detail, dimension strings, dashed lines and some poché and rendering techniques. Dashed lines are used to denote hidden features, centerlines and section lines in plan. Heavier line widths help distinguish foreground elements, edges and sectioned elements from background features. A thoughtful hierarchy of lineweights can present a user with an easily recognizable visual organization which may even impart a third dimension to the image. A simple test for clarity is to stand back and "test" the drawing—to what is your eye drawn first? Is that area or verbal information the first thing a viewer ought to notice? If not, changes in linewidth, lettering size and style may be necessary.

In linework, corners should meet cleanly, without overruns or mismatches, as should curves and tangents. If you stop an inking stroke before reaching the end of a line, start the new stroke just beyond the end of the old stroke. This technique avoids misaligned overruns due to starting a new stroke over the end of the last one (see Figure 9.32).

Crosshatching should be regularly spaced. It is best to slide an electrostatic copy of an engineer's scale (20 feet to the inch or less) beneath the Mylar and use the scale tics to guide hatch line spacing, rather than rely on spacing by eye. Refer to the chart in Figures 9.33 and 9.34 for standard pochés for common and obsolete building materials. It may be wise to include a poché key in a drawing, especially if some pochés represent unusual materials or features. On double-matte Mylars, it is advisable to ink pochés on the back of the sheet, away from linework, so that errors and changes do not require reworking linework as well as, pochés.

Figure 9.32. Magnified image of an interrupted technical pen line which has been restarted prior to the line end (top), and just at the line end (bottom). The bottom version isn't noticeable to the eye on lines smaller than #2. (Adapted from U.S. Department of the Interior, National Park Service, Historic American Buildings Survey/Historic American Engineering Record, Larry D. Lankton and Richard K. Anderson, Jr., *Historic American Engineering Record Field Instructions,* Washington, DC. 1981,)

Some pochés require stippling (a random pattern of dots) in addition to crosshatching. Stippling can be achieved with technical pens or an airbrush.

Older drafting techniques are frequently effective graphics for indicating solids by means of shading or shadows. Nineteenth-century drawings and engravings often imparted the illusion of a third dimension to rounded metal objects such as tanks, flywheels and boilers by using graded line shading. Less time-consuming line shadowing can also be used. When light is assumed to shine from the upper left at a 45-degree angle, edges struck by light are drawn with light lines, those on shadowed sides are drawn with heavier lines. Both of these antique techniques have been used effectively in HAER drawings for improving clarity, but they do run the

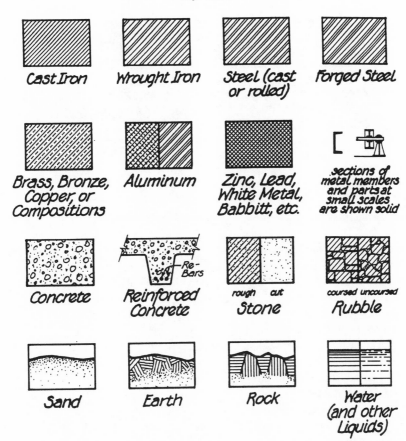

Figure 9.33. Standard pochés or crosshatching for various materials. (Adapted from U.S. Department of the Interior, National Park Service, Historic American Buildings Survey/Historic American Engineering Record, Larry D. Lankton and Richard K. Anderson, Jr., *Historic American Engineering Record Field Instructions,* Washington, DC. 1981, pp. 152–153.)

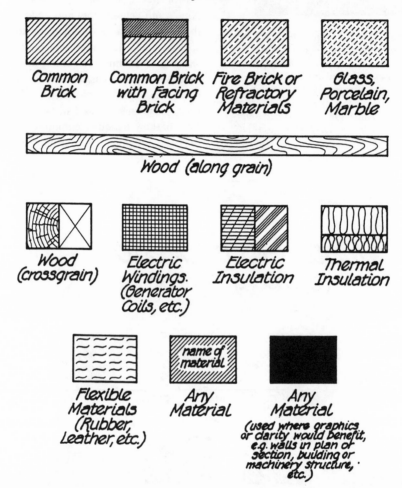

Figure 9.34. Standard pochés or crosshatching for various materials. (Adapted from U.S. Department of the Interior, National Park Service, Historic American Buildings Survey/Historic American Engineering Record, Larry D. Lankton and Richard K. Anderson, Jr., *Historic American Engineering Record Field Instructions,* Washington, DC. 1981, pp. 152–153.)

risk of creating the impression that the drawings themselves are old rather than recent unless a user pays careful attention to annotations and delineator dates. More modern engineering drafting practice relies on a schedule of line widths for particular functions. Solid objects receive heavy lines, lighter lines being relegated progressively to recessed or hidden features, dimension strings, centerlines and arrows. Architectural drafting practice has used "outlining" as a method for emphasizing distinct planes as advancing or receding from the plane of the drawing surface. This method is effective when used intelligently—small projecting features should receive lighter outlining than large ones, and outlines should encompass a single plane or feature, not several of different "depths" in the drawing (Figure 9.35). Stippling may be used to impart "roundness" or a third dimension to

structures, but closely spaced fine dots (less than 0.010″ diameter closer than 0.015″ spacing, as well as closely spaced fine lines) should be avoided since they either "drop out" or blur together in reproductions and reductions.

Interpretive Drawings: Axonometrics and Process Diagrams

Interpretive drawings can be much more efficient and effective than orthographic views alone in displaying how buildings and site are related, how structures and machinery were assembled. They include axonometric drawings, projected perspectives (derived from scale drawings) and process diagrams.

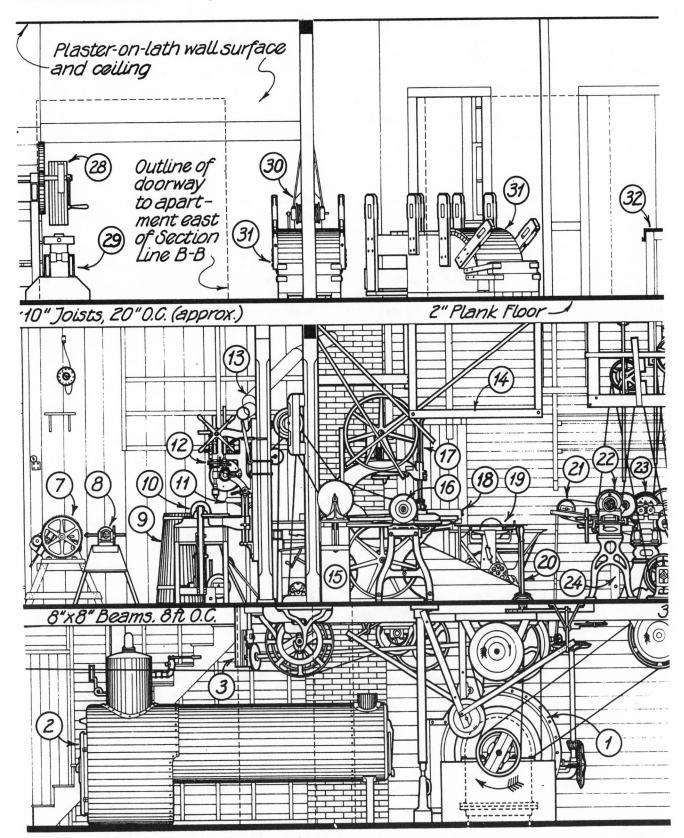

Plaster-on-lath wall surface and ceiling

Outline of doorway to apartment east of Section Line B-B

10" Joists, 20" O.C. (approx.)

2" Plank Floor

8"x8" Beams, 8 ft. O.C.

Figure 9.35. Outlining has been used with a very strong graphic sense in this HAER drawing of a woodworking shop. (Historic American Engineering Record, National Park Service; delineated by Anastasios Kokoris, 1979, and Richard K. Anderson, Jr., 1980. Ben Thresher's Mill, Barnet Center vicinity, Caledonia Co., VT {HAER No. VT-10}, sheet 9 of 11.)

Axonometric drawings are projections produced to a scale along three different axes. The scales may vary from axis to axis, or they may be the same on all axes (isometric). The axes may be at various angles as well to facilitate clarity and avoid distortion. Such drawings can be developed into assembled views that more clearly display the organization of parts or machinery than orthographic views. They may also display disassembled or "exploded" views describing how a machine or structure is built or operates. Annotations should accompany such drawings, as well as axonometric graphic scales where applicable (see Figure 9.36).

Process diagrams are interpretive drawings that may take many forms, from the purely schematic "box and arrow" flow diagram to more illustrative cutaway axonometrics (Figure 9.36). Sometimes such diagrams can be combined with plans or sections of a structure, building or site if the process and the view are reasonably "parallel." Standard IV requires that these drawings "read" well—that they impart information with clarity and conciseness, but this does not necessarily mean simplicity. If machinery and process steps must be keyed (rather than labeled) for identification, make sure the key numerals progress with the process flow. If a verbal description of a process accompanies a schematic diagram, try to make sure the diagram and any number key system flow left-to-right in the direction users read.

Annotations

Annotations come in many forms from blocks of descriptive text (columns or "blurbs") to one- or two-word labels. In all cases, attention should be paid to correct terminology, data, grammar and spelling. Annotations should cite sources for drawings, call attention to features "omitted for clarity" and where a user might find the omitted information (viz. a photograph included in the documentation package). Annotations should also label parts, label rooms, give dates, report machinery specifications, label materials, point out significant features, account for discrepancies between the drawing and field work, or the drawing and photographic coverage, etc. All annotations should be for purposes and information significant to the documentation process, the recorded site and its context.

Sometimes space is too crowded in a drawing to label areas directly. In such cases a number or letter key tag with an arrow should be used. Do not omit arrows in hopes that proximity of a numeral or label to a part will suffice to associate the two unambiguously in a user's mind—an arrow removes all doubt.

Color

Archival measured drawings are black and white, so where color is significant, a verbal means of denoting it is required. It is best to refer to colors by their Munsell Color Number rather than rely on descriptive terms such as "bright red," "blue green" and the like, however, such descriptive terms are better than nothing in the absence of access to a Munsell Color Book. Contemporary market terms (Charleston Green, South Bay Yellow) are virtually useless to future researchers.[7]

Archival color photography or photocopies of colored drawings might be conducted by producing *on site* a series of three archivally stable black-and-white color separations, each separation containing a color key with Munsell color numbers of each key color clearly labeled on the color key in the view. This would permit accurate color correction in photographic prints or later computerized image processing.

Specialized Techniques: Video, Animation and Stereo Imagery

Some operations and processes are not easily communicated by static drawings. Video tapes and motion picture film may not be able to record essential operative principles of a process or machinery clearly since these formats will by nature record distractions or machine and structural elements which conceal the process partially or completely. There are also diagrams which record "reconstructed" processes not recordable by video methods because the process machinery no longer exists or is not in operation. These observations by no means exclude video recordation of a process as a valuable format, but in many cases, some form of animated drawings may perform as well as, instead of or in conjunction with video formats to "explicate and illustrate what is significant or valuable" about a site. CAD systems and animation programs are available to produce such sequences, and they can be transcribed to video tape, optical disks, film or printed out on paper as simple flip animation booklets.

An example of an application for animation could include illustration of the stresses in bridge members as various loads travel across bridges. Such images could be highly accurate mathematically and at the same time visually educational to laymen. Animation can elucidate other functions that are invisible or hard to imagine from a drawing because they take place through time or involve very complex interactions of stresses, forms of energy, chemicals, etc. In the future it is likely that computerized drawing and photo data may be so easily manipulated that a documentation user may "travel" through a site, stopping to analyze anything anywhere, using virtual reality displays.

Stereo photographs add a delightful dimension to photographic coverage and it is presumed stereodrawings would do the same as a form of interpretive drawing. Stereodrawings have been used to display molecular structure for chemists and stereophoto views of Mars taken by Viking spacecraft have been published for study by scientists and the public.[8] Although the employment of stereo imagery is not required by the Secretary's Standards, it is not excluded either. Stereocameras are difficult to come by, and the

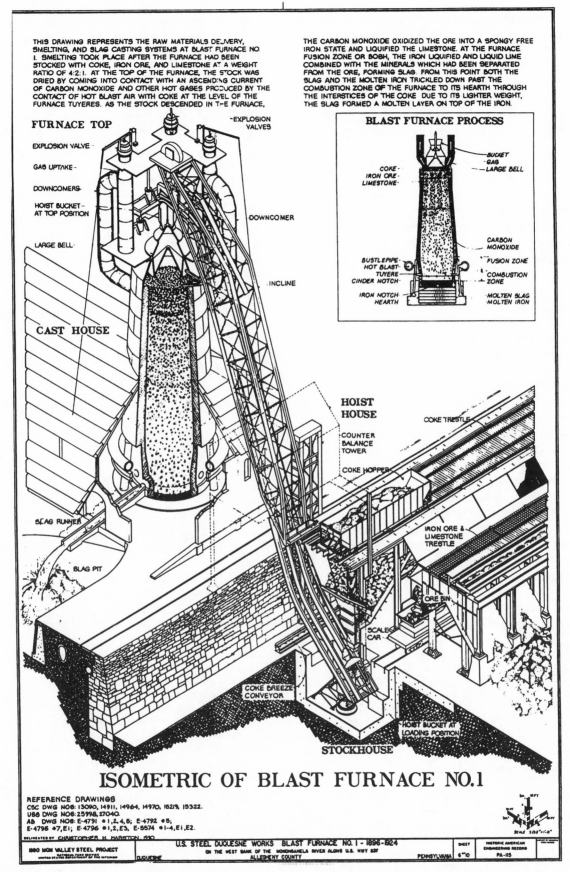

THIS DRAWING REPRESENTS THE RAW MATERIALS DELIVERY, SMELTING, AND SLAG CASTING SYSTEMS AT BLAST FURNACE NO. I. SMELTING TOOK PLACE AFTER THE FURNACE HAD BEEN STOCKED WITH COKE, IRON ORE, AND LIMESTONE AT A WEIGHT RATIO OF 4:2:1. AT THE TOP OF THE FURNACE, THE STOCK WAS DRIED BY COMING INTO CONTACT WITH AN ASCENDING CURRENT OF CARBON MONOXIDE AND OTHER HOT GASES PRODUCED BY THE CONTACT OF HOT BLAST AIR WITH COKE AT THE LEVEL OF THE FURNACE TUYERES. AS THE STOCK DESCENDED IN THE FURNACE,

THE CARBON MONOXIDE OXIDIZED THE ORE INTO A SPONGY FREE IRON STATE AND LIQUIFIED THE LIMESTONE. AT THE FURNACE FUSION ZONE OR BOSH, THE IRON LIQUIFIED AND LIQUID LIME COMBINED WITH THE MINERALS WHICH HAD BEEN SEPARATED FROM THE ORE, FORMING SLAG. FROM THIS POINT BOTH THE SLAG AND THE MOLTEN IRON TRICKLED DOWN PAST THE COMBUSTION ZONE OF THE FURNACE TO ITS HEARTH THROUGH THE INTERSTICES OF THE COKE DUE TO ITS LIGHTER WEIGHT, THE SLAG FORMED A MOLTEN LAYER ON TOP OF THE IRON.

BLAST FURNACE PROCESS

FURNACE TOP

EXPLOSION VALVES
EXPLOSION VALVE
GAS UPTAKE
DOWNCOMERS
HOIST BUCKET AT TOP POSITION
LARGE BELL
DOWNCOMER
INCLINE

CAST HOUSE

BUCKET
GAS
LARGE BELL
COKE IRON ORE LIMESTONE
CARBON MONOXIDE
FUSION ZONE
COMBUSTION ZONE
BUSTLE PIPE HOT BLAST TUYERE
CINDER NOTCH
IRON NOTCH HEARTH
MOLTEN SLAG MOLTEN IRON

HOIST HOUSE
COUNTER BALANCE TOWER
COKE HOPPERS
COKE TRESTLE

SLAG RUNNER
SLAG PIT

IRON ORE & LIMESTONE TRESTLE
ORE BIN
SCALES CAR

COKE BREEZE CONVEYOR
HOIST BUCKET AT LOADING POSITION
STOCKHOUSE

ISOMETRIC OF BLAST FURNACE NO. 1

REFERENCE DRAWINGS
CSC DWG NOS: 13090, 14911, 14964, 14970, 15219, 15322.
USS DWG NOS: 25998, 27040.
AB DWG NOS: E-4791 #1,2,4,5; E-4792 #5;
E-4795 #7,E1; E-4796 #1,2,E3, E-5574 #1-4,E1,E2.

DELINEATED BY CHRISTOPHER H. MARSTON, 1990

1990 MON VALLEY STEEL PROJECT
NATIONAL PARK SERVICE
UNITED STATES DEPARTMENT OF THE INTERIOR

U.S. STEEL DUQUESNE WORKS BLAST FURNACE NO. 1 - 1896-1924
ON THE WEST BANK OF THE MONONGAHELA RIVER ALONG U.S. HWY 837
ALLEGHENY COUNTY
DUQUESNE | PENNSYLVANIA

SHEET 6 OF 10

HISTORIC AMERICAN ENGINEERING RECORD
PA-115

Figure 9.36. This cutaway isometric of a blast furnace reveals the integrated materials handling systems in use at U.S. Steel's Duquesne, Pennsylvania, works much more effectively than possible with mere sections or photographs. (Historic American Engineering Record, National Park Service; delineated by Christopher H. Marston, 1990. U.S. Steel Duquesne Works Blast Furnace No. 1, 1896–1924, sheet 6 of 10.)

"stereo" photographs produced for stereophotogrammetry or digital imagery analysis are intended for calculation purposes, not visual display. Widespread camera viewpoints aid the accuracy of photogrammetric work, but for visual observation, they are too widely spread in viewpoint or made at angles that interfere too much for the human eye and mind to perceive them in a realistic fashion.

Stereo drawings containing cutaway views, process information and the like can be produced by hand (Figure 9.37), but they take a great amount of time and may not be justified economically for what they bring to documentation, except in very rare cases. With the advancement of computer programs, however, the author anticipates a time when stereo images can be easily generated by computer from existing orthogonal views or photographic information, thus adding another dimension to industrial archaeological documentation.

Field Reports

Where historical and field investigation have led a team to make complex decisions about the content, accuracy and display of documentary drawings, these issues may best be documented in a field report included as an appendix to the written history rather than verbally included in the drawings. Indeed, such reports might be said to be required by Standard II. This does not mean drawings should not outline field methods and decision processes in annotations, but it may mean that complete discussion and reporting will take too much space to incorporate anywhere else but in a field report. In complex situations, such a report may be vital to a user's comprehension of methods used, background of team members, decisions and limitations in the techniques and equipment used, site access and conditions, budget and other factors that have contributed significantly to the form and content of the documentation. A user may need to know all of these things in order to reach a properly and professionally informed opinion about the merits and limitations of the documentation.

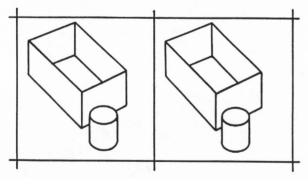

Figure 9.37. This stereo drawing is simplified to make a point. Readers can view the three-dimensional effect by looking at something about 3 feet away and then holding the image at about 16″ away. Fusion of the two images can be made easier for some readers by placing a 3″x5″ card vertically on the line between the images. Maximum size for stereo views is about 2 1/4″ square without the use of specialized viewers containing prisms or mirrors. (Drawing by Richard K. Anderson, Jr.)

BIBLIOGRAPHY

Bartlett, Frank W. and Theodore W. Johnson. *Engineering Descriptive Geometry and Drawing.* New York: John Wiley & Sons, Inc., 1927.

Baynes, Ken and Francis Pugh. *The Art of the Engineer.* Woodstock, N.Y.: The Overlook Press, 1981.

Breed, Charles B. and George L. Hosmer. *The Principles and Practices of Surveying. Volume I: Elementary Surveying.* New York: John Wiley & Sons, Inc., 1977.

Burns, John A. ed. *Recording Historic Structures.* Washington, D.C.: The American Institute of Architects Press, 1989.

Duff, Jon M. *Industrial Technical Illustration.* New York: Van Nostrand Reinhold Company Inc., 1982.

French, Thomas E. and Carl L. Svensen. *Mechanical Drawing.* New York: Webster Division, McGraw-Hill Book Company, 1962.

French, Thomas E. and Charles J. Vierck. *A Manual of Engineering Drawing for Students and Draftsmen.* New York: McGraw-Hill Book Company, Inc., 1953.

Lombardo, Albert J., ed. *Engineering Drawing.* New York: Barnes & Noble, 1956.

Low, Julian W. *Plane Table Mapping.* New York: Harper & Brothers, 1952.

Luzadder, Warren J. *Basic Graphics.* New York: Prentice-Hall, 1962.

Maurello, S. Ralph. *The Complete Airbrush Book.* New York: Leon Amiel Publisher, Inc., 1980.

Mette, C. Michael. *Airbrush Techniques: Basic Skills Workbook 1.* Cincinnati, OH: North Light Books, 1986.

Munsell Color, Macbeth, Division of Kollmorgen Corporation, 405 Little Britain Road, New Windsor, N.Y. 12553–6148. (phone: 914-565-7660, fax: 914-565-0390)

Tufte, Edward R. *The Visual Display of Quantitative Information.* Cheshire, Conn.: Graphics Press, 1983.

——— *Envisioning Information.* Cheshire, Conn.: Graphics Press, 1983.

Worthen, W.E., C.E. *Appleton's Cyclopaedia of Technical Drawing.* New York: D. Appleton and Company, 1885.

ENDNOTES

1. Secretary of the Interior's Standards and Guidelines for Architectural and Engineering Documentation; HABS/HAER Standards, (Washington, D.C.: U.S. Government Printing Office, 1990) Reprinted from the Federal Register, Vol. 48, Number 190, Thursday, September 29, 1983 pg. 44370-44374.

2. For example, the quality and methods of iron production at some blast furnace sites has been deduced from chemical analysis of buried slag. At some mill sites, accumulated silt has been excavated from turbine pits in order to gain access to surviving machinery.

3. See Guidance for Controlling Asbestos-containing Materials in Buildings by Exposure Evaluation Division, Office of Toxic Substances, Office of Pesticides and Toxic Substances, U.S. Environmental Protection Agency, Washington, DC 20460.

4. Compared to hand-sketched notes and hand-made measurements, what constitutes "field notes" for primary source verification (Standard II) when state-of-the-art computerized analytical plotting methods, computer programs, data storage and

retrieval technology and other equipment become obsolete and inaccessible? There are no technological interfaces required between a researcher's eyes and a hand-made document, except perhaps a pair of glasses.

In my opinion it would be an important test to have two teams independently measure the same industrial site and produce the same set of drawings at the same scales—one team using traditional "hand" techniques, the other "high tech" data gathering and computer technology—while keeping strict accounts of time, methods, costs (including all equipment), errors, and quality of final product. A thorough comparison of the two teams' products should follow along with all factors involved. It would be interesting to compare the drawings at the end of the projects by overlaying them, looking for dimensional discrepancies, and analyzing where and why they occurred. (See Chapter 7 for more information on photogrammetric recording.)

5. Mylar is a copyrighted trademark for a product of the DuPont Company.

6. Lighter fluid is commonly naphtha, a hydrocarbon mixture. Spot removers are composed primarily of 1,1,1 trichloro*ethane,* a common solvent that has not been linked with serious health hazards at the low exposures one would see in a laundry room or at a drawing board; it is available in food markets, drug stores and hardware stores. 1,1,1 trichloroethane should not be confused with 1,1,1 trichlor*ethylene,* a known carcinogen.

7. Munsell color numbers are the professionally accepted means of recording color, not use of printers' color systems such as "Pantone." Certain lighting conditions and surface characteristics are also required for correct color documentation. There is at present (1993) no cross-reference between the Munsell system and printers' color sample books due to the variety of ink manufacturers, paper bases and other variables. Munsell references are manufactured in three sets of color reference books, and numerous instruments are available for color measurement. The "glossy" color set (recommended by the Department of the Interior and the National Park Service) presents 40 hues and 1600 colors in removable, indexed chips. The lacquer colors are stable for at least eight years. Printers' charts rely on translucent inks, and colors may vary depending on paper and inks used for the charts; printers' color references have a lifetime of about six months under ordinary use and exposure. No standards are currently available for recording the colors of translucent or transparent materials, such as stained glass. Requests for information and orders for Munsell color books and ancillary equipment should be addressed to Macbeth, Division of Kollmorgen Instruments Corporation, 405 Little Britain Road, New Windsor, NY 12553-6148 (914) 565-7660 (phone), (914) 565-0390 (fax).

8. The Martian Landscape, Washington, DC: Scientific and Technical Information Office, National Aeronautics and Space Administration, 1978.

CHAPTER 10

Large Format Photography

Robert J. Hughes

INTRODUCTION

Almost anyone can "take a picture," especially with the many fully automatic cameras on the market. Film loading, light metering, flash, focusing, film advance, even wide angle and telephoto lens adjustments have become automatic in today's world of still photography. The photographer need only point the camera and press a button to make a photograph of a chosen subject.

However, contrary to popular belief, the production of good photographs remains a rather complex process involving a combination of the following:

1. the nature of the subject,
2. the personality of the photographer,
3. the photographer's concept of the subject,
4. the technical execution of the photograph,
5. the audience for which the picture is intended.

It is impossible to list these factors in order of priority as all are necessary and interrelated. A good photographer regards them as a unit and balances the components to create a photograph in harmony with all demands.

Anyone can indeed "take a picture." Not everyone will be a photographer. As my college photography professor, who was fond of instilling some paranoia into his students, used to say, "Everything you are is summed up the moment you release the shutter!" If that does not scare you, it should.

For the most part, those of us who deal with architectural and archaeological recordation work with subjects that are static, and not likely to run off before we have the chance to trip the shutter. Static subjects allow the photographer all the time needed to make the best possible picture, and this influences both the approach to the subject and choice of technique.

The key to successful photographic recordation of static subjects is contemplation. The process should not be rushed, time should be taken to study the subject carefully from different angles and points of view. Texture, tone, background and composition are key as is the need to wait, when appropriate, for the light to be just right. And if your audience requires technical quality, the subject should be photographed on the largest film size that can be used for a perfect job under prevailing conditions.

DOCUMENTATION: HABS/HAER STANDARDS

This chapter will deal primarily with photography according to HABS/HAER standards (Historic American Building Survey/Historic American Engineering Record). Therefore we will consider the fine folks of HABS/HAER our intended audience and this will greatly affect technique, composition and film/print processing and packaging.

The subject of composition pertains equally to the many facets of creativity: painting, drawing, sculpting, textiles, photography and even the culinary arts, and is worthy of a more comprehensive treatment than I can give it in this writing. The "eye" of the photographer must be developed in accordance with understanding balance of light, mass, form, texture and movement (yes, even stationary objects can describe movement to the eye!).

In the field of recordation photography, composition is often dictated by the subject itself and the requirements of the recording team. Each object or section of an object will be the primary subject of the photograph and should occupy the greater proportion of the image area with only enough surrounding visual "information" to place it in context.

To meet HABS/HAER standards, it must be, at minimum, a 4″ × 5″ black and white negative with all aspects of the subject in sharp focus, archivally processed and placed in an acid-free negative sleeve. The photographs are referenced in both the measured drawings and the documentation text, and the envelope for each photo is labeled with view or negative number, the name of the site, date of the photograph and brief description of the view and photographer's name

This chapter is intended to address the practical use of the large format, or view, camera as it applies to photographic recordation of buildings, IA sites and other structures and objects. It also deals with the care and handling of sheet or "cut" film, and the loading and unloading of the film in the film holders that are an integral part of camera operation. Film processing and darkroom techniques are a subject best left to another book at another time. For the purposes of this article, the science of light sensitive emulsions and the chemical process of rendering them into negative and/or positive images on film and paper will be accredited to "magic," and left to the wizards of the dark. For more information on film processing and darkroom technique, consult any of the books listed in the bibliography.

THE CAMERA

The large format, or view, camera is larger than most other types of cameras and is usually mounted on a tripod during use. Some models (press-type cameras), however, can be hand-held and, using a range finder or sight mounted on top of the camera, lend themselves to a "point and shoot" technique.

Nothing about the view camera is convenient, but given the use of good quality lenses, nothing can match it for resolution, general image quality and the range of creativity it affords.

View cameras are most commonly available in three sizes: 4″ × 5″, 5″ × 7″ and 8″ × 10″, and are made of wood, metal and/or plastic. The size relates to the size of the sheet of film each will accommodate. There are larger cameras as well. However, in this essay, we will deal with only the three common sizes above and, in particular, the 4″ × 5″ model (see Figure 10.1).

The large format cameras bear some operational similarity to 35mm SLR (Single Lens Reflex) cameras, in that the image is viewed on a ground glass plate as it passes through the lens. Whereas the SLR camera incorporates a mirror that reflects the light upward into a prism for an offset, corrected image, the view camera has no mirror, the ground glass is directly behind the lens and the image is seen upside down and backwards.

The view camera body consists mainly of two movable planes (or frames) connected by a light-tight bellows. The back frame holds the ground glass viewing plate and, when ready to make an exposure, a film holder and film. The inner surface of the ground glass defines the film plane and, when the film holder is in place, the film occupies the exact same position. The front frame holds the lens board and most cameras allow for interchangeable lenses.

The frames are mounted on a rail or track and are moved back and forth to focus the camera. Both front and back frames are usually mounted such that they can be tilted up or down,

Figure 10.1. A 4×5 format view camera with fully adjustable front and back frames, showing 150mm (standard) lens and accordion bellows. Both frames can be shifted, tilted and swung independently.

turned left or right and shifted vertically and horizontally. This range of movement gives the view camera a versatility not found in other types of camera. Although manufacturers of 35mm and medium format cameras are marketing "tilt and shift" lenses, their products cannot match the view camera for adaptability.

The camera's simple construction results in simplicity of operation, unequaled reliability, infrequent repairs and, for many models, a comparatively low purchase price.

Lens aperture, shutter speed and the shutter release are controlled in the lenses themselves and are mechanically or, in some newer cameras, electronically operated. Film holders are thin, two-sided "boxes" with dark slides on both sides. Each holder accommodates one sheet of film on each side and must be loaded by hand in total darkness. Once loaded, the slide is only removed when the holder is in the camera and an exposure is about to be made. The slide is replaced immediately after exposure and then only removed in total darkness to retrieve the film for processing.

LIGHT

Available Light

As stated before, patience and contemplation are the operational words for large format recordation photography. If working outdoors, watch the subject as the sun moves across it during the course of the day. Is it best captured with the sun full upon it, or would the early morning or late afternoon sun render better detail? To avoid shadows, glare or bright spots altogether, you may want to wait for the diffused light of pre-dawn, dusk or a cloudy day. If you wish to record all sides of the subject, you may have to make the photographs at different times of the day as the sun changes position.

Perhaps the greatest challenge to the photographer is photographing the north side of a structure (or the south side if working in the southern hemisphere). The north side never receives direct sunlight and on bright, sunny days will always be in shadow. If the exposure is made for the shadowed north side, the background can be overexposed and detail lost. If the photograph is made when the sun is at its zenith, the sun can glare through the camera lens, washing out the image and destroying detail. The best possible solution to this problem is to wait for the diffused light of a cloudy day or, if the weather does not cooperate, to make the exposure early or late in the day when the sun is well to one side. In any case, cameras pointed directly toward the sun's position will yield poor quality photographs.

The same can hold true for interior photography as well. Nevertheless, artificial lighting may be necessary and is much more practical inside a structure or in deep shade than outside under the open sky.

Artificial Light

Generally speaking, artificial light is brought to a subject by flash or by fixed lighting or by a combination of both. Modern flash equipment is usually in the form of an electronic strobe light and is available in many forms, sizes and strengths or intensities. Elaborate sets can include separate stands, multiple flash heads, and reflectors and diffusers that the photographer can arrange to achieve the desired result. Fixed lighting comes in the form of incandescent modeling and floodlamps and can also employ reflectors and diffusers. In either case, they allow mobility, choice and placement options that are not present when dealing with available or natural light.

Color and Black and White Film

When using black and white film, the color of the light striking the subject need not be of concern, but when using color film, the kind and source of the light become all important. Color film is balanced for either sun light (daylight) or artificial light (tungsten) and should be matched to the type of light illuminating the subject. Lens filters are available to change the light balance and make it possible to use artificial light (tungsten) film in daylight or vice versa, but this should be done only when there is no alternative.

Strobe flash systems are balanced to simulate sunlight while fixed lighting, flood lamps, etc., usually require the photographer to use tungsten (indoor) film to achieve correct color balance. Film packages contain information on film type, speed, exposure, filters, color balance, handling, processing, etc, which can help the photographer make the proper choice to meet specific requirements or to accommodate a particular situation.

FILM AND LOADING

Most of the same types of film available in 35mm format are also available in sheet form for use in a view camera, so that the photographer has a wide range of choices for color or black and white, negative or transparency, high or low speed film. For view cameras, the film comes cut into individual sheets (hence the term "cut" film) and is notched in the upper right hand corner of each sheet (see Figure 10.2). The notches are a code that identifies the type of film and helps the photographer determine the emulsion side of the film sheet. When holding the sheet of film so that the notches

Figure 10-2. A sheet of 4×5 cut film (note notches in upper right indicating film type and emulsion side).

are in the upper right-hand corner, the emulsion side is facing you. This position is critical in the dark when loading film into film holders.

Types of Film

Film, both black and white and color, is rated according to the speed with which the emulsion will accept light (register an image). The "speed" of film is marked as a number and the higher the number, the "faster" the film. This number appears on film packages following the initials "ASA/DIN" or "ASA/ISO." In the world of photography, faster is not necessarily better. High speed films generally render a course or "grainy' image when processed which results in a loss of detail. Consequently, HABS/HAER limits film speed to ASA/ISO 400.

It is a good idea to practice loading and unloading cut film by using some spoiled or exposed sheets of film. Assemble some empty film holders and the sheets of film, blindfold yourself and practice "feeling" for the notches on the film edge without getting fingerprints all over the film surface. Practice arranging and finding things in the dark and handling the film holders with their folding ends, dark slides and film rails. In this operation neatness and organization are absolute necessities. (You might find yourself performing this operation in closets, motel/hotel bathrooms or under piles of blankets.) Some photographers use a "light-tight" box (often homemade) in which they place the carton of unexposed film and the film holders. They then insert their arms through holes in one side of the box which have sleeves that close snugly around the wrists preventing light leaks.

The slides in the film holders usually have indicators on one side to show whether or not the film in that frame has been exposed (see Figure 10.3). Note that one sheet of film can be inserted into each side of the film holder. The slides on each side are turned accordingly when the film has been exposed and when unexposed film is about to be loaded. Film loading and unloading MUST TAKE PLACE IN TOTAL DARKNESS one sheet of film at a time. The photographer must be sure the notches are in the upper right-hand corner as the film sheet is slid into the holder, taking care to insure that the film edges are caught under the guides or rails located on both sides of the holder. Once the film is in position in the holder, close the end of the holder and push the dark slide into place.

USING THE CAMERA

Camera Placement

The view camera is not a device for the impatient. It is usually large, somewhat heavy, operationally slow and, with its appurtenances, bulky. (You do not usually find them on the sidelines at a sporting event.) The ideal location for camera placement is at the exact horizontal and vertical center of the

Figure 10.3. A 4×5 format cut film holder with dark slides in place and locked: Exposed white edge of slide (top) indicates unexposed film inside. After the exposure is made, the slide is replaced with the other side (black) showing, to indicate exposed film inside.

image area you wish to photograph. Since this often is not possible, we can achieve the desired results by other means. Once mounted on a tripod, the camera should be leveled, particularly when doing recordation work. A standard lens, that is one that gives you an image on the ground glass that is the same size as the image seen by the naked eye, is best because it will cause the least distortion. The camera should be placed far enough from the subject so that the entire subject is contained within the field of view as seen through the lens. If the subject location does not allow camera placement at the proper distance, if you cannot get far enough away or close enough to your subject, then a wide-angle or telephoto lens will be necessary.

The Lenses

The lenses made for use on view cameras have a mechanism for holding the aperture and shutter open while the photographer views the subject and focuses the image on the ground glass plate at the back of the camera (see Figure 10.4). A dark cloth or hood is usually used to shade the camera back and the photographer's head to facilitate this process. Some photographers also use a viewing "loup" or magnifying glass against the ground glass to obtain sharp focus. In any case all parts of the image must be in sharp focus.

The mobility of the front and back frames on the camera allows the photographer to correct the perspective of the subject if, as mentioned before, the camera cannot be placed in the exact center of the image area. Moving or "shifting" the lens upwards (or downward if the camera is located above the image center) will center tall subjects in the image area. Shifting the lens to the left or right will move subjects horizontally to achieve the same result if the camera must be placed to the side of center. More information on this follows later.

Once the image is composed and focused on the ground glass plate, and the light level checked using any good light meter, the aperture and shutter speed must be set in the camera's lens. The smaller the aperture or lens opening is during exposure, the greater will be the depth-of-field (the amount of the image area from foreground to background that will be in sharp focus). The process of setting the aperture (or diaphragm) is called "stopping down" the lens. While the shutter can be tripped by hand, the use of a cable release makes it easier and minimizes the possibility of camera shake.

Light metering is an automatic function on many cameras available today. Most 35mm cameras have through-the-lens metering systems built into the camera which measure the light actually striking the film plane. This is not true for the view camera. Light must be measured independently by means of a separate hand-held light meter (see Figure 10.5).

It may be possible to use the built-in metering system in another camera to get a light reading, provided that the camera is set for the correct film speed (ASA/ISO). Such built-in metering systems are often tailored (or "dedicated") to the camera in which they are installed, and many are "integrated" with miniature computer systems that control both shutter speed and aperture (diaphragm) settings automatically. Consequently, they may give a false reading in relation to any other camera.

The best possible method to measure light intensity is to use a separate, good quality, hand-held light meter. Such meters must be set to match the speed (ASA/ISO) of the film in

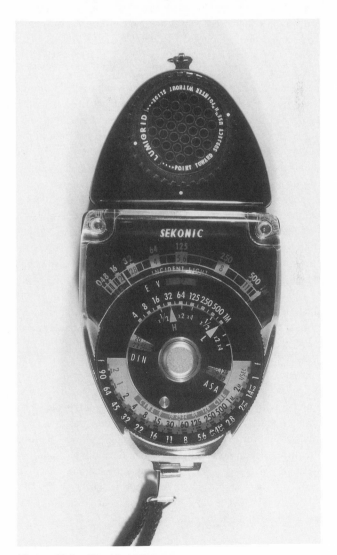

Figure 10.5.   Hand-held light meter:
light sensor
film speed setting
incident light scale
aperture settings
shutter speed settings

Figure 10.4.   150MM STANDARD LENS:
aperture lock
aperture scale
shutter release lever shutter
speed scale

use and usually have a needle or pointer that moves up and down a scale depending on the available light level. They also have switches or some other means to change from high light level to low light level if needed. Once the needle or pointer registers, the scale will show a number of shutter speed/aperture combinations that will give the correct exposure. Any camera store that caters to professional photographers will carry a full range of light meters.

Focal Length and Subject Distance

Popular thought has it that wide-angle and telephoto lenses alter perspective because wide-angle lenses seem to distort the subject and exaggerate depth while telephoto lenses seem to compress space. Nevertheless, these effects are not faults in the respective lens designs but are the results of the way in which these lenses are used. All lenses (standard, wide-angle and telephoto) PRODUCE IDENTICAL PERSPECTIVES IF THEY ARE USED AT THE SAME DISTANCE FROM THE SUBJECT.

The following simple experiment will prove this point. Take three photographs of the same subject from the same camera position, one with a standard lens, one with a wide-angle lens and one with a telephoto lens. If you enlarge the negatives respectively to make the main subject the same size on all the prints and compare, you will discover that, allowing for slight differences in sharpness and grain due to differences in image magnification, the three will be identical in perspective, and if superimposed, would register perfectly.

Take three additional photographs of the same subject with a standard, wide-angle and telephoto lens respectively. Begin with the telephoto shot and make it from a distance at which the main subject exactly fills the height of the negative. The other two shots are made from distances at which the height of the main subject is the same as it was in the telephoto shot, meaning that the shots with the standard and wide-angle lenses are made respectively closer to the subject. Enlarge the three negatives to the same size prints and compare. Although the main subject will be the same size in each, space relationships will be totally different. The background will appear large and close in the telephoto shot, smaller and farther away in the standard shot and even smaller and farther away in the wide-angle view. This time the difference in perspective is real and cannot be equalized through enlarging. The experiment demonstrates that it is NOT the focal length of the lens, but the DISTANCE BETWEEN SUBJECT AND CAMERA that determines the perspective of a photograph.

TILT AND SHIFT: PERSPECTIVE CONTROLS

The term "perspective" usually means rectilinear perspective, not cylindrical or spherical perspective, and there are two kinds of rectilinear perspective: academic and true. The specifications of academic rectilinear perspective are as follows:

1. Straight lines are rendered straight.
2. All two-dimensional forms parallel to the plane of the film are rendered distortion free: parallels are rendered parallel, circles are rendered round, angles are rendered in their true shapes.
3. Receding horizontal lines converge toward vanishing points, and all such vanishing points are located on the true horizon, whether the horizon is visible in the picture or not.
4. Vertical lines must appear parallel and vertical.

True rectilinear perspective is identical to academic rectilinear perspective in regard to points one, two and three; it differs in regard to point four: verticals are rendered parallel only if they fall under point two. If the film is not parallel to the verticals and/or horizontals (if the camera is tilted upward or downward, or if placed to one side of the plane of the subject giving a three-quarter view) verticals and/or horizontals will converge in the picture. This convergence is, of course, nothing but the natural manifestation of perspective in the vertical (and/or horizontal) plane. This phenomenon, if unwanted, can be avoided by one of the following controls.

Vertical Control

The film must be parallel to the vertical lines of the subject. This is accomplished by leveling the camera. However, if the subject is a tall building, and the photograph is made with the camera level, the top of the building will be cut off in the picture and the foreground will appear unduly prominent. On the other hand, if the camera is tilted to include the top of the building and reduce the amount of foreground shown, the vertical lines will converge. In such a case the only way to make a satisfactory negative is to raise the front frame (the lens) of the camera as follows:

Place the camera on a tripod. Aim and focus as usual observing the image on the ground glass—the vertical lines will converge. Tilt the camera forward until it is level. The vertical lines will now appear parallel, but the top of the building will be cut off. Without altering the camera position, elevate the lens by raising the front until the entire building appears on the ground glass. Stop down as usual and make the photograph (see Figure 10.6).

Horizontal Control

Horizontal control may become necessary if the camera cannot be placed at the center of the subject and it is achieved in much the same manner as vertical control. The film must be parallel to the horizontal lines of the subject. Place the

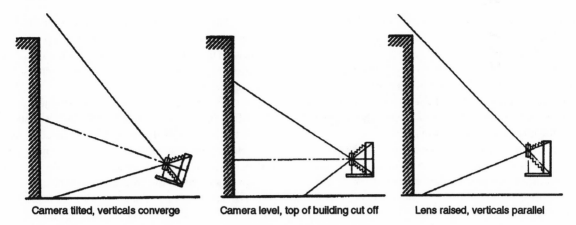

Camera tilted, verticals converge   Camera level, top of building cut off   Lens raised, verticals parallel

Figure 10.6. Vertical control

camera on a tripod, aim and focus the image on the ground glass. The horizontal lines will converge. Turn the camera until the film is parallel with the plane of the building. The horizontal lines will now appear parallel but one side of the building will be cut off. Without altering the camera position, shift the lens to the right (or left as the case may be) until the entire building appears on the ground glass. Stop down and make the photograph.

The "Swings" of a View Camera

The SWINGS of a view camera are the possible movements (vertical, horizontal, turn and tilt) of the front frame (the lens) and the back frame (the film plane) that may be employed to control perspective and achieve sharp focus on the ground glass (see Figure 10.7).

In order to control successfully the perspective of a picture the photographer must realize two points:

1. Only the planes, forms and angles of the subject that are parallel to the film plane can be rendered distortion-free. Any forms and angles not parallel to the film plane will be rendered distorted. The photographer can accomplish parallel placement by situating the camera accordingly in relation to the subject, by placing the subject accordingly in relation to the camera, or if neither is possible, by adjusting the camera back to move the film parallel to the part of the subject that must be rendered free of distortion regardless of the direction in which the lens is pointed. If none of the above can be done, distortion-free rendition in the negative is impossible.

2. The lens must have more than average covering power or accommodate a wider field of view because it may be necessary to adjust it in such a way that it no longer points at the center of the film. Otherwise, use of the front swings may move the image so that part of the film would be outside the area of sharp focus, and that part would be rendered either unsharp or, in extreme cases, blank. To avoid this problem, either a lens with extra covering power (a higher quality lens

that holds accurate image resolution to its edges), or a wide angle lens of equal focal length designed to cover the next larger film size must be used as above.

EXPERIMENT

The best way to understand the principles of perspective control is to experiment by photographing a large box so that three of its sides are visible in the picture, one of which—the

Figure 10.7. Swings of a view camera

front—must be rendered distortion-free (its vertical lines parallel, its horizontal lines parallel and its angles 90 degrees). Proceed as follows:

1. Mount a swing-type view camera on a tripod and place it to show two sides of the box and high enough to capture an oblique view of the top. With the lens wide-open and all swings (or frames) in neutral position, center the image of the box on the ground glass and focus.

2. Adjust (tilt) the back of the camera so that the film is parallel with the vertical lines of the box. This will render the vertical lines of any subject parallel instead of converging. The image will be partly out of focus, but disregard this for the time being.

3. If adjusting the back (or making any of the following adjustments) results in displacement of the image on the ground glass, DO NOT CHANGE THE CAMERA POSITION. Instead, center the image of the box by using the vertical (rising) or horizontal (sliding) adjustments of either the lens or the camera back.

4. Swing the back of the camera laterally until it is parallel to the front of the box. In this position, the horizontal lines of the front of any subject will be parallel instead of converging. While making this adjustment be careful not to spoil the parallel relationship between the camera back and the vertical lines of the box. The box will now appear very much out of focus.

5. Refocus the lens for the best possible focus (large sections of the box will still be out of focus).

6. Tilt and swing the lens until the plane of sharpest focus is the principle plane of the box (until you get the best possible overall focus). This is a delicate job because only slight movements from the neutral position of the lens are required. Continue to refocus the lens while making the front adjustments, checking the sharpness of the image on the ground glass. Although this will not bring the entire subject into sharp focus, it will improve overall sharpness to a point where stopping down the lens aperture will be sufficient to render a critically sharp picture of the entire box.

DEPTH OF FIELD

All of us at some time or another have squinted our eyes in order to see a distant object more clearly. The squint, partially closing the eye lids, reduces the size of the aperture of our eyes and lengthens our field of focus. This same principal holds true for camera lenses as well—the smaller the lens opening or aperture, the greater the amount of the field of view that will be in focus. However, the second function of the movable frames of a view camera (lens and camera back) is to extend the depth-of-field, the sharply focused zone from foreground to background, in oblique angle shots of relatively flat subjects (and only these), for example, a floor or the facade of a building. Any part of the subject that projects beyond this inclined plane (inclined in relation to the film plane) must be brought into sharp focus by stopping down

the lens. However, the overall gain in sharp focus by adjusting the camera frames is so great that the entire depth of a subject can be rendered sharp with considerably less aperture adjustment (stopping down) than would otherwise be necessary (see Figure 10.8).

To achieve overall sharpness, we must adjust the position of the film in relation to the lens and subject in such a manner that near areas of the subject are focused at the top (or one side) of the ground glass (greater ground glass-to-lens distance) and far areas of the subject are focused at the bottom (or other side) of the ground glass (shorter ground glass-to-lens distance). This is done by tilting (or laterally turning) the back of the camera accordingly. The entire depth of the subject will appear sharp without stopping down the lens if the photographer tilts (or turns) the camera back such that imaginary lines drawn through the principal planes of the subject, the lens (diaphragm) and the film converge at a common point.

The photographer can achieve the same sharpness in depth by tilting the lens forward instead of tilting the camera back backward (to photograph a horizontal subject, i.e., a floor). This method must be used when the camera back must be kept vertical to render vertical lines parallel (furniture standing on the floor). However, tilting the lens in this manner throws its axis off the center of the ground glass and, if the covering power of the lens is insufficient, it could result in vignetting. (Vignetting is the loss of image at the corners or, in more severe instances, the creation of blank areas on the negative.) The photographer can usually avoid this problem by lowering the lens vertically or raising the camera back until the lens axis is once again centered on the ground glass (Figure 10.9).

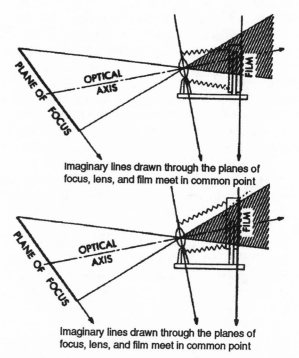

Imaginary lines drawn through the planes of focus, lens, and film meet in common point

Imaginary lines drawn through the planes of focus, lens, and film meet in common point

Figure 10.8. Depth of field

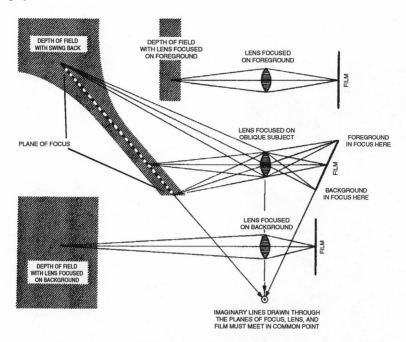

DEPTH OF FIELD WITH SWING BACK

DEPTH OF FIELD WITH LENS FOCUSED ON FOREGROUND

LENS FOCUSED ON FOREGROUND

FILM

PLANE OF FOCUS

LENS FOCUSED ON OBLIQUE SUBJECT

FOREGROUND IN FOCUS HERE

FILM

BACKGROUND IN FOCUS HERE

LENS FOCUSED ON BACKGROUND

FILM

DEPTH OF FIELD WITH LENS FOCUSED ON BACKGROUND

IMAGINARY LINES DRAWN THROUGH THE PLANES OF FOCUS, LENS, AND FILM MUST MEET IN COMMON POINT

Figure 10.9. Depth of field

LOAD THE HOLDER

The film holder is slipped into the back of the camera and is held in place by means of a spring-loaded frame which also holds the ground glass focusing plate. Once in place, the film plane in the holder will occupy the same position as the ground glass focusing plate. Some view cameras allow this frame to rotate on the camera to accommodate either horizontal or vertical images.

Double check to be sure the lens is closed, the shutter speed and aperture set and the shutter cocked for exposure. Remove the dark slide from the holder, release the shutter and replace the slide. Most slides, as mentioned before, are marked on one side to indicate the film has been exposed. As the slide is replaced, the photographer can turn the slide so marking the exposed frame. Film holders also usually have catches or locks that prevent the slide from being removed unintentionally (see Figure 10.10).

The film holder can be removed, turned to the second side and replaced in the camera for a second exposure.

FILTERS

Since HABS/HAER photographers work primarily in black and white, they can use color filters to enhance the final image and create more interest in the overall photograph. The filters most often employed are yellow, orange and/or red. They have the effect of increasing contrast and giving more tone to the sky, rendering clouds very visible against the blue sky in the black and white image. The effect is usually very pleasing.

Filters change the response of photographic emulsion to light and color. Their function is to alter the rendition of color in terms of either black and white or color to produce a picture that is clearer, more accurate, more interesting or more beautiful than it would be if no filter were used. Roughly stated, a filter transmits light of its own color and absorbs light of a complementary color.

Using a filter will affect a photograph in two ways: (1) As stated above, it affects the response of the film to light and color; (2) A filter affects the exposure—since every filter absorbs a certain amount of light, the exposure must be increased to compensate for light loss. The amount of increase is based upon four factors: the color sensitivity of the film; the spectral composition of the light; the color of the filter; and the density of the filter.

Filter manufacturers provide a basis for calculating exposures by assigning specific factors to each filter by which the exposure is multiplied when the filter is used with specific types of film and light. For example, if the correct exposure without a filter is 1/100 sec. at f/16 and a filter is used that, in conjunction with the type of film and light, has a factor of 2, the exposure would be either 1/50 sec. at f/16 or 1/100 sec. at f/11. (Each time the shutter speed is decreased by one setting or the aperture is opened by one stop the amount of light reaching the film plane doubles. Conversely, each time the shutter speed is increased by one setting or the aperture is closed by one stop the amount of light is decreased by one-half.)

COPY PHOTOGRAPHY

View cameras can be employed to photograph other photographs, documents and/or important records. This procedure is usually accomplished indoors using a copy stand or table constructed for this purpose. The camera is mounted

Figure 10.10.   Loading the film holder:
holder end folded open
cut film sheet (notches in upper right)
films rails
dark slide partially opened with "unexposed" indicator(s) showing

vertically or horizontally and pointed at a flat surface designed to hold the subject matter to be photographed and the flat copy surface is flooded with artificial light. The camera moves along a vertical or horizontal track closer to or further back from the copy surface to accommodate the size of the subject to be copied. Light is measured with a meter and the aperture and shutter speed are set accordingly with some important variations.

When making a photograph of another photograph, the aperture and shutter should be set as the light meter indicates. However, when photographing drawings, charts,

graphs, any text document or any subject that is strictly line art, that is black or dark lines on a plain white or near-white background, the aperture should be opened one-half to one full stop further than indicated by the meter. This will prevent a gray or darkened background in the photograph.

ACCESSORIES

As with most other cameras on today's market, there are many accessories available for the view camera, items which, although almost indispensable, must be considered as extras. Apart from a good carrying case and plenty of film holders, the view camera all but commands the use of a tripod, a light-proof focusing hood, a light meter and a shutter release cable. Other goodies and gadgets might include lens hoods, a Polaroid film back, flash holders and brackets and a blister or bag bellows, interchangeable with the accordion bellows, for use with wide-angle lenses.

Film manufacturers are now marketing pre-loaded film packets (currently called "Ready-Loads") for use in view cameras. The sheets of film are placed by the manufacturer in light-proof, removable paper sleeves, two to a unit (just like traditional film holders), which can be slipped into the camera back using a special holder. The paper packets, available at a higher price, eliminate the need for hand loading film and eliminate the risk of dust contamination.

There are some items, however, that the photographer will not find in any camera catalog or on a camera store shelf. These are things not usually associated with photography in any way.

1. A good pocket knife with, perhaps, a screw driver blade (to tighten things that come loose);
2. String and tape to fasten things which might not otherwise get fastened;
3. Work gloves, hedge clippers and garden shears (for landscaping as needed to clear the field of view);
4. A big flash light serves two purposes—to find your way in and out of dark cavernous places, and to serve as a focusing point in dimly lit or dark spaces;
5. A magnifying loup or glass to aid in sharp focusing;
6. Heavy shoes, insect repellent and protective clothing and gear for you and your camera as dictated by field conditions; and
7. Extra everything.

THE FUTURE OF STILL PHOTOGRAPHY

With the development of television, videography, videotape and disk, computer imaging, digitized electronic recording and storage mechanisms and cameras that provide instant photo images, it's hard to imagine a place for the "old" technology of still photography. Each day seems to bring new and more versatile "imaging" systems to the marketplace and the effect on the speed and accuracy of communication is staggering. However, the printed photograph has one distinct advantage over any of the electronic image systems: once processed, a printed photograph does not require any electric energy in order to view it.

Another point to consider is that the very malleability of computer-generated images creates a place for a visual record that cannot be enhanced or altered so easily. The still photograph cannot be altered easily, and when it is changed, such changes or alterations are usually obvious even to the naked eye. Thus the still photograph continues to play a role as a valuable recording medium.

BIBLIOGRAPHY

Feininger, A. *The Complete Photographer*. Englewood Cliffs, NJ: Prentice-Hall Inc., 1968.

National Park Service. "Guide for the Preparation of Photographic Documentation in Accordance with the Standards of the Historic American Building Survey/Historic American Engineering Record (HABS/HAER)." Preservation Planning Branch, Resource Planning and Preservation Division, Cultural Resource Management, Mid-Atlantic Region, December 1989.

Niece, R. C. *Photo-Imagination*. New York: Amphoto, 1966.

CHAPTER 11

Land Surveying Methods Employed By Industrial Archaeologists

Edward H. Winant

INTRODUCTION

Surveying plays an important role in any industrial archaeology project. The reason for a land survey is to locate relevant points both horizontally and vertically for preparing a site map, and to measure structural dimensions that would be too hazardous to obtain by hand-held measuring tapes. The site map should show all relevant historical and archaeological points. This map then provides the context for the important features of the site.

A horizontal survey, for these purposes, is best accomplished by using a plane table, which directly maps points of interest. The vertical survey is done after the horizontal by means of an instrument called the level. This two-step procedure of surveying is most suited for the beginning surveyor and lends itself to small, open sites that are relatively level.

For forested sites, or rugged terrain, the theodolite, also known as the transit, is useful. This instrument is able to accomplish both horizontal and vertical surveys in one step, although it is more difficult to use. However, for some purposes, such as measuring vertical dimensions, it is indispensable, because it has pivotal motion in both the horizontal and vertical planes, while other surveying instruments turn only in the horizontal.

This chapter will address both types of surveying, giving the novice some idea on how to conduct an industrial archaeology survey. Besides field work, it will also cover supplemental topics such as mapping, necessary calculations, and special forms of field measurements.

EQUIPMENT

For any survey, certain equipment besides the instrument is needed. A field book for recording notes and some pencils, a 100-foot surveyor's tape measure, (you could use a 30-meter tape if you happen to have one),[1] a plumb bob, several wooden hubs and tacks (hubs are small stakes, about 6 inches long that are driven flush into the ground, and hold the tack in place) and a hammer. Additionally, brightly colored flagging is quite helpful. A surveying tape is marked off in tenths of a foot, rather than inches, and is easier to use. Site mapping in the United States is based on decimals of the foot, whereas Canada has converted to the metric system.

Measurements using a surveyor's tape will also convert more easily to mapping, as map distances are plotted using an engineer's scale and not a ruler. The scale is simple to use, and is based on the premise of an even number of divisions per inch. For example, a 10 scale has ten ticks per inch. If you are plotting a map with a $1'' = 10'$, then each tick on the scale represents one foot. Likewise, on a 20 scale, there are twenty ticks per inch (see Figure 11.1, Engineer's Scale).

In addition to modern measurements, the historian should also be familiar with antiquated surveying units. These units include the rod, also known as a pole or perch, and the chain. As a unit, one rod is 16 1/2 feet long, and was originally a measuring rod of about that length. A chain is four rods, or 66 feet. It is quite useful for measuring areas, as 10 square chains equals an acre. These units may be encountered in researching old deeds or in locating surveying markers in the field.

Scales can be expanded, after a fashion, for larger numbers. For instance, a 10 scale can be used to represent $1'' = 100'$, where each tick would represent 10 feet. This representation scheme allows you to make much more use out of the standard 10, 20, 30, 40, 50 and 60 engineering scales. Additionally, some maps, such as topographic maps, use a scale marked as 1:24000. This means that one map inch is the same as 24,000 ground inches. If you convert this, it comes to $1'' = 2000'$, so you could use the 20 scale, with each tick representing 100 feet.

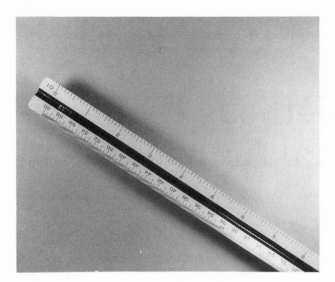

Figure 11.1. Engineer's scale

THE PLANE TABLE

The most basic type of horizontal survey would be to draw a rough sketch of the site and measure all the distances with a tape.[2] Essentially, however, that is what the plane table allows you to do, only in a much more controlled manner. The plane table is the most basic surveying instrument. It consists of a telescope or sighting arm (the alidade) mounted on a drawing board (see Figure 11.2, Alidade). The drawing board sits on a tripod so that it may be leveled and rotated. At the base of the telescope is a straightedge, which is marked as a 10 scale. Thus, when the alidade is sighted on a relevant point, the line to that point on the map lies along the straightedge. Distances from the instrument to the various points should be measured with the 100 foot tape. On the drawing, then, the point lies along the line of the straightedge, and the map distance may be scaled off at a convenient setting.

To set up the plane table, select a flat spot in the middle of the ground to be surveyed with good visibility of much of the site as possible. Avoid spots where trees block the line of sight to important features. Also, for locating buildings, it is better to set up off a corner in order to see two sides, rather than setting up in front and measuring only one.

The plane table consists of an alidade, or sighting device, which is equipped with a straightedge and engineering 10 scale; a drawing table; and a tripod. Prior to setting up the instrument, you should assemble these items, setting the alidade on the table and screwing the table onto the tripod head (see Figure 11.3). Now you may set the plane table over your first point. The tripod legs should be spread wide enough to give stability, but may be adjusted to place the alidade at a good viewing level. Setting up an instrument has two main objectives: getting the instrument over a point on the ground and insuring that the table is level. Both of these operations require multiple adjustments.

Coarse adjustments are made with the tripod legs. Moving individual legs in or out will both adjust the center of the instrument and the relative levelness of the table. If you are fortunate, your tripod will have adjustable legs, allowing for lengthening or shortening without removing the leg from the ground. Once the coarse adjustments are finished, press the tripod legs firmly into the ground.

For fine adjustments use the tripod head. This is an attachment, (a Johnson Head, to be specific), that will allow you to level the table (see Figure 11.4). The Johnson Head is a universal joint, where the bottom section is used for leveling and is then locked into place, while the upper section allows the board to be rotated horizontally to orient the board with regard to the site. A little practice will allow you to manipulate the table with ease. The drawing paper, usually cut from a large roll of vellum, may either be taped to the table or fastened with special screws at the edge of the table.

With the drawing table and paper attached to the tripod and the alidade resting on top, you may begin your survey. The first point you should mark on your map will be the point where you are set-up (A). The alidade is then pivoted around this point to take sights. To mark other relevant points, such as building corners or trees, sight the alidade so that it shows the object in question. Then draw a line, along the straightedge, from the center point for a suitable distance, and make some note of what the point is. The length of the line should be drawn to scale, using the scale provided on the straight-

Figure 11.2. Alidade.

Figure 11.3. Plane table.

Figure 11.4. Johnson head.

edge or an engineer's scale. The ground distance should be measured with a 100 foot surveyor's tape.

It may be necessary to have a person hold a surveying rod on the point to be sighted to insure that it is easily seen. A "rodman" is also necessary to pick up important ground points that are below the level of the alidade. When using a rod, simply sight the alidade on the center of the rod.

Some relevant ground points to pick up are high points and low points in the terrain. These points will be of use when doing the leveling survey, discussed later in this chap-

ter. It is also useful in doing the leveling survey to establish a grid on the ground as the base for determining contours of equal elevation. This grid should be about 25 or 50 feet square (6 or 12 meters).[3] Grid points should be marked on the map as such, and some temporary marker, (a long pin, or a stick with a bit of flagging), left on the ground point for the later leveling operation.

It is quite probable that it will not be possible to see the whole site from one set-up. The first step in moving the instrument is deciding where you will set it up next (B). Send the rodman to this point, and mark it on your map. You may then move the instrument and set it up again on the new point.

At the new set-up, place the pivot point of the alidade on point B. Now, with the alidade sighted at point (A) move the map so that line (BA) (on the map) lines up with the straight-edge. Then place the alidade on the drawing board (see Figure 11.5, Plane Table Traversing). You may now continue with the survey, drawing lines from the new setup to relevant points. Further setups are conducted in the same manner, plotting the new point, moving the instrument and back-sighting the instrument to the last occupied setup.

Creating a final map from a plane table survey is relatively easy. You already have the direction of the lines and scaled distances from one point to the others, and need only add relevant symbols for the objects and clean up the radial lines (from setup point to object point). Cleaning up the radial lines will probably mean redrawing the map on a clean sheet

SIDE SHOT

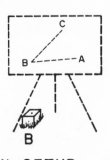

NEW SETUP

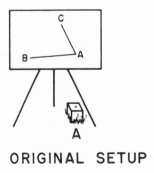

ORIGINAL SETUP

Figure 11.5. Plane table traversing (Drawing by Paul Boxley).

of paper. Once all the points are located, you may draw in symbols for building walls, fences, trees, roads, etc. Such symbols may be as you desire, and should be referenced in a legend on the map.[4]

STADIA

A second method of finding the distance is known as the stadia method. This is easier than using the tape, but not quite as accurate. The stadia method makes use of the upper and lower cross hairs of the telescope and the rod. To make a stadia reading, simply read the upper cross hair where it falls on the rod, and then take the lower cross hair reading. Subtract the lower reading from the upper, and multiply this difference by 100. The product will give you the difference in feet from the instrument to the rod. This operation is similar, in theory, to focusing a 35mm camera. In focusing, you adjust the lens to bring the picture in focus and then may read the numbers to get a rough distance, such as 2, 6 or 8 meters. Of course, most distances show up as infinity, so you can not really use a camera to calculate survey distances.

THE LEVEL

To perform the vertical survey, you need a level (see Figure 11.6). The surveying level is a telescope with sensitive level bubbles mounted on a tripod. The level is also equipped with three or four leveling screws that allow for fine adjustments in keeping the instrument level. Setting up the level will become quite easy with practice. The tripod legs should be spread wide enough to provide stability and even enough to keep the top roughly level. The leveling screws are then operated in pairs to bring the instrument into its final position.

This positioning is accomplished by aligning the telescope across two screws that are opposite one another. Then, turn both screws, either both outwards or both inwards. (This may also be seen as turning one clockwise and its opposite number counterclockwise.) When the level bubble is centered, rotate the telescope across the other pair of screws, assuming

you have four. If you only have three, place the telescope perpendicular to the third screw. Adjust these screws. This operation may have to be preformed several times, with each subsequent adjustment being finer than the previous one.

Once the instrument is level, you may begin taking sights. The first sight necessary is a backsight on a known or assumed elevation. This known elevation is called a benchmark. The government places permanent benchmarks periodically across the country. For most sites, however, it is sufficient to pick a stable point (telephone pole, building corner, a big rock, etc.) and assume an elevation for it, thus creating a temporary benchmark. The rod should be held vertical, or plumb, over this point. Read the number on the rod that is intersected by the center cross hair in the telescope and record that number in the backsight column of your field notebook (see Figures 11.7 and 11.8).

As you can see from Figure 11.7 (of the Philadelphia rod), the rod is marked off so that you may read to the nearest hundredth of a foot. The large red numbers are feet, the black numbers are tenths of feet and the bars are spaced so that every top or bottom of a bar is one-one hundredth of a foot. For your convenience, every fifth hundredth bar is longer than the rest. Since it is not always possible to see one whole foot of rod through the telescope, smaller red numbers are repeated to show the foot markings.

As mentioned before, read the rod at the center cross hair and record this reading in the backsight column (BS) of the

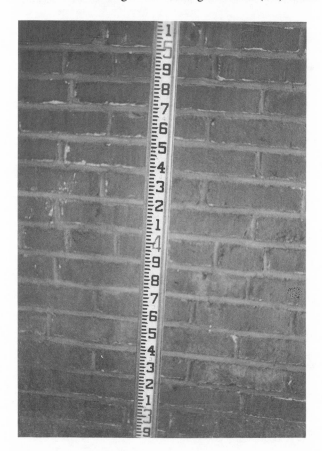

Figure 11.7. Philadelphia rod.

Figure 11.6. Dumpy level.

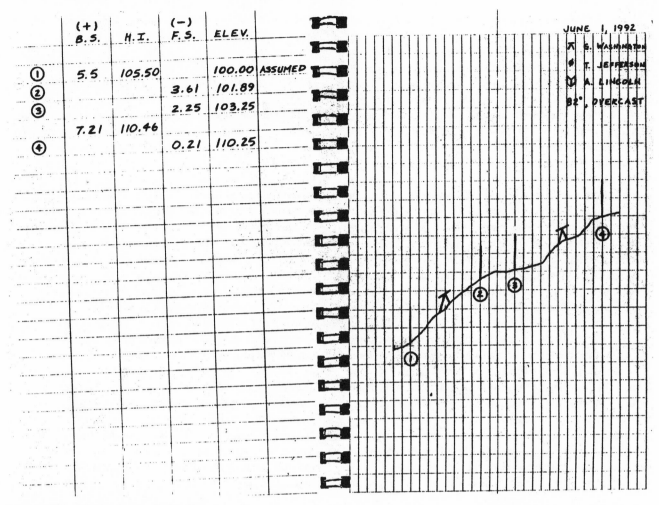

	(+) B.S.	H.I.	(−) F.S.	ELEV.	
①	5.5	105.50		100.00	ASSUMED
②			3.61	101.89	
③			2.25	103.25	
	7.21	110.46			
④			0.21	110.25	

JUNE 1, 1992
G. WASHINGTON
T. JEFFERSON
A. LINCOLN
82°, OVERCAST

Figure 11.8. Notebook setup for leveling.

field notebook. The backsight is added to the elevation of the ground point to give the elevation of your instrument's line of sight, also known as height of instrument (HI).

To move the instrument, you will need to take a foresight (FS). Send the rodman to the point in question, and take a reading on the rod. This should be recorded in the foresight column in the fieldbook. Before moving the instrument, though, you should take sights on all other relevant points to determine their elevation. Take a rod reading on each unknown point, and record this as an intermediate foresight (IFS) in another column of your field book. Any foresight is subtracted from the height of instrument to give the elevation of the unknown point.

When you are ready to move the instrument and have recorded the foresight, you may pick up the instrument and move it to a spot where you may see the foresight point and also may see more points to survey. Set up the instrument at a convenient spot, level it and take a backsight, as before, on the point which gave you the previous foresight. Record this in your field book as shown in Figure 11.8.

To do a complete topographical survey, you need to record all local high and low spots, which is why the points were earlier located with the plane table. Further, the accuracy of any contour map will increase with the number of known ground elevations. This is the rationale behind the grid system, to provide a reasonable number of ground points that will cover the whole site.

Besides normal ground points, it is necessary to record the elevations of building corners and other important industrial archaeological features. This is done in the same way as for ground points.

TOPOGRAPHIC MAPS

Once the elevations have been calculated in the field book, they should be recorded on the plan map (from the plane table survey) by each point that they represent. From these elevations a contour or topographical map may be constructed.[5]

Contours are lines of equal elevation. They are usually drawn, for this scale of mapping, every foot or every two feet apart in elevation. A simple method of interpolation will show you where these lines should go in between your known elevation points. An example calculation will best demonstrate how to construct these contour lines.

Assume there are two known elevations, 96.4 feet and 103.2 feet, and that they are 36 feet apart on a straight line. Further, the contour interval for the map is set at two feet. The contours that will fall between these points are then: 98, 100 and 102 feet (see Figure 11.9). First calculate the total difference in elevation between the two points, which is 103.2 − 96.4 = 6.8 feet. Then determine the differences in elevation from each contour line to the lower elevation (this makes the math easier). These are 98 − 96.4 = 1.6 feet, 100 − 96.4 = 3.6 feet and 102 − 96.4 = 5.6 feet. Now comes the interpolation, which is simply a matter of ratios. Thus, the ground distance from the point 96.4 to the 98 contour divided by the total distance (36 feet) is equal to the ratio of elevations (1.6/6.8). The ratio of elevations here is .235. Multiply this by the total distance (36 feet) and you will find that the 98 contour lies 8.46 feet (call it 8.5) from the 96.4 foot point, along a straight line to the 103.2 foot point. Similarly, the ratio of elevations for the 100 foot contour is 3.6/6.8 = .529. Multiplying by the distance, one finds that this contour is 19 feet from our first control point. Lastly, the 102 contour can be determined to be 29.65 feet (round to 29.5) from the first point.

To draw the contour map, first mark these three contours as points on the map. Then, using combinations of other known points, calculate the positions of other contour points for the entire site (this can be quite a long process, as you may have many points). When all the contour points have been plotted, merely connect points with equal elevations together.

There are, of course, some rules involved in connecting these points. Contour lines may not end, so that you must either make them into closed circles or show them going off the edge of the map. The lines may not cross one another, unless you have the unusual case of an overhang.

THE TRANSIT OR THEODOLITE

The previous operations using plane table and level can be used to produce a complete topographic map. However, it requires covering the same ground in field twice—once for the plane table and once for the level. The same data can be obtained in one sweep with a transit, but while this reduces time in the field, it requires more office time for mapping and some more complicated calculations.

The transit or theodolite is one of the more delicate and sophisticated surveying instruments. It consists mainly of a telescope. This telescope, however, is mounted so that it may traverse and measure horizontal and vertical angles. Further, it has several knobs that allow it to be "locked" into any angular position (see Figures 11.10 and 11.11).

Setup of the transit is similar to setting up a plane table. It must be accurately positioned over a ground point, which is achieved by positioning and repositioning the tripod legs. In addition, the transit has a slight range of motion on the head of the tripod for fine adjustments. After positioning, the transit must be set level. For this operation, there are three or four leveling screws, so this is done in the manner of leveling the level. Mark the setup location with a hub, which is a semi-permanent marker such as a tack in a wooden stake (driven flush with the ground) or a railroad spike. The center of the transit should be directly above the

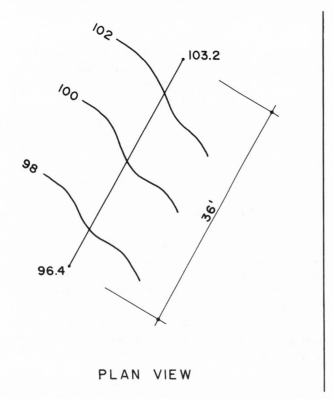

PLAN VIEW

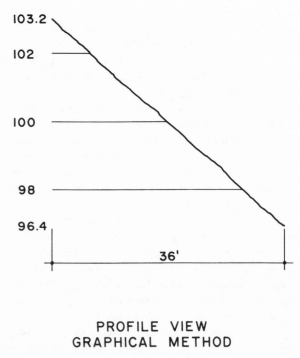

PROFILE VIEW
GRAPHICAL METHOD

Figure 11.9. Contour mapping (Drawing by Paul Boxley).

Figure 11.10. Digital theodolite.

tack, and to insure this you should use a plumb bob. The plumb bob hangs from a convenient hook on the transit, and you should adjust the instrument until the bob hangs over the tack in the hub.

When using the level, set a 186benchmark, or known elevation. With a transit, you must set a zero azimuth, or baseline to measure angles. A convenient starting azimuth is magnetic north,[6] although any direction is usable. It should be marked on the final map with some symbol such as a north arrow. You should mark the baseline with one or two wooden stakes in case you need to set up on this hub in the

Figure 11.11. Digital theodolite.

future. If you use a building corner or other permanent point to set your baseline, you can just make note of that.

To measure angles, the transit has two horizontal motions, or an upper circle and a lower circle. The lower circle is used to set the baseline and then it is locked in place. Motion of the upper circle will then show the angle from the baseline, and allow you to make a measurement.

To set the baseline, then, lock the bottom circle and turn the upper circle so that it reads zero. Lock the upper circle. Unlock the lower circle and turn it until the telescope points towards your baseline. Lock the lower circle and make fine adjustments with the proper knob. When this is set do not touch the lower knobs until you are finished with this setup and ready to move on. To finish the setup procedure, measure the height of instrument (a folding rule is best, but you could use the surveying rod if you are careful) and record this in your field book (see Figure 11.12).

The baseline for vertical angles is the level line of sight from the instrument. It will measure positive angles up from this line, and negative angles below this line. It is important when recording vertical angles to include the sign.

The horizontal angles are measured from the zero azimuth around the circle for 360 degrees. They may be measured clockwise or counterclockwise, and either is allowable as long as you are consistent and remember which method you used. Measuring clockwise is preferred, as this follows the convention for magnetic compass readings.

You may now begin to use the transit. For each point to be recorded (these will be the same points you would survey with the plane table and level) turn the transit, remembering to use the upper circle until the crosshairs bisect the rod. Use the vertical motion of the telescope to put the crosshairs on a convenient marking. A reading equal to the height of your instrument is preferred. Record this number as your rod reading. Then record the horizontal and vertical angles, remembering the sign for the vertical angle. For each point, you will also need the distance, which you can get by using a tape or get a stadia reading. For important points, use the 100-foot tape. You may use stadia for ground shots.

If you need to move the instrument, you must first set another hub at the new location. Have the rodman drive the hub into the ground, place a tack in it, and then take a shot on it as usual. Move the transit and set it up over that hub.

When it is set up, you will need a backsight to tie it in to the first hub, which is similar to the backsighting operation for the plane table. This time, though, you must set the correct angle for the baseline. The baseline for the second hub is the backsight line to the first hub. The angle to set on the lower circle is the measured angle from the first hub to the second hub minus 180 degrees. For example, if your measurement to the second hub was 200 degrees, the backsight will be 20 degrees. If your measurement was 90 degrees, your backsight will be −90 degrees, which you do not have room for on the transit. For negative numbers, simply add in a complete circle (360 degrees). In the second case this will give you a backsight of 270 degrees.

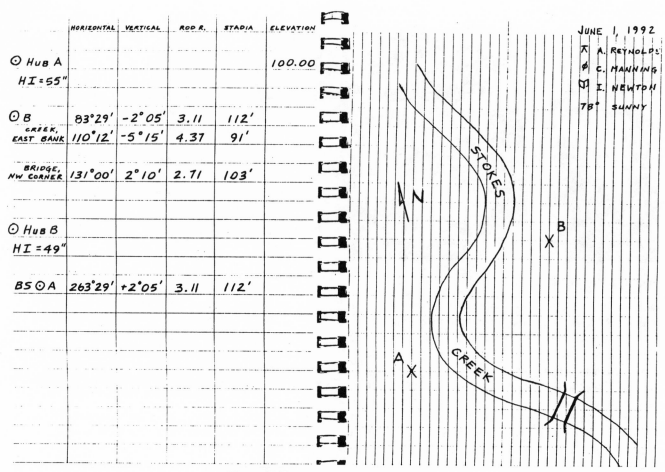

	HORIZONTAL	VERTICAL	ROD R.	STADIA	ELEVATION
⊙ HUB A HI = 55"					100.00
⊙ B	83°29'	-2°05'	3.11	112'	
CREEK, EAST BANK	110°12'	-5°15'	4.37	91'	
BRIDGE, NW CORNER	131°00'	2°10'	2.71	103'	
⊙ HUB B HI = 49"					
BS ⊙ A	263°29'	+2°05'	3.11	112'	

Figure 11.12.   Notebook setup for transit.

Set this azimuth using the lower circle and orient it on the first hub. The rodman will have to walk there and give you the backsight. Lock the lower circle and continue taking sights with the upper.

ELEVATIONS

Using the vertical angles and distances from your field book, you can calculate the elevation of each point. Knowing, or assuming the elevation of the first hub, add in the height of instrument. From this, subtract the rod reading. Note that, if the rod reading is equal to the height of instrument, these will cancel and you will have saved a step of your calculations. To this, add or subtract the difference in elevation, depending on the sign of the angle (see Figure 11.13).

The difference in elevation is equal to the distance times the sine of the angle. There is no need to worry over complicated trigonometric functions, because even the simplest scientific calculator will give you the sine of an angle. Further, your field book has many trigonometric functions on the front and back inside covers. The equation for elevation becomes:

(1) Elev. = Known Elev. + HI − Rod + Sin (∝) × Distance
For the example shown in Figure 12, the elevation of Hub B would be calculated as:

Elev. B = 100' + 4.5' − 3.11 + Sin (−2°o5') × 112'
Elev. B = 97.40'

MAPPING

Drawing the map from a transit survey is somewhat similar to the plane table survey. First, draw in a point for the first hub and sketch in the azimuth line. Then, for each point in your field book, turn the horizontal angle from the azimuth, scale off the proper distance and place your point. A circular protractor is the best way to turn angles for your map, since it models the action of the transit.

Remember to map each ground point from the hub from which it was measured from in the field. Thus you will map Hub 2 from Hub 1, and then all the next points will be measured from Hub 2.

For each point, you will also have an elevation. From these, you can construct contour lines in the same method as you did for the leveling survey. You may wish to pencil in the elevations by each point on your map when you first draw them.

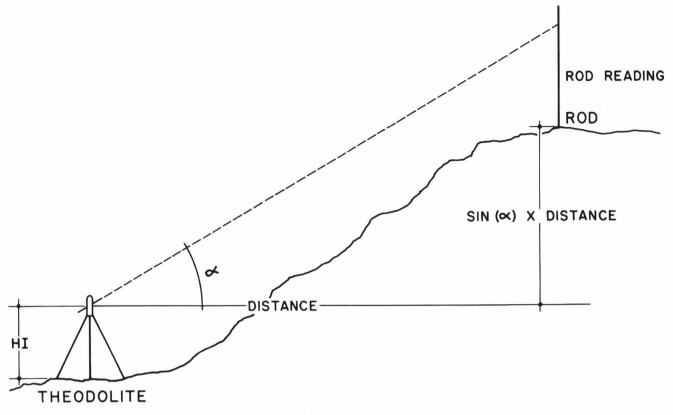

Figure 11.13. Elevations with theodolite (Drawing by Paul Boxley).

Vertical and Horizontal Dimensions

A transit is very useful in measuring dimensions that may be too difficult or dangerous to obtain with a measuring tape. A good example would be building heights, or second story horizontal measurements of condemned and dangerous buildings. Of course, it is far less accurate than a measuring tape, and so should only be used to get measurements that would otherwise be impossible.

To get vertical measurements, set the transit up on a line perpendicular to the desired height. The farther back you set-up, the higher measurements you will be able to take. Make a note of the distance from the instrument to the object. For each dimension, you will need two angle measurements, to the upper and lower lines marking off the dimension. For each angle, calculate the vertical difference between the line and the transit, as $y = \sin(\text{alpha}) \times d$, where d is the distance. Take the difference of the two heights, upper minus lower, to get the vertical dimension (see Figure 11.14).

Horizontal dimensions can be measured in the same way, although the calculations are complicated somewhat by the difference in angle notation. When making horizontal measurements, make sure that the zero azimuth is perpendicular to the building. Measure the angles to the edges of the dimension desired. These angles will be from 0 to 360 degrees, and you will want to convert them to declination angles. Azimuth refers to degrees of a circle, of which there are 360,

while declination angles measure differences in the lay of separate lines. For angles that vary from 0 to 180, the azimuth and declination are the same. To get declination angles for azimuths of from 180 to 360 subtract the angle from 360 and note it as a negative angle.

As with the vertical dimensions, calculate the distance from the instrument for each dimension line. Then take the difference to get the total dimension, remembering that subtracting a negative is the same as adding.

COMPARISON

It seems useful here to enumerate the differences between the plane table and transit to help select the proper instrument for any surveying job. A plane table is much easier to use, requires no trigonometry and produces a map in the field which may be checked for errors while on the job site. On the other hand, it is bulkier and harder to move, and requires the use of a level for elevations.

The transit can be used for both the horizontal and vertical survey, and is more compact and easier to carry and move. This makes it preferable for wooded or hilly sites. Its major drawback is that all information must be recorded in the field book and mapped out in the office, so mistakes are not readily noticed. Further, this system requires using trigonometry and calculating. Of course, computers and

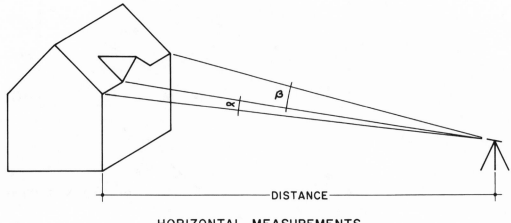

HORIZONTAL MEASUREMENTS

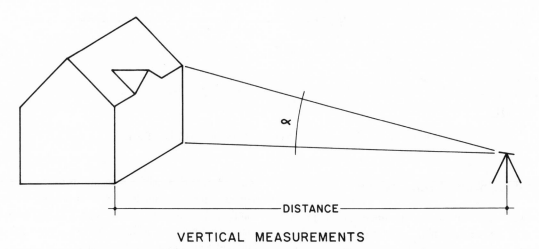

VERTICAL MEASUREMENTS

Figure 11.14.   Horizontal and vertical measurements (Drawing by Paul Boxley).

electronic field books reduce computation time, but the cost of such systems, and the necessary field instruments is staggering. One other advantage of the transit is the ability to measure building dimensions remotely.

TRAVERSING

Historical site work in the United States may include some work with deeds to determine land ownership. Traversing is surveying a circuit around a plot of land to determine the boundaries, and can be used to duplicate the deed work.

If you have referenced the deeds in question for the traverse information, you should plot out all the relevant lines with directions and lengths. You should also compute all the angles from one line to another. These can be done later in the office. Many early deeds in the eastern United States used a haphazard type of surveying called "metes and

bounds." This subject is dealt with in an appendix to this chapter. As western lands were developed from Ohio west, more foresight was applied and the lands were parceled out and surveyed on a grid system.

When this information is ready, begin the field traverse. Set the instrument on the first point and align it with the reference angle.[7] Turn off the first angle (calculated from your office work) and measure off the distance. Move the instrument to this point, reference it to the first point with a backsight, and turn off the next angle.

Continue this until the instrument is at the last point and is pointed at the first. When you have this last measurement, you have closed the traverse. All traverses must have closure. Of course, when you plot up a traverse from the field notes there will inevitably be errors and it will not close precisely on paper. If you are within a foot or two, you are doing well. You may even feel smug if your traverse is closer than the deed book.

CONCLUSION

This lesson on surveying is intended to allow a novice surveyor to make a credible survey of an industrial archaeology site. Surveying may seem to be a monumental task, but with proper attention to detail, careful study and practice, it will soon become quite easy.

It is important to keep in mind that the final map is the reason for the survey, and the map needs to be useful to the IA site. Therefore, you should include all relevant items and points to provide a meaningful context for the site. If you accomplish this, your final map will add greatly to the understanding and study of the site in question.

If you are interested in this topic and wish to pursue it further, you should get a surveying textbook, such as one used by freshman or sophomore civil engineering students. Such a textbook will cover the topics in this lesson more completely, and will also include such topics as instrument calibration, practical astronomy, different types of surveys and will give a scholarly justification for all these topics. Examples of textbooks are

Moffitt, F. H. and H. Bouchard, *Surveying,* 7th ed., (New York: Harper and Row, 1982).

Breed, C. B. and G. L. Hosmer, *The Principles and Practice of Surveying,* vol. 1, "Elementary Surveying", 7th ed., (New York: John Wiley and Sons, 1938).

Field books are also good references, and indispensable in the field. Besides being weatherproofed, they are lined for survey work and contain trigonometric tables on the inside covers. They are available from any engineering supply store or surveying instrument retailer, and are published by the surveying instrument manufacturers.

APPENDIX

"Tracing Property Boundaries using Metes and Bounds Surveys," by Dr. Robert T. Howe, Professor Emeritus of Civil Engineering, University of Cincinnati.

These are the surveys that you will find in the rural areas of West Virginia and states that do not use the public land survey system of sections, ranges and townships. The measuring systems used in the surveys will likely be rods, chains and links, and directions will be referred to as x number of degrees in a certain compass direction (see Figure 11.15). Remember: 1 rod = 16.5 feet, 1 chain = 66 feet or 100 links.

Start by converting all measurements to feet or some other common unit to get a feel for the relative lengths of the measurements. To convert chains and links to feet, write the distance, that is, 5 chains 40 links as 5.40 chains; then multiply by 66 to get the correct number of feet. Never go closer than 1 foot when multiplying the number.

Make a sketch of the property described, using graph paper ruled 4 or 5 squares to the inch. Sketch the property out

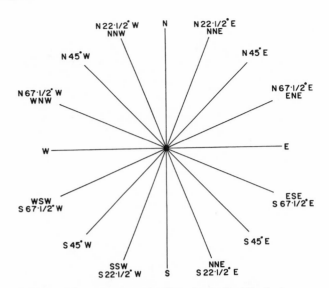

Figure 11.15. Bearing angles (Drawing by Paul Boxley).

roughly first, and then use a scale and protractor to make a more precise copy later (see Figure 11.16).

Almost invariably, the property lines will not close when you try to sketch them out. The rule here is to make the fewest possible changes to create closure. Change the fewest number of measurements. Change compass bearings before you change distances. When changing bearings, anticipate the results if you changed North to South, South to North, East to West or West to East. Do not take the deed description too literally the first time through. You can also sketch out parcels that are supposed to be contiguous and piece them together, hoping they will fit. If these do not work, try drawing the first line to get your beginning point, and then draw the last line and proceed to draw it backwards, changing North to South, South to North, East to West and West to East as you go. If you are dealing with adjacent parcels, you can also look for calls (references, citations) to the same objects; note every object, such as the old oak tree or the stream bed, on your sketch map. If all your dimensions are in rods or poles, you can just draw your sketch map using those as the unit of measurement if you wish.

Bearings are the angles to the East or West from the North or South. Lay the 0 line of a protractor on a North/South line that you draw, with the center of the protractor at the end of the line. Always start by drawing the North/South line. Then measure x number of degrees to the East or West from this line, depending on how the deed reads. Each bearing is independent of the previous one, so you will need to make a new north/south line each time and put the protractor on the east or west side of the line each time. Use an engineer's scale to measure the distance the line should go once the direction is established. Assume a one (1) degree tolerance (margin of error) on any point on the compass.

Finally, the sum of the latitudes of the lines must equal zero and the sum of the departures of the lines must equal zero, or

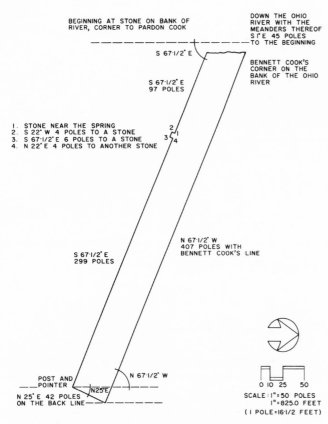

BEGINNING AT STONE ON BANK OF
RIVER, CORNER TO PARDON COOK

DOWN THE OHIO
RIVER WITH THE
MEANDERS THEREOF
S1°E 45 POLES
TO THE BEGINNING

S 67·1/2° E

BENNETT COOK'S
CORNER ON THE
BANK OF THE OHIO
RIVER

S 67·1/2° E
97 POLES

1. STONE NEAR THE SPRING
2. S 22° W 4 POLES TO A STONE
3. S 67·1/2° E 6 POLES TO A STONE
4. N 22° E 4 POLES TO ANOTHER STONE

N 67·1/2° W
407 POLES WITH
BENNETT COOK'S LINE

S 67·1/2° E
299 POLES

POST AND
POINTER
N 25° E 42 POLES
ON THE BACK LINE

N 67·1/2° W

N 25° E

0   10 25   50

SCALE: 1"= 50 POLES
1"= 825.0 FEET
(1 POLE= 16·1/2 FEET)

Figure 11.16. Example of deed plat (Drawing by Paul Boxley).

you will not get closure. The latitude is "its projection onto a reference meridian (North/South line)." If a line bears southerly the latitude will be negative, if it bears northerly it will have a positive latitude. "The departure (Dep.) of a line is its projection onto a line at right angles to the reference meridian." Lines bearing easterly will have a positive departure, and lines bearing westerly will have a negative departure. If one makes a table of the direction of the lines, you can see if mov-

ing a latitude or departure from + to − , or vice versa, will create a closure. (Source: Legauly, Adrian R., et al., *Surveying: An Introduction to Engineering Measurements.* Englewood Cliffs, NJ: Prentice-Hall, Inc., 1956, p. 210.)

ENDNOTES

1. Archaeologists use metric, or System International (S.I.), units in their profession. Engineers, at least in the U.S., use the English or U.S. Customary system. Most surveying equipment sold domestically uses the U.S. Customary system, although modern electronic equipment is capable of either. The point is, the modern surveyor must also be capable of using both systems.

2. This is, of course, an accepted method but one not covered in this chapter. For more information on this type of survey, see Bodey, H and Hallas, M., Elementary Surveyinq for Industrial Archaeologists (Shire Publications: 1978) or some such other work.

3. Twenty-five feet is not equal to 6 meters, actually being 7.6 m. However, 6 meters is close to the distance and is a nice round number. Further, surveys are done in one measuring system and need not transfer easily to another.

4. There are, of course, standard map symbols. HABS/HAER has a set of symbols they prefer, and this then becomes the standard for industrial archaeology in the United States. Their symbols may be found in Historic American Engineering Record, Field Instructions (Washington, DC: HABS/HAER, National Park Service, January, 1981).

5. For a more involved discussion on topographical surveys, see Francis H. Moffitt and Harry Bouchard, Surveyinq, Seventh Edition, Chapter 15, "Topographic Surveys" (New York: Harper and Row, 1982).

6. Older transits have a magnetic compass built into the instrument. Digital theodolites do not, but an attachable compass may be purchased and set on the carrying handle. It is almost necessary to have the compass attached to the transit in order to get the precision needed. Aligning the instrument by a hand-held compass will not work.

7. This reference could be magnetic north, or may say "From the large rock, to the corner of Mr. Smith's property." In any case, align the instrument's 0 angle with the proper sight just like you do in the site survey. If the deed uses magnetic compass readings, you should worry about changing declinations over the years.

CHAPTER 12

Integrating Geographic Information Systems and Industrial Archaeology: Exploring the Potential and the Limitations

Trevor M. Harris
Gregory A. Elmes

INTRODUCTION

The field of Geographic Information Systems (GIS) is currently experiencing something of an explosion in its widespread adaptation to a variety of application areas. In essence, GIS are concerned with the computer manipulation, analysis and output of data that have a spatial or geographical component. By spatial, it is meant that the data have a locational constituent that is usually represented in the form of an X, Y coordinate. Very often this is expressed in terms of a cartesian coordinate system such as latitude and longitude or UTM, though a variety of other coordinate forms could be used. Additionally, though less commonly used, are "nominal" location identifiers such as place names or arbitrary identification numbers. Traditionally, archaeologists have extensive spatial data handling requirements. Archaeological phenomena are underpinned by their unique position in space and time, and by the relationships which exist between them. The use of maps to both record and analyze archaeological data is a standard ingredient of archaeological analysis and can involve both small scale regional distribution maps as well as detailed intrasite plans. Not least, maps provide both a convenient storage medium whereby vast quantities of complex thematic and locational data may be stored on a single map sheet, and yet provide a convenient means of analysis through visualization of the mapped data. For these reasons archaeologists have often emulated developments in spatial analysis within geography (Hodder 1977; Bintliff, 1986; Grant, 1986; Goudie, 1987; Gamble, 1987).

This chapter contends that the adoption of GIS within archaeology represents an important continuation of this process.

GIS was born out of a demand-driven need for a computer-based capability to manipulate and analyze geographical data. Its rapid growth in recent years has been fueled by supply-side technological improvements as in the price-performance ratio of computer hardware and the availability of off-the-shelf GIS software packages. Geographic Information Systems are specially designed computer software systems which input, store, transform, manipulate, analyze and display spatial data traditionally represented in the form of maps or plans. In essence such systems are characterized by their ability to store many sets of locational data, usually representing a series of maps layers, and enable these layers to be compared, integrated, and analyzed (see Figure 12.1). The power of a GIS lies in its ability to store not only the locational and attribute data for each spatial entity but also the topological relationships that exist between them. This permits the different spatial features which make up each map layer to be integrated with those of other map coverages, examined in the same analysis, and interpreted maps and new information produced. It is the ability to handle spatial data from several map layers with different scales and projections, to seek relationships, to produce composite variables and maps and to model the information in graphical and numerical fashion, which makes GIS so potentially important to archaeology. Thus GIS are well suited for "what if" type queries, encouraging an exploratory approach to spatial data

GIS DATA LAYER PRINCIPLE

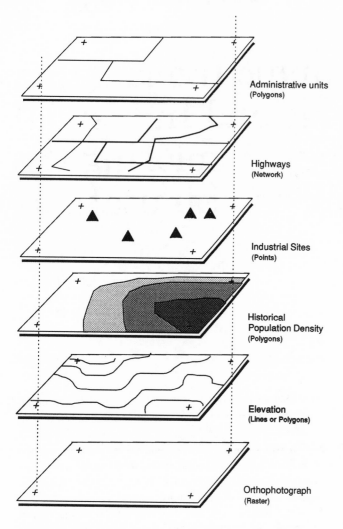

Administrative units
(Polygons)

Highways
(Network)

Industrial Sites
(Points)

Historical
Population Density
(Polygons)

Elevation
(Lines or Polygons)

Orthophotograph
(Raster)

+   Geo-registration marks

Figure 12.1. GIS data layer principle

analysis not unlike that proposed by Tukey (1977) in his development of Exploratory Data Analysis (EDA) techniques. Besides the considerable data management capabilities of GIS, the data models enable more realistic portrayals of archaeological entities to be recorded for analysis and obviate the crude reduction of archaeological sites to single point data regardless of their actual size and shape (see Figure 12.1).

Information processing about historical structures and their environments is becoming increasingly important in industrial archaeology. This need ranges from the basic necessity to create and maintain an inventory of archaeological sites with associated site information to issues of regulation and legal compliance, and to undertake more sophisticated research tasks to explain the origins, evolution and demise of industrial sites in their social, economic, cultural and physical landscapes. The nature of the questions asked while realizing these activities invariably entails the use of geographic information. If the question of "where," or "where and when,"

or "what if" are important considerations to the understanding of a site, then the application of geographic information systems (GIS) will probably contribute substantially to the quality of the explanation and also to the effectiveness of the industrial archaeologist in exploring, analyzing, displaying and managing the site.

Currently, GIS are just beginning to appear in the archaeological literature and yet this chapter contends that GIS has the potential to revolutionize the way in which archaeologists record, manipulate and analyze archaeological data. The chapter contributes to the literature in two ways. First, it outlines the principles which underlie GIS and identifies those areas within industrial archaeology where GIS could be expected to make a significant contribution. In particular, it emphasizes the potential for GIS applications in inventorying, cultural resource management, analysis and education within industrial archaeology. Secondly, industrial archaeology is used as a basis for identifying current limitations in the GIS technology itself. The needs of archaeologists with regard to issues of temporality, three-dimensionality, spatial and temporal fuzziness and to incorporate a rich diversity of information sources and media, make additional demands on GIS which it is currently ill-equipped to handle. In examining the strengths and limitations of GIS in the context of industrial archaeology the paper contributes to a greater understanding of GIS potential, and identifies those areas where the nature of the questions pursued by industrial archaeology could contribute to the development and integration of GIS within archaeology proper. In this regard the paper concludes by seeking to identify future trends in which GIS are likely to provide a powerful computer environment within which to meet the needs of industrial archaeology into the twenty-first century.

THE APPLICATION OF GIS IN ARCHAEOLOGY

Despite what appears to be a very recent history, GIS have been in existence since the 1960s (Tomlinson, 1967; Rhind, 1976; Nagy and Wagle, 1979; Rhind, 1981; Burrough, 1986; Tomlinson, 1987). The Canada Land Inventory, established over twenty years ago, first began the process of converting immense quantities of analog map data into digital form. By 1972, the Canada Geographic Information System (CGIS) had become the world's first operational integrated GIS. The system achieved this distinction through its ability to not only input, store and display coverage maps, such as forestry reserves or soil type, but to overlay two or more coverages for a region and compute the areas of simple or compound coverages, thereby providing cross-tabulations of vegetation associated with particular soil types, for example (Nagy and Wagle, 1979, 171). In this functional respect the CGIS differed from earlier, purely cartographic systems. The ability to undertake such operations is due to the geo-referencing of each map layer to a set of common locations and the generation of a data structure which then permits data integration, manipulation and analysis to be performed. This characteristic functionality of GIS is crucial to understanding the potential and important rise of GIS vis a vis digital mapping or Computer Aided Design—Computer Aided Mapping (CAD/CAM) systems (Cowen, 1988). At about the same time the seminal text on GIS edited by Tomlinson was published under the aegis of the International Geographical Union (Tomlinson, 1972).

Until very recently, basic GIS texts were few and the newcomer to the field was served primarily by documentation of specific GIS software packages or articles in conference proceedings. In 1991, a key work, *Geographical Information Systems,* edited by Maguire, Goodchild and Rhind, was published. This wide-ranging compilation represents the culmination of nearly thirty years work in GIS, most of which was available only in scattered and often inaccessible papers and proceedings. A veritable flood of published works in GIS are now becoming available on a wide range of specialized topics. The GIS literature is also benefitting from the relatively recent proliferation of GIS-focused journals and its appearance in periodicals directed towards the remote sensing community. The *International Journal of Geographical Information Systems; Cartography and Geographic Information Systems; International Journal of Imaging, Remote Sensing and Integrated Geographical Systems* and *Photogrammetric Engineering and Remote Sensing* are the primary sources of research and development in GIS.

One pioneering work by Burrough (1986) defines GIS as being "a powerful set of tools for collecting, storing, retrieving at will, transforming and displaying spatial data from the real world." This definition, however, represents a somewhat narrow perspective in that it excludes the very important institutional and decision-making contexts, and the human setting of the system (de Man, 1988). Geographic data are voluminous, multidimensional and dynamic; frequently they describe diverse, often complex subject matter ranging from the characteristics of the physical environment to social, historical, economic and cultural aspects of human spatial organization. In relating physical and human phenomena, geographic data are generally acquired at many scales to explain and understand past and present processes. As a result GIS should be considered to be simultaneously a set of tools to create and modify map data, a technology for combining and interpreting maps, and a revolution in map structure, content and use that affords new horizons in spatial analysis and communication.

Typically GIS consist of four main components embodying computer hardware, software, geographical data and the human organizational context. The minimal physical configuration to support GIS requires a high speed central processing unit (CPU), ample mass storage devices such as hard disk drives and CD-ROM, a digitizing table for cartographic data entry, editing and update, a plotter, a printer and a high resolution display monitor. GIS software normally includes routines for data input, manipulation and spatial analysis, display and hard copy functions and usually a database man-

agement system (DBMS). Contemporary systems provide either an easy to use graphical interface or the tools to develop human-computer interactions tailor-made to the application at hand. In addition the arrival of electronic networks has permitted the configuration of connected GIS in disparate locations. These so-called distributed systems promise ever greater integration of electronic media, and connectivity between users.

The application of GIS is best understood as a process consisting of an integrated sequence of steps permitting the definition, implementation and continual refinement of the problem at hand (Figure 12.2). The GIS data input system may capture data in digital form from a variety of sources, such as paper maps and manuscripts, field surveys, or magnetic media, and stores them in a spatial database to be retrieved, edited and updated at will. The data manipulation and analysis parts of the system permit multiple layers of spatial features to be geo-referenced along with their characteristics or attributes, thereby enabling multivariate analysis to be performed at a given location, across areas or regions, and through time. GIS will process interactive queries to the geographical database either from the display monitor or as keyboard commands, and deliver the output to a variety of output devices for the presentation of information as maps and in other graphical, tabular and report forms.

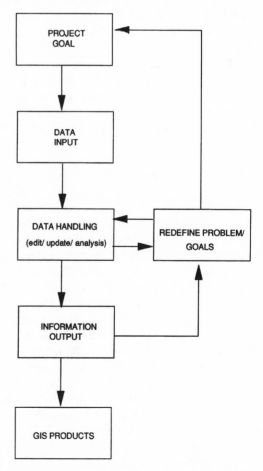

Figure 12.2. The GIS environment: iterative problem solving

What little integration of GIS into archaeology has occurred to date has focused predominantly on landscape archaeology. No GIS applications specific to industrial archaeology at the site scale are known to exist at the present time. Recognition of the potential of GIS for archaeological work first entered the literature in North America in the early 1980s (Brown and Rubin, 1982). By 1985 both Commission IV of the Union International des Sciences Pre et Proto Historiques and the Society for American Archaeology had sessions on GIS (Gill and Howes, 1985; Kvamme, 1985a). Papers covered both methods and principles (Kvamme, 1985b; Ferguson, 1985), and specific regional applications (Bailey et al., 1985; Creamer, 1985). North America has continued to lead in GIS applications because of its early start in GIS and, until recently, the greater availability of off-the-shelf GIS software. The publication of a major landmark volume in 1990 documenting over 20 archaeological applications in GIS in North America began the process of establishing GIS as a tool in archaeology in the minds of archaeologists (Allen, Green and Zubrow, 1990). That process has now proceeded to a point where at least most, if not all, archaeologists are now aware of the technology. Awareness of GIS potential can be expected to be followed by expansion (Harris and Lock, 1990) and although only a limited number of GIS applications in archaeology have appeared in published form, many more can be expected in the near future as the technology diffuses through the archaeological community (see, for example, two edited volumes by Maschner, forthcoming).

With the exception of parts of Western Europe, the adoption of GIS in archaeology elsewhere in the world has been much slower, with the lead often coming from geographers rather than archaeologists. In the United Kingdom Harris (1986) showed the need for computerized spatial data handling procedures at the regional level for archival, educational and research purposes as well as, for cultural resource management within a comprehensive planning system. He outlined a GIS application to the archaeology of the Brighton area, a theme which was followed up by the addition of draped images on Digital Terrain Models and three dimensional graphics (Harris, 1988). Two other geographers have also shown the potential of GIS in archaeology with their work on remote sensing techniques in the Fens of East Anglia (Donoghue and Shennan, 1988; Donoghue, 1989). The prospects for the widespread adoption of GIS in U.K. archaeology have been discussed by Harris and Lock (1991) as well as, in the specific application area of cultural resource management (Lock and Harris, 1990; Harris and Lock, 1992). Other European GIS applications include the work of Wansleeben (1988) in the Netherlands, Arroyo-Bishop (1991) in France and Gaffney and Stancic in Yugoslavia (1991, 1992). The publication of a recent volume focusing on the application of GIS to national archaeological resource management issues (National Museum of Denmark, 1992), and annual publications of Computer Applications in Ar-

chaeology (Rahtz, 1988; Rahtz and Richards, 1990; Lockyear and Rahtz, 1991; Lock and Moffett, 1992) indicate that, as in North America, GIS based archaeology is similarly at the point of take-off in Western Europe.

THE BASIC PRINCIPLES OF GIS

Spatial data are fundamentally different from other types of data in that many aspects of spatial knowledge are difficult to express in natural language. The linear, sequential form of written and spoken language is poorly equipped to describe and logically manipulate the parallel, simultaneous nature of spatial data. The creative use of graphical skills, or scientific visualization, is often needed to understand and depict concepts of spatial relationships that exist between objects. Spatial relationships, as characterized by proximity, adjacency, direction, distance, shape and boundaries, for example, are essential to the documentation and explanation of an historic site within its economic and cultural landscape and are central to the functionality of GIS. Major advances in computer-based information technology have transformed the way in which spatial data are stored, handled and analyzed. The following discussion seeks to outline the basic principles of GIS through the identification and evaluation of its components, varied functions and organization within a human setting.

Initially, many industrial archaeologists may have encountered computer applications in the form of CAD/CAM. Despite many claims, not all systems that display maps and diagrams in a computer environment are fully functional GIS (Cowen, 1988). Automated cartography and CAD/CAM emphasize the graphical and symbolic elements for representing spatial objects. CAD systems are powerful graphical tools able to depict solid forms and can provide apparent movement to the objects on the screen. In contrast to GIS, CAD systems deal with limited quantities of data and are incapable of supporting the spatial database and analytical functions necessary for the continual data transactions, maintenance and handling that characterize information production within a management setting. In many instances CAD/CAM systems are admirable for industrial archaeology purposes for documenting historic structures at engineering scales, and indeed they overlap in some graphical functions with GIS. However, as indicated earlier, GIS are primarily distinguished from other graphical digital systems by virtue of the linkages between the cartographic features and their attributes, the organization of the data in geo-referenced layers, and by the potential of continuous spatial coverage embodying many scales.

A fundamental characteristic of any GIS is the linkage between the spatial features of interest to the archaelogist and their attributes (Figure 12.3). Spatial features, such as buildings, artifacts, soil units, may be represented by geometric primitives: points, lines, polygons (areas) and volumes, or

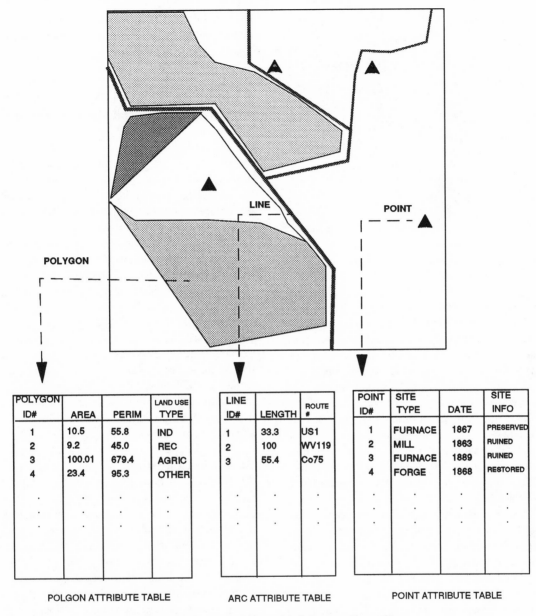

Figure 12.3. Vector data model: links to attribute tables

are sampled by means of regularly-spaced grid cells. In the GIS spatial data are stored in one of these two basic forms: either as grid-cells or as linked sets of points, lines and areas. Grid-based systems are usually called raster systems. Those comprised of geometric elements are called vector systems. In either case, spatial data captured and stored in a GIS represent abstractions or models of the real world and like all representations have their strengths and limitations. In order to increase their effectiveness most contemporary systems provide both alternatives.

The vector data model developed from the spatial primitives is particularly useful for handling data in the familiar form of the topographical map, encountered most frequently in the United States as the U.S. Geological Survey 1:24000 map quadrangle. Topology, a branch of geometry dealing

with spatial relationships such as adjacency and connectivity, enables the computer system to maintain the relationships between the spatial features and their attributes no matter what transformations or analytical manipulations are applied. Because it can precisely represent the outlines and position of features, the principal utility of the vector GIS lies in map overlays, modeling spatial relations, networks and interactions, and in producing high quality map output from coordinate data.

The raster, or grid based, data model implicitly records location spatial relationships by virtue of the ordering of the rows and columns of cells in which the map features are sampled (see Figure 12.4). In the raster model the accuracy of representation of real world features is determined by the cell size. Spatial resolution, the size of the smallest object that

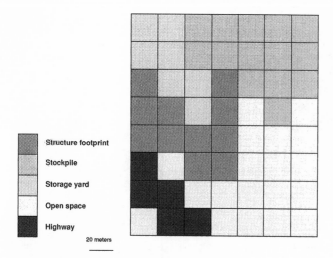

Structure footprint

Stockpile

Storage yard

Open space

Highway

20 meters

Figure 12.4. Raster data model: land cover example

can be represented, is limited by the length of the side of a cell. Although the grid-like form of display is not as familiar as the vector format, the raster GIS is often cheaper and more simple to learn and use. Raster models are not necessarily inferior to vector models for they provide many advantages in their analytical functions, efficiency of operation, and ease of integration with spatial models (for a more detailed discussion of the various strengths of the two approaches see Burrough, 1986, Aronoff, 1989; Star and Estes, 1990; and Tomlin, 1990). GIS analysis often involves the use of both vector and raster models and as suggested previously many systems offer both options. Since most contemporary graphic screen displays and many hard copy devices employ a raster format, vector structures are frequently converted to this structure for output. Additionally, images from remote sensing and digital orthophotographs, which are in raster form in their unprocessed state, have enormous interpretive value when stored and displayed as a background to topographical, vector data.

Feature-based or object-oriented modes of handling spatial data have emerged from the GIS software developers (Aronson, 1987). Unlike the vector and raster models, common standards have not been established as yet, the term "object-oriented" is applied to various approaches and there is no general agreement on what exactly it means (Healey, 1991). An object not only has information related to its characteristics but also the set of operations or methods that are applicable. Some elements of this emerging data structure are important; one is the relaxation of the concept of multiple layers of data so that the user works with any and all features at will. The integration of behavioral rules or "intelligence" with the objects dictates how they may or may not relate to other features in the landscape or through time. Object-oriented systems offer the possibility of preventing anachronisms in historical applications, for example. Perhaps the most immediate impact on the user community of object-oriented methods will be the prevention of inappropriate analysis being performed.

Increased flexibility of analysis and richness of representation of reality, however, will contribute to the future effectiveness of GIS applications.

GIS FUNCTIONALITY AND INDUSTRIAL ARCHAEOLOGY: THE POTENTIAL

The power of GIS, then, stems from the availability of operations that, alone or in combination, allow the processing of map data stored in various formats to identify or produce useful output. Rhind (1981) has suggested that basic GIS questions may be grouped into six classes which relate to location (what is at a given place), condition (where are objects of a given type located), trend (what changes are or have occurred), routing over a network, pattern identification and spatial modeling. For most users, as the use of GIS evolves, a progression through these classes of operation will occur.

Initially in industrial archaeology GIS applications will be used primarily to record sites and make inventories, requiring site identification, location and the recording of condition, status and characteristics in the database. Even without further analysis these GIS functions will provide considerable computer capability for research and cultural resource management purposes. The use of GIS for on-site recording and analysis in real time would seem to be somewhat further off, partly because of the prevailing limitations of GIS to handle multidimensional data, and partly because of the practical difficulties of incorporating this computer technology into the excavation and recording process. Current operational needs call for the development and implementation of data models able to record objects at engineering scales in three, or possibly four, dimensions, while at the same time able to retain a larger geographical perspective (see Figure 12.5, for example). Industrial archaeological applications can be expected to proceed subsequently to greater use of the on-line query, analytical, and modeling functions as the user community perceives greater operational potential for decision support and analysis.

Usually multiple datasets are required to establish information for a particular research question, resource management decision or administrative task. Digital physical and environmental data (e.g., elevation, hydrology, soils, and land cover) will be required along with cultural, social and economic data. Resource managers or researchers frequently require map layers containing land ownership, governmental jurisdiction, viewshed, rights-of-way, surface water, elevation, land cover, land-use, natural hazards and endangered species. Typical data layers necessary for an application in industrial archaeology might include a base map for orientation, various environmental overlays, natural resources, cultural artifacts, transportation networks, engineering diagrams (plan, elevation and profile drawings), parcel maps, area boundary maps, current and

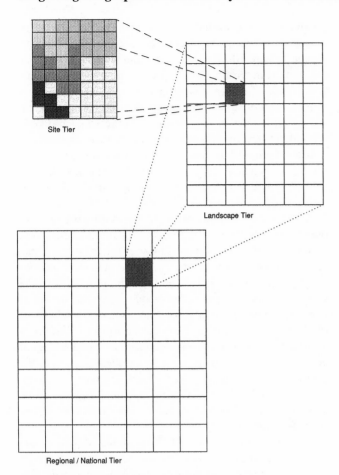

Figure 12.5. GIS data model: map scale hierarchy

Table 12.1 *Typical Questions Which May Be Asked in a GIS for Industrial Archaeology*

a) Where is industrial site A?
b) Where is A in relation to a geographical distribution B?
c) How many occurrences of type A are there within a specified distance of location C?
d) What is the value of function Z at position X?
e) How large is A? (area, perimeter, count)
f) What is the intersection of two . . . n types of spatial data layers?
g) What is the path of least cost or distance between place X and place Y?
h) What objects are at point, along a line, or in an area defined by a series of coordinates?
i) What is next to objects at place A? Where A is unconstrained or has specific attributes (Note the concept of adjacency can be extended from space into time).
j) Reclassify objects which have attribute A.
k) Simulate the effect of process P over time T for scenario S.

(modified from Burrough, 1986).

Although Table 12.1 provides only a limited selection of potential GIS operations, it reflects the progression, suggested previously in this chapter, from inventorying and monitoring, through network and trend operations, towards full-blown time-space modeling. The many command types available within GIS may be grouped according to major classes of functions which they perform. Many taxonomies of GIS operations have been proposed and no single approach is comprehensive (see Tomlin, 1990, and Star and Estes, 1990 for contrasting approaches). Berry (1991) has proposed a fourfold classification that has some merits for the present discussion. The four classes of primitive operations identified by Berry are reclassification of map categories; overlay of two or more maps; distance and connectivity measurement; and neighborhood, zone or regional characterization.

The first of these classes, reclass operations, assign new thematic values of an attribute on a single map layer by grouping observations into meaningful categories, often with the purpose of creating input for a subsequent analytical step. New values may be assigned on the basis of their initial attribute class, descriptive statistics such as quartiles or deviation from a mean, their position, shape, or size. A simple reclassification of historical industrial sites, for example, could group all sites that exceed a critical threshold of their attribute data, such as in the number of people employed, or the nature and quantities of material produced. A weighted reclassification generates a quantitative map layer from a categorical one, as in the production of a relative site-suitability index for an industrial process, for example, or a map representing the combined effects of distance and slope on accessibility to certain places, usually thought of as a cost surface. The buffering operation in Figure 12.6a shows a reclassification of the map layer on the basis of a threshold distance from selected historic structures, perhaps with the goal of identifying associated features at the landscape scale.

historical data, local demographic characteristics, migration data, economic data, trade flows and the like. Because each map layer is registered to a set of common coordinates, the data themes may be manipulated, cross-referenced, interrogated, analyzed and further valuable information generated.

At present the most advantageous use of GIS in archaeology is at the intersite level (i.e., between sites) and usually involves site inventorying and comparison of archaeology at the landscape scale. Analysis of intrasite data, that is, those detailing data within a given site, present problems to the current generation of GIS so the following discussion is applicable mainly to multiple site comparisons. Once a database has been established a formidable range of questions may be posited in order to display and understand the spatial and temporal relations between sites (see Table 12.1). Identifying the distribution of sites involved in a given industrial process, such as iron-making for example, enables concepts to be developed which relate the siting decision and site operation to its historical setting and to the regional landscape, past and present. The exploration of hypotheses relates and explains industrial operations in the context of prevailing economic, social and physical conditions.

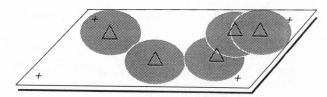

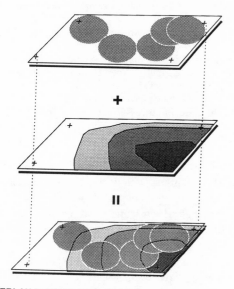

a. BUFFERING AROUND HISTORIC SITES

b. OVERLAY BUFFER ZONE ON POPULATION DENSITY

Figure 12.6. Typical GIS analysis functions

Areal association provides the basis for many explanations of past locational decisions. The second of Berry's class of GIS operations, overlay operations, create new maps on the basis of the values occurring at the same location in two or more other maps in a manner analogous to cross tabulation in statistical analysis (Figure 12.6b). In the case of a site suitability index, for example, it is possible to evaluate aggregate suitability for a particular process by integrating the site suitability of all the necessary and sufficient factors of production. Where the data type permits, overlay functions may use mathematical operations such as addition, subtraction, multiplication and division; or statistical techniques may be invoked, or Boolean or set operators, such as .AND., .OR. and .NOT. applied to generate new information.

Any thorough explanation of geographical and historical patterns and processes in human social organization, however, requires the ability to model spatial interactions, the movements or flows of people, goods, communications, and ideas. Measuring distance and connectivity, the third class of GIS functions, is the initial step towards understanding the dynamic relationships of a site to its socioeconomic setting, as measured by the migration of settlement, the journey to work of laborers, the transportation of raw materials, or the distribution of product to market. Network analysis is a ma-

jor strength of vector-based GIS although it demands large quantities of high quality data to produce meaningful results. Raster GIS are effective where continuous surfaces may be inferred, as in terrain models, for example. Recreating historical lines-of-sight and viewsheds, based on the past or present location of structures or features, contributes to the education of the general public and to the researcher alike in the ability to create former landscapes and to ascertain visual impacts (Figure 12.7). In combination with time-series data, interaction functions hold the potential of revealing historical developments and change both graphically and numerically.

According to Berry's taxonomy, the fourth group of GIS operations is based on sampling information gathered from a moving grid or window passing over the underlying map data, an action known as filtering. A new map layer describing zones or regions is created from the properties of the sample of data captured in the window. Arguably, the most frequent use of this class of operation is in the development of slope and aspect maps from elevation data. Filtering is also valuable in estimating the population characteristics of geographic areas from spatial samples. Identification of the maximum and minimum values, central tendency, variation, and diversity provide tools for in-depth investigation of the conditions surrounding a site, and the similarities and differences between sites.

While these four classes of GIS operations provide a wide array of analytical methods, the GIS user must also consider the organizational context of the data to be processed, and the uses to which the generated information is put (de Man, 1988). Meaningful information takes the form of answers to specific questions arising from research, educational or managerial functions which themselves are part of an institutional and societal environment. Thus, in order to achieve a sustained, productive life, the design of a GIS must anticipate and respond to the purposes of the organization for which it will provide information, and the legal and bureaucratic conditions that prevail. In the context of cultural resource management, for example, the GIS must produce information that managers actually need and use. Given the visual characteristics of its output, the tendency can be to generate impressive but superfluous products. Additionally,

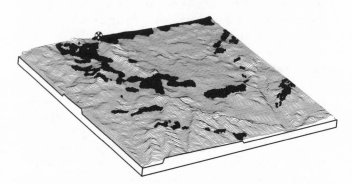

Figure 12.7. Viewshed analysis

it must reflect the cultural needs, norms, values and behavior of the organization. Thus, the physical subcomponents of a GIS only become productive in relation to the people who use them and the tasks and information which they generate. Without a comprehensive needs assessment of the nature of the information actually used to make decisions, a GIS may become a technological burden.

GIS are often employed to provide routine, well understood information but equally they can explore types of information that might provide innovative knowledge. Examples of the latter are accomplished by the simulation of alternative outcomes, the use of probability reasoning, and of fuzzy set concepts. Well-defined problems lead to the straight-forward application of GIS in a problem-solving mode. In contrast, poorly defined problems may require a strategy based on iterative procedures, with increasing refinement of the problem in successive rounds. More frequently, the use of a GIS is made more difficult by complex institutional structures involving several organizational "cultures" embodying various branches of federal, state and local government, research groups and universities, as well as those of the general public.

As GIS matures, related technologies are adding to its versatility and promise in applications to the documentation of historic structures. Two important developments are satellite-based Global Positioning Systems (GPS) and the integration of remote sensing. The positional accuracy of GPS, allied with its universal coverage now that the full complement of navigational satellites is operational, can provide a major source of precise spatial information for incorporation within a GIS. Typically, depending on model and system, GPS can provide positional accuracy to within a few meters and sometimes to sub-centimeter accuracy in horizontal and vertical control. The ability to traverse a site and record both locational and thematic information with a high degree of precision which can then be downloaded into a GIS may prove to be as significant an advance to industrial archaeology as GIS itself.

Similarly, processing systems for aerial or satellite remotely sensed images are designed to handle very large quantities of digital information and possess great strength in classification. Image processing currently lacks the functional links to attribute information characteristic of GIS, and the normal practice is to include classified images as data layers geo-registered to the other map information. Image processing functions such as edge-enhancement and smoothing have been modified for use in several raster-based GIS, and most large GIS now have integrated facilities for image processing.

The increasing use of remotely-sensed data, digital aerial and orthophotographs (digital aerial photographs corrected for distortion) in the GIS environment requires ever greater storage, processing power and analytical capabilities for their graphic display and investigation as well as, the close integration of vector and raster capabilities. Two developments in this respect are exemplified by Environmental Systems Research Institute's ARC/GRID (TM) and IMAGE INTEGRATOR (TM) which are illustrative of system developments being pursued by many commercial GIS vendors. ARC/GRID permits the spatial analytical power of raster (grid cell) operations to be combined directly with the cartographic qualities of vector-based data in an interactive window environment. Eventually, such developments will lead to a full integration of the analytical advantages of each data model. As previously indicated, the rectification, classification and analysis of remotely sensed data is of growing importance in GIS applications, and contemporary technical developments are reducing the difficulties in handling the raster and vector data models in combination.

Similarly IMAGE INTEGRATOR permits the user to superimpose GIS output products on images of many types, such as digital orthophotographs; scanned aerial photographs and classified remotely-sensed images. This function greatly enhances the ability to verify locational accuracy, land cover, land parcels and to portray interpreted data on a familiar background.

GIS AND ARCHAEOLOGY: THE WEAKNESSES

It has been proposed above that GIS and related technologies have much to offer the world of archaeology. This transferral of opportunity, however, should not be seen as merely a one way flow. In the same way that GIS technology brings archaeological phenomena into sharper focus in the minds of researchers and resource managers, so, too, can archaeology act as a lens on the utility, strengths and limitations of GIS itself. There can be no doubt that already the needs of archaeologists cannot be fully met by the GIS technology currently available (Harris and Lock, forthcoming). In reviewing the diffusion of GIS in many disciplinary areas it is astounding as to the speed at which user expectations of the technology grows. This growth in user maturity is invariably exponential and very quickly pushes the technology to its limits. In this respect, theoretical developments within a discipline are symbiotically linked to methodological developments in GIS, for one acts in very close style upon the other. Identifying these lacunae provides directions as to the possible future areas in the development of GIS and in the application of that technology to research in archaeology. This paper identifies five such areas of GIS functionality whereby the requirements of archaeologists could contribute to the development and application of GIS technology. These areas comprise fuzzy space and fuzzy time, temporality, multidimensionality, cognition and behavioralism, and the integration of a variety of media sources. It would be a misconception to imply that these themes are not being pursued in other areas but the field of industrial archaeology does exhibit a number of needs, such as temporality and three-dimensional space, which if brought to bear could drive some of this developing technology.

There can be little doubt that GIS represents progress in the advancement of computer-based spatial accuracy with regard to the recording and interrelating of archaeological phenomena. What becomes apparent, however, is that the demands of the digital technology to record site boundary information "accurately" can be somewhat spurious in terms of the implied accuracy. At one level, perceived or affected accuracy can arise simply from the representation of an archaeological feature in the computer or on a hard copy plot. This aspect is already acknowledged within the GIS world for the routine process of encoding a feature can in itself contribute to a misleading perception of accuracy which the source data and encoding accuracy does not actually support. In this respect the issue of scale, accuracy and error in data capture and reproduction becomes critical. The temptation to push data interpretation beyond the limits which the scale or accuracy of data capture will permit is unfortunately all too prevalent in GIS applications and represents a gross misuse of GIS technology. The issue of multiplicative cascading errors which arise from the combination of data layers captured at varying levels of accuracy is also a well known, if little understood, element of GIS. What archaeology brings to this discussion is that the boundaries of archaeological sites are often in themselves fuzzy in nature and do not conveniently lend themselves to digital capture in either vector or raster form. The need to deal with imprecise or fuzzy archaeological information parallels similar questions raised in geography (for an early origin to this debate see Gale, 1972). In the recording of soil distribution maps, for example, the soil type rarely changes as abruptly as the line demarcating the distributions on a map would suggest. There is invariably a transition zone of varying width between the respective soil types, but because of the crudity of both the survey information and current computer spatial data handling technology, this transition is only represented at present as a linear division (Fisher, 1987).

The issue of fuzzy space is equally applicable to the definition and recording of archaeological site boundaries. This concern for recording either the "cartographic" representation of archaeological phenomena or a "symbolic" representation of site has important implications for GIS applications in industrial archaeology. For the purpose of a national or state site location and retrieval system, for example, a case might be made that the detailed cartographic representation of individual archaeological buildings is not required or warranted. Thus complex building footprints or infrastructural features would be grouped into a single entity or feature. It would not be intended as a true record of an actual site description. The highly accurate descriptions of sites which accompany excavation or detailed site survey would represent the other extreme for archaeologists. Thus, the issue of scale of data capture, for between site and on-site purposes, becomes a significant issue for the design and construction of an industrial archaeological database.

Furthermore, the detailed recording of a building, by plan and elevation, clearly does not represent the known limits of human use of the space surrounding such a construction. Consequently, GIS in this respect forces archaeologists to return to earlier archaeological issues concerning the definition of site boundaries. The issue as to what level of accuracy should site information be "captured" and for what purposes is evident. Defining an optimal scale of data capture, identifying the level of accuracy or error involved and the qualifications which this level of data accuracy imposes on archaeological research questions is something that will become an important issue to industrial archaeologists as GIS are adopted.

A similar and related issue which arises in the context of GIS applications in industrial archaeology concerns the addition of the third dimension, either in the form of time, depth or height. To an extent, in archaeology both depth and temporality are closely interwoven, in that the depth at which an artifact is found often indicates its temporal sequence relative to other contexts which may occur on top (later), underneath (earlier), or to the side (contemporaneous). This situation is invariably more complex, in that one period may intrude on another, as in the excavation of a pit or the presence of post-holes. Traditionally, GIS applications in archaeology have been firmly rooted in two-dimensional abstractions of reality, which represents the continuation of traditional manual or CAD approaches to handling archaeological information. In part, it also represents certain limitations in GIS functionality to handle spatial information in more than two dimensions. Where an application calls for the handling of a third dimension, such as depth, height or time, then the usual approach has been to construct, integrate and analyze within a vertical series of two-dimensional geographies (Jones, 1989; Raper, 1989; Turner, 1991). In many instances, two-and-one-half dimensional graphics are achieved via the draping of two-dimensional coverages over a wire frame representation of a landform or other surface. This facility adds to the visual interpretation of the archaeological phenomenon, but the approach is limited by the restriction to two-dimensional GIS functionality.

However, archaeologists operate in a multidimensional world. It is no happenstance that the majority of GIS applications in archaeology to date have occurred at the inter-site, regional scale. Here, GIS functionality is at its strongest in identifying distribution patterns and exploring latent relationships between sites and their surroundings. At the intra-site level, however, the recording of excavation data, or of plan and elevation, above or below the surface, necessitates the need for a third dimension. At this point conventional GIS approaches are inadequate and limited in their utility. Only in a few instances of the dollar rich commercial world of petroleum and gas exploration has GIS been developed and implemented which possess true three-dimensional functionality, and even here implementation falls short of what can reasonably be envisioned. The demands of archaeologists would clearly indicate a similar need for three dimensional capabilities. Visualization software moves some way toward this goal but still stops short of providing GIS functionality.

There exist a variety of ways in which three-dimensional data models can be constructed and it is likely that GIS capability to handle three dimensional data is not far from being a reality (Belcher and Paradis, 1991; Fisher and Wales,1991). Three aspects arise from consideration of three-dimensional functionality as applied to archaeological analysis and theory. The first aspect is related to the recording and analysis of archaeological phenomena in-situ at the intrasite scale. The concern here is with replacing the traditional hand-drawn or CAD plans by three dimensional GIS recording which is capable of sustaining subsequent digital analysis. One immediate analytical outcome of such a system would be the ability to record the excavation of a site within a GIS and include the unique position of an artifact or feature in three-dimensional space. Seeking linkages and relationships between archaeological contexts would then be possible, and the generation of Harris Matrix diagrams from the stored three-dimensional relationships in the GIS could be an automatic outcome. (See Harris 1975 and Harris 1979 for an explanation of the Harris Matrix method of analysis of three-dimensional data.) A second area of inquiry is related to the investigation of change through time at both the intra- and intersite scales. A continuous z-axis would permit the construction of dynamic models based on the combined temporal attributes of different archaeological elements from within the same site. In this, the possibility of using topology traditionally used to explore spatial relationships, to examine spatio-temporal patterns is particularly attractive. Not least, the ability to address issues associated with fuzzy space and fuzzy time as outlined above raises a number of potentially rewarding avenues of inquiry. Third, three dimensional capability would enable the development of spatial statistics capable of heuristically seeking adjacency and other spatial relationships in three dimensions simultaneously. Although perhaps initially of less direct application in industrial archaeology such a development could greatly benefit the creation of powerful spatial statistical algorithms which would draw upon the full data and functionality available within such three-dimensional systems.

The final deficiency in GIS which industrial archaeology brings to the fore is related to questions concerning the incorporation of cognition and behavioralism within a GIS, and with the inclusion of source materials from disparate media. It is perhaps here that industrial archaeology does focus a number of needs which would push GIS beyond its limits. To an extent, while a GIS takes us some way down the road toward an integrated information system it is still relatively crude when compared with the rich breadth of media and sources upon which industrial archaeologists have traditionally drawn. While the GIS is designed to handle data which has a spatial component, there are many sources which archaeologists regularly call upon but which would represent major problems if integrated within a GIS. For ex-

ample, an industrial archaeologist may wish to use old and present-day survey plans of an industrial site; utilize oral histories as passed on by those who may have worked in a building; incorporate old and recent photographs or paintings of a structure and its surroundings; peruse documents, ledgers or letters concerning everyday life in a particular structure; or examine other studies written about a site. There may even be moving images and film which could illustrate the operational nature of an industrial site far better than any text or GIS attribute could impart. Much of this information would clearly provide an understanding of a site from the perspective of those who lived and worked there when it was in operation. This cognitive perspective could be invaluable to those seeking to understand the human experience in the context of a relic's structure and the landscape in which it stood. Because of the difficulties encountered in incorporating such diverse media into a GIS there has been a noted tendency for archaeological explanation to focus on seeking causal explanation from data which is more readily available. Invariably, this data pertains to the physical environment and great care should be taken not to move toward the discredited notions of environmental determinism because of limitations in the handling of non-standard information. For these reasons GIS must seek additional means for recording and displaying material which can aid and facilitate explanation. The development of multimedia applications is only now becoming available, and yet if integrated within a GIS would provide tremendous possibilities to utilize the full power of a GIS linked to the enormous explanatory power of visualization and multimedia presentation. This powerful combination would add another dimension to the exploratory and explanatory power of a GIS.

CONCLUSION

Industrial archaeology is one application area of GIS technology that presents both immediate opportunities and significant limitations for the prospective user. Considerable opportunities exist for a wide range of user applications including documentation, inventorying, cultural resource management and the explanation of sites, artifacts and the historical geography of technology, production and labor. One immediate use of such an information system is in support of the cultural resource manager's ability to make decisions and target limited financial and human resources efficiently based on site priorities. The administration of industrial archaeology and historic structures as a cultural resource requires the reliable production of accurate and timely information for policy making, management-level decision making and routine daily operations. GIS has proven capabilities to fulfill these needs. On the other hand, current GIS technology exhibits a number of deficiencies likely to impact on areas of importance to industrial archaeologists, including consideration of the cognitive and intangible aspects of society. There is a necessity to represent people in history as vital, dynamic and decisive individuals, rather than as merely a catalogue of their effects and accoutrements. A significant danger exists for the technological developments of GIS to outstrip the conceptual and methodological progress necessary to represent the elements and principles of industrial archaeology and related fields. Linking industrial archaeology with GIS represents a considerable challenge, but is an area where the rewards could be substantial both in the conservation and understanding of our historical heritage and in the functional development of GIS.

BIBLIOGRAPHY

Allen, K. M. S., S. W. Green, and E. B. W. Zubrow, eds. *Interpreting Space: GIS in Archaeology*. London: Taylor and Francis, 1990.

Aronoff, S. *Geographic Information Systems: a Management Perspective*. Ottawa, Canada: WDL Publications, 1989.

Aronson, P. "Attribute Handling for Geographic Information Systems." Proceedings of AUTOCARTO 8. American Society for Remote Sensing and Photogrammetry/American Congress on Surveying and Mapping (Falls Church, VA): 346–355, 1987.

Arroyo-Bishop, D. "The ArcheoDATA System—Towards a European Archaeological Document." In *Computer Applications and Quantitative Methods in Archaeology 1990*, edited by K. Lockyear and S.P.Q. Rahtz, 61–69. Oxford: British Archaeological Reports International Series 565, 1991.

Bailey, R. D., S. Howes, S. Hackenberger, and D. Wherry. "Geographic Information Processing in Land Use Modeling and Testing in the Columbia River Basin." Paper presented at the 50th Annual Meeting of the Society for American Archaeology, 1985, Denver.

Belcher, R. C. and A. Paradis. "A Mapping Approach To Three Dimensional Modeling." In *Three Dimensional Modeling With Geoscientific Information Systems*, edited by A.K. Turner, 107–122. Dordrecht, The Netherlands: Kluwer Academic Publ., 1991.

Berry, J. K. *Map Analysis Tutor (maTUTOR)*. Springfield, Virginia: Spatial Systems Inc., 1991.

Bintliff, J. L. "Archaeology At the Interface: An Historical Perspective." In *Archaeology at the Interface: Studies in Archaeology's Relationships with History, Geography, Biology and Physical Science*, edited by J. L. Bintliff and C. F. Gaffney, 4–31. Oxford: British Archaeological Reports, 1986.

Brown, P. E. and B. H. Rubin. "Patterns of Desert Resource Use: An Integrated Approach To Settlement Analysis." In *Granite Reef: A Study in Desert Archaeology*, edited by P. E. Brown and C. L. Stone, 28, 267–305. Arizona: Arizona State University, Anthropological Research Papers, 1982.

Burrough, P. A. *Principles of Geographical Information Systems For Land Resources Assessment*. Oxford: Clarendon Press, 1986.

Burrow, I., ed. *County Archaeological Records: Progress and Potential*. Somerset: Association of County Archaeological Officers, 1985.

Cowen, D. J. "GIS Versus CAD Versus DBMS: What Are the Differences?" *Photogrammetric Engineering and Remote Sensing* 54 (1988): 1551–4.

Creamer, W. "The Upper Klethia Valley: Computer Generated Maps of Site Location." Paper presented at the 50th Annual Meeting of the Society for American Archaeology, Denver, 1985.

de Man, E. "Establishing a Geographical Information System in Relation To Its Use: A Process of Strategic Choice." *International Journal of Geographical Information Systems* 2 (1988): 245–61.

Department of the Environment. *Handling geographic information: the Government's response to the Report of the Committee of Enquiry chaired by Lord Chorley*. London: H.M.S.O., 1988.

Donoghue, D. "Remote Sensing and Wetland Archaeology." In The Archaeology of Rural Wetlands in England, edited by J. M. and B. Coles, 42–45. WARP Occasional Paper 2, Department of History and Archaeology. Exeter: University of Exeter, 1989.

Donoghue, D. and I. Shennan. "The Application of Multispectral Remote Sensing Techniques To Wetland Archaeology." In *The Exploitation of Wetlands*, edited by P. Murphy, and C. French, 47–59. Oxford: British Archaeological Reports, 1988.

Ferguson, T. A. "Use of Geographic Information Systems to Recognize Patterns of Prehistoric Cultural Adaption." Paper presented at the 50th Annual Meeting of the Society for American Archaeology, Denver, 1985.

Fisher, P. F. "The Nature of Soil Data in GIS: Error or Uncertainty." In *Proceedings of International Geographic Information Systems (IGIS) Symposium: The Research Agenda*, edited by R. T. Aangeenbrug and Y. M. Schiffman, Vol. 3, 307–18. Washington, DC: NASA, 1987.

Fisher, T. R. and R. Q. Wales. "Three Dimensional Solid Modeling of Geo-objects Using Non-uniform Rational B-splines (NURBS)." In *Three Dimensional Modeling with Geoscientific Information Systems*, edited by A. K. Turner, 85–105. Dordrecht, The Netherlands: Kluwer Academic Publ., 1991.

Gaffney, V. and Z. Stancic. *GIS Approaches to Regional Analysis: A Case Study of the Island of Hvar*. Ljubljana: University of Ljubljana, 1991.

Gaffney, V. and Z. Stancic. *Diodorus Siculus and the Island of Hvar, Dalmatia: Testing the Text With GIS*. In Computer Applications and Quantitative Methods in Archaeology 1992, edited by G. R. Lock and J. Moffett, 113–125. BAR International Series S577. Oxford: Tempus Reparatum, British Archaeological Reports, 1992.

Gale, S. "Inexactness, Fuzzy Sets and the Foundation of Behavioral Geography." *Geographical Analysis* 4 (1972): 337–49.

Gamble, C. "Archaeology, Geography and Time." *Progress in Human Geography* 11 (1987): 227–246.

Gill, S. J. and D. Howes. "A Geographical Information System Approach To the Use of Surface Samples in Intra-site Distributional Analysis." Paper presented at UISPP Commission IV Symposium on Data Management and Mathematical Methods in Archaeology, Denver, 1985.

Goudie, A. S. "Geography and Archaeology: The Growth of a Relationship." In *Landscape and Culture*, edited by J. M. Wagstaffe, 11–25. London: Blackwell, 1987.

Grant, E., ed. *Central Places, Archaeology and History*. Sheffield: Department of Archaeology and Prehistory, University of Sheffield, 1986.

Harris, E. C. "The Stratigraphic Sequence: a Question of Time." World Archaeology 7, 109–121, 1975.

Harris, E. C. *Principles of Archaeological Stratigraphy*. London: Academic Press, 1979.

Harris, T. M. "Geographic Information System Design For Archaeological Site Information Retrieval." *Computer Applications in Archaeology 1986*. (University of Birmingham, 1986): 148–161.

Harris, T. M. "Digital Terrain Modelling and Three-dimensional Surface Graphics for Landscape and Site Analysis in Archaeology and Regional Planning." In *Computer and Quantitative Methods in Archaeology 1988*, edited by S.P.Q. Rahtz, 161–172. Oxford: British Archaeological Reports, 1988.

Harris, T. M. and G. R. Lock. "The Diffusion of a New Technology: A Perspective on the Adoption of Geographic Information

Systems Within UK Archaeology." In *Interpreting Space: GIS in Archaeology,* edited by K. M. S. Allen, S. W. Green and E. B. W. Zubrow, 33–53. London: Taylor and Francis, 1990.

Harris, T. M. and G. R. Lock. "Toward a Regional GIS Site Information Retrieval System: the Oxfordshire Sites and Monuments Record (SMR) Prototype," *Sites and Monuments: National Archaeological Records.* DKC: The National Museum of Denmark, 1992.

Harris, T. M. and G. R. Lock. "Archaeology, Multi-dimensionality and 3D GIS." In *Geographic Information Systems and the Advancement of Method and Theory,* edited by H. D. G. Maschner. Carbondale, Illinois: Southern Illinois University Press, forthcoming.

Healey, R. G. "Database Management Systems." In *Geographical Information Systems: Principles and Applications,* Volume 1: Principles, edited by D.J. Maguire, M.F. Goodchild, and D.W. Rhind, 251–67. London: Longman, 1991.

Hodder, I. "Spatial Studies in Archaeology." *Progress in Human Geography* (1977): 33–64.

Jones, E. R. "Data Structures for 3D Spatial Information Systems." *International Journal of Geographical Information Systems* 3, no. 1 (1989): 15–31.

Kvamme, K. L. "Geographic Information Systems Techniques for Regional Archaeological Research." Paper presented at UISPP Commission IV Symposium on Data Management and Mathematical Methods in Archaeology, Denver, 1985a.

Kvamme, K. L. "Fundamentals and Potential of Geographic Information System Techniques for Archaeological Spatial Search." Paper presented at the 50th Annual Meeting of the Society for American Archaeology, Denver, 1985b.

Kvamme, K. L. and T. A. Kohler. "Geographic Information Systems: Technical Aids for Data-collection, Analysis and Displays." In *Quantifying the Present and Predicting the Past: Theory Method and Application of Archaeological Predictive Modelling,* edited by J. W. Judge and L. Sebastian, 493–547. Washington D.C.: U.S. Government Printing Office, 1988.

Limp, W. F. "Continuous Cost Movement Models in Behrens." In *Applications of Space-Age Technology in Anthropology,* edited by C. A. and T. L Sever, 237–250. Mississippi: NASA, John C. Stennis Space Center, 1990.

Lock, G. R. and T. M. Harris. "Integrating Spatial Information in Computerised SMRs: Meeting Archaeological Requirements in the 1990s." In *Computers and Quantitative Methods in Archaeology 1990,* edited by K. Lockyear and S. P. Q. Rahtz, 165–173. Oxford: British Archaeological Reports International Series 565, 1991.

Lock, G. R. and T. M. Harris. "Visualizing Spatial Data: The Importance of Geographic Information Systems." In *Archaeology and the Information Age: A Global Perspective,* edited by P. Reilly and S. P. Q. Rhatz, 81–96. London: Routledge, One World Archaeology 21, 1992.

Lock, G. R. and T. M. Harris. "Integrating Spatial Information in Computerized Sites and Monuments Records: Meeting Archaeological Requirements in the 1990s." In *Computer Applications and Quantitative Methods in Archaeology 1990,* edited by K. Lockyear and S. P. Q. Rahtz, 165–173. Oxford: British Archaeological Reports International Series 565, 1991.

Lock, G. R. and T. M. Harris. "Visualizing Spatial Data: The Importance of Geographic Information Systems." In *Archaeology in the Information Age,* edited by S. P. Q. Rahtz and P. Reilly. London: Routledge, 1992.

Lock, G. R. and J. Moffett, eds. *Computer Applications and Quantitative Methods in Archaeology 1991.* Oxford: British Archaeological Reports International Series S577, Tempus Reparatum, 1992.

Lockyear, K. and S. P. Q. Rahtz, eds. *Computer Applications and Quantitative Methods in Archaeology 1990.* Oxford: British Archaeological Reports International Series 565, 1991.

Maguire, D. J., M. F. Goodchild and D. W. Rhind, eds. *Geographical Information Systems: Principles and Applications.* 2 volumes. London: Longman, 1991.

Maschner, H. D. G., ed. *Geographic Information Systems and the Advancement of Method and Theory.* Carbondale, Illinois: Southern Illinois University Press, forthcoming.

Maschner, H. D. G. and M. Aldenderfer, eds. *Anthropology through Geographic Information and Spatial Analysis.* Oxford: Oxford University Press, forthcoming.

Nagy, G. and S. Wagle. "Geographic Data Processing." Association of Computer Machinery *Computing Surveys* 11, no. 2,(1979): 139–79.

National Museum of Denmark *Sites and Monuments: National Archaeological Records,* DKC, 1992.

Rahtz, S. P. Q., ed. *Computer and Quantitative Methods in Archaeology 1988.* Oxford: British Archaeological Reports, 435–451.

Rahtz, S. P. Q. and J. D. Richards, eds. *Computer Applications and Quantitative Methods in Archaeology 1989.* Oxford: British Archaeological Reports International Series 548, 1990.

Raper, J. F., ed. *Three Dimensional Applications in Geographic Information Systems.* London: Taylor and Francis, 1989.

Rhind, D. W. "Geographical Information Systems." *Area 8,* no. 1, (1976): 46–52.

Rhind, D. W. "Geographical Information Systems in Britain." In *Quantitative Geography: Retrospect and Prospect,* edited by R. J. Bennett and N. Wrigley, 17–35. London: Routledge and Kegan Paul, 1981.

Star, J. and J. Estes. *Geographic Information Systems: An Introduction.* Englewood Cliffs, New Jersey: Prentice Hall, 1990.

Tomlin, C. D. *Geographic Information Systems and Cartographic Modeling.* Englewood Cliffs, New Jersey: Prentice Hall, 1990.

Tomlinson, R. F. *An Introduction to the Geographic Information System of the Canada Land Inventory.* Ottawa, Canada: Department of Forestry and Rural Development, 1967.

Tomlinson, R. F., ed. *Geographic Data Handling.* Commission on Geographical Data Sensing and Processing. Ottawa, Canada: International Geographical Union, 1972.

Tomlinson, R. F. "Current and Potential Uses of Geographical Information Systems—The North American Experience." *International Journal of Geographical Information Systems 1,* no. 3 (1987): 203–8.

Tomlinson, R. F. "Canadian GIS Experience." *CISM Journal* 43, no. 3 (1989): 227–32.

Tukey, J. W. *Exploratory Data Analysis.* Addison-Wesley Publishing Co., Reading, MA, 1977.

Turner, A. K. ed. *Three Dimensional Modeling With Geoscientific Information Systems.* Dordrecht, The Netherlands: Kluwer Academic Publications, 1991.

Wansleeben, M. "Geographic Information Systems in Archaeological Research." In *Computer and Quantitative Methods in Archaeology 1988,* edited by S.P.Q. Rahtz, 435–451. British Archaeological Reports, 1988.

Note: The term *industrial archaeology* is abbreviated to *IA* in index subentries.

Abstracts, microfilm, 55

Access, quad clues to site, 86–87. *See also* Company records, accessing; Federal records, accessing

Accessories, view camera, 176

Aerial photographs, 199; advantages of, 123; film for, 125; of industrial dereliction, 130; interpretation of, 127–31; and maps contrasted, 123; on-site verification of, 130; types of, 123–24. *See also* Orthophotographs

Aerial photography, 4, 7, 123–24; and thermography contrasted, 126

Agriculture: aerial photograph focus on, 127, 128; information on, 42; Library of Congress photographs re, 53; U.S. focus on, 43

Aiken Street (Lowell, Mass.) Bridge, 64

Airbrushing, 158, 159

Air pollution, co-generation of, 52

Alaska, on quads, 63, 64n.2

Alcohol, as drawing cleanser, 157–58

Algorithms, GIS-generated, 201

Alloys, 152–53

Aluminum, 152

American Association for State and Local History, 54

American Concrete Institute, 51

American Folklife Center, Library of Congress, 45–47

American Institute of Architects, 51

American Revolution, 42

American Society of Civil Engineers, 51

American Society of Mechanical Engineers, 51

American Society of Photogrammetry, 104

American State Papers, 42, 46

America's Industrial Heritage Project, 3, 5n.18

Anderson, Richard K., Jr., xv, 133–65

Annotations: on field notes, 143, 150–52; on measured drawings, 137, 156, 162, 164

Annual reports, as IA resource, 51

Antarctica, mapping of, 93n

Antietam, Battle of, 32

Aqueducts, cement in, 9

ARC/GRID, 199

Archaeology, 2; GIS and, 191–92, 194, 199–201; landscape, 194; prehistoric and historic, 5n.13; topography as element of, 89. *See also* Industrial archaeology

Architecture: engineering and, 1–2; photogrammetry and, 103–104

Archives, public: as IA resource, 44, 49–58. *See also* National Archives

Army Corps of Engineers, U.S., 43; and Bonnet Carre Spillway, 43–44; as IA resource, 47

Army Corps of Engineers Historical Centers, 44

Army Map Service, U.S., 92–93, 97

Arrows, as drawing elements, 162. *See also* North arrows

Artifacts, 2; as central to IA, 1–3; depth of subterranean, 200; GIS focus on, 194, 196; LANDSAT identification of, 126

Artillery, coordinates used in aiming, 91–92

Assembly views, exploded, 133, 137

Association of Industrial Archaeology (Brit.), 3

Astronomy: data on, 43; as surveyor consideration, 188

Axonometrics, 133, 137, 160–62

Azimuths, 184–86; and declination angles contrasted, 187

Backsight (BS) (surv.), 182–83, 185, 188

Baldwin Locomotive Works, 51

Bales, Fred, 103, 106

Baltimore, Md.: iron industry of, 42

Baltimore & Ohio Railroad, 88; bridges of, 73

Bearings (angles), 189

Bedstead pony truss bridges, 108–10, 116–21

Behavioralism, GIS and, 199, 201

Benches (side-hill right-of-way cuts), 79

Benchmarks, surveyor's, 182, 184

Bethlehem Steel Company, 86, 87

Bibliographies: as IA resource, 50–51, 57; for National Register nominations, 54

Black (color), in quads, 60, 61

Blast furnaces, on quads, 82

Blue (color), in quads, 60

Blueprints: distortion in, 157; as IA resource, 46

Bonnet Carre Spillway, 43–44

Books, as IA resource, 49–50, 54. *See also* Textbooks

Boteler, Henry, 28, 31, 34

Boteler Cement Mill. *See* Shepherdstown Cement Mill

Breakwaters, cement, 9

Bricks, manufacture of, 85, 130

Bridges, 134; on aerial photographs, 127; animated-drawing approach to reporting on, 162; bascule, 110, 118–20; calculating age, size, etc., of, 71–75; cement in, 9; courthouse data on, 55, 56; covered, 112–14; expansion/contraction of steel, 147; failure of, 107; field notes on, 143–44; photogrammetry and, 104; photographing, 106–21; on quads, 61, 64, 71–75, 88; railroad, 34, 46, 73, 75; over Red River, 44–46; as stereocard subject, 53; stress in, 133; toll, 44, 45; truss, 107–10, 112–21, 133, 147. *See also* Drawbridges; Viaducts

Brown (color), in quads, 60

Buffer zones, GIS-generated, 197

Builder's plates, machinery: as IA resource, 151

Buildings: on aerial photographs, 127; field analysis of, 152; field notes on, 143; GIS focus on, 194, 200; on quads, 61, 64n.4, 80–85, 88; safety precautions in old, 140; on topographic maps, 89. *See also* Blast furnaces; Depots, railway; Factories; Kilns; Mills; Power plants

CAD (Computer Aided Design) system, 4, 156–58, 162, 193, 194, 200, 201

Calcining, 9, 22, 28

Calibration, surveying-instrument, 188

Calligraphy, in drawing lettering, 156

CAM (Computer Aided Mapping) system, 193, 194

Cameras, 182; large-format, 168, 170–76; metric vs. nonmetric, 104; single vs. stereometric, 104; SLR (Single Lens Reflex), 168; video, 125; view. *See also* Film; Lenses; Photographs; Stereocameras

Canada: GIS in *see* Canada Geographic Information System; maps of, 90, 91, 94 & n.18, 99, 192 [(*see also* Canada Geographic Information System; Canada Map Office)]; quads for, 63

Canada Geographic Information System (CGIS), 192

Canada Land Inventory, 192

Canada Map Office, 91 & n.10, 97, 99

Canadian Inventory of Historic Buildings, 91n.9

Canals, 1, 51; on aerial photographs, 127; of Britain, 3; cement, 9; data on U.S., 43; photographing, 125; power, 61, 64, 65; of Shepherdstown Cement Mill complex, 29, 33, 35; on typographic maps, 89. *See also* Chesapeake and Ohio Canal

Captions, photo, 153. *See also* Legends

Carbider, The (Union Carbide house organ), 51

Cartography: alphanumeric approach to, 97; automated, 194 (*see also* CAM). *See also* Maps

Cartoons, drawings prefigured in, 137, 155

Case histories/studies: of aerial-photographed sites, 130–31; federal records–related, 43–45; photogrammetry, 105–14

Castings, machinery, 144

Cast iron, 152

Catalogues, company/parts: as IA resource, 51, 151

Causeways, cement, 9

Cement industry, 7–9, 31, 33. *See also* Calcining; Limestone; Portland cement; Shepherdstown Cement Mill

Cement Mill, Battle of. *See* Shepherdstown, Battle of

Census, U.S. Bureau of the, 43, 44, 46

Censuses, U.S., 52; as IA resource, 43

Chadwyck-Healey, Inc., 54

Chain (unit of length), 179, 188

Chambers of commerce, as IA resource, 54

Charcoal, as cement-production fuel, 22

Charts: nautical, 63; schematic, 134

Chesapeake and Delaware Canal, 9

Chesapeake and Ohio Canal, 22, 23, 28, 31–34; cement for, 9–10

Child labor: photographic record of U.S., 53; in W.Va., 56

Chimneys, industrial: on aerial photos, 130

Church of Jesus Christ of Latter Day Saints, record-keeping of, 56

Cincinnati, O.: written history of, 50

Civil War, Shepherdstown Cement Mill during, 9, 26, 31–33, 35 (*see also* Shepherdstown, Battle of). *See also* Slavery

Coal, 57, 130; as cement-production fuel, 22, 27; of Virginias, 57

Coal Age (journal), 51

Coasts, charting of U.S., 63. *See also* Shorelines

Co-generation, energy, 52

Cognition, GIS and, 199, 201

"Coke Making at Bretz" (film), 53

Coking, film treatment of, 53

Color(s): field use of contrasting pen(cil), 140, 147; in measured drawings, 162; in quad symbology, 60

Company records: accessing, 57; as IA resource, 134, 151. *See also* Annual reports; Ledgers

Compass, as transit element, 189n.6

Computers: drawings generated by, 164 (*see also* CAD); in-camera, 171; as IA resource, 157, 164–65n.4 (*see also* CAD; CAM; Geographic Information Systems [GIS]); lettering by, 156; maps generated by (*see* CAM); photography and, 154; as site-documentation aid, 141

Congress, U.S.: and American industry, 42

Conowingo Dam, 68, 69

Conrail, 73, 75

Consol News (Consolidation Coal house organ), 51

Contact sheets, 153

Contour gauges, 150

Contours, map, 183–84, 186. *See also* Maps, contour

Convention bureaus, as IA resource, 54

Coordinates, cartographic, 91–94 & n.16; Cartesian, 91, 191; GIS, 197; UTM, 158

Copies, electrostatic, 157. *See also* Blueprints; Photocopies

Corrosion: 109, 117–20; of wrought iron, 152

Cotton: New England Milling of, 65, 67; Oklahoma, 45

Courts, U.S.: records of, 43, 47

CROMPTON quad, 67

Crosshatching, 158–59

Cryptococcosis, 140

Culverts, railroad, 46

Curtis Bay Tank (Baltimore), 81

Cutaway drawings, 133

Dams: cement in, 9; impounding, 61; photogrammetry and, 107; Potomac River, 22, 28–29, 33, 34, 36; on quads, 61, 64, 67, 69. *See also* Reservoirs; Spillways

Dashed lines, use of, 158

Database management system (DBMS), for GIS, 193

Datum planes, 144–47

Declination angles, 187

Deeds: checking dimensions of (*see* Traversing); as IA resource, 44, 55–57; language of, 189n.7

Defense Mapping Agency Topographic Center, 90n.3

Dehydration, as site hazard, 140

Delaware and Hudson Canal, 96

Delaware Aqueduct, 96, 97, 101

Denmark, GIS in, 194

Departure (line projection), 189

Depots, railway, 46

Depression, Great: data on, 46

design, computer-aided. *See* CAD

Detailed Land Maps, ICC, 45–46

Determinism, environmental, 201

Diagonals, measurement of room, 149

Diameters, estimating, 144

Diapositives, 104, 106

Dimensions: from datum planes, 146–47; without measuring, 151. *See also* Multidimensionality

Directories: business, 51, 52; city, 51–52; telephone, 51, 52

Dissertations, doctoral: as IA resource, 50–51

Distance, GIS focus on, 198

Ditches, in aerial photos, 128. *See also* Irrigation ditches

Docket books, as IA resource, 56

Documentation, site, 4, 133–65; remote sensing and, 123–32. *See also* Measured drawings

Drawbridges, on quads, 75

Drawings: animated, 162; axonometric (*see* Axonometrics); composite 115; engineering, 151; for HABS/HAER documentation, 54; HAER perspective on, 115; as IA resource, 46, 134, 137; interpretive (*see* Axonometrics; Perspectives, projected; Process diagrams); isometric, 134, 162; literal vs. nonliteral, 115, 120–21; measured (*see* Measured drawings); multiple, 157; photogrammetric, 103–22; and photographs contrasted, 134; planimetric vs. topographic, 105; schematic (*see* Schematic drawings); site (*see* Site drawings); tools for on-site, 139; touching up, 105, 107–10, 112, 114, 120, 121 (*see also* Stereoplotting). *See also* Airbrushing; Axonometrics; Blueprints; Cartoons; Crosshatching; Cutaway drawings; Flow diagrams; Force diagrams; Linework; Measured drawings; Pochés; Process diagrams; Schematic drawings; Site drawings; Sketches; Stippling

Drift mines, 76

Earth, photographs of, 126

Eck, Ronald W., xv, 123–32

Eckhart Mines, 76

Economic development agencies, state, 56

Edge-enhancement (image-processing function), 199

Electronic Distance Measurement (EDM) equipment, 147

Elmes, Gregory A., xv, 191–202

Engineers, U.S., 189n.1

England: antilabor legislation in, 41; GIS in, 194; IA in, 2–3; industrial squalor of, 49

English system. *See* U.S. Customary system

Environmentalism, industry and, 56

Environmental Systems Research Institute, 199

Equator, UTM focus on, 94 & n.16

Eratosthenes, 91

Erie Canal, 9

Erie-Lackawanna Railroad, 75

Erie Railroad, 75

Error, margin of: in field notes, 147; surveyor's, 189; in tape readings, 149

Europe: cement in, 9; GIS in, 194; IA-related journals of, ix; photogrammetry in, 103; university perspectives in, 1. *See also* England

Excavations, site, 5n.13, 200; as archaeological necessity, 2; IA and, 137, 164n.2

Exploratory Data Analysis (EDA), 192

Factories: On aerial photos, 130; British, 3; data on U.S., 42; Library of Congress photos of, 53; of Ohio, 49; on quads, 61. *See also* Mills

Federal records: accessing, 46–47; as IA resource, 41–48

Federal Writers' Project (FWP), 50

Ferry(-ies): on quads, 71; Red River, 44

Field books, surveyor's, 186–88

Field maps, surveyor's. *See* Maps, plan

Field notes, 8, 10–11, 179; Army Engineers, 44; photogrammetric, 115, Railroad Valuation Board, 46; as site-documentation preliminary, 134, 140–53, 155, 164n.4; surveyor's, 180, 182–83, 185, 187, 188. *See also* Rubbings

Field reports, formal, 164

Field work, IA, x, 1, 4–5, 133–34; accuracy of, 147–52; equipment for, 137–40; measured drawings and, 133–65. *See also* Surveying

Film: care of, 153; as IA resource, 53, 201; motion-picture, 162; photographic, 124–25; tungsten, 169; view-camera, 169–70, 173–76. *See also* Mylar

Filtering (map-"reading" technique), 198

Filters, camera, 175

Final Land Reports, ICC, 45

First Aid, on-site, 139–40

Floodplains, on aerial photos, 130

Floods: aerial photos of, 128; on Red River, 44

Floor plans, building: as IA resource, 134

Flow diagrams, 162

Folklore, oral history and, 55

Force diagrams, 133

Foresight (FS) (surv.), 183

France, GIS in, 194

Furnace, Md., 82

Fuzzy space, 199–201

Fuzzy time, 199–201

Gauges, for field work, 139, 150

Genesee River, 75

Geocode, Canadian Inventory of Historic Buildings, 91n.9

Geographic Information Systems (GIS), 191–202; background of, 192–93; basic principles of, 194–96; and CAD contrasted, 194; described, 191, 193; literature on, 193; operation of, 192–93; raster-based, 199; vector-based, 199; vector vs. raster, 195–96, 198; weaknesses of, 199–202

Geological Survey, U.S. *See* U.S. Geological Survey

Geology, federal focus on, 43

Georadar, 137

GIS. *See* Geographic Information Systems

Glass industry, 152; as film subject, 53; in W. Va., 56

Global Positioning Systems (GPS), GIS and, 199

Grade, as right-of-way consideration, 79

Granite, quarrying of, 77

Green (color), in quads, 60

Grids: coordinate-governed, 92 & n.13; reference, 150

Grist mill, Shepherdstown, 9, 32

HABS. *See* Historic American Building Survey

HAER. *See* Historic American Engineering Record

Hand-lettering, of drawings, 155–56

Hardware, GIS computer, 193

Harpers Ferry National Historic Park, x, 7

Harris, Trevor M., xv–xvi, 191–202

Harris Matrix diagrams, 201

Hawaii, on quads, 63

Hazardous wastes, detection of, 130

Haze, photographing through, 125

Height of instrument (HI) (surv.), 183

Highways. *See* Roads

Hills, on quads, 87, 88

Hinks, A. R., 92n.13

Histoplasmosis, 140

Historical societies: as IA resource, 49, 50, 53, 54, 57; and oral histories, 55; publications of, 50, 51

Historic American Building Survey (HABS), 4, 5nn.17, 18, 53, 54, 104; documentation parameters of, 10–11; as IA resource, 46; literature of, 54, 139; map symbols preferred by, 189n.4; photographic standards of, 167, 170

Historic American Engineering Record (HAER), 4, 5nn.17, 18, 53, 54, 157; accuracy parameters of, 147; documentation parameters of, 10–11; drawings produced by, 115, 159; as IA resource, 46; literature of, 54, 139; map symbols preferred by, 189n.4; photographic standards of, 167, 170

Histories, as IA resource: company, 50; local, 49–50; oral (*see* Oral histories)

Hodge's Ferry bascule bridge, 110, 118–20

Horizon, as aerial photo element, 124

Horseshoe Curve (P.R.R.), 79

Howe, Barbara J., xvi, 46, 49–58

Hughes, Robert J., xvi, 167–77

Humpback covered bridges, 110, 112–16, 120

IA Journal, ix, 5n.12

Imaging, and photography contrasted, 125. *See also* Thermal infrared imagery

Index(es): American Folklife Center, 46; of corporate records, 57; county court–maintained, 55–56; Dun & Co., 57; ICC *Reports*, 45; for measured-drawing sets, 158; newspaper, 52; using, 53. *See also* Maps, index

Indian Affairs, Bureau of, 44

Industrial archaeology (IA), 1–5; background of, 2–3; birth of American, 3; defined, ix, x, 2; Geographic Information Systems and, 191–202; techniques of, 1, 3–5

Industrialization, history of, ix. *See also* Industrial revolution; Industry

Industrial revolution, 2–3, 5, 51; and cement, 9, 23; intellectual reaction to, 1

Industry(-ies): British controls on, 41; of Cincinnati, 50; HABS/HAER studies of, 54; interstate competition for U.S., 56; state monitoring of, 56; U.S. focus on, 43 (*see also* Manufactures, U.S.); written information on U.S., 50–57. *See also* Bricks, manufacture of; Cement industry; Factories; Glass industry; Iron industry; Mills; Railroads; Textile industry; Timber industry

Infrared region, 125. *See also* Thermal infrared imagery

Ink(s), 157, 165; Library of Congress focus on, 157

Institute for the History of Technology and Industrial Archaeology, ix–x, 7, 10, 11

Instruments, imaging, 125. *See also* Tools

Intermediate foresight (IFS) (surv.), 183

International Map of the World (IMW), 90 & n.3; Millionth-Scale, 93

Interstate Commerce Commission (ICC), records of, 43, 45–46

Interstate highway system, 73

Interviews, taped. *See* Oral histories

Inventions, IA focus on, 134

Inventories, site, 3–4

Iron, alloys of, 152

Iron Bridge Gorge Museum, 3

Iron industry: Baltimore as hub of U.S., 42; underground artifacts of, 164n.2; of W.Va., 56

Irrigation ditches, imaging of, 126

James River, 112

James River and Kanawha Company, 51

Jeep trails, 61

Johnson Heads, 180

Journals: GIS-focused, 193; IA-focused, ix (*see also* SIAN); as IA resource, 1, 51, 98; trade, 51. *See also* Newsletters; Periodicals

Kemp, Emory L., ix, xvi, 1–39

Kilns: on aerial photos, 130; brick, 85; of Shepherdstown Cement Mill, 7, 9–11, 22–23, 25, 28, 29, 31–33, 35

Labels, drawing, 162

Labor, British curbs on, 41

Landmarks, as IA resource, 91

LANDSAT (spaceflight), 126–27

Laser levels (tools), 146

Laser printers, 158

Latitude: longitude and, 64n.1; as surveying factor, 189

Latrobe, Benjamin Henry, 9

Law Revision Counsel, U.S. House of Representatives, 47

Laws, data on federal, 47

Lawsuits, court records of, 56

Lead, 152

Ledgers, as IA resource, 201

Legends, on surveyor's maps, 182. *See also* Captions

Lenses, camera, 153–54, 182; "stopping down" of, 171–74; telephoto, 172; view-camera, 168, 170–75; wide-angle, 172, 173

Lettering: of drawings, 156; process, 158. *See also* Hand-lettering

Letters (correspondence), as IA resource, 201

Levels (tools), 137; on-site use of, 144–46, 153; surveyor's, 179, 182–85, 187

Libraries, as IA resource, 45, 46, 50–54, 151. *See also* Library of Congress

Library of Congress, 43; as IA resource, 44–47, 50, 53; ink-related studies of, 157. *See also* American Folklife Center

Licenses, courthouse data on, 55

Light: artificial, 169; as central to photography, 167, 169; measurement of, 124. *See also* Spectrum, electromagnetic; Wavelength

Lighter fluid, 165n.6; Mylar cleaned with, 157

Light meters, 171–72, 176

Limestone, as cement source, 8–9

Linework (graph.), effective, 158, 160

Link (unit of length), 188

Lithographs, 53

Loading docks, on aerial photos, 130

Locks, waterway: on aerial photos, 130; Potomac River, 31, 34; on quads, 64

Lowell, Mass., 61, 67; Dickens in, 49; quad of, 64–65

Lowell (Mass.) Machine Shop, 65

Lumber camps, Maine, 46

Luten, Daniel, 107

Luten concrete arch bridge, 107, 116–18

Machinery: construction of, 147; field notes on, 143–44, 151; safety precautions near, 140

McKee, Harley, 4

Magnetometers, 127

Maine, state of: American Folklife Center research in, 46

Manuals, HABS/HAER, 139

Manufactures, data on U.S., 42–43

Mapping, 179; digital, 193

Maps, 57; aerial, 4, 125; aerial photographs as complement to, 130; and aerial photographs contrasted, 123; aspect, 198; boundary, 196 (*see also* Traversing); Canadian (*see* Canada, maps of); computer-generated (*see* CAM; Geographic Information Systems); contour, 7 GIS-directed overlay of, 197, 198; as IA resource, 45, 134, 191; index, 61–63, 91; large-scale, 90; Library of Congress and, 47; as measured-drawing complement, 158; military, 92–93; of New York state, 94; Ordnance Survey, 63; paramountcy of, 89; parcel, 196; plan, 125, 180–83, 187; printing information on, 100n.27; quadrangle (*see* Quad[rangle map]s); remote sensing images as, 132; Sanborn insurance, 52, 57; site, 4, 5, 7, 10, 39, 134, 137, 179; sketch, 54; slope, 198; small-scale, 90, 93; soil-distribution, 200; state/provincial, 63, 100; topographic, 60, 89–93, 98n, 103, 118, 130, 133, 179, 183–84, 186, 188, 195 (*see also* UTM metric grid reference system); USGS, 43, 46, 54, 59, 91, 94, 99–100, 158, 195 (*see also* Quad[rangle map]s). *See also* CAM; Charts; Detailed Land Maps, ICC; International Map of the World; Thematic Mapper

Measured drawings: annotations on, 137, 156, 162, 164; field work and, 133–65; final, 157–64; goal of, 157; preliminary, 155–57 (*see also* Sketches, as field-note complement); types of, 133

Measurement(s): as GIS function, 197, 198; on-site, 143–50, 153, 155, 164–65n.4; running, 148. *See also* Dimensions; Measuring tapes; Surveying

Measuring tapes, 148, 153, 154; for site work, 137; surveyor use of, 179, 181, 185; and transits contrasted, 186

Mechanics' liens, as IA resource, 55

Media, GIS integration of, 199, 201

Meridians, cartographic-zone, 94 & n.17

Merrimack River, 61, 64, 65

Metals, field identification of, 152–53

Meteorology, data on, 43

Metes and bounds, 188–89

Metric system, 179; archaeologists and, 189n.1

Microwave region, 125, 126

Middlesex Canal, 9

Mileposts, railroad, 45

Mills: British, 3; excavations at, 164; of Lowell, 64–65; Maine lumber, 46; natural lighting of 19th century, 67; Rhode Island cotton, 67. *See also* Grist mill; Shepherdstown Cement Mill

Minerals, data on U.S., 42. *See also* Mines; Quarries

Mines, 57; on aerial photos, 130; coal, 130; of Ohio, 49; open-pit vs. deep, 76; on quads, 61, 76; wastes of, 127; working conditions in, 46. *See also* Subsidences, mine

Minutes, county-government, 56

Mississippi River, Army Engineers vs., 43–44

Models, scale: of machinery, 151–52

Morgantown, W.Va., 52, 53, 130–31

Morgantown Energy Associates, 52

Morgues, newspapers, 53

Mortar, cement as, 9

Mortgages, as IA resource, 55

Mosaic, photographic: controlled vs. uncontrolled, 124

Moving pictures. *See* Film; Video

Multidimensionality, GIS and, 199–201

Munsell Color Book, 162, 165n.7

Museums, as IA resource, 50, 53, 57

Mylar: cleaning of, 157–58; drawing on, 155, 157, 165n.5

"'Nailers' Consumption,' and Other Disease Peculiar to Workers in Iron and Glass" (Dickey), 56

Naphtha, 165n.6

Nassawango blast furnace, 82

National Aeronautics and Space Administration (NASA), 126

National Archives, 42, 48n.3, 53; as IA resource, 4, 43–47

National Conference of State Historic Preservation Officers, 54

National Endowment for the Humanities, 52

National Historic Landmarks, 3

National Historic Preservation Act, 3

National Ocean Survey (NOS), 63, 64n.7

National Park Service, 4, 46; cartographic philosophy of, 96; and IA, ix, 3; and photogrammetry, 104; publications of, 54. *See also* Historic American Building Survey (HABS); Historic American Engineering Record (HAER)

National Register of Historic Places, 3, 4, 53, 54; bridges on, 107; as IA resource, 46; nomination for, 54; Shepherdstown Cement Mill bid to, 7, 8, 10, 19–39

National Topographic Mapping Program, USGS, 91n.5. *See also* Maps, USGS

Native Americans: information on, 42; LANDSAT focus on pre-Columbian, 126–27

Natural gas, GIS focus on, 200

Navigation, information on interstate, 42

Netherlands, GIS in, 194

Newsletter(s): as IA resource, 98; Society for Industrial Archaeology (*see* SIAN)

Newspapers, as IA resource, 44, 46, 52–53. *See also* Obituaries

New York, state of: cement industry of, 9; maps of, 100n.29

New York State Transverse Mercator System, 94n.16

Norfolk and Western Railway, 31, 34

North arrows, 156, 184

Northing. *See* Y coordinates, UTM

Notes, to measured drawings, 157. *See also* Field notes

Numeration, engineering, 108

Obituaries, as Ia resource, 52

Office, of Shepherdstown Cement Mill, 7, 10, 22, 23, 27–28, 31, 33, 35

Ohio, state of, 49; in lithographs, 53. *See also* Cincinnati

Ohio River, 88

Oklahoma, state of: Texas vs., 44. *See also* McAlester; Muskogee

Oral histories: as IA resource, 54, 201; techniques of recording, 55

Orchards, on aerial photos, 127

Orthophotographs, 196, 199

Ouelette Bridge (Lowell, Mass.), 64

Outlining (drafting technique), 160

Overbeck, Ruth Ann, xvii, 41–48

Overexposure, photographic, 169

Paintings, as IA resource, 201

Pamphlets, archival, 54

Pantographs, 104

Parallax error, as site hazard, 144

Parking lots, on aerial photos, 128

Patents, in U.S., 42, 48n.3; data on, 43

Pawtuxet River, 67

Pelikan-FT (ink), 157

Pencil, ink vs., 157

Pennsylvania Railroad, 73. *See also* Horseshoe Curve

Pentel Ceran-O-matic ink, 157

Periodicals: government, 51; trade, 151. *See also* Journals

Permission forms, for interviewees, 55

Perspective(s), 133; academic vs. true, 172; photographic, 172–74; projected, 160

Petitions, congressional, 42

Petroleum, GIS focus on, 200

Petroleum tank farms, on aerial photos, 130–31

Philadelphia rods, 182

Philadelphia, Wilmington and Baltimore Railroad, 73

Photocopies, 175–76; use of, 156–57

"Photogrammetric Recording of Historic Transportation Sites, The" (Spero), 105, 106

Photogrammetry, 134, 141, 153, 164; advantages of, 120–22; aerial, 103; defined, 103; as IA resource, 1, 4, 5, 7, 103–22; medical applications of, 103; problems of, 121; terrestrial, 103–21; terrestrial vs. aerial, 103; weather and, 117–19, 121. *See also* Remote sensing

Photographs: aerial (*see* Aerial photographs); of Army Engineers, 44; of earth, 126; field, 137, 141, 143, 153; grid-referenced citation of, 99; historical-society, 50; as IA resource, 44, 46, 52–54, 57, 134, 137, 201; in local histories, 50; as measured-drawing complement, 16; measurements from (*see* Photogrammetry); of National Archives, 47; oblique, 104, 121, 124, 155; as oral-history complement, 55; overlapping, 154; of photographs, 175–76; rectified, 153–54; stereo, 162, 164; survey-related, 54. *See also* Cameras; Film; Prints; Texture; Tone

Photography, 134; advances in 19th century, 103; aerial (*see* Aerial photography); elements of good, 167; as IA resource, 1, 4, 5, 7; large-format, 167–77; multiband, 126; "near-infrared," 125; quad-assisted, 88; for Shepherdstown Cement Mill project, 7–8, 11, 39. *See also* Cameras; Contact sheets; Film; Lenses; Photogrammetry; Prints; Separations; Transparencies

Photo keys, 130

Pink (color), in quads, 60–61, 65, 88

Pipelines, aerial photo–detected, 127, 128, 131

Plane tables, 179–82, 184–86; and transits contrasted, 187–88

Plans, survey: as IA resource, 201

Plants (bot.), irritating, 140

Pochés, 155, 158–59

Population, GIS focus on, 198

Portage, N.Y., 75

Portage Tunnel. *See* Staple Bend Tunnel

Portage Viaduct, 75

Portland cement, 9

Postal Service, U.S.: as IA resource, 43. *See also* Post offices

Postcards, as IA resource, 53

Post offices: National Archives data on, 47; of W.Va., 49

PostScript (font), 158

Potomac Cement Mills. *See* Shepherdstown Cement Mill

Potomac Mills, Mining and Manufacturing Company, 32

Potomac River, 7, 10, 11, 22, 28–29, 31. *See also* Shepherdstown Cement Mill

Power generation, as news item, 52

Power plants: on aerial photos, 130; photogrammetry and, 107; on quads, 61

Pratt truss bridges, 107

Prints, photographic: prudent handling of, 153

Process diagrams, 133, 160, 162

Processes, industrial: field notes on, 151–52

Profile gauges, 150

Puerto Rico, quad coverage of, 63, 64n.2

Pullman Palace Car Company, 50

Purple (color), on quads, 61, 65

Pythagorean Theorem, 92

Quad(rangle map)s, 59–88, 90–91, 94 & n.17, 97, 100; availability of, 63; inconsistent quality of, 67; indexing, 62, 64n.6; nomenclature of, 60, 76; "reading," 61, 64–88; revision of, 60, 64n.3; working with, 62, 64n.6, 98n

Quarries: limestone, 9, 22, 23, 31, 33; on quads, 77

Queries, GIS-directed responses to, 193, 198

Quicklime, 9, 22

Racks, brick-drying, 85

Radar, 125, 126; airborne, 123. *See also* Georadar

Radiation, remote sensing of, 125–27

Radiometers, 127

Railroads: advent of, 1; on aerial photos, 127, 128, 130; British, 3; data on U.S., 43; ICC focus on, 45–46; on quads, 60, 61, 63, 65, 73, 87, 88; quarries on, 77, 79; Shepherdstown Cement Mill reliance on, 10, 31; on topographic maps, 89. *See also* Bridges, railroad; Depots; Track; Tunnels

Railroad Valuation Board, ICC, 45, 46

Railroad Valuation Reports, ICC, 45–46

Raster data-storage system, 195–96, 198–200

Ready-Loads (film packets), 176

Recording Historic Structures (Burns), 4, 5n.17

Records: company (*see* Company records); credit, 57; federal (*see* Federal records). *See also* Valuation records

Red (color), in quads, 60. *See also* Pink; Purple

Red River, bridges over, 44–46

Red River Bridge Company, 44

Reference angles, 188, 189n.7

Relief, as quad feature, 60

Remote sensing, 194; applications of, 131–32; defined, 123; GIS and, 196, 199; as IA technique, 1, 4; and site documentation, 123–32. *See also* Sensors, remote

Reservoirs: in aerial photos, 128; on quads, 81

Resolution, photographic, 124

Reynolds (Shepherdstown Cement Mill co-owner), 32

Rhode Island, state of: textile industry in, 67

Rivers: charting of U.S. navigable, 63; logging on Maine, 46; photographing, 125, 128, 130; as power generators, 67–70; on quads, 75. *See also* Ferries; Floods; Locks; Potomac River; Spillways; Streams

Roads, 43; on aerial photos, 127, 128, 131; courthouse data on, 55, 56; "light-duty," 86; on quads, 61, 63, 71, 86–87; "unimproved," 87; of Virginia, 56; of West Virginia, 51. *See also* Causeways; Interstate highway system; Trails

Robert E. Lee Bridge, 112

Rod (unit of length), 179, 188

Rodman (surveyor assistant), 181, 183, 185

Romers (cartographic tools), 96

Rosendale Cement Mill, 9

Round Top (Md.) cement plant, 9, 32, 34

Rubbings, as IA resource, 150

Ruins, on aerial photos, 127

Runways, on aerial photos, 128

Safety, on-site, 140, 152, 153

Satellites: NASA, 126; navigational, 199

Scaffolding, bridge photogrammetry–related, 122

Scale(s): of aerial photos, 124, 127; axonometrics and, 162; cartographic, 60, 89–91, 124; drawing, 150; English/metric, 156; engineer's, 179, 181, 189; errors related to, 153; field-note, 141; map (*see* Scale, cartographic); for on-site measurement, 137, 139; pantographic, 105; photogrammetric, 116–18; of photograph dimensions, 155; on preliminary drawings, 155, 156; process diagrams and, 133. *See also* Models, scale; Philadelphia rods

Scale sticks, 153, 155

Scanning, multispectral, 125, 126

Scatterometers, 127

Schematic drawings, 162; site plans preliminary to, 147. *See also* Process diagrams

Scherzer rolling lift bridge, 110

Science, federal data on, 42–43

Sensors, remote, 123–32; imaging, 125–27; nonimaging, 127; nonphotographic, 125–27; passive vs. active photographic, 125; photographic, 123–25; types of, 123. *See also* Aerial photography; Remote sensing

Separations, color-coded, 162

Shading, as drafting technique, 159

Shadow(s): draftsman use of, 159; as photo-interpretation aids, 127, 128, 130, 131

Shepherdstown, W.Va., 7; Battle of, 9, 31–33, 35

Shepherdstown Cement Mill, x, 7–39; end of, 10, 32; history of, 9

SHEPHERDSTOWN quad, 67

SHOHOLA, PA quad, 94n17, 97

Shorelines, photographing, 125

Silt, 164

Site drawings, 4, 5, 7, 8; field notes preliminary to, 8, 10–11; of Shepherdstown Cement Mill, 11

Sites, historic industrial, 11; accessing, 131; documentation of (*see* Documentation, site); GIS reclassification of, 197, 199; grid-referenced citation of, 98–101; literature available at, 54. *See also* Field work; Shepherdstown Cement Mill

Sketches: for metes-and-bounds surveys, 188–89; as field-note complement, 140–43, 153, 164n.4. *See also* Drawings; Grids, reference; Thumbnail sketches

Skylab (spaceflight), 126

Slag, 153, 164n.2

Smoothing (image-processing function), 199

Society for American Archaeology, 194

Society for Industrial Archeology (SIA), ix, 2, 5n.12

Society for the History of Technology, 2

Software, GIS, 191, 193, 194, 196, 201

Soils: aerial-photo clues to, 128, 130; GIS and, 194; map focus on, 200

South Carolina, state of: photogrammetry used in, 104

Spaceflights, NASA, 126, 162

Spectrometers, 127

Spectrum, electromagnetic, 125–26. *See also* Scanning, multispectral

Spero, Paula A. C., xvii, 103–22

Spillways, Army Engineer–designed, 43–44

Spot remover, 165n.6; Mylar cleaned with, 157

Springs, thermographic detection of, 126

Stadia method (of surveying), 182, 185

Stainless steel, 152

Standpipes, on quads, 80

Staple Bend Tunnel, 86–87

Steam engines: British interest in, 3; data on, 43

Stereocards, as IA resource, 53

Stereocameras, 162

Stereodrawings, 162, 164

Stereophotogrammetry, 103, 105, 164

Stereoplotting, 104–106, 112, 114, 115, 118, 120; problems of, 121

Stereoscopes, 124, 128–29

Stippling, 158–60

Story boards, 137, 155

Stott, Peter H., xvii, 64n.5, 89–102

Streams, on aerial photos, 127, 128

Subsidences, mine, 130

Survey(s): data on U.S., 42; historic-site, 53–54; photogrammetry and architectural, 104; of Shepherdstown Cement Mill, 10. *See also* Surveying; U.S. Geological Survey

Surveying: by industrial archaeologists, 1, 7, 179–89; metes-and-bounds, 188–89. *See also* Plans, survey; Traversing; Trilateration

Surveying (Moffitt/Bouchard), 188

Survey of Federal Writers' Project Manuscript Holdings in State Depositories (Banks/Carter), 50

Surveys and Mapping Branch, Canadian Department of Energy, Mines, and Resources, 91

Susquehanna River, 68

Swamps, photographing, 125

Symbols: quad, 61; surveyor's, 182, 189n.4

System International (S.I.) *See* Metric system

Technology: federal data on, 42–43; historical geography of, 201; history of, 1–3; literature on, 50; military, 43; society and, 2. *See also* Industry; Machinery

Telegraphy, federal focus on, 43

Telescopes, surveying. *See* Transits

Television: as IA resource, 53; images viewed on, 125

Templates, drafting, 158

Temple University Urban Archives Center, 53

Temporality, GIS and, 199, 200

Textbooks: as IA resource, 151; surveying, 188

Textile industry: in New England, 61, 67; in W.Va., 57

Texture, as photograph element, 127

Thacher truss bridge, 107–109

Thematic Mapper (TM), 126

Theodolites. *See* Transits

Thermal infrared imagery, 125–26

Thermal scanners, 123

Thermography. *See* Thermal infrared imagery

Theses, master's: as IA resource, 50–51

Thumbnail sketches, as measured-drawing preliminary, 137

Timber, on aerial photos, 127, 128

Timber industry, of Maine, 46

Titles, drawing-view, 156

Title sheets, for measured drawings, 158

Tone, as photograph element, 128, 130

Tools: drawing, 157; site-analysis, 137–39, 144, 147. *See also* Levels; Measuring tapes; Scale sticks; Transits

Topographic System of Canada, 90

Topography: defined, 89; quads and, 60

Topology, GIS and, 195, 201

Townships, as map-referencing guides, 91

Track, railroad: ICC data on, 45–46; shared, 45

Trails, on quads, 71. *See also* Jeep trails

Tramways, cable-car, 22, 31, 33, 35

Transits, 7, 144, 146, 149, 152, 153, 179, 184–87, 189n.6; digital, 189n.6; and plane tables contrasted, 187

Transparencies, infrared color–film, 125

Transportation, in U.S., 42–43; GIS focus on, 196, 198; IA focus on, 103–22; as journal topic, 51; literature on, 50. *See also* Canals; Interstate Commerce Commission; Railroads; Roads

Travel agencies, as IA resource, 54

Traversing, 188–89

Trials, records of, 55–56

Trichloroethane, and trichloroethylene contrasted, 165n.6

Trigonometry, surveying and, 186–88

Trilateration, 149–50

Tripod, surveying, 180, 182, 184

TrueType (font), 158

Tunnels, on quads, 61, 79, 86–87

Ultraviolet region, 125

"Unified Plane Co-ordinate Reference System, A" (Colvocoresses), 91n.8

Union Agency for the Five Civilized Tribes, 44

Union International des Sciences Pre et Proto Historiques, 194

United Nations Cartography Section, 90n.3

Universal Polar Stereographic (UPS) Grid, 93n

Universal Transverse Mercator system. *See* UTM metric grid reference system

University Microfilms, Inc., 51

U.S. Coast and Geodetic Survey, 64n.7, 93

U.S. Customary system, 179, 189n.1

U.S. Geological Survey, 43, 54, 63, 91; accessing, 91; as IA resource, 46; maps of (*see* Maps, USGS; Quads); mission of, 91n.5

UTM (Universal Transverse Mercator) metric grid reference system, 54, 61, 89–102, 158, 191

Valuation records, railroad, 45

Vector data-storage system, 195–96, 198–200

Vellum, drawing on, 155, 157

Viaducts, 75; on quads, 79, 88

Video, as IA resource, 53. *See also* Television

Video tapes, as IA resource, 162

Viewsheds, GIS recreation of, 196, 198

Vignetting (photography problem), 174

Viking (spacecraft), 163

Virginia, commonwealth of: bridges of, 107–21; coal of, 57; maps of, 118; photogrammetry in, 104; public/private developmental partnerships in, 56

Virgin Islands, quads of, 63

Virginius Island, 7

Visible region (of electromagnetic spectrum), 125

Visitor bureaus, as IA resource, 54. *See also* Chambers of commerce

Vital statistics, courthouses as repositories of, 55

Vogel, Robert M., xvii, 57, 59–88, 98n; Foley and, 2

Walsworth Publishing Company, 50

Washington, D.C.: as Shepherdstown Cement Mill client, 10, 31, 32, 34

Washington Monument, Shepherdstown cement in, 34

Watercourses: data on U.S., 43; GIS focus on, 196; photographing, 125; on quads, 60, 61, 63, 64. *See also* Breakwaters; Canals; Coasts; Culverts; Irrigation ditches; Navigation; Reservoirs; Rivers; Springs; Streams; Wharves

Water tanks, on quads, 80

Wavelength, 126

Weather, as photogrammetry consideration, 117–21

Weights and measures, federal focus on, 43

Weirs: on aerial photos, 130; on Mississippi, 44; on quads, 64

West Virginia, state of: coal of, 57; local histories of, 50; postal patterns in, 49; roads of, 51; surveying in, 188; and workplace health, 56. *See also* Morgantown

West Virginia Geological Survey, 50

West Virginia University, ix. *See also* Institute for the History of Technology and Industrial Archaeology

Wharves, on aerial photos, 130

Wheeling Cotton Mill, 52

White, Canvass, 9

Wills, as IA resource, 55

Winant, Edward H., xvii–xviii, 179–89

Wood, types of, 152

World War I, use of cartographic coordinates in, 92

X coordinates, UTM, 93–94, 96, 97n.24, 100, 101

X, Y coordinates, GIS, 191

Y coordinates, UTM, 93–94, 96, 97n.24, 100, 101

Yugoslavia, GIS in, 194

Zero azimuth, 184, 185, 187

Zones, cartographic, 93–97, 101